Sentencing and Human Rights

Sentencing and Human Rights

The Limits on Punishment

SARAH J SUMMERS

Professor of Criminal Law, Criminal Procedure Law and Criminology, School of Law, University of Zurich

OXFORD
UNIVERSITY PRESS

OXFORD
UNIVERSITY PRESS

Great Clarendon Street, Oxford, OX2 6DP,
United Kingdom

Oxford University Press is a department of the University of Oxford.
It furthers the University's objective of excellence in research, scholarship,
and education by publishing worldwide. Oxford is a registered trade mark of
Oxford University Press in the UK and in certain other countries

First Edition published in 2022

Impression: 1

Published in the United States of America by Oxford University Press
198 Madison Avenue, New York, NY 10016, United States of America

British Library Cataloguing in Publication Data

Data available

Library of Congress Control Number: 2022940285

ISBN 978–0–19–287038–4

DOI: 10.1093/oso/9780192870384.001.0001

Printed and bound by
CPI Group (UK) Ltd, Croydon, CR0 4YY

Acknowledgements

In the process of writing this book, I have benefited from the support of a number of colleagues. In particular, I would like to thank Andreas Donatsch, a constant source of encouragement, Lindsay Farmer, Marc Thommen, and, as always, Stefan Trechsel. I am also indebted to two anonymous reviewers for their comments and to Fiona Briden and her team at OUP for their assistance. Special thanks are reserved for Sararard Arquint for his willingness to spend not just his days but also his evenings discussing crime and punishment.

Contents

Table of Cases before the European Court and the European Commission of Human Rights

Table of Cases before the National Courts

AUSTRALIA

CANADA

ENGLAND AND WALES

GERMANY

IRELAND

SCOTLAND

SOUTH AFRICA

SWITZERLAND

USA

1

Sentencing and Human Rights

I. Sentencing Theory and the Principles of Punishment

Sentencing law and theory is closely bound up with the justification of punishment.[1] It is thus unsurprising that sentencing theory is generally perceived as falling squarely within the domain of moral philosophy.[2] Much of the debate has focused on whether retribution or consequentialist notions of deterrence or rehabilitation should serve as the principal aim on which the sentencing system is based. There are numerous articles by proponents of the various theories explaining why their theory should provide the primary basis for the determination of the sentence.[3] The importance of the moral philosophical discussion transcends national boundaries. Despite considerable diversity in the legal cultures and traditions of the various legal systems, '[p]rinciples of uniformity and retributive proportionality are now recognised to some extent in almost all systems, but sentences in these systems are also designed to prevent crime by means of deterrence, incapacitation and rehabilitation'.[4] Whereas broadly 'correctionalist' accounts of punishment underpinned the penal welfare model of punishment for much of the twentieth century,[5] the 'just deserts' movement[6] of the 1980s was in line with a transfer of focus away from the individualized treatment of offenders and towards a vision of punishment which

[1] See notably HLA Hart, *Punishment and Responsibility: Essays in the Philosophy of Law* (J Gardner, 2nd edn, Oxford: OUP 2008) 1.

[2] The same might be said of theories of criminalization. See, though, L Farmer, *Making the Modern Criminal Law: Civil Order and Criminalisation* (Oxford: OUP 2016).

[3] For a useful overview see A Ashworth, *Sentencing and Criminal Justice* (6th edn, Cambridge: CUP 2015) 80; S Trechsel, P Noll, and M Pieth, *Schweizerisches Strafrecht: Allgemeiner Teil I: Allgemeine Voraussetzungen der Strafbarkeit* (7th edn, Zurich: Schulthess 2017) 16. These theories are considered in more detail in Ch 6.

[4] RS Frase, 'Comparative Perspectives on Sentencing Policy and Research' in M Tony and RS Frase (eds), *Sentencing and Sanctions in Western Countries* (Oxford: OUP 2001) 259 at 261.

[5] On the decline of the welfarist rationale, see F Allen, *The Decline of the Rehabilitative Ideal* (New Haven, CT: Yale University Press 1981).

[6] See A von Hirsch, *Doing Justice: The Choice of Punishment* (Report of the Committee for the Study of Incarceration, New York, NY: Hill & Wang 1976); A von Hirsch, *Past or Future Crimes: Deservedness and Dangerousness in the Sentencing of Criminals* (Rutgers, NJ: Rutgers University Press 1985). For criticism E van der Haag, 'Punishment: Desert and Crime Control' (1986–87) 85 *Michigan Law Review* 1250.

Sentencing and Human Rights. Sarah J Summers, Oxford University Press. © Sarah J Summers 2022.
DOI: 10.1093/oso/9780192870384.003.0001

not only favoured a more standardized approach to the treatment of offenders, but which also expressly legitimized retributivist penalties and practices.[7]

It is interesting, though, that despite the depth and cross-border reach of the discussion of the aims and principles of punishment and notwithstanding the importance of retributivism in modern sentencing theory, none of the theories has been able to assert itself as the principal sentencing rationale in practice. In fact, it is quite common for the sentencing judge to choose between aims in determining the sentence. In England and Wales, for instance, the sentencing judge is not just entitled but is in fact obliged to consider five (!) essentially competing aims in determining the sentence: 'the court must have regard to the following purposes of sentencing— (a) the punishment of offenders, (b) the reduction of crime (including its reduction by deterrence), (c) the reform and rehabilitation of offenders, (d) the protection of the public, and (e) the making of reparation by offenders to persons affected by their offences.'[8]

In other countries, greater emphasis is placed in the statutory regulation on establishing what might be described as a more principled approach to sentencing. In Switzerland, for instance, the focus on culpability in the main sentencing provision has been taken to indicate that retribution is the principal aim of punishment.[9] This view contrasts sharply, however, with the case law of the Swiss Federal Supreme Court (SFSC) which frequently notes that the purpose of the sentence cannot solely be described in terms of 'commensurate desert'[10] (*Schuldausgleich*) because the 'criminal law is not principally concerned with retribution but with prevention'.[11] The conflation here of the aims of the 'criminal law' and those of 'punishment' is not explained and calls for

[7] For an excellent overview of the 'history of the present' see D Garland, *The Culture of Control: Crime and Social Order in Contemporary Society* (Oxford: OUP 2001) 9. See further Ch 6.

[8] Sentencing Act 2020, s 57(2). This provision (in its guise as s 142(1) of the Criminal Justice Act 2003) has been described by Ashworth as representing 'the worst of "pick and mix" sentencing', Ashworth, *Sentencing and Criminal Justice* (n 3). See also the criticism in C Wells and O Quick, *Lacey, Wells and Quick Reconstructing Criminal Law* (4th edn, Cambridge: CUP 2010) 60.

[9] See eg S Trechsel and M Thommen, 'Art 47' in S Trechsel and M Pieth (eds), *Schweizerisches Strafgesetzbuch: Praxiskommentar* (3rd edn, Zurich: Dike 2018) N 7: '*Art 47 schreibt die Strafzumessung nach dem Verschulden vor, was den Gedanken der Gerechtigkeit (Vergeltung) in den Vordergrund rückt*'; G Arzt, 'Strafzumessung—Revolution in der Sackgasse' (1994) 12 *Recht* 141–55 (part 1) and 234–48 (part 2): '*In der Vordergrund rückt Art 63 die Schuld (und mit ihr die Sühne). Der Täter «verdient» die Schuldangemessene Strafe*.'

[10] See the terminology used by C Roxin, 'Prevention, Censure and Responsibility: The Recent Debate on the Purposes of Punishment' in AP Simester, A du Bois-Pedain, and U Neumann (eds), *Liberal Criminal Theory: Essays for Andreas von Hirsch* (Oxford: Hart Publishing 2014).

[11] See eg BGE 134 IV 121, 128 E 3.3.3: '*Der Zweck der Strafe erschöpft sich denn auch keineswegs bloss im Schuldausgleich. Denn das Strafrecht dient in erster Linie nicht der "Vergeltung", sondern der Verbrechensverhütung*.' See similarly BGE 134 IV 1, 12 E 5.4.1; BGE 129 IV 161, 164, E 4.2; BGE 119 IV 125, 126, E.3; BGE 118 IV 337, 340, E.2.

closer consideration.[12] For now, it is sufficient to note that the Swiss courts have felt it necessary to have recourse to other rationales beyond retribution.

In view of the apparent difficulties in establishing a principal sentencing aim in practice, it may be unsurprising perhaps that the focus of much of the literature on sentencing has been on formal rather than substantive issues, such as the importance of providing reasons for, and of reducing disparity between, sentencing decisions.[13] As Lacey has argued, however, '[a] focus on form and procedure avoids controversy and unites those who, were they to dig deeper into the issues, would find themselves disagreeing about the substantive values which should underlie the rules, standards or guidelines which they can agree should be consistently and certainly enforced.'[14]

The result of this state of affairs is that the power of the sentencing judge and indeed the legislator remains virtually unfettered, while the legitimacy of important sentencing practices, such as sentence discounts for confessions or sentence enhancements for previous convictions, remains under-theorized. Missing from sentencing theory is detailed consideration of a constitutional or rights-based approach to the sentencing exercise. This seems surprising. As Garland has noted: 'The philosophies of punishment, at least in their traditional form, are based upon a rather idealized and one-dimensional image of punishment: an image which poses the problem of punishment as a variant of the classic liberal conundrum of how the state should relate to the individual.'[15] In view of the state monopoly on punishment,[16] coupled with the dramatic

[12] See eg Farmer, *Making the Modern Criminal Law* (n 2) 21: 'the aims or social function of punishment are not necessarily the same as those of the criminal law.' See also RA Duff, *The Realm of the Criminal Law* (Oxford: OUP 2018) 15 and V Chiao, *Criminal Law in the Age of the Administrative State* (New York, NY: OUP 2019) ch 4.

[13] M Wasik, 'Towards Sentencing Guidelines in England' in I Dennis (ed), *Criminal Law and Justice: Essays from the WG Hart Workshop 1986* (London: Sweet & Maxwell 1987) 237.

[14] See N Lacey, 'Discretion and Due Process at the Post-Conviction Stage' in I Dennis (ed), *Criminal Law and Justice: Essays from the WG Hart Workshop 1986* (London: Sweet & Maxwell 1987) 221, 227. See too Arzt, 'Revolution in der Sackgasse' (n 9) 141–55.

[15] D Garland, *Punishment and Modern Society: A Study in Social Theory* (Oxford: OUP 1990) 9 arguing that 'the solutions offered by philosophy are unlikely to match up to the problems of the institution'; see too D Garland, 'Philosophical Argument and Ideological Effect' (1983) 7 *Contemporary Crises* 79–85.

[16] This reflects an understanding of the criminal law and indeed punishment as falling principally within the domain of the nation state, see A Harel, 'Why Only the State May Inflict Criminal Sanctions: The Case against Privately Inflicted Sanctions' (2008) 14 *Legal Theory* 113–33. Attempts to interfere with state sovereignty in the identification and classification of criminal conduct are viewed with considerable scepticism, while the imposition of punishment outwith the boundaries of the nation state has given rise to questions of legitimacy, see S Gless, 'Strafe ohne Souverän?' (2007) 125 *Schweizerische Zeitschrift für Strafrecht* 24; M Dubber, 'Common Civility—The Culture of Alegality in ICL' (2011) 24 *Leiden Journal of International Law* 923, 928; K Ambos, 'Punishment without a Sovereign? The Ius Puniendi Issue of International Criminal Law: A First Contribution towards a Consistent Theory of International Criminal Law' (2013) 33 *Oxford Journal of Legal Studies* 1.

interference in the rights of an individual brought about by its imposition,[17] one might expect human rights principles to have taken on considerable importance in this context.

In fact, there has been little analysis of the ways in which human rights principles act to protect individuals from *substantive* unfairness or injustice in the attribution of criminal liability and the imposition of punishment.[18] This stands in stark contrast to the importance of notions of procedural fairness which have been developed in an attempt 'to instantiate at the level of the criminal law and criminal justice system a form of procedural justice which corresponds to the legitimacy of procedural democracy at the level of the political sphere'.[19] Just as theoretical accounts of criminal procedure law are concerned not only with justifying criminal proceedings, but also with examining the nature of restraints on the process, so too might consideration of constitutional constraints provide an alternative basis for thinking about sentencing law and practice.

II. The Criminal Law and Human Rights Restraints

The influence of constitutional law on criminal procedural law has been so substantial that the claim that criminal procedure law has been 'almost completely constitutionalized'[20] does not seem wildly exaggerated. In Europe, the dominance of Article 6 of the European Convention on Human Rights (ECHR) has resulted in criminal procedure law being constrained by a particular understanding of procedural fairness framed in terms of adversarial opportunities.[21] Similarly, in the United States (US) the constitutionalization of criminal procedure has revolutionized criminal proceedings, affording the accused a host of procedural rights.[22] It is important to note, however,

[17] V Tadros, *The Ends of Harm* (Oxford: OUP 2011) 1: 'Punishment is probably the most awful thing that modern democratic states systematically do to their own citizens.'

[18] Frase, 'Comparative Perspectives' (n 4) 271.

[19] S Veitch, 'Judgment and Calling to Account: Truths, Trials and Reconciliations' in RA Duff and others (eds), *The Trial on Trial II: Judgment and Calling to Account* (Oxford: Hart Publishing 2007) 155, 169.

[20] WJ Stuntz, 'Substance, Process and the Civil-Criminal Line' (1996) 7 *Journal of Contemporary Legal Issues* 1; see too J Cédras, 'La Constitutionnalisation de la Procédure Pénale en France et aux États-Unis' (2011) 82 *Revue Internationale de Droit Pénal* 445–56.

[21] See eg S Trechsel, *Human Rights in Criminal Proceedings* (Oxford: OUP 2005); J Jackson and S J Summers, *The Internationalisation of Criminal Evidence: Beyond the Common Law and Civil Law Traditions* (Cambridge: CUP 2014).

[22] RJ Allen and others, *Comprehensive Criminal Procedure* (4th edn, New York, NY: Wolters Kluwer 2016) 63–66; N Kuckes, 'Civil Due Process, Criminal Due Process' (2006) 25 *Yale Law and Policy Review* 8.

that such notions of fairness or due process are not (principally) concerned with just outcomes. Those charged with criminal offences are to be given the opportunity to challenge the criminal charge in line with principles of adversariality in a public forum supervised by an independent and impartial judge. The right is to procedural fairness rather than outcome-related justice.[23] Procedural fairness has little to say about the substance of the decision, beyond perhaps the idea that the decision of the judge must not be 'arbitrary or manifestly unreasonable'.[24] The right to a fair trial is 'perfectly consistent with the reality of social injustice in a democratic polity'.[25] This highlights the limits of procedural rules in addressing unfairness inherent in the substantive law itself.[26]

Just as procedural fairness has become the guiding principle for courts in determining the conduct of the authorities in criminal proceedings, so too might one expect notions of substantive fairness to have played a role in the regulation of the attribution of criminal liability and the imposition of punishment.[27] In fact, the dominance of constitutional constraints in the criminal procedural context contrasts noticeably with their relevance in relation to the substantive law.[28] This applies both to the attribution of criminal liability and the imposition of punishment.

A sustained effort by renowned US academics in the second half of the twentieth century to advocate for more judicial supervision of the substantive criminal law proved unsuccessful.[29] In particular, the argument that *mens rea* should be afforded constitutional status did not find support. This is well illustrated by the fact that the US Supreme Court (USSC) has since 'nurtured' the concept of strict liability offences, now said to be 'deeply entrenched' in the US

[23] S Trechsel, 'Why Must Trials be Fair?' (1997) 31 *Israel Law Review* 94, 102. In the words of Reed and Murdoch, the 'right under the ECHR article 6 is to "fairness" rather than to justice', R Reed and J Murdoch, *Human Rights Law in Scotland* (4th edn, Edinburgh: Bloomsbury, 2017).

[24] See eg *Navalnyy and Ofitserov v Russia* App nos 46632/13 and 28671/14, 23 Feb 2016, para 101; *Van Kück v Germany* App no 35968/97, ECHR 2003-VII, paras 46–47; *Khamidov v Russia* App no 72118/01, ECHR 2007-XII, para 170; *Berhani v Albania* App no 847/05, 27 May 2010, paras 50–56; *Ajdarić v Croatia* App no 20883/09, 13 Dec 2011, paras 47–52; *Anđelković v Serbia* App no 1401/08, 9 Apr 2013, paras 26–29.

[25] Veitch, 'Judgment and Calling to Account' (n 19) 170.

[26] S J Summers, *Fair Trials: The European Court of Human Rights and the European Criminal Procedural Tradition* (Oxford: Hart Publishing 2007) ch 6.

[27] See B Waldmann, 'Das Strafrecht im Spannungsfeld zwischen Grundrechtverwirklichung und Grundrechtsbindung' in MA Niggli, J Hurtado Pozo, and N Queloz (eds), *Festschrift für Franz Riklin* (Zurich: Schulthess 2007) 273, 277.

[28] See too M Kremnitzer, 'Constitutionalization of Substantive Criminal Law: A Realistic View' (1999) 33 *Israel Law Review* 720.

[29] See notably HM Hart, 'The Aims of the Criminal Law' (1958) 23 *Law and Contemporary Problems* 401, 422; HL Packer, 'The Aims of the Criminal Law Revisited: A Plea for a New Look at "Substantive Due Process"' (1971) 44 *California Law Review* 490.

criminal justice system.[30] Dubber, writing about US criminal law, notes that '[i]t has become commonplace that there are no meaningful constraints on substantive criminal law',[31] while Bilionis has suggested that 'we are inclined to see no meaningful relationship between the Constitution and the substantive criminal law because we expect the relationship to manifest itself only in the trappings of substance, in rights-based restraints on the criminal sanction that are grounded in some satisfactory theory of crime, punishment and individual liberty'.[32] Even in countries, such as Germany, where the constitution expressly provides for judicial consideration of the compatibility of statutes with the constitution, there is considerable reluctance on the part of the judiciary to declare criminal law unconstitutional.[33]

The comparatively restricted role of human rights principles is also evident in the context of sentencing law. Such principles might be expected to play an important role at the sentencing stage, regulating the process and substance of the sentencing exercise, delineating the state's role, and affording it legitimacy in the imposition of punishment. If the values underpinning the sentencing decision are not clearly articulated, there is a danger that the sentencing exercise could be arbitrary and serve to undermine the legitimacy of the state in the attribution of punishment. It is generally accepted that the sentencing system must operate in accordance with the principles of human rights law.[34] Indeed, provisions such as the Eighth Amendment to the US Constitution or Article 3 ECHR would seem to expressly demand judicial oversight of sentencing. In spite of this, however:

[30] A Saltzman, 'Strict Criminal Liability and the United States Constitution: Substantive Criminal Law Due Process' (1978) 24 *Wayne Law Review* 1571; see also HL Packer, 'Mens Rea and the Supreme Court' [1962] *Supreme Court Review* 107.

[31] MD Dubber, 'Toward a Constitutional Law of Crime and Punishment' (2004) 55 *Hastings Law Journal* 509, 509, citing WJ Stuntz, 'The Pathological Politic of Criminal Law' (2000) 100 *Michigan Law Review* 505; C Finkelstein, 'Positivism and the Notion of an Offence' (2000) 88 *California Law Review* 335; SH Kadish, 'Fifty Years of Criminal Law: An Opinionated Review' (1999) 87 *California Law Review* 943; LD Bilionis, 'Process, the Constitution, and Substantive Criminal Law' (1988) 96 *Michigan Law Review* 1926; Stuntz, 'Substance, Process, and the Civil-Criminal Line' (n 20) 1.

[32] Bilionis, 'Process' (n 31) 1271.

[33] O Lagodny, 'Basic Rights and Substantive Criminal Law: The Incest Case' (2011) 61 *University of Toronto Law Journal* 761, highlighting the tension between criminal legal theory (*Rechtsguttheorie*) and constitutional law; C Nestler, 'Constitutional Principles, Criminal Law Principles and German Drug Law' (1998) 1 *Buffalo Criminal Law Review* 661, arguing that '[c]onstitutional and criminal law principles have had little, if any, significance in the historical development of criminal drug legislation in Germany'.

[34] See eg D van Zyl Smit, 'Human Rights and Sentencing Guidelines' (2001) 5 *Law, Democracy and Development* 45, 45: 'It is widely accepted that human rights principles of constitutional and international law set outer limits within which any sentencing system must operate.'

> The relationship between human rights and sentencing is highly complex. Although human rights are often invoked when sentencing is discussed, little systematic thought has been given to the impact that human rights should have on the sentencing framework as a whole. Part of the reason is that insufficient attention is paid to the reality that sentencing takes place within the overall criminal justice environment.[35]

This failure to take seriously the core constitutional or human rights values underpinning the criminal law has been subject to considerable criticism. Constitutional regulation of criminal procedure seems to 'logically require substantive limits on the law of crimes';[36] it makes little sense to constitutionalize only one aspect of criminal justice while leaving the substantive criminal law 'without constitutional constraint'.[37] In addition, it has been argued that the aggressive constitutional regulation of policing and trial procedure at the expense of the substantive law has meant that 'legislators find it easy to expand criminal codes and raise sentences but harder to regulate policing and the trial process'.[38]

It is true that neither the constitutionalization of criminal procedure nor acceptance of the existence of disparity between sentencing theory and practice explains the importance of expressing sentencing values in human rights terms. Indeed, one response might be to question the importance of human rights theory in this context. Certainly, it is unlikely to provide much of an answer to the problem of the one-dimensional image of punishment identified by Garland.[39] Nevertheless, this exercise might be of use first, in explaining the importance of principles underpinning the criminal law orthodoxy and second, in providing a basis for a critique not just of the reluctance of the courts to follow these principles, but also the lawfulness of their failure to do so. It is necessary to express the values underpinning the sentencing decision in constitutional or human rights terms precisely because the theoretical arguments are not always understood by the courts as of essential importance to ensuring that the sentencing decision can be characterized as just. The importance of the expression of sentencing values as human rights is underscored by the fact

[35] ibid.

[36] Stuntz, 'Substance, Process and the Civil-Criminal Line' (n 20) 1; Hart, 'The Aims of the Criminal Law' (n 29) 401; Packer, 'Mens Rea and the Supreme Court' (n 30); Packer, 'Aims of the Criminal Law Revisited' (n 29) 490.

[37] Dubber, 'Toward a Constitutional Law' (n 31) 520.

[38] WJ Stuntz, 'The Political Constitution of Criminal Justice' (2006) 119 *Harvard Law Review* 780, 782.

[39] Garland, 'Philosophical Argument' (n 15) 79–85.

that theoretical or philosophical arguments, irrespective of their coherence or sense, may simply be ignored by the courts. Sentencing principles may be well established in law, but this does not guarantee that they will be adhered to in practice. The human rights principles, on which the principles of the imposition and attribution of criminal liability are based, cannot simply be discounted and thus act as important restraints both on the legislature and on the judiciary in its application of the law.

III. The Importance of Expressing Sentencing Values as Human Rights

Commitment to 'justice' at sentencing requires recognition of the human rights principles underpinning the state's mandate to impose punishment. The potential for the most fundamental of sentencing principles, for even the most established of principles of criminal legal theory to be rejected by the courts is well illustrated by a judgment of the SFSC from 2010 on 'diminished culpability' (*verminderte Schuldfähigkeit*).[40] The case involved the intentional homicide of a small child by the partner of the child's mother, who was sentenced to twelve years' imprisonment. The child's mother was convicted of intentionally killing her daughter by omission for failing to intervene to protect the child. The cantonal court determined that the mother could only be held partially culpable for her actions. The sentencing judge was required, in accordance with the Swiss Criminal Code, to reduce the sentence of an offender who was only partially capable of appreciating the wrongfulness of their behaviour or acting accordingly.[41] This led the judge to impose a sentence of six years' imprisonment, instead of the twelve years which would have been imposed had the offender been determined to be fully culpable. The prosecution appealed on the grounds that the sentence was unduly lenient, arguing that that the sentence reduction granted by the court to take account of the mother's 'diminished culpability' was too substantial. In its judgment, the SFSC initiated a major modification of its approach to sentencing in cases involving 'diminished culpability'.

[40] BGE 136 IV 55 (on appeal by the prosecutor of the Canton of Zurich).

[41] Art 19(2) SCC: 'If the person concerned was only partially able at the time of the act to appreciate that his act was wrong or to act in accordance with this appreciation of the act, the court shall reduce the sentence.' The English language version of SCC is available at: https://www.fedlex.admin.ch/eli/cc/54/757_781_799/en (accessed 9 Nov 2021).

Prior to this case, the law regulating the extent of sentence reductions in cases involving those deemed to have acted with 'diminished culpability' was clear and, from a theoretical perspective at least, uncontroversial.[42] In determining the sentence to be applied in such cases, the following sentencing principles applied. First, an offender deemed to be only partially culpable for the offence was to receive a lesser sentence than that which would have been imposed had they been deemed fully culpable.[43] Second, the judge was not bound by mandatory minimum sentencing laws.[44] Third, the only relevant factor in determining the extent of the sentence reduction was the degree of the reduced culpability of the offender (and the impact of this on the offence committed); in particular, this meant that other matters, such as the seriousness of the offence at issue, were essentially irrelevant.[45] Finally, in acknowledgment of the impact of diminished culpability on the blameworthiness of the offender and in order to take proper account of the principle of culpability (*Schuldprinzip*), the sentencing judge was first to consider the sentence that would have been imposed had the offender been fully culpable and then to reduce this accordingly in order to reflect the offender's diminished culpability. Over the years, the SFSC had developed an approach which consisted of defining the extent of the reduced culpability as 'low', 'medium', or 'high' and providing for a corresponding reduction of the sentence that would have been imposed in event of full culpability by 25%, 50%, or 70% respectively.[46]

These sentencing principles mirrored, unsurprisingly, the general approach to the attribution of criminal liability in Swiss law according to which a clear distinction is to be made between the determination of subjective and objective liability for the prohibited act or omission (*Tatbestandsmässigkeit*) and the issues of unlawfulness (*Rechtswidrigkeit*) and culpability (*Schuld*).[47] (1) Of

[42] See H Wiprächtiger and S Keller 'Art 48a' in MA Niggli and H Wiprächtiger (eds), *Basler Kommentar: Strafrecht I* (4th edn, Basel: Helbing Lichtenhahn Verlag 2019) N 4f; D Jositsch, G Ege, and C Schwarzenegger, *Strafrecht II: Strafen und Massnahmen* (9th edn, Zurich: Schulthess 2018) 85 f; S Trechsel and M Thommen, 'Art 48a' in S Trechsel and M Pieth (eds), *Schweizerisches Strafgesetzbuch: Praxiskommentar* (3rd edn, Zurich: Dike, 2018) N 2. But see H Mathys, 'Zur Technik der Strafzumessung' (2004) 100 *Schweizerische Juristen Zeitung* 173. It is perhaps no coincidence that Judge Mathys was one of the Federal Supreme Court judges on the bench in the case in question.

[43] See eg BGer 6B_585/2008, 19 June 2009, E 3.5; BGE 118 IV 1, 4, E 2; BGE 116 IV 300, 303, E bb.

[44] According to Art 48a para 1 of the Criminal Code, the sentencing judge is not bound by the minimum sentence set out in law if they decide it is necessary to reduce the sentence (*Strafmilderung*). According to Art 111 StGB the minimum sentence to be imposed in a case involving intentional homicide is five years' imprisonment.

[45] See eg BGE 134 IV 132, 136, E 6.1: '*Die Verminderung der Schuldfähigkeit ist bei der Strafzumessung ungeachtet der Schwere der Tat im ganzen Ausmass der Verminderung zu berücksichtigen.*' See also BGE 118 IV 1, 4, E 2; BGE 129 IV 22, 35, E 6.2.

[46] A practice subsequently criticized in BGE 136 IV 55, 62, E 5.6 as '*systemwidrig*'.

[47] See GP Fletcher, *Rethinking Criminal Law* (New York, NY: OUP 2000) 575 for a comparative discussion of the structure of offences.

particular theoretical importance in the context of the attribution of criminal liability is the conceptual separation of culpability (a mixture of capacity and fault) and intention. Only those who are deemed to have acted culpably can be punished.[48] (2) A person deemed wholly to lack culpability cannot be punished for their actions, irrespective of the seriousness of the criminal offence committed or whether or not they intended to commit the offence.

Similarly, in the context of sentencing in cases of diminished culpability this separation between culpability and intent was clearly maintained: the sentencing judge was to determine the sentence that would have been imposed had the accused been fully culpable and to reduce this sentence in accordance with the extent of diminished culpability, irrespective of the extent of the accused's subjective liability.

In its judgment, the SFSC called into question not just its long-standing sentencing principles on diminished culpability, but arguably also the general principles governing the attribution of criminal liability in Swiss law. It set out by acknowledging the importance of the culpability principle and the fact that the sentencing judge was permitted by the Criminal Code to impose a sentence outwith the generally applicable sentencing framework in cases of diminished culpability, if a lower sentence was deemed appropriate. It went on to hold, however, that diminished culpability was just 'one of several criteria' to be considered 'in determining the extent of an offender's guilt'; a number of other factors, including notably *dolus eventualis*, were also considered by the SFSC as indicative of 'lesser blameworthiness' (*geringer Schuldvorwurf*).[49]

It set out an alternative approach for the sentencing judge in dealing with such cases. First, the judge was to ascertain the extent of the offender's diminished culpability and the extent to which this impacted on their culpability for the offence committed (*Tatverschulden*) and on this basis to determine the overall culpability of the offender for the offence (*Gesamtverschulden*). In a second step, the judge was then to determine, within the sentencing framework for the offence at issue, the (hypothetical) sentence appropriate to the offender's culpability. In a third step, the judge could then have regard, where appropriate, to offender-related sentencing components (*Täterkomponeneten*)

[48] Vgl G Stratenwerth, *Schweizersiches Strafrecht, Allgemeiner Teil I: Die Straftat* (Bern: Stämpfli 2011) 33: '*Zu den Grundprinzipien des schweizerischen Strafgesetzbuchs gehört, wie der Rückblick auf die Entstehungsgeschichte gezeigt hat, die strenge Bindung der Strafe an die Schuld*'; A Donatsch and B Tag, *Strafrecht I: Verbrechenslehre* (9th edn, Zurich: Schulthess, 2013) 269.

[49] BGE 136 IV 55, 60, E 5.6: '*Bei der Frage, in welchem Umfang die Einschränkung der Schuldfähigkeit die Verschuldensbewertung beeinflusst, gilt es vor Augen zu halten, dass die verminderte Schuldfähigkeit im Sinne von Art. 19 Abs. 2 StGB (bzw. aArt. 11 StGB) eines von mehreren Kriterien sein kann, wenn auch—je nach Grad der Verminderung—von wesentlichem Gewicht. So trifft etwa denjenigen ein geringerer Schuldvorwurf, dem lediglich eventualvorsätzliches Handeln anzulasten ist.*'

and to the issue of attempts.[50] In addition, and again in a major departure from its earlier case law, the SFSC held that mandatory minimum sentences should generally be respected and a sentence outside the sentencing framework only imposed if this were justified by exceptional circumstances.[51]

The judgment was subject to considerable criticism and described as incoherent and as breaking away without explanation from the earlier case law of the SFSC.[52] It is important to emphasize two distinct but related problems with this approach to sentencing in cases involving diminished culpability. First, the SFSC's insistence on treating culpability and intent both simply as aspects of '*Tatverschulden*' (blameworthiness) seems to be at odds with the dominant and widely accepted principles of the attribution of criminal liability in substantive criminal law theory. Indeed, it seems to share a certain affinity with the widely rejected *kausale Handlungslehre* which considers the subjective markers of liability (such as intention) to be forms of culpability.[53] Essentially, the judgment collapses at the sentencing stage the distinction, considered central to the theory of the criminal law in the context of the attribution of criminal liability, between culpability and subjective liability for the criminal offence.

Second, the consequence of this approach is that instead of establishing the sentence which would have been imposed had the offender been fully culpable and reducing that sentence in accordance with the extent of the offender's 'diminished culpability', the sentencing judge must consider the reduced culpability of the offender simply as one factor which might necessitate a sentence reduction. After establishing the appropriate sentence taking into account the offender's diminished culpability, the sentencing judge is entitled to make

[50] ibid 62 E 5.7: '*Liegt eine Verminderung der Schuldfähigkeit vor, hat der Richter im Sinne einer nachvollziehbaren Strafzumessung somit, in Abänderung der bisherigen Rechtsprechung (vgl BGE 134 IV 132), wie folgt vorzugehen: In einem ersten Schritt ist aufgrund der tatsächlichen Feststellungen des Gutachters zu entscheiden, in welchem Umfange die Schuldfähigkeit des Täters in rechtlicher Hinsicht eingeschränkt ist und wie sich dies insgesamt auf die Einschätzung des Tatverschuldens auswirkt. Das Gesamtverschulden ist zu qualifizieren und mit Blick auf Art 50 StGB im Urteil ausdrücklich zu benennen, wobei von einer Skala denkbarer Abstufungen nach Schweregrad auszugehen ist. Hierauf ist in einem zweiten Schritt innerhalb des zur Verfügung stehenden Strafrahmens die (hypothetische) Strafe zu bestimmen, die diesem Verschulden entspricht. Die so ermittelte Strafe kann dann gegebenenfalls in einem dritten Schritt aufgrund wesentlicher Täterkomponenten (sowie wegen eines allfälligen blossen Versuchs im Sinne von Art. 22 Abs. 1 StGB) verändert werden (Urteil 6B_585/2008, 19 June 2009 E 3.5 mit Hinweis auf BGE 134 IV 132, E 6.1, S 135).*'

[51] BGE 136 IV 55, 63, E 5.8.

[52] See F Bommer, 'Die strafrechtliche Rechtsprechung des Bundesgerichts im Jahr 2010' (2015) 151 *Zeitschrift des Bernischen Juristenvereins* 350, 356.

[53] On the various theories, see Trechsel, Noll, and Pieth, *Schweizerisches Strafrecht* (n 3) 76ff; Donatsch and Tag, *Strafrecht I* (n 48) 93; G Stratenwerth, 'Die Bedeutung der Finalen Handlungslehre für das Schweizerische Strafrecht' (1965) *Schweizerische Zeitschrift für Strafrecht* 179; P Noll, *Der Strafrechtliche Handlungsbegriff* (*Kriminologische Schriftenreihe, vol 54*, Kriminalistik Verlag: Heidelberg 1971) 54. P Graven and B Sträuli, *L'Infraction Pénale Punissable* (2nd edn, Bern: Stämpfli 1995) 59. For a useful discussion of these theories of acting in English see Fletcher, *Rethinking Criminal Law* (n 47) 476–83.

further deductions for other factors such as the fact that the offence was only attempted. Essentially, this means that the sentence reduction afforded for the diminished culpability of the offender is not deducted from the full sentence which would have been imposed had the offender been deemed fully culpable. This means that the sentence imposed will not necessarily take proper account of the extent of the offender's diminished culpability.

The judgment is not only problematic from the perspective of criminal law theory; it is also questionable whether the approach espoused is in line with human rights. A state is only permitted to punish a person if they can be held to be *culpable* for the conduct at issue.[54] The imposition of punishment on a person who entirely lacks culpability violates both the principle of legality[55] and the presumption of innocence.[56] Such individuals must not be punished, although a court might be entitled to make a treatment order, in cases involving mental illness: 'Our collective conscience does not allow punishment where it cannot impose blame.'[57] This reflects the fact that, '[w]hatever doubts [theologians, philosophers, and scientists] have entertained as to the matter [exercise of free will], the practical business of government and administration of the law is obliged to proceed on more or less rough and ready judgments based on the assumption that mature and rational persons are in control of their own conduct.'[58]

In the same sense, a person whose culpability is deemed to be diminished is entitled to a reduction of the sentence that would have otherwise been imposed had they been fully culpable. It would be unjust to sentence and punish the person to the same extent as a fully culpable person;[59] the sentence must be reduced in proportion to the diminished culpability. The failure to properly take into account the scope of the offender's culpability violates an individual's rights in precisely the same way, as would the imposition of punishment on a person who cannot be held culpable for their behaviour. It would seem clear that irrespective of the extent of the reduction, the entire sentence that would have otherwise been imposed must be reduced in proportion to the diminished

[54] See eg Trechsel, Noll, and Pieth, *Schweizerisches Strafrecht* (n 3) 142.

[55] See eg *Vevara v Italy* App no 17475/09, 29 Oct 2013, paras 44–45.

[56] *AP, MP and TP and EL, RL and JO-L v Switzerland*, 29 Aug 1997, Reports 1997-V.

[57] *Durham v United States*, 214 F.2d 862, 876 (DC Cir 1954).

[58] *Gregg v United States*, 316 US 74, 79–80 (1942) per Justice Jackson; see also *Holloway v United States*, 148 F.2d 665, 666–67 (DC Cir 1945); *Steward v Davis*, 301 US 548, 590 (1937). For discussion see M Lydon, 'Criminal Law—Rehabilitation, A Thesis; Punishment, the Antithesis—Insanity Defence in the Balance (1969) 19 *DePaul Law Review* 140, 142.

[59] This would be incompatible with the culpability principle: see S Trechsel and M Jean-Richard, 'Art. 19' in S Trechsel and M Pieth (eds), *Schweizerisches Strafgesetzbuch: Praxiskommentar* (3rd edn, Zurich: Dike 2018) N 16: '*Verzicht auf Herabsetzung der Strafe bei verminderter Schuldfähigkeit ist mit einem Schuldstrafrecht nicht vereinbar.*'

culpability of the offender. Legality demands that only those who had capacity and a fair opportunity to obey the law can be justly punished and then only to the extent that this equates to the extent of their culpability. In practical terms and in direct contrast to the judgment of the SFSC, this means that the deduction for the diminished culpability must be undertaken after the sentence has otherwise been established; there can then be no further deductions.[60]

One of the most interesting things about this judgment, for our purposes here, is that the SFSC felt able to depart so substantially not just from its established practice, but also from the criminal law orthodoxy. The judgment highlights an important difference in practice between theoretical principles and human rights standards and the possibility for the legislature and the courts to simply discount the criminal law theory on the attribution of criminal liability. This underscores the relevance of clearly articulating the relationship between the fundamental principles of criminal legal theory and the individual rights on which these are based. Failure to ensure that these rights are upheld at the sentencing stage can lead to very real injustice, which goes to the very heart of the legitimacy of both the attribution of criminal liability and the imposition of punishment. This suggests that there is room for an alternative theoretical account of the sentencing exercise as understood as a practice within the context of a liberal conception of criminal law and justice. This requires consideration of the values, which might be expected to underpin the sentencing decision in light of human rights principles and indeed the criminal law orthodoxy.

IV. Human Rights as Limits on Punishment

This book sets out to demonstrate, even if this is seldom acknowledged in theory or practice, that human rights are of considerable importance at sentencing. In this regard, reference is made principally to the guarantees as set out in the European Convention on Human Rights.[61] In identifying those human rights guarantees, which are of particular relevance at the sentencing stage, a number of issues fall to be examined. First, it is important to consider why or for what the offender is to be sentenced. Modern criminal law is dominated by principles of individual responsibility and culpability. This reflects

[60] These issues are discussed in more detail in Ch 2.

[61] Although the Court has been subject to considerable criticism, see eg P Popelier, S Lambrecht, and K Lemmens (eds), *Criticism of the European Court of Human Rights* (Antwerp: Intersentia 2016), it occupies an undeniably central position in interpreting and developing human rights in Europe.

the commitment to liberalism, particularly in the context of the attribution of liability, in western criminal justice systems.[62] Here the culpability of the offender takes centre stage. Punishment is only to be imposed on a culpable offender for conduct which was clearly marked as criminal at the time of the commission of the offence.[63]

This understanding of the criminal law is accepted in the leading theories on, and indeed practice concerning, the attribution of criminal liability.[64] It has been subject, however, particularly in the context of the imposition of punishment to a number of challenges. One of the most important of these has been from orthodox positivism which advocates less consideration of the responsibility of the offender and more focus on their dangerousness. According to this vision, the individualization of punishment is based an offender's social responsibility or dangerousness rather than on any notion of moral responsibility.[65] This view of punishment, however, is difficult if not impossible to reconcile with established principles regulating the attribution of criminal liability. If the descriptive understanding of the criminal law as a reaction to individual culpability for clearly defined prior wrongs is accepted in the context of the attribution of liability, the role of human rights in the context of the imposition of punishment is clear. Both the attribution of criminal law and the imposition of punishment are subject to the same liberal constraints as a means of ensuring that violations of the criminal law are justly or fairly sanctioned.[66] It seems to follow from this that in determining the sentence the judge should only be concerned with the culpability of the accused for the specific conduct at issue.[67] In the words of Hall: 'it is unjust that what was legal when done should be subsequently held criminal, that what was punishable by a minor sanction when committed should later be punished more severely.'[68]

Of interest, however, is the fact that sentencing practice does not (always) appear to be in alignment with these principles. Whereas liability for an antecedent act or omission is the defining factor in the substantive criminal law

[62] Farmer, *Making the Modern Criminal Law* (n 2) especially ch 6. See further N Lacey, *In Search of Criminal Responsibility: Ideas, Interests and Institutions* (Oxford: OUP 2016); N Lacey, 'Socializing the Subject of Criminal Law? Criminal Responsibility and the Purposes of Criminalization' (2016) 99 *Marquette Law Review* 541.

[63] See eg S Trechsel and M Jean-Richard, 'Art 1' in S Trechsel and M Pieth (eds), *Schweizerisches Strafgesetzbuch: Praxiskommentar* (3rd edn, Zurich: Dike 2018) N 1, N 6.

[64] See eg Trechsel, Noll, and Pieth, *Schweizerisches Strafrecht* (n 3) 65ff.

[65] M Foucault, 'About the Concept of the "Dangerous Individual" in the 19th-Century Legal Psychiatry' [1978] *International Journal of Law and Psychiatry* 1.

[66] Y Cartuyvels and G Cliqennois, 'The Punishment of Mentally Ill Offenders in Belgium: Care as Legitimacy for Control' (2015) 12 *Champ Pénal* N 6.

[67] Fletcher, *Rethinking Criminal Law* (n 47) 461.

[68] J Hall, 'Nulla Poena Sine Lege' (1937) 47 *Yale Law Journal* 165, 171.

orthodoxy, marking the boundaries between criminal and police law,[69] many important sentencing practices seem principally occupied with future risk or with factors which do not appear *prima facie* to go to the culpability of the perpetrator for a specific offence. Other factors, which seem to have little to do with the blameworthiness of an accused for a specific offence, such as previous convictions, confessions, or the length of the proceedings, are commonly taken into account in the sentencing decision. An examination of the principle of legality allows for consideration of the extent to which these practices might be said to infringe human rights principles.

Second, it is important to consider limits on the extent of punishment: how much punishment should be imposed? The notion of proportionality is usually referred to in the sentencing literature in the context of the relationship between the sentence and seriousness of the offence.[70] Proportionality as a rights-based restraint is quite different in that it regulates the relationship between the sentence and the relevant human right. In its guise as a rights-based restraint, proportionality is generally understood in terms of 'liberty-interest proportionality', whereby incursions on liberty or life or expression are required to be proportionate to the offence for which they were imposed.[71]

Human rights are not infrequently discussed in the context of the proportionality of the sentencing decision.[72] The practical relevance of these safeguards is less clear. Commentators in the US have pointed to the fact that the US Supreme Court, for example, takes very different approaches to substantive sentencing law depending on whether a capital sentence is available to the sentencing court. In the context of capital sentencing, its review process has been described as 'robust' while in non-capital cases its oversight has been referred to as 'virtually non-existent'.[73] Consideration of the case law of the European Court of Human Rights (ECtHR) meanwhile suggests that proportionality at the sentencing stage might well have relevance beyond the confines of the

[69] MA Niggli and S Maeder, 'Was Schützt Eigentlich Strafrecht (und Schützt es Überhaupt Etwas)?' (2011) *Aktuelle Juristische Praxis* 443.

[70] See eg in the context of just deserts theory, von Hirsch, *Doing Justice* (n 6).

[71] A Ristroph, 'Proportionality as a Principle of Limited Government (2005) 55 *Duke Law Review* 263, 301.

[72] See M Bagaric, S Gopalan, and MR Florio, 'A Principled Strategy for Addressing the Incarceration Crisis: Redefining Excessive Imprisonment as a Human Rights Abuse' (2017) 38 *Cardozo Law Review* 1663, 1710, 1712 focusing on how much to punish. See also the Canadian case *R v Smith (Edward Dewey)* [1987] 1 SCR 1045 and the Irish judgment in *Lynch and Whelan v Minister for Justice, Equality and Law Reform* [2010] IESC 34.

[73] See RE Barkow, 'The Court of Life and Death: The Two Tracks of Constitutional Sentencing Law and the Case for Uniformity' (1996) 107 *Michigan Law Review* 1145. Mandatory life sentence without parole in the context of juveniles was deemed to constitute 'cruel and unusual punishment' by the USSC in *Graham v Florida* 560 US 48 (2010) and *Miller v Alabama* 567 US 460 (2012).

prohibition on inhuman and degrading punishment[74] and might extend to a number of other fundamental rights, notably liberty[75] and the freedom of expression. Consideration of the scope of proportionality as a human right provides the basis for considering sentencing laws and practices, such as the resort to mandatory minimum sentences or the imposition of indeterminate sentences of imprisonment.

Third, to what extent do human rights demand consistency or a lack of disparity between sentences? Proportionality might also be understood as encompassing what Ristroph has referred to as 'equality-interest proportionality',[76] which requires that punishment be imposed 'consistently and nonarbitrarily'.[77] Although this might be considered to constitute an aspect of proportionality, it will be argued here that it is more helpful to consider the issue in the context of the right to equality. To what extent might disparity at the sentencing stage be said to interfere with the right to equality and the right to freedom from discrimination? In the sentencing literature, disparity is often concerned with sentencing outcomes, with ensuring that similar sentences are imposed for similar crimes. Equality in this sense is taken to mean ensuring consistency of outcome. But consistent with what? An examination of the human rights principles and in particular the prohibition on discrimination provides the basis for examining the relationship between consistency, equality, and justice.[78] This in turn will allow for consideration of the issue of disparity in the development of a variety of sentencing practices and theory, notably in the context of the development of sentencing guidelines and mandatory sentencing regimes.

Fourth, it is important to consider who should have the responsibility for the sentencing decision and the consequences of legislative or executive interference at sentencing. The right to a judge might be considered to be more of a procedural than a substantive guarantee. It will be argued here, however, that the role of the judge is not just essential to guaranteeing procedural fairness but is also of considerable importance in the context of ensuring freedom

[74] *Harkins and Edwards v UK* App nos 9146/07 and 32650/07, 17 Jan 2012; *Rrapo v Albania* App no 58555/10, 25 Sept 2012; *Babar Ahmad and Others v UK* App nos 24027/07, 11949/08, 36742/08, 66911/09, and 67354/09, 10 Apr 2012; *Laszlo Magyar v Hungary* App no 73593/10, 25 May 2014.

[75] D van Zyl Smit and S Snacken, *Principles of European Prison Law and Policy: Penology and Human Rights* (Oxford: OUP 2009) 95.

[76] Ristroph, 'Proportionality' (n 71) 301.

[77] ibid 269. 'Equality-interest proportionality is perhaps more accurately called uniformity but to follow common practice, I will refer to uniformity as a variant of proportionality' and at 304 citing *Furman v Georgia*, 408 US 238 (1972) at 245 where the majority was not prepared to hold that the death penalty was disproportionate per se to any offence, but did hold that the manner in which the death penalty was applied was disproportionate.

[78] See further Ch 4.

from arbitrariness and guaranteeing adherence to substantive human rights. Although it might seem clear that a judicial authority should have the primary responsibility for setting the sentence, a number of sentencing laws and practices seem to undermine this notion. Examples include mandatory sentencing provisions, the conceptual separation of sentencing and other aspects such as the enforcement of the sentence, and, in more recent times, the introduction of summary proceedings, which afford the prosecutor a considerable role in determining the sentence. It is important to note in this regard that the limited constitutional review in sentencing takes on particular importance in criminal justice systems, which rely on cooperation of the accused in criminal proceedings as a case disposal mechanism. In view of the fact that the vast majority of cases are 'settled' without a trial by way of pre-trial pleas on the part of the accused, there is little control of 'disproportionate or arbitrary sentences except the discretion of the prosecutor bringing the charges'.[79] It is essential therefore to consider the ways in which human rights principles might be said to regulate who is entitled to set the sentence.

One response to this might be to question not just the relevance of human rights but also the authority of the ECtHR. In this regard, it is important to note that modern sentencing practice has been profoundly affected by populist punitiveness[80] and penal populism,[81] which has led to a period of continually increasing sentencing severity, largely unrelated to the introduction of more punitive sentencing guidelines or legislation.[82] At the same time, human rights, and the ECtHR in particular, have been under sustained criticism,[83] which is probably best understood in the context of the rise of political populism.

[79] Barkow, 'The Court of Life and Death' (n 73). For criticism of the prosecutor as an effective control mechanism see RE Barkow, 'Institutional Design and the Policing of Prosecutors: Lessons from Administrative Law' (2009) 61 *Stanford Law Review* 869.

[80] AE Bottoms, 'The Philosophy and Politics of Punishment and Sentencing' in C Clarkson and R Morgan (eds), *The Politics of Sentencing Reform* (Oxford: Clarendon Press 1995) 40; AE Bottoms, 'Reflections on the Criminological Enterprise' (1995) 46 *Cambridge Law Journal* 240.

[81] JV Roberts and others, *Penal Populism and Public Opinion: Lessons from Five Countries* (Oxford: OUP 2002); J Pratt, *Penal Populism* (London: Routledge 2006); J Pratt, 'Penal Populism and the Contemporary Role of Punishment' in T Anthony and C Cuneen (eds), *The Critical Criminology Companion* (Annandale: Hawkins Press 2008) 265.

[82] Garland, *The Culture of Control* (n 7).

[83] See notably Lord Sumption's Reith lectures, available at https://www.bbc.co.uk/programmes/m00057m9 (accessed 11 Nov 2021). For a useful discussion of the issues see H Kennedy and J Sumption, 'Are Our Human Rights Laws Working?' *Prospect* (12 July 2019), in which Lord Sumption refers to judicial decision-making under the ECHR as an 'unholy mixture of grandeur and officious meddling. It achieves nothing that cannot be achieved with perfect democratic legitimacy by ordinary legislation.' For discussion of the critique of human rights see M Mahlmann, 'One Step Too Far—Some Philosophical and Political Reflections on the Current Critique of Human Rights' in A Sajó and R Uitz (eds), *Critical Essays on Human Rights* (The Hague: Eleven International Publishing 2020) 67; P Popelier, S Lambrecht, and K Lemmens (eds), *Criticism of the European Court of Human Rights* (Antwerp: Intersentia 2016).

Although penal populism clearly preceded the more recent resurgence of political populism, these phenomena might nevertheless be seen to be 'structurally connected'.[84] In the words of Lacey:

> It is probably more accurate to see overcriminalization and penal severity as themselves products of some of the large economic, social and political forces that have created populism itself: perceived weaknesses in national state sovereignty, prompting a resort to criminalization as one few tools of governance still within nation-state control; social conflict; a failure to ensure that an adequate majority feel that they have a stake in the prevailing order; and persistent inequality.[85]

Nevertheless, there can be no denying that human rights guarantees referred to earlier are common to all criminal justice systems in liberal democracies. The commitment to liberal constitutionalism means that adherence to human rights principles cannot be considered to be in any sense radical. In fact, quite to the contrary, one would expect these principles to be upheld. It is interesting, then, to think about why this is not the case and why these principles do not enjoy broader recognition in sentencing practice.

Consideration of the principles underpinning the sentencing decision provides the basis for revisiting important sentencing practices in the light of these principles. In addition, it allows for analysis of the extent to which these sentencing practices deviate from the orthodoxy and how they can be reconciled with a human rights-based understanding of the sentencing decision. The methodology employed here is not comparative. Various sentencing practices from different jurisdictions are examined with a view to illustrating the relevance and potential impact of the human rights principles in practice. Although there are obviously considerable differences between the various sentencing systems, many of the issues in question, such as the legitimacy of relying on confessions or previous convictions, are of common concern. The approach is necessarily selective. The aim here is not to produce a definitive or comprehensive account of human rights and sentencing but rather to begin to identify some human rights principles, which might govern or constrain the sentencing decision. This in turn will provide the basis for consideration of the role of human rights guarantees in the justification of punishment.

[84] N Lacey, 'Populism and the Rule of Law' (2019) 15 *Annual Review of Law and Social Science* 79, 91.
[85] ibid.

V. Human Rights and the Justification of Punishment

The determination of the sentence is generally considered to be one of the most difficult tasks facing a judge.[86] Judges are bound by what are sometimes characterized as competing expectations. They are required to pass a sentence which is not only appropriate in the case at issue, but which fits with the values of the sentencing system more broadly. This focuses attention on the importance of the rationale(s) on which the imposition of punishment is based. Even if it is accepted that human rights serve to restrict the sentence which is to be imposed, the question is whether and to what extent this conception of punishment in a liberal democracy has the potential to contribute to the debate on the justification of punishment.

The justification of punishment is focused on aims and in this context fundamental disagreement exists between those who support broadly retributivist theories and those who argue in favour of consequentialist approaches, such as rehabilitation or deterrence. Part of the reason why consequentialist theories have fallen out of favour is that they are unable to explain why only the guilty should be punished. In the words of Gardner:

> any broadly utilitarian defence of the rule against punishment of innocents leaves that rule too vulnerable to exigencies at the margins. One can always imagine extreme cases in which punishing the innocent would bring more benefit than following the rule would bring, even allowing for the value of the rule itself and the value of its combination with other rules.[87]

Retributivist accounts, on the other hand, are generally assumed to be better placed to account for the importance of ensuring that only the guilty are punished.

Much of the recent discussion of justified punishment should be understood in this context as an attempt to limit retributivist accounts of punishment.[88] It is questionable, however, whether such perceptions of justice or fairness are in fact tied to notions of retribution or desert. Tonry has argued that:

[86] See eg Trechsel and Thommen, 'Art 47' (n 9) N 5.

[87] J Gardner, 'Introduction' in HLA Hart, *Punishment and Responsibility: Essays in the Philosophy of Law* (J Gardner, 2nd edn, Oxford: OUP 2008) xx.

[88] Notably von Hirsch, *Doing Justice* (n 6) 79. See Garland, *The Culture of Control* (n 7) 9 citing A von Hirsch, *Censure and Sanctions* (Oxford: Clarendon Press 1993) who suggests that 'the reappearance of "just deserts" retribution as a generalized policy goal in the US and UK' was initially prompted 'by the perceived unfairness of individualised sentencing'. See also S Trechsel, 'Die Entwicklung der Mittel und Methoden des Strafrechts' (1974) 90 *Schweizerische Zeitschrift für Strafrecht* 271.

> Desert does not have widespread appeal . . . because all reasonable people believe that retribution rather than general prevention is the general justification of punishment, but instead because there is a widely shared intuition that justice is inexorably linked with fairness and that fairness consists in treating like cases alike. Even in an incapacitative or rehabilitative scheme of punishment, most people would find it inappropriate that cases be dealt with inconsistently. Fairness, not desert, is the key idea. Because desert implies a comprehensive approach to setting sentencing standards that can then be consistently or inconsistently applied, desert often serves as a proxy concept for fairness.[89]

This, though, gives rise to questions about what this notion of fairness at sentencing might entail.

This book sets out, then, to examine the theoretical importance and extent of human rights principles at the sentencing stage, while analysing the consequences of acceptance of these principles for sentencing practice. Notwithstanding the gap between sentencing theory and practice, it will be argued that human rights principles do in fact have a role to play in constraining the sentencing exercise and that this has considerable implications for some of the most common sentencing practices. At the heart of this study is the contention that punishment will only be justified if the human rights principles restricting the state in its imposition of punishment are adequately recognized and guaranteed. The argument is not that justice is exhausted by adherence to the human rights principles, but rather that these are preconditions of justice. In this sense, the book is concerned primarily with the limits on punishment rather than with the appropriate sentence. Consideration of these limits nevertheless provides the basis for reconsideration of some of the most important assumptions underpinning the debate between retributivists and consequentialists on the justification of punishment.

[89] M Tonry, *Sentencing Matters* (New York, NY: OUP 2006) 184.

2
Legality and the Sentence

I. Legality and Punishment

Offenders are to be punished for their crimes and not for other reasons such as lifestyle or character. This is one of the most fundamental principles of the criminal law in liberal societies. Punishment is contingent on a determination that the offender has committed a criminal offence. This reflects a commitment to the notion that the power to punish is constrained by law. Legality demands that disputes be resolved by reference to pre-existing legal rules; punishment is only to be imposed for behaviour which is expressly marked in law as criminal at the time that it was committed.[1] This principle serves as an important protection against the arbitrary application of the law and the misuse of power.[2] In addition, it underscores the importance of the commitment to individual agency. Laws must be sufficiently clearly defined in order to ensure that individuals are aware of the limits on their activities. Only those who had a fair opportunity to act in accordance with the law and who were capable of doing so can be held accountable—and punished—for their actions.

The legality principle is complemented in the procedural context by the presumption of innocence. The criminal law defines the nature of the unlawful conduct. It is this conduct which the prosecution must prove occurred and a failure to do so will result in the acquittal of the accused. Legality and the presumption of innocence thus share a certain symmetry, which explains why creating broad criminal law provisions can interfere with the standard of proof

[1] See Art 1 CC: 'A penalty or measure may only be imposed for an act that has been expressly declared to be an offence by law'; and BGE 118 Ia 305, 319: 'Criminal sanctions constitute serious infringements of personal liberty and thus must be founded on a formal legal basis, which defines the nature of the punishment and the criminal conduct'. See also J Horder, *Ashworth's Principles of Criminal Law* (9th edn, Oxford: OUP 2019) 85; SH Kadisch, S Schulhofer, and RE Barkow, *Criminal Law and its Processes* (10th edn, New York, NY: Aspen Publishers, 2016).

[2] *Streletz, Kessler and Krenz v Germany* [GC] App nos 34044/96, 35532/97, and 44801/98, ECHR 2001-II, para 50. See also S Trechsel and M Jean-Richard, 'Art 1' in S Trechsel and M Pieth (eds), *Schweizerisches Strafgesetzbuch: Praxiskommentar* (3rd edn, Zurich: Dike 2018) N3: 'effective safeguards against arbitrary prosecution, conviction and punishment'.

Sentencing and Human Rights. Sarah J Summers, Oxford University Press. © Sarah J Summers 2022.
DOI: 10.1093/oso/9780192870384.003.0002

requirement and the presumption of innocence by making it easier for the state to prove its case.[3]

These principles are widely accepted in the writing on criminal law and indeed procedure[4] and are reflected in the leading theories governing the attribution of criminal liability.[5] They are rarely considered, however, in any detail at the sentencing stage. Much is made of the importance of the definition of crime, of placing the burden of proof on the prosecution to prove the various aspects of the charge and yet at the sentencing stage, it appears commonplace for factors to be considered, which seem to have little to do with the offence committed. At the sentencing stage, the importance of 'character' seems to re-emerge from the shadows, while legality is relegated to the background.

This chapter sets out to address the failure to consider carefully the relevance of legality at sentencing and begins with an examination of the relationship between legality and the generally accepted principles governing the attribution of criminal liability. Despite considerable differences in these theories of attribution, even across Europe, some common principles do exist. The basis for this consensus, it will be argued, is the common commitment to legality. The state is only entitled to call culpable individuals to account for clearly defined criminal behaviour and not for other reasons, such as status or character. The same principles must regulate the imposition of punishment. A lack of symmetry in this regard would give rise to serious questions about the coherence of the criminal law. It would make little sense to insist, for instance, that criminal offences be strictly defined and then to allow punishment to be imposed for reasons not connected to the commission of these offences.

Consideration of the definition and scope of legality as a human right as guaranteed by Article 7(1) of the European Convention on Human Rights (ECHR) demonstrates the relevance of legality both in the context of the attribution of liability and in relation to the imposition of the sentence. Article 7(1) ECHR requires not just that criminal liability and punishment only be imposed on culpable individuals following a violation of clearly defined laws; it also requires causality between the ascription of liability and the imposition of punishment. The analysis of the scope of Article 7(1) ECHR provides the basis

[3] V Tadros and S Tierney, 'The Presumption of Innocence and the Human Rights Act' (2004) 67 *Modern Law Review* 402.

[4] See eg RA Duff and others, *The Trial on Trial: Volume 3: Towards a Normative Theory of the Trial* (Oxford: Hart Publishing 2007).

[5] See eg S Trechsel, P Noll, and M Pieth, *Schweizerisches Strafrecht, Allgemeiner Teil I: Allgemeine Voraussetzungen der Strafbarkeit* (7th edn, Zurich: Schulthess 2017) 50; A Donatsch and B Tag, *Strafrecht I: Verbrechenslehre* (9th edn, Zurich; Schulthess, 2013) 30; G Stratenwerth, *Schweizerisches Strafrecht, Allgemeiner Teil I: Die Straftat* (4th edn, Bern, Stämpfli 2011) 83. Horder, *Ashworth's Principles* (n 1); GP Fletcher, *Rethinking Criminal Law* (New York, NY: OUP 2000).

for detailed consideration of the role of legality in the context of the imposition of punishment.

Several important sentencing practices, including those involving previous convictions and confessions, seem difficult to reconcile with legality. If legality prohibits the imposition of more severe punishment on an offender for reasons not connected to their culpability for the offence at issue, then treating previous convictions as an aggravating factor seems problematic. Similarly, the practice of treating a lack of remorse or a failure to plead guilty or confess as an aggravating factor gives rise to the suspicion that a higher sentence is being imposed for (bad) character, rather than in response to the offender's blameworthiness for the offence at issue. Equally, assuming punishment should reflect an offender's culpability for the offence, it seems unlikely that a failure to reduce the sentence to reflect an offender's reduced culpability could be deemed compatible with legality. Consideration of these issues provides the basis for an examination of the disconnect between the importance of legality in the context of the attribution of liability and its relevance in relation to the imposition of punishment and for discussion of the extent of the legality principle as constraint on sentencing law and practice.

II. Legality and Theories of the Attribution of Criminal Liability

Legality is of particular importance in the criminal law context.[6] A state is only permitted to hold individuals accountable for conduct which is clearly set out in law as criminal. There is considerable academic discussion about the scope of the legality principle, the rationale(s) on which it is based, and even about whether or not it can be characterized as one legal principle. Some have argued that there is 'no such thing as a single "principle of legality" ';[7] while others have called into question the characterization of the principle as a legal rule, arguing that it is preferable to think of it as 'a legal concept embodied in a series of doctrines'.[8] These include the prohibition on retrospective legislation (*nullum*

[6] F Allen, *The Habits of Legality: Criminal Justice and the Rule of Law* (New York, NY: OUP 1996) 5: 'The legality ideal confronts its sternest test in the areas of criminal justice'.

[7] See eg P Westen, 'Two Rules of Legality in Criminal Law' (2007) 26 *Law and Philosophy* 229, 229 arguing that the principle 'consists of two distinct norms that derive from two fundamental principles of criminal justice, viz. the principle, "No person shall be punished in the absence of a bad mind," and the principle that underlies the maxim, "Every person is presumed innocent until proven guilty" '.

[8] PH Robinson, 'Fair Notice and Fair Adjudication: Two Kinds of Legality' (2005) 154 *University of Pennsylvania Law Review* 335.

crimen, nulla poena sine lege praevia);[9] the requirement that criminal activity be clearly defined in law (*nullum crimen, nulla poena sine lege certa*);[10] and the notion that the law itself be strictly construed (*nullum crimen, nulla poena sine lege stricta*).[11] It is generally agreed that the principle embodies the concept of law as a means of restricting state authority and that it serves to prevent arbitrariness and in particular the arbitrary imposition of punishment.[12] In this regard, the principle has both an *ex ante* function in announcing rules of conduct and an *ex post* role in the context of the adjudication of contraventions of the law.[13] Individuals are only to be subject to the power of the prosecuting and investigating authorities for behaviour which is clearly and prospectively defined as a criminal wrong and punishment is only to be imposed on those who have committed such activities.

The commitment to legality is clearly evident in the process of the attribution of criminal liability. This is a carefully regulated affair, governed by strict substantive and procedural rules that determine whether a person can be held criminally responsible for a particular act or omission. A considerable amount of energy has been invested in examining and defining the general principles of criminal liability and there is a vast body of literature dedicated to the task of explaining the manner in which this liability is to be established.[14] Despite considerable differences between legal systems, even within Europe, as regards the manner in which criminal liability is determined, it is possible to identify two principles, which might be considered to constitute 'universal principles of criminal liability'.[15] The 'universality' of these principles might be seen as closely connected to, or even a direct result of, the common commitment to legality.

First, the focus of the criminal law is said to be 'act-based', in that it is designed to attribute liability for acts or omissions committed or attempted, and not simply for bad character.[16] The emphasis of the substantive criminal law

[9] F Allen, 'The Erosion of Legality in American Criminal Justice: Some Latter-Day Adventures of the Nulla Poena Principle' (1987) 29 *Arizona Law Review* 385.

[10] H Packer, *The Limits of the Criminal Sanction* (Stanford, CA: Stanford University Press 1968) 73.

[11] For a good overview of the principle see J Hall, 'Nulla Poena Sine Lege' (1937) 47 *Yale Law Journal* 165.

[12] Trechsel and Jean-Richard, 'Art 1' (n 2) N 3.

[13] Robinson, 'Fair Notice' (n 8) 375.

[14] See eg Stratenwerth, *Schweizerisches Strafrecht, Allgemeiner Teil I* (n 5); Donatsch and Tag, *Strafrecht I* (n 5); Trechsel, Noll, and Pieth, *Schweizerisches Strafrecht* (n 5); Horder, *Ashworth's Principles* (n 1).

[15] Fletcher, *Rethinking Criminal Law* (n 5) 420 refers to the requirement of an act as 'a primary candidate for a universal principle of criminal liability'.

[16] Stratenwerth, *Schweizerische Strafrecht, Allgemeiner Teil I* (n 5) 74–76 (*Tatstrafrecht* as opposed to *Täterstrafrecht*); Fletcher, *Rethinking Criminal Law* (n 5) 420, 426–33 (contrasting acts and conditions); O Wendell Holmes, *The Common Law* (New York, NY: Barnes and Noble 2004) 33: 'the reason for requiring an act is, that an act implies choice, and that it is felt to be impolitic and unjust to make a man answerable for harm, unless he might have chosen otherwise.'

is not on who a person 'is', but rather on what they have (or indeed have not) 'done'.[17] The criminal law is concerned with particular 'types of conduct' and not with 'character or disposition'.[18] The requirement that the state clearly define the conduct considered criminal dictates that something concrete must have occurred before the state is entitled to intervene.[19] The close relationship between the legality principle and the 'act requirement' is unmistakable. In the words of Fletcher, 'there is nothing controversial about saying that criminal punishment presupposes an unlawful act. It seems indeed to follow from the maxim '*nulla poena sine lege*'.[20] Without this requirement, it would be possible for those charged with enforcing the law to pick and choose those to be subjected to punishment.[21] The criminal justice authorities would be able to subject individuals to the might of the criminal justice system on the basis that they considered the individuals to be dangerous or simply of bad character.[22] Provisions which allow for the detention or punishment of certain categories of people not for specific behaviour but essentially for being 'anti-social' are at odds with act-based criminal law and are impossible to reconcile with the principle of legality.[23] This indicates that legality not only requires that offences be

[17] Stratenwerth, *Schweizerisches Strafrecht, Allgemeiner Teil I* (n 5) 76, 'Ein Täterstrafrecht ist daher grundsätzlich abzulehnen'; V Schwander, *Das Schweizerische Strafgesetzbuch* (2nd edn, Zurich: Polygraphischer Verlag 1964) 22.

[18] Stratenwerth, *Schweizerisches Strafrecht, Allgemeiner Teil I* (n 5) 126: 'Bei Strafe verboten oder geboten sein können, wo wurde oben ... bereits ausgeführt, nicht Charaktereigenschaften oder Gesinnungen, sondern allein bestimmte Verhaltensweisen.'

[19] Trechsel, Noll, and Pieth, *Schweizerisches Strafrecht* (n 5) 73: '*Das Verständnis und die Anwendung des positiven Rechts müssen vom Gesetz ausgehen. Das Gesetz knüpft die Strafen und Massnahmen immer an die Erfüllung bestimmter Tatbestände*'; see too Donatsch and Tag, *Strafrecht I* (n 5) 84. Hall, 'Nulla Poena' (n 11) 184: 'What is actually done is the basis for judgment.' G Gordon, *The Criminal Law of Scotland* (3rd edn, Edinburgh, W Green 2000): it is 'axiomatic that before there can be a conviction for a crime there must have been created a situation forbidden by the criminal law'.

[20] Fletcher, *Rethinking Criminal Law* (n 5) 468.

[21] See eg *Papachristou v Jacksonville*, 405 US 156 (1972) in which the USSC held so-called 'status crimes' (being a 'dissolute person', a 'common gambler', 'a habitual loafer') to be unconstitutional. See also AG Amsterdam, 'Constitutional Restrictions on the Federal Punishment of Crimes of Status, Crimes of General Obnoxiousness, Crimes of Displeasing Police Officers, and the Like' (1967) 3 *Criminal Law Bulletin* 205, 234.

[22] A good example of such law is provided by the Soviet criminal law of the 1930s which provided for the punishment of 'socially dangerous acts' and in the absence of any specific statute allowed for judicial determination of those acts or omissions determined to be 'socially dangerous', see HJ Berman, 'Principles of Soviet Criminal Law' (1947) 56 *Yale Law Journal* 803, 804; see also FJ Feldbrugge, 'Soviet Criminal Law—The Last Six Years' (1963) 54 *Journal of Criminal Law and Criminology* 249, 261, noting that 'in various periods (particularly in the thirties), criminal law policy was, for the most part, determined by the need to supply fixed numbers of forced laborers'.

[23] Hall, 'Nulla Poena' (n 11) 182. English law famously allowed for the preventive detention of vagabonds and mendicants and the concept of 'dangerousness' has considerable current importance with the 'rejuvenation of protectionism as a central goal of penal policy', see E Baker, 'Dangerousness, Rights and Criminal Justice' (1993) 56 *Modern Law Review* 528; Home Office, *Crime, Justice and Protecting the Public* (1990) Cm 965, para 2.15. In addition, such preventative detention is incompatible with Art 5 ECHR, see eg *Lawless v Ireland (No 3)*, 1 July 1961, Series A no 3; *Jecius v Lithuania* App no 34578/97, ECHR-IX, para 5; *A and Others v UK* [GC] App no 3455/05, ECHR 2009; *Blokhin v Russia* [GC] App no 47512/06, 23 Mar 2016, para 171.

set out in law, but also imposes some constraints on criminalization in that the legislator is prohibited from enacting offences that criminalize individuals on the basis of 'status' or 'character'.

Another fundamental principle of criminal liability, which is common to western criminal justice systems and which again is closely connected to the legality principle, is the notion of 'subjective attribution'. In the context of the attribution of criminal liability, it is not sufficient that the person committed an unlawful act, it is also essential that the wrongdoing can be attributed to them (subjective attribution; culpability; *Schuld*).[24] This notion is quite separate from subjective state of mind requirements, or *mens rea*, such as intent. Individual agency and the capacity of individuals to adapt their behaviour to ensure compliance with the law lies at the heart of the legality principle. An individual can only be held accountable if they could have been expected to act otherwise.

There is a clear connection, here, between the requirement evident in the legality principle that a person have a fair opportunity to ascertain what conduct is prohibited in order that they are afforded the opportunity to act otherwise[25] and the criminal law principle, which states that only those who were both capable of recognizing the wrongful nature of their behaviour and able to modify their behaviour accordingly are to be held to be culpable for that behaviour. A good exposition of this connection between legality and culpability was provided by Judge Wright in the case of *United States v Moore*:

> The concept of criminal responsibility is, by its very nature, 'an expression of the moral sense of the community'. In western society, the concept has been shaped by two dominant value judgments—that punishment must be morally legitimate, and that it must not unduly threaten the liberties and dignity of the individual in his relationship to society. As a result, there has historically been a strong conviction in our jurisprudence that to hold a man criminally responsible, his actions must have been the product of a 'free will' . . . Thus criminal responsibility is assessed only when through 'free will' a man elects to do evil, and if he is not a free agent, or is unable to choose or to act voluntarily, or to avoid the conduct which constitutes the crime, he is outside the postulate of the law of punishment.[26]

[24] Trechsel, Noll, and Pieth, *Schweizerisches Strafrecht* (n 5) 143; Fletcher, *Rethinking Criminal Law* (n 5) 459.

[25] BGE 112 Ia 107, 113, E 3: 'the characteristics of criminal behaviour and the consequences of the behaviour must, at the time of the conduct, be defined and must be clearly recognisable for every person.'

[26] *Moore v United States*, 485 F2d 1139, 1240 per Judge Wright.

Similarly, the German Federal Criminal Court has held that '[c]ulpability is a prerequisite of punishment' and implies that 'the offender committed the wrong even though he could have acted lawfully, could have decided to obey the law'. This notion of culpability is based on the understanding of the individual as a 'free, responsible, moral agent capable of choosing to obey the law'.[27]

If there might be said to be consensus about the existence of this requirement, it would certainly be an over-statement to claim that the culpability principle is uniformly defined, even within the various European jurisdictions.[28] The scope of the principle is very much contested. In the words of Fletcher: 'The major difference between German and Anglo-American theory is that the German analysis of the distinction between wrongdoing and attribution goes far beyond the questions of insanity and infancy.'[29] This reflects disagreement as to the categorization of matters which go to the subjective elements of the offence or to culpability.[30] In Swiss criminal law, for instance, it is settled that culpability and intention are quite separate notions. This reflects an understanding of criminal liability (for intentional conduct[31]) as based on three distinct pillars: the subjective and objective elements of the criminal offence, unlawfulness, and culpability.[32] Issues which are considered as affecting the culpability of the accused include insanity, error of law, and necessity.[33] The

[27] BGHSt 2, 200 cited by Trechsel, Noll, and Pieth, *Schweizerisches Strafrecht* (n 5) 143: '*Strafe setzt Schuld voraus. Schuld ist Vorwerfbarkeit. Mit dem Unwerturteil der Schuld wird dem Täter vorgeworfen, dass er sich nicht rechtmässig verhalten hat, dass er sich für das Unrecht entschieden hat, obwohl er sich rechtmässig verhalten, sich für das Recht hätte entscheiden können. Der innere Grund des Schuldvorwurfes liegt darin, dass der Mensch auf freie, verantwortliche, sittliche Selbstbestimmung anlegt und deshalb befähigt ist, sich für das Recht und gegen das Unrecht zu entscheiden, sein Verhalten nach den Normen des rechtlichen Sollens einzurichten und das rechtlich Verbotene zu vermeiden, sobald er die sittliche Reife erlangt hat und solange die Anlage zur freien sittlichen Selbstbestimmung nicht durch die in § 51 StGB (Schuldfähigkeit) genannten krankhaften Vorgänge vorübergehend gelähmt oder auf die Dauer zerstört ist.*'

[28] This reflects too differences in the understanding of notions of responsibility, see eg M Renzo, 'Responsibility and Answerability in the Criminal Law' in RA Duff and others (eds), *The Constitution of the Criminal Law* (Oxford: OUP 2013); V Tadros, *Criminal Responsibility* (Oxford: OUP 2007); MS Moore, 'Causation and the Excuses' (1985) 73 *California Law Review* 1091.

[29] Fletcher, *Rethinking Criminal Law* (n 5) 456. Fletcher's detailed and careful consideration of the problem of working out a 'sound distinction' between the categories of wrongfulness and attribution 'beyond the questions of insanity and infancy' is essential reading.

[30] These are evident in the considerable literature on theories of acting or, in the words of Fletcher, theories 'about the relationship of acting and intending'. See Fletcher, *Rethinking Criminal Law* (n 5) 437. See notably H Welzel, *Das Deutsche Strafrecht: Eine Systematische Darstellung* (11th edn, Berlin: De Gruyter 1969). J Horder, 'Criminal Law: Between Determinism, Liberalism and Criminal Justice' (1996) 49 *Current Legal Problems* 159.

[31] For consideration of criminal liability in the context of negligence see eg Donatsch and Tag, *Strafrecht I* (n 5) 332–74.

[32] On the tripartite understanding of the attribution of liability see Trechsel, Noll, and Pieth, *Schweizerisches Strafrecht* (n 5) 77.

[33] ibid 142–70.

position in England and Wales is considerably less clear.[34] There is certainly some indication in Anglo-American theory of support for a broad understanding of this notion of culpability or subjective attribution. HLA Hart, for instance, argues that the various situations which indicated that the 'capability and opportunities to abide by the law were absent' included 'cases of accident, mistake, paralysis, reflex action, coercion, insanity'.[35] There is little clarity, though, in the law of England and Wales regarding the definition and scope of the culpability requirement. This is evident, even in the context of insanity, as is illustrated by the controversy surrounding the availability of insanity as a defence to strict liability offences.

Until relatively recently insanity was not considered to be a defence to strict liability offences. In the context of strict liability offences, the motivation of the offender is considered irrelevant and there is no need to prove intent in order for the individual to be held criminally liable.[36] The position was that outlined in *DPP v Harper*, in which the court (in)famously held that 'insanity can be a defence in the magistrates' court, but only if the offence charged is one in which *mens rea* is an element … The defence is based on the absence of *mens rea*, but none is required for the offence of driving with an excess of alcohol. Hence the defence of insanity has no relevance to such a charge as it is an offence of strict liability'.[37] This position was subject to considerable criticism[38] and subsequently held to be 'misleading'.[39] In *Loake*, the High Court made it clear that it was erroneous to regard the insanity defence as negating *mens rea*, noting that it was 'not correct … to simply regard insanity reductively, as operating simply on the basis that someone suffering from a disease of the mind will always lack *mens rea* for the offence'[40] and that it was possible for someone 'to have the full *mens rea* for a criminal offence, whilst at the same time, because of a defect of reason arising from a disease of the mind, not know what

[34] For discussion of culpability in English law in the context of insanity see Horder, *Ashworth's Principles* (n 1) 157; RA Duff, 'Law, Language and Community: Some Preconditions of Criminal Liability' (1998) 18 *Oxford Journal of Legal Studies* 189.

[35] HLA Hart, *Punishment and Responsibility: Essays in the Philosophy of Law* (J Gardner, 2nd edn, Oxford: OUP 2008) 152.

[36] See for detailed discussion G Sullivan, 'Strict Liability for Criminal Offences in England and Wales Following Incorporation into English Law of the European Convention on Human Rights' in A Simester (ed), *Appraising Strict Liability* (Oxford: OUP 2010).

[37] *DPP v Harper* [1997] 1 WLR 1406 followed in *R v Horseferry Road Magistrates Court, ex p K* [1997] QB 23.

[38] See eg T Ward, 'Magistrates, Insanity and the Common Law' [2017] *Criminal Law Review* 796.

[39] *Loake v Crown Prosecution Service* [2017] EWHC 2855 (Admin) [55], [2018] Cr App R 16, [2018] 2 WLR 1159.

[40] ibid para 40.

he is doing in wrong'.[41] The court held that it was crucial that 'those whom we punish should have had, when they acted, the normal capacities, physical and mental, for doing what the law requires and abstaining from what it forbids and a fair opportunity to exercise these capabilities'.[42]

The attribution of criminal liability requires that the offender knew what they were doing was wrong. In short, while there might be consensus, in Europe at least, that this means that those who were criminally insane at the time of the commission of the offence cannot be held liable, the scope of the principle is likely to be broader and to include necessity and unavoidable (excusable) errors of law.

It is important to stress that this understanding of the criminal law theory on the attribution of criminal liability as requiring both an act and culpability is in no sense radical, but rather represents the criminal law orthodoxy. Stratenwerth identifies the nineteenth century as a crucial moment in the movement away from reliance on the character of the offender in the context of the attribution of criminal liability and notes the connection of this to the growing acceptance of liberal conceptions of the state and to the notion of individual agency.[43] As Lacey has argued:

> a freely choosing, responsible citizen stood centre stage, posing new legitimation problems as well as new challenges of coordination ... the proposition that the proof of a subject's guilt should be facilitated by mechanisms based on the assumption that his or her previous behaviour manifested a criminal character suggestive of a propensity to commit crime was at odds with the vision implicit in the emerging social imaginary, and might moreover be seen as introducing information which was irrelevant to the charge at issue.[44]

It is unsurprising, then, that the notion of legality owes much, despite the prominence of the concept of law as limitation in documents such as Magna Carta, to the prevailing ideology of nineteenth century.[45] Although often

41 ibid para 41, referring to the formulation of Lord Diplock in *R v Sullivan* [1984] AC 156, 173.

42 *Loake v Crown Prosecution Service* [2017] EWHC 2855 (Admin) [35]; [2018] Cr App R 16; [2018] 2 WLR 1159, citing Hart, Punishment and Responsibility (n 35) 15. See also SJ Morse and MB Hoffman, 'The Uneasy Entente between Insanity and Mens Rea: Beyond Clark v Arizona' (2007) 97 *Journal of Criminal Law and Criminology* 143.

43 Stratenwerth, *Schweizerisches Strafrecht, Allgemeiner Teil I* (n 5) 76.

44 N Lacey, 'The Resurgence of Character: Responsibility in the Context of Criminalization' in A Duff and S Green (eds), *Philosophical Foundations of Criminal Law* (Oxford: OUP 2011) 155, 159.

45 Strathenwerth, *Schweizerisches Strafrecht, Allgemeiner Teil I* (n 5) 76; see also Robinson, 'Fair Notice' (n 8) 336. For an overview of the history of the principle see Hall, 'Nulla Poena' (n 11) 165.

referred to by its Latin idiom, the modern principle and in its restatement as *nulla poena sine lege, nulla poena sine crimine, nullum crimen sine poena legali*, is generally attributed to Feuerbach.[46] The development of the principle was closely connected to the rise of parliament and the English conception of the rule of law, which was later championed by the liberal revolutionary reformers on the European continent.[47] Many of the European criminal codes of the late nineteenth century were influenced by the neo-classical school of penology.[48] Legality lies at the heart of this conception of criminal liability. The state is entitled to call people to account for violating the criminal law but only those who are capable of being called to account can be held liable.

This draws attention to the relationship between criminal law theory and legality. The act requirement and the principle of subjective attribution or culpability are considered important ethical principles underpinning the criminal law. HLA Hart refers, for instance, to the 'moral protest', which arises when someone is punished because ' "he could not have helped it" or "he could not have done otherwise" or "he had no real choice" '.[49] There is less recognition of the fact, though, that these moral principles are based on—or at the very least align with—'political' principles, such as legality. Put another way, the 'political' protest, when individuals are held liable even though they 'could not have done otherwise', is that the state is only entitled to attribute liability to—and by extension impose punishment on—those who were able to act in accordance with the law and as a response to a violation of a clearly defined criminal offence. Equally, it underlines the fact that the attribution of liability and the imposition of punishment must be subject to the same constraints. The imposition of punishment for reasons other than those which apply in the context of the attribution of criminal liability violates the legality principle. In order to explore this further, it is important to consider the regulation of legality as a human right.

[46] PJA Feuerbach, *Lehrbuch des Gemeinen in Deutschland Gültigen Peinlichen Rechts* (11th edn, Giessen: Heyer 1832) 12, 19. See also Trechsel, Noll, and Pieth, *Schweizerisches Strafrecht* (n 5) 50: '*Nicht etwa ein römischer Jurist, sondern Feuerbach hat den Grundsatz lateinisch formuliert: nullum crimen, nulla poena lege.*'

[47] J-A Roux, *Cours de Droit Criminel Français* (2nd edn, Paris: Sirey 1927); A Schottlaender, *Die Geschichtliche Entwicklung des Satzes: Nulla Poena Sine Lege* (Heidelberg: Ruprecht-Karls-Universität Heidelberg 1911) 1.

[48] Notably Zanardelli's Italian Code of 1889 and Haus's Belgian Penal Code of 1867. For discussion see Y Cartuyvels and G Cliquennois, 'The Punishment of Mentally Ill Offenders in Belgium: Care as Legitimacy for Control' (2015) 12 *Champ Pénal* N 6.

[49] Hart, *Punishment and Responsibility* (n 35) 152.

III. Legality as a Human Right: Article 7(1) ECHR

A. 'No Punishment without Law'

> *No one shall be held guilty of any criminal offence on account of any act or omission which did not constitute a criminal offence under national or international law at the time when it was committed. Nor shall a heavier penalty be imposed than the one that was applicable at the time the criminal offence was committed.*[50]

The legality principle, protected by Article 7(1) ECHR, is 'an essential element of the rule of law'.[51] Its importance is underscored by the fact that the contracting states are not permitted to derogate from the provision even in times of war or emergency.[52] The European Court of Human Rights (ECtHR) has stated that Article 7(1) ECHR serves to protect against 'arbitrary prosecution, conviction and punishment' and that it comprises several distinct requirements.[53] According to the first sentence of Article 7(1) ECHR, criminal offences must be prescribed in law and must not be retrospectively applied. The second sentence prohibits the retrospective imposition of a more severe penalty. Finally, the ECtHR has read into Article 7(1) ECHR the requirement of *lex mitior*:[54] if the sentencing options at the time of the commission of the offence differ from criminal penalties enacted before the final judgment, the *lex mitior* guarantee dictates that the court must apply those provisions which are most favourable to the accused.[55] The judgment of the Grand Chamber in *Scoppola* reversed the earlier position of the ECtHR, reaffirmed on numerous occasions, according to which the *lex mitior* principle was not protected by Article 7(1) ECHR. The ECtHR justified its change in approach by reference to the emergence of a consensus in Europe that the guarantee is a fundamental principle of criminal

[50] Art 7(1) ECHR. The ECtHR has held that Art 7(1) ECHR does not apply to civil proceedings, see eg *Kot v Russia* App no 20887/03, 18 Jan 2007, para 38.

[51] See *Del Río Prada v Spain* [GC] App no 42750/09, ECHR 2013, para 77.

[52] ibid.

[53] See eg *SW v UK*, 22 Nov 1995, Series A no 335-B, para 34; *CR v UK*, 22 Nov 1995, Series A no 335-C, para 32; *Kafkaris v Cyprus* [GC] App no 21906/04, ECHR 2008-I, para 137.

[54] *Scoppola v Italy (no 2)* [GC] App no 10249/03, 17 Sept 2009, paras 103–9, thirty-year prison sentence instead of a life sentence. See also *Ruban v Ukraine* App no 8927/11, 12 July 2016, paras 41–46; *Gouarré Patte v Andorra* App no 33427/10, 12 Jan 2016, paras 28–36; *Koprivnikar v Slovenia* App no 67503/13, 24 Jan 2017, para 59. The guarantee is referred to in other international human rights instruments such as Art 15(1) ICCPR and Art 9 ACHR.

[55] *Scoppola v Italy (no 2)* [GC] App no 10249/03, 17 Sept 2009, paras 103–9.

law.[56] It is useful to consider the guarantees in the first and second sentences of Article 7(1) ECHR before turning to consider the relationship between the attribution of liability and the imposition of punishment in the context of the legality principle.

B. Imposition of 'Guilt' for 'Acts or Omissions' Set Out in Criminal Law

1. Definition of Criminal Offences and the Prohibition on Retrospectivity

The first sentence of Article 7(1) ECHR requires that criminal offences be prescribed in law and prohibits their retrospective application. The principle of non-retrospectivity of criminal law is quite clear.[57] The principle will be violated if a person is convicted on the basis of criminal laws which only came into force after the commission of the criminal offence (*lex praevia*).[58] The requirement that criminal offences be clearly defined in law has given rise to more discussion.[59] The ECtHR has interpreted the certainty requirement (*lex certa*) as demanding the accessibility, foreseeability, and clarity of the law.[60] In addition, Article 7(1) ECHR prohibits the extension of existing offences to cover behaviour which was not previously considered to be criminal in nature and requires that 'the criminal law must not be extensively construed to an accused's detriment, for instance by analogy' (*lex stricta*).[61]

The requirement that criminal offences be clearly and precisely defined is a crucial aspect of the legality principle, but the contracting states are afforded considerable leniency in interpreting the requirement. Broad public order laws, such as 'breach of the peace-type' offences or, in more recent times,

[56] ibid para 108: according to the ECtHR: 'inflicting a heavier penalty for the sole reason that it was prescribed at the time of the commission of the offence would mean applying to the defendant's detriment the rules governing the succession of criminal laws in time. In addition, it would amount to disregarding any legislative change favourable to the accused which might have come in before the conviction and continuing to impose penalties which the State—and the community it represents—now consider excessive'. See further L Gonin and O Bigler, *Convention Européen des Droits de l'Homme* (Bern: Stämpfli 2018) 465–66.

[57] One exception to the clarity here concerns the issue of continuing offences, see eg *Rohlena v Czech Republic* [GC], no 59552/08, ECHR 2015, paras 57–64.

[58] See eg *Vasiliauskas v Lithuania* [GC] App no 35343/05, ECHR 2015-VII, para 165.

[59] There is an obvious connection between these principles, as the determination of whether a law has been retrospectively applied will often turn on whether the law was sufficiently clearly defined in the first place. See eg *Kafkaris v Cyprus* [GC] App no 21906/04, ECHR 2008-I.

[60] *Kokkinakis v Greece*, 25 May 1993, Series A no 260-A, para 40.

[61] *Del Río Prada v Spain* [GC] App no 42750/09, ECHR 2013, para 77, citing *Coëme and Others v Belgium* App nos 32492/96, 32547/96, 32548/96, 33209/96, and 33210/96, ECHR 2000-VII, para 145; *Başkaya and Okçuoğlu v Turkey* [GC] App nos 23536/94 and 24408/94, ECHR 1999-IV, paras 42–43.

anti-terrorism provisions,[62] which take the form of all-encompassing catch-all provisions, exist in many jurisdictions.[63] Similarly, it is not particularly difficult to pinpoint cases where the judiciary has been afforded considerable freedom in 're-interpreting' conduct previously considered legal as criminal.[64]

The ECtHR has held that 'absolute certainty' while 'highly desirable' also has the potential to 'entail excessive rigidity'. It has frequently stressed the importance of ensuring that the law is 'able to keep pace with changing circumstances'[65] and it has noted that 'many laws are inevitably couched in terms which, to a greater or lesser extent, are vague and whose interpretation and application are a question of practice'.[66] This means that 'however clearly drafted a provision may be, in any system of law, including criminal law, there is an inevitable element of judicial interpretation' and this unavoidably necessitates 'elucidation of doubtful points' and 'adaptation to changing circumstances'.[67]

In determining whether laws are sufficiently certain, the ECtHR has focused on the requirement of foreseeability. This emphasizes the importance of the definition of law to the ECtHR's understanding of legality, which, the ECtHR has held, 'implies qualitative requirements, including those of accessibility and foreseeability'.[68] The ECtHR has consistently held that '[a] norm cannot be regarded as a "law" unless it is formulated with sufficient precision to enable the individual to regulate his conduct: he must be able—if need be with appropriate advice—to foresee, to a degree that is reasonable in the circumstances, the consequences which a given action may entail'.[69] This means that '[a]n individual must know from the wording of the relevant provision and, if need

[62] See A Donatsch and W Wohlers, *Strafrecht IV: Delikte gegen die Allgemeinheit* (4th edn, Zurich: Schulthess, 2011) 213. See also eg *Kobe v UK* (dec) App no 48278/09, 14 June 2011; and for commentary on the UK provisions J Hodgson and V Tadros, 'How to Make a Terrorist out of Nothing' (2009) 72 *Modern Law Review* 984.

[63] See eg Donatsch and Wohlers, *Strafrecht IV* (n 62) 190. See also the Advisory Opinion of 29 May 2020 of the GC of the ECtHR 'concerning the use of the "blanket reference" or "legislation by reference" technique in the definition of an offence and the standards of comparison between the criminal law in force at the time of the commission of the offence and the amended criminal law', Request no P 16-2019-001.

[64] See eg *SW and CR v UK*, 22 Nov 1995, Series A no 335-B (marital rape). See also the report of the Eminent Jurists Panel of the International Commission of Jurists, *Terrorism, Counter-terrorism and Human Rights: Assessing Damage, Urging Action* (Geneva, International Commission of Jurists 2009) 49.

[65] See eg *Flinkkilä and Others v Finland* App no 25576/04, 6 Apr 2010, para 65.

[66] *Kokkinakis v Greece*, 25 May 1993, Series A no 260-A, para 40; *Sunday Times v UK (no 1)*, 26 Apr 1979, Series A no 30, para 49; *Flinkkilä and Others v Finland* App no 25576/04, 6 Apr 2010, para 65.

[67] See eg *Liivik v Estonia* App no 12157/05, 25 June 2009, para 94; *Kafkaris v Cyprus* [GC] App no 21906/04, ECHR 2008-I, para 141.

[68] *Coëme and Others v Belgium* App nos 32492/96, 32547/96, 32548/96, 33209/96, and 33210/96, ECHR 2000-VII, para 145; *EK v Turkey* App no 28496/95, 7 Feb 2002, para 51.

[69] *Sunday Times v UK (no 1)*, 26 Apr 1979, Series A no 30, para 49; *Flinkkilä and Others v Finland* App no 25576/04, 6 Apr 2010, para 64.

be, with the courts' interpretation of it, what acts and omissions will make him criminally liable'.[70]

Individuals will be required to take suitable precautions in order to comply with the law, particularly in the context of 'regulatory-type' offences. In *Cantoni*, for instance, the manager of a supermarket argued that his conviction for selling medicinal products as defined by the Public Health Code violated the legality principle.[71] He claimed that it was not clear that the products in question fell within the code's definition of 'medicinal products'. In holding that there was no interference with Article 7 ECHR, the ECtHR referred to the fact that it was a 'logical consequence of the principle that laws must be of general application' that 'the wording of statutes' was 'not always precise'. It held that 'one of the standard techniques of regulation by rules is to use general categorisations as opposed to exhaustive lists' and in the case at issue the position had been sufficiently clarified in the case law of the courts. The applicant, in his capacity as a professional responsible for managing a supermarket, could have been expected to take special care in assessing the risks that he was taking in offering such products for sale.[72]

In the case of *SW and CR*, which concerned the convictions of two men for raping their wives, despite previous settled case law to the effect that a husband could not be convicted of raping his wife, the ECtHR held that there was 'an evident evolution, which was consistent with the very essence of the offence, of the criminal law through judicial interpretation towards treating such conduct generally as within the scope of the offence of rape'. Here there seems to be an underlying suggestion that all 'reasonable' people would recognize that such conduct was prohibited. The ECtHR stated that this evolution had 'reached a stage where judicial recognition of the absence of immunity had become a reasonably foreseeable development of the law'.[73]

Similarly in *Flinkkilä*, which concerned journalists and newspaper editors convicted of publishing the name of an offender, the ECtHR was not convinced that the applicants had been unable to foresee that criminal sanctions could be

[70] *Jorgic v Germany* App no 74613/01, ECHR 2007-III, para 140; *Cantoni v France* [GC], 15 Nov 1996, Reports 1996-V, para 35; *Achour v France* [GC] App no 67335/01, ECHR 2006-IV, para 54.

[71] *Cantoni v France* [GC], 15 Nov 1996, Reports 1996-V.

[72] ibid para 31. Other cases have involved the interpretation of the term 'insult', *Grigoriades v Greece* [GC] App no 24348/94, 25 Nov 1997, para 38; the definitions of the 'offence of proselytism', *Larissis and Others v Greece* App no 23372/94, 24 Feb 1998, para 34; *Kokkinakis v Greece*, 25 May 1993, Series A no 260-A, para 53; the 'crime of propaganda', *Erdogdu and Ince v Turkey* App nos 25067/94 and 25068/94, 8 July 1999, para 59; the term 'dissemination of propaganda against the individuality of the State', *Başkaya and Okçuoğlu v Turkey* [GC] App nos 23536/94 and 24408/94, ECHR 1999-IV, para 40, and the interpretation of the crime of genocide, *Jorgic v Germany* App no 74613/01, ECHR 2007-III. The ECtHR did not find a violation of Art 7 ECHR in any of these cases.

[73] *SW and CR v UK*, 22 Nov 1995, Series A no 335-B, para 43.

imposed on them.[74] It held that 'the scope of criminal liability had gradually been clarified through judicial interpretation in a manner which had been consistent with the essence of the offence and with good journalistic practice' and that although there had only been two judgments on the provision at issue, 'the possibility that a sanction would be imposed for invasion of private life was not unforeseeable'.[75] These cases illustrate the importance of foreseeability in the ECtHR's approach. The suggestion is that the applicants ought to have known that they could have been convicted or should have taken more care to ensure that they complied with the law.

These cases can be contrasted with the judgment in *Parmak and Bakır*. In this case, the applicants had been convicted of being members of a terrorist organization. They complained that the criminal provisions had been 'extensively applied to secure their conviction', and that 'the domestic courts had based their findings ... on an interpretation—by analogy, in particular—that violence, which is an essential component of terrorist offences, could be taken to include moral coercion'.[76] The ECtHR noted 'that the domestic courts did not explain how the concept of moral coercion relates to the constitutive elements of the offence, including with respect to the degree of coercion and the severity it must attain to warrant the conclusion that it amounts to terrorism'.[77] It found a violation of Article 7(1) ECHR, noting that 'domestic courts must exercise special diligence to clarify the elements of an offence in terms that make it foreseeable and compatible with its essence'.[78]

The failure to define offences sufficiently gives rise to the worry that the criminal law might be (mis)used to criminalize opponents of governments or those deemed socially dangerous. This leads to the suspicion that the investigation, prosecution, and imposition of liability is based on 'character' or 'dangerousness' rather than the contravention of clearly defined laws. This is precisely the type of situation which legality is designed to prohibit. The case law of the ECtHR highlights that the first sentence of Article 7(1) ECHR contains an 'act' requirement: a person must have done, or failed to have done,[79] something in order to be held liable. Criminal liability is only to be imposed for conduct and not for character or some abstract notion of 'social dangerousness'. In addition,

74 *Flinkkilä and Others v Finland* App no 25576/04, 6 Apr 2010.
75 ibid para 47.
76 *Parmak and Bakır v Turkey* App nos 22429/07 and 25195/07, 3 Dec 2019, para 53.
77 ibid para 75.
78 ibid para 77.
79 Art 7(1) ECHR refers to 'acts' and 'omissions'.

the emphasis on foreseeability as a means of guarding against arbitrariness highlights the commitment to individual agency.

2. Guilt, Culpability, and the Attribution of Liability

The ability of an individual to obey the law is a precondition of legality and thus for the imposition of criminal liability. The reference in the first sentence of Article 7(1) ECHR to the 'guilt' of an accused person indicates that the guarantee requires 'a finding of liability by the national court enabling the offence to be attributed to … its perpetrator'.[80] This notion might be seen as espousing Fletcher's principle of 'subjective attribution', according to which 'no one may be properly punished for a wrongful act unless the act is attributable to him'.[81] Individuals are presumed to be responsible citizens or 'reasonable persons' capable of obeying the instructions set out in the law.[82] The culpability requirement is essentially the manifestation of the principle that only those who had capacity and a fair opportunity to obey the law can be justly punished.[83] This in turn 'sits happily with a familiar species of legal individualism that adopts a contractual model of law and the state'.[84]

It is important to distinguish clearly between this requirement of culpability or subjective attribution[85] and the subjective state of mind requirement of criminal laws, such as intent. The ECtHR has consistently held that Article 7(1) ECHR[86] does not contain any sort of subjective state of mind requirement. It has repeatedly held that the contracting states are free to define the constituent elements of offences[87] and that 'the lack of subjective elements does not necessarily deprive an offence of its criminal character; indeed, criminal offences based solely on objective elements may be found in the laws of the Contracting States'.[88] In this regard, it has referred to its case law on the presumption of innocence and the importance of ensuring coherence between the various provisions of the Convention.[89] The reference to 'innocence' in Article 6(2) ECHR,

[80] *Varvara v Italy* App no 17475/08, 29 Oct 2013, para 71.

[81] Fletcher, *Rethinking Criminal Law* (n 5) 455.

[82] See eg RA Duff, 'Responsibility, Citizenship, and Criminal Law' in RA Duff and SP Green (eds), *Philosophical Foundations of Criminal Law* (Oxford: OUP 2011) 125; L Farmer, 'Criminal Responsibility and Proof of Guilt' in L Farmer and MD Dubber (eds), *Modern Histories of Crime and Punishment* (Stanford, CA: Stanford University Press 2007).

[83] See eg HLA Hart, 'Prolegomenon to the Principles of Punishment', 21–24; 'Legal Responsibility and Excuses', 28; 'Punishment and Elimination of Responsibility, 181–83; 'Responsibility and Retribution', 227–30, all in Hart, *Punishment and Responsibility* (n 35).

[84] RA Duff, 'Choice, Character and Criminal Liability' (2003) 12 *Law and Philosophy* 345, 380f.

[85] Fletcher, *Rethinking Criminal Law* (n 5) 459.

[86] *Varvara v Italy* App no 17475/08, 29 Oct 2013, para 70.

[87] ibid.

[88] *Janosevic v Sweden* App no 34619/97, ECHR 2002-VII, para 68.

[89] See eg *G v UK* (dec) App no 37334/08, 30 Aug 2011: 'It is not the Court's role under Article 6 §§ 1 or 2 to dictate the content of domestic criminal law, including whether or not a blameworthy state of mind

like the reference to 'guilt' in Article 7(1) ECHR, implies that the accused can be held accountable for their conduct.[90]

In the context of Article 6(2) ECHR, the ECtHR has held that the contracting states may, 'in principle and under certain conditions, penalise a simple or objective fact as such, irrespective of whether it results from criminal intent or from negligence'.[91] Some commentators have argued that the presumption of innocence ought to be interpreted as prohibiting strict liability offences by demanding that the prosecution have the obligation to prove that the accused had a blameworthy state of mind (*mens rea*).[92] The ECtHR has rejected this approach, noting that it is not its role to 'dictate the content of domestic criminal law, including whether or not a blameworthy state of mind should be one of the elements of the offence or whether there should be any particular defence available to the accused'.[93] Equally, though, the ECtHR has also distinguished in the context of Article 6(2) ECHR the subjective state of mind requirement (such as intention) integral to the definition of the offence from the notion of the attribution of wrongdoing (culpability). In *AP, MP and TP v Switzerland*, it held that it was a 'fundamental rule of criminal law that criminal liability does not survive the person who has committed the criminal act' and that this rule was 'also required by the presumption of innocence enshrined in Article 6 § 2 of the Convention'.[94] This judgment emphasizes the principle that individuals can only be punished if they can be held to be personally culpable for the conduct at issue. This suggests support for the position that it is 'a fundamental principle of criminal law that no one be punished for an offence if he or she could not have acted otherwise'.[95]

In view of this, it should come as little surprise that the ECtHR has held that strict liability offences, which do not require intent on the part of the accused,

should be one of the elements of the offence or whether there should be any particular defence available to the accused', citing *Salabiaku v France*, 7 Oct 1988, Series A no 141-A, para 27; *Radio France and Others v France* App no 53984/00, ECHR 2004-II, para 24. This is discussed further in what follows.

[90] The presumption of innocence is a procedural rather than a substantive safeguard. For a forceful defence of this distinction see P Roberts, 'Strict Liability and the Presumption of Innocence: An Exposé of Functionalist Assumptions' in Simester, Appraising Strict Liability (n 36).

[91] *Salabiaku v France*, 7 Oct 1988, Series A no 141-A, para 27; *Vastberga Taxi Aktiebolag and Vulic v Sweden* App no 36985/97, 23 July 2002, para 112; *Janosevic v Sweden* App no 34619/97, ECHR 2002-VII.

[92] See eg Tadros and Tierney, 'The Presumption of Innocence' (n 3) 402; A Paizes, 'A Closer Look at the Presumption of Innocence in our Constitution: What is an Accused to be Presumed *Of*?' (1998) 11 *South African Journal of Criminal Justice* 409; JC Jeffries, Jr and PB Stephan III, 'Defences, Presumptions, and the Burden of Proof in Criminal Law' (1979) 88 *Yale Law Journal* 1325.

[93] *G v UK* (dec) App no 37334/08, 30 Aug 2011, para 27, citing *Salabiaku v France*, 7 Oct 1988, Series A no 141-A, para 27; *Radio France and Others v France* App no 53984/00, ECHR 2004-II, para 24.

[94] *AP, MP and TP v Switzerland*, 29 Aug 1997, Reports 1997-V, para 46.

[95] See S Trechsel, *Human Rights in Criminal Proceedings* (Oxford: OUP 2004) 157.

are not incompatible per se with Article 7(1) ECHR.[96] A charitable take on this position might be that it reflects considerable differences in the regulation of the 'subjective' elements of criminal liability in the member states. This does not mean, however, that states are permitted to impose liability in cases in which the accused did not know that what they were doing was wrong and were thus unable to act in accordance with the law. This is clearly illustrated by the decisions of the ECtHR in a series of Italian cases involving the imposition of 'punitive penalties', despite the fact that the Italian Court of Cassation had acquitted the applicant companies' representatives on the basis of 'an inevitable and excusable error' of law.[97]

In these cases, the applicants could not be found guilty because they could not, on account of the lack of foreseeability of the criminal laws in question, have been expected to act otherwise. In *Sud Fondi SRL and Others*, the ECtHR explained that 'the logic of the sentence, punishment and the notion of "guilty" (in the English version) and "personne coupable" (in the French version) were consistent with an interpretation of Article 7(1) which required, for the purposes of punishment, an intellectual link (knowledge and willingness) to enable an element of responsibility in the behaviour of the person who committed the crime to be established'.[98] This was subsequently endorsed by the Grand Chamber in *GIEM SRL and Others*, in which the ECtHR noted the 'clear correlation between the degree of foreseeability of a criminal-law provision and the personal liability of the offender' and held that 'Article 7 requires the existence of a mental link through which an element of liability may be detected in the conduct of the person who physically committed the offence'.[99] In *Vervara*, the ECtHR concluded that '[i]t would be inconsistent on the one hand to require an accessible and foreseeable legal basis and on the other to permit punishment where, as in the present case, the person in question has not been convicted'.[100]

The imposition of criminal liability on a person who cannot be held accountable or culpable for their failure to obey the criminal law will violate Article 7(1) ECHR. These cases make it clear that the legality principle includes

[96] See eg *Valico SRL v Italy* (dec) App no 70074/01, ECHR 2006-III.

[97] *Sud Fondi SRL and Others v Italy* App no 75909/01, 20 Jan 2009, para 116; *Varvara v Italy* App no 17475/08, 29 Oct 2013; *GIEM SRL and Others v Italy* [GC] App nos 1828/06, 34163/07, and 19029/11, 28 June 2018. See for discussion F Meyer, *Systematischer Kommentar zur Strafprozessordnung mit GVG und EMRK, Band X: EMRK* (Cologne: Carl Heymanns Verlag 2019) 718–19.

[98] *Sud Fondi SRL and Others v Italy* App no 75909/01, 20 Jan 2009, para 116.

[99] *GIEM SRL and Others v Italy* [GC] App nos 1828/06, 34163/07, and 19029/11, 28 June 2018, para 242.

[100] *Varvara v Italy* App no 17475/08, 29 Oct 2013, para 71.

a type of 'culpability' requirement, yet the scope of the requirement remains far from clear. The case law suggests support for an understanding of the culpability requirement in Article 7(1) ECHR as prohibiting a finding of guilt in cases involving unavoidable errors of law or in the absence of personal liability. In view of the fact that an individual charged with committing the act or omission at issue must be able to ascertain that their behaviour is contrary to the criminal law in order to enable them to take the appropriate steps to obey the provisions, Article 7(1) ECHR must also be taken to prohibit the punishment of those who, on account of insanity, were unable to act in accordance with the law.

C. Prohibition on the Imposition of a Heavier 'Penalty' than that Set Out in Law

1. Defining 'Penalties'

a) The Autonomous Notion of Penalty

The second sentence of Article 7(1) ECHR prohibits the imposition of a heavier *penalty* than was applicable at the time of the commission of the criminal offence. An individual must be able to establish 'from the wording of the relevant provision, if need be with the assistance of the courts' interpretation of it and after taking appropriate legal advice', not just the acts and omissions, which will result in criminal liability, but also the penalty which will be imposed.[101]

It is essential to note that this guarantee is broader in scope than the guarantee set out in the first sentence of Article 7(1) ECHR. The reference here is to a 'penalty' imposed following the 'commission of a criminal offence' rather than to 'punishment' following a finding of 'guilt' as employed in the first sentence. The prohibition on the retrospective application of a heavier penalty protects not just those who have been 'convicted' of a criminal offence, but also those on whom other penalties have been imposed.[102] This distinction is of crucial importance to establishing the scope of the guarantee. It reflects the creation of an 'autonomous' notion of 'penalty' and the ECtHR's desire to ensure a prohibition on the de facto imposition of punishment in the absence of

[101] *Del Río Prada v Spain* [GC] App no 42750/09, ECHR 2013, para 79, citing *Cantoni v France* [GC], 15 Nov 1996, Reports 1996-V, para 29 and *Kafkaris v Cyprus* [GC] App no 21906/04, ECHR 2008-I, para 140.

[102] See eg *Varvara v Italy* App no 17475/08, 29 Oct 2013, paras 215–19; *GIEM SRL and Others v Italy* [GC] App nos 1828/06, 34163/07, and 19029/11, 28 June 2018.

conviction or after acquittal.[103] In each case, the ECtHR will assess for itself whether a particular measure amounts in substance to a 'penalty' within the meaning of Article 7(1) ECHR.[104]

The wording of the second sentence of Article 7(1) ECHR indicates that 'the starting point in any assessment of the existence of a penalty is whether the measure in question is imposed following conviction for a "criminal offence" '.[105] Even in the absence of a criminal conviction, a measure might nevertheless be deemed to constitute a 'penalty' if it is determined by the Strasbourg authorities to be punitive in nature. The reason for this is that:

> if the criminal nature of a measure were to be established, for the purposes of the Convention, purely on the basis that the individual concerned had committed an act characterised as an offence in domestic law and had been found guilty of that offence by a criminal court ... States would be free to impose penalties without classifying them as such, and the individuals concerned would then be deprived of the safeguards under Article 7(1).[106]

The definition of 'penalty' is thus of essential importance to ensuring the effectiveness of the provision. Equally, though, it gives rise to difficult questions regarding the relationship between the definition of penalty and 'punishment'.

In determining whether a measure is to be considered a penalty for the purposes of the second sentence of Article 7(1) ECHR, the ECtHR will consider, inter alia, 'the characterisation of the measure under domestic law, its nature and purpose, the procedures involved in making its implementation, and its severity'.[107] The ECtHR has concluded that measures imposed in addition to

[103] *GIEM SRL and Others v Italy* [GC] App nos 1828/06, 34163/07, and 19029/11, 28 June 2018, para 242.

[104] See eg *GIEM SRL and Others v Italy* [GC] App nos 1828/06, 34163/07, and 19029/11, 28 June 2018, para 215; *Welch v UK*, 9 Feb 1995, Series A no 307-A, para 27, where the ECtHR held that it must 'remain free to go behind appearances and assess for itself whether a particular measure amounts in substance to a "penalty" within the meaning of this provision'; *Jamil v France*, 8 June 1995, Series A no 317-B, para 30; *Uttley v UK* (dec) App no 36946/03, 29 Nov 2005.

[105] See eg *Welch v UK*, 9 Feb 1995, Series A no 307-A, para 27.

[106] *GIEM SRL and Others v Italy* [GC] App nos 1828/06, 34163/07, and 19029/11, 28 June 2018, para 216.

[107] *Welch v UK*, 9 Feb 1995, Series A no 307-A, para 28; *Jamil v France*, 8 June 1995, Series A no 317-B, para 31; *Adamson v UK* (dec) App no 42293/98, 26 Jan 1999; *Van der Velden v Netherlands* (dec) App no 29514/05, ECHR 2006-XV; *Kafkaris v Cyprus* [GC] App no 21906/04, ECHR 2008-I, para 142. The severity of the measure is not, however, in itself decisive, since, for instance, many non-penal measures of a preventive nature may have a substantial impact on the person concerned, see eg *Welch v UK*, 9 Feb 1995, Series A no 307-A, para 32. The criteria are very similar to the Engel criteria applied in order to determine whether the matter at issue concerned a criminal charge for the purposes of Art 6(1) ECHR. See too M Villiger, Handbuch der Europäischen Menschenrechtskonvention (3rd edn, Zurich: Schulthess 2020) 347 and for further discussion Ch 6.

a criminal sentence, such as confiscation orders,[108] or as an alternative to a prison sentence, such as measures involving imprisonment in default,[109] or punitive measures imposed in the context of administrative proceedings,[110] all constitute penalties for the purposes of Article 7(1) ECHR. Some assistance in the definition of penalty is provided by examining those measures which have been determined not to be punitive in nature, notably treatment orders, preventative measures, and measures which are to be understood as involving the enforcement of a penalty rather than a penalty itself.

b) Treatment Orders

Treatment and hospital orders imposed on those acquitted on the grounds of criminal insanity have consistently been held not to constitute punishment and thus to fall outwith the scope of the definition of penalty.[111] In *Berland*, for instance, the applicant was found to be 'criminally insane', thus precluding the imposition of criminal liability. He argued that the hospitalization measure imposed on him constituted a penalty. The ECtHR disagreed, holding that 'the compulsory hospitalisation measure' was not a penalty as it could only be imposed 'where a psychiatric assessment has established that the mental disorders of the person found to lack liability "require treatment and present a risk for the safety of others or seriously undermine public order"'.[112] It noted that the measure was imposed in the context of a specialized hospital (and not an ordinary prison) 'to receive treatment and at the same time to prevent him from reoffending' and was not imposed 'following a conviction for a "criminal offence"'.[113] This led the ECtHR to conclude that as the measure was imposed for the purposes of treatment rather than punishment, it did not constitute a penalty for the purposes of Article 7(1) ECHR.[114] The judgment was criticized by Judge Zupančič and Judge Yudkivska in their dissenting opinion on the

[108] *Welch v UK*, 9 Feb 1995, Series A no 307-A, paras 29–35.

[109] *Sud Fondi SRL and Others v Italy* App no 75909/01, 20 Jan 2009; *Varvara v Italy* App no 17475/08, 29 Oct 2013, para 55; *GIEM SRL and Others v Italy* [GC] App nos 1828/06, 34163/07, and 19029/11, 28 June 2018.

[110] *Valico SRL v Italy* (dec) App no 70074/01, ECHR 2006-III.

[111] *Berland v France* App no 42875/10, 3 Sept 2015, para 39. In this case, the ECtHR agreed with the finding of the national court, which had held that '[t]he declaration of the existence of sufficient evidence that the person ha[d] committed the offence as charged [did] not constitute a conviction but a finding that there [was] a factual situation which could have legal consequences'. See also *Claes v Belgium* App no 43418/09, 10 Jan 2013, para 110; and *Moreels v Belgium* App no 43717/09, 9 Jan 2014, para 43, in which the ECtHR held that the detention in treatment facilities of those with mental disorders who are declared criminally insane 'do[es] not engage Article 5 § 1 (a) of the Convention, as they do not follow a "conviction"'.

[112] *Berland v France* App no 42875/10, 3 Sept 2015, para 44.

[113] ibid.

[114] ibid para 45.

basis that 'incarceration in a mental hospital ward for the criminally insane is often much worse than ordinary imprisonment' and that 'to maintain that the applicant here was not punished is simply not true'.[115]

This dissenting opinion and the suggestion that treatment orders might amount to 'de facto punishment' draws attention to the potential for the breadth of the notion of 'penalty' to introduce tension between the 'state's purpose and the objective impact of the sanction' in the context of constitutional deliberations about the concept of punishment. As Fletcher notes:

> Though a philosophical inquiry into the nature of punishment may distinguish cleanly between therapy and punishment, the same distinction does not necessarily control the constitutional debate. The pressure to extend the procedural guarantees of the criminal trials has generated a subtle shift away from what the court regards as the euphemism of treatment to the impact of confinement on the individual. Thus, in the constitutional debate, the impact of coercive confinement leads to a potentially broader view of punishment than one would generate under a philosophical analysis that stresses the purpose for which the punishment is imposed.[116]

The case law of the ECtHR suggests, though, that the commitment to legality means that the same constraints apply in relation to both the philosophical and the constitutional debate. The distinction between treatment and punishment in the second sentence of Article 7(1) is of central importance precisely because of the commitment in the first sentence of Article 7(1) ECHR to the culpability requirement. A person who is found to be criminally insane cannot be punished without violating the guarantee in the first sentence of Article 7(1) ECHR. The imposition of a measure amounting to punishment in the absence of a finding of guilt would clearly violate Article 7(1) ECHR.[117] The ECtHR has rightly resisted the temptation to focus on the impact of the detention for the individual and has instead concentrated on the nature of the measure itself. In order to determine whether a measure is a penalty, it is necessary to consider the reasons for its imposition. Is the order imposed because an individual needs treatment or is it to be understood as

115 ibid dissenting opinion, para 33, attached to the judgment.

116 Fletcher, *Rethinking the Criminal Law* (n 5) 414.

117 *GIEM SRL and Others v Italy* [GC] App nos 1828/06, 34163/07, and 19029/11, 28 June 2018, para 251: Art 7 precludes the imposition of a criminal sanction on an individual without his personal criminal liability being established and declared beforehand. Otherwise, the principle of the presumption of innocence guaranteed by Art 6(2) of the Convention would also be breached.

a response to criminal conduct for which an individual could not be held accountable?

On this point, the ECtHR's reasoning in *Berland* is not particularly convincing. The ECtHR held that the nature and purpose of the compulsory hospitalization measure was to allow the applicant to 'receive treatment and at the same time to prevent him from reoffending'.[118] The reference to 'reoffending', in particular, seems difficult to square with the idea that the measure was not imposed as a response to the criminal conduct. Were the measure to have been imposed and its length determined purely in respect of medical reasons, then its characterization as preventative and remedial rather than punitive might be considered appropriate. Here, though, by tying the applicant's release to evidence concerning his likelihood of 'reoffending', the authorities seem to suggest that the imposition of the measure was at least partially motivated by the offence, thereby suggesting that it ought to be considered at least in part as punitive. Such measures should only be viewed as therapeutic if they are imposed in line with the civil standards for the commitment of those with psychiatric problems.[119]

c) *Distinguishing between Preventative and Punitive Measures*

The ECtHR has held that measures which are solely preventative in nature will not fall within the scope of Article 7(1) ECHR. The distinction between preventative and punitive measures is extremely difficult to maintain in practice, however, precisely because many measures will have both a punitive and a preventative character. This has led the ECtHR to conclude that even measures which are primarily 'preventative' might be regarded as also having punitive character.[120] This distinction is of particular relevance in the context of measures imposed on an offender in addition to a sentence of imprisonment. The prohibition on the imposition of *ex post facto* penalties might also apply to preventative orders, if they are to be classed as at least partly 'punitive' in nature.[121]

In *M v Germany*, for instance, the applicant was convicted and sentenced to five years' imprisonment and a period of up to a maximum of ten years of preventative detention.[122] This preventative detention was subsequently extended in violation, the applicant claimed, of Article 7(1) ECHR. The German government argued that while the sentence was 'fixed with regard to the offender's

[118] *Berland v France* App no 42875/10, 3 Sept 2015, para 44.
[119] This type of detention is regulated by Art 5(1)(e) ECHR.
[120] *Welch v UK*, 9 Feb 1995, Series A no 307-A, paras 29–35.
[121] See eg *OH v Germany* App no 4646/08, 24 Nov 2011, para 103.
[122] *M v Germany* App no 19359/04, ECHR 2009-VI.

personal guilt', measures of 'correction and prevention' were of a 'preventive nature and were ordered because of the danger presented by the offender, irrespective of his or her guilt'. This was representative of the 'twin-track' system of sentences and measures introduced in 1933. The benefit of preventative detention was that 'it could be suspended on probation at any time, provided that it could be expected that the detainee would no longer commit serious criminal offences outside prison'; the problem, though, was that its duration was not fixed in law. Preventative measures were thus not to be considered as penalties.[123]

The ECtHR did not agree with this approach, noting that preventive detention orders, which could only be imposed on those who had been repeatedly found to have committed 'criminal offences of a certain gravity', were to be classed as penalties for the purposes of Article 7 ECHR.[124] Such measures were to be understood as constituting punishment, precisely because they are imposed on an individual *for* (by reason of) the commission of a criminal offence. Thus, although the measure was certainly primarily 'preventive' in nature, the fact that it was imposed for a criminal offence meant that it had to be classed as 'punitive' and thus as a penalty for the purposes of Article 7(1) ECHR.[125]

In *Ilnseher v Germany*, this reasoning was put to the test by German legislation designed to provide a lawful basis for detention in the types of case found in *M* to violate Article 7(1) ECHR.[126] The applicant had been convicted of murder as a young offender and sentenced to ten years' imprisonment. On completion of the sentence, the applicant was not released but instead remanded in preventative detention. He complained that the 'subsequent' order[127] that he be placed in preventative detention violated his right under Article 7(1) ECHR not to have a heavier penalty imposed than the one applicable at the time of his offence. The government argued, and the Grand Chamber agreed, that the subsequent detention was not to be characterized as based on the criminal conviction in the sense of Article 5(1)(a) ECHR. Instead, it was justified on the grounds that the applicant was suffering from a mental disorder in the sense of Article 5(1)(e) ECHR.[128]

123 ibid.
124 ibid paras 128 and 135; see also *Glien v Germany* App no 7345/12, 28 Nov 2013, paras 120–30.
125 *Welch v UK*, 9 Feb 1995, Series A no 307-A, paras 29–35.
126 *Ilnseher v Germany* [GC] App nos 10211/12 and 27505/14, 4 Dec 2018.
127 On the decision to translate 'nachträglich' as 'subsequent' rather than 'retrospective' see *Ilnseher v Germany* [GC] App nos 10211/12 and 27505/14, 4 Dec 2018, paras 104–6 and for criticism the dissenting opinion of Judge Albuquerque, attached to the judgment, at 142.
128 ibid para 171.

This represented a change of approach from earlier cases in which the ECtHR had indicated that the term 'of unsound mind' within the meaning of Article 5(1)(e) ECHR only covered 'mentally ill persons who could not be held criminally responsible for their acts' and that those who 'suffered only from a personality disorder were, as a rule, not covered by that notion'.[129] The ECtHR's focus in its more recent case law seems to be on the nature and conditions of detention rather than on any particular medical diagnosis or differentiation between mental illness and personality disorder.[130] The position of the ECtHR in the context of Article 5(1) ECHR was based on acceptance of the applicant's (continued) detention (after expiry of the sentence) as therapeutic rather than punitive in nature and thus as falling with the scope of Article 5(1)(e) ECHR rather than Article 5(1)(a).

For the purposes of Article 7(1) ECHR, however, the problem remained that the detention was imposed because the applicant had been convicted of a criminal offence. The ECtHR accepted that although the measure had not been imposed in the judgment of the criminal court, it was nevertheless 'linked' to the conviction and thus 'following' the latter.[131] Despite this finding, which would strongly suggest that the measure was at least partially punitive, the ECtHR held that while the measure was initially punitive, it had morphed into a purely preventative measure with time. It justified this conclusion on the basis that:

> in some rare cases ... especially if national law does not qualify a measure as a penalty and if its purpose is therapeutic, a substantial change, in particular in the conditions of execution of the measure, can withdraw the initial qualification of the measure as a penalty within the meaning of Article 7 of the Convention, even if that measure is implemented on the basis of the same order.[132]

[129] *Glien v Germany* App no 7345/12, 28 Nov 2013, para 87; *Bergmann v Germany* App no 23279/14, 7 Jan 2016, para 83.

[130] See in particular *Bergmann v Germany* App no 23279/14, 7 Jan 2016, para 83: the ECtHR was influenced by the fact that the applicant was detained in a newly constructed preventive detention centre, a separate building located on the premises of the prison. In this regard, his detention differed from that at issue in earlier cases, in which the applicants were detained in 'separate wings for persons in preventive detention' of various prisons and not 'in institutions suitable for the detention of mental-health patients'; *Kallweit v Germany* App no 17792/07, 13 Jan 2011, para 57; *OH v Germany* App no 4646/08, 24 Nov 2011, paras 87–92; *Kronfeldner v Germany* App no 21906/09, 19 Jan 2012, paras 80–85; *Glien v Germany* App no 7345/12, 28 Nov 2013, paras 92–106.

[131] In *Bergmann v Germany* App no 23279/14, 7 Jan 2016, the measure had been imposed by the sentencing judge at the same time as the sentence.

[132] *Ilnseher v Germany* [GC] App nos 10211/12 and 27505/14, 4 Dec 2018, para 206.

It held that 'a measure may continue to be "imposed" over a longer period of time while changing its manner of execution, and thus its characteristics, during its imposition'.[133] Further, any assessment of whether a measure amounts to a penalty was to be determined 'on the basis of criteria which are both "static" or not susceptible to change after the point in time when the measure was ordered, particularly the criterion whether the measure in question was imposed following conviction for a "criminal offence" or that of the procedures involved in its making' and 'other criteria, including those of the nature and purpose of the measure and of its severity', which were to be understood as ' "dynamic" or susceptible to change over time'. This led the ECtHR to conclude that '[t]he applicant's preventive detention was imposed because of and with a view to the need to treat his mental disorder, having regard to his criminal history'. It accepted, though, that:

> the nature and purpose of his preventive detention, in particular, was substantially different from those of ordinary preventive detention executed irrespective of a mental disorder. The punitive element of preventive detention and its connection with the criminal offence committed by the applicant was erased to such an extent in these circumstances that the measure was no longer a penalty.[134]

The idea seems to be that the aim of some measures might be regarded as dynamic in nature and thus some punitive measures might change with time and turn into purely preventative orders. This, though, makes little sense, not least because the focus for the purposes of Article 7(1) ECHR is on the *reason* for the imposition of the measure, not on its aims.[135] If the link to the conviction is not completely severed, then it cannot be 'erased'[136] or 'eclipsed'.[137] The judgment seems at odds with the essence of legality and focuses attention on the failure of the ECtHR to insist on the determination of the character of the measure at the

[133] ibid para 207.
[134] ibid para 236.
[135] See also the dissenting opinion of Judge Sicilianos, para 16: 'More generally, the use of a criterion which is "dynamic", and therefore ongoing and changeable by definition, could well lead to uncertainties incompatible with the substance of the nullum crimen nulla poena sine lege principle. It is almost platitudinous to reiterate that that principle is the cornerstone of criminal law and criminal proceedings, and that it forms part of the hard core of the Convention, as a provision from which no derogation is permissible. Any attempt to limit its scope would require recourse to criteria which are reliable and stable enough to ensure the certainty of the law necessary in criminal matters.'
[136] *Ilnseher v Germany* [GC] App nos 10211/12 and 27505/14, 4 Dec 2018, para 236.
[137] *Bergmann v Germany* App no 23279/14, 7 Jan 2016, paras 181–82.

time of its initial imposition. In the words of Judge Pinto de Albuquerque in his dissenting opinion:

> The retrospective conversion of a time-limited punitive security measure into a potentially life-long pseudo-medical confinement measure imposed on convicted offenders with *ex nunc* established 'mental disorders' is an historically and dogmatically unreasonable, let us say it, abusive interpretation that not only goes beyond the nature and purpose of the measure of preventive detention, but circumvents the prohibition of *nulla poena sine lege praevia* guaranteed in a State governed by the rule of law.[138]

Any attempt to exclude such measures from the definition of punishment is particularly insidious.[139] Measures imposed (even for the purposes of treatment) as a response to the commission of a criminal offence (rather than, say, purely on mental health grounds) must be understood as constituting punishment. In this regard, the ECtHR's judgments in cases such as *Bergmann* and *Ilnseher* fall particularly short.[140] The imposition of measures of the sort at issue must be understood as constituting punishment, precisely because they are imposed on an individual *for* (on the grounds of) the commission of a criminal offence.

d) Imposition and Enforcement of Penalties

The notion of 'penalty' does not extend to procedural laws.[141] In addition, the ECtHR has continually insisted on a conceptual separation of penalties on the one hand and measures which relate to the enforcement of the penalty on the other, even though this distinction may not always be clear. Enforcement measures, such as provisions on early release, do not fall within the scope of Article 7(1) ECHR.[142] The ECtHR has held that if 'the nature and purpose of a measure' relates to the 'remission of a sentence or a change in a regime for early release' then this does not form part of the 'penalty' in the sentence of Article 7(1) ECHR.[143] The ECtHR has itself recognized that 'in practice, the distinction between the two may not always be clear cut'.[144] It has also noted

138 ibid dissenting opinion, attached to the judgment.

139 Hart, *Punishment and Responsibility* (n 35) 166.

140 See also the dissenting opinion of Judge Pinto de Albuquerque, attached to the judgment, in *Ilnseher v Germany* [GC] App nos 10211/12 and 27505/14, 4 Dec 2018.

141 See eg *Scoppola v Italy (no 2)* [GC] App no 10249/03, 17 Sept 2009, para 110.

142 *Kafkaris v Cyprus* [GC] App no 21906/04, ECHR 2008-I.

143 ibid citing *Hogben v UK* (dec) App no 11653/85, 3 Mar 1986; *Hosein v UK* (dec) App no 26293/95, 28 Feb 1996; *Grava v Italy* App no 43522/08, 10 July 2003, para 51; *Uttley v UK* (dec) App no 36946/03, 29 Nov 2005.

144 *Kafkaris v Cyprus* [GC] App no 21906/04, ECHR 2008-I, para 142.

that '[i]ssues relating to release policies, the manner of their implementation and the reasoning behind them fall within the power of the Member States to determine their own criminal policy'.[145]

In *Del Río Prada*, the applicant was a member of *Euskadi Ta Askatasuna* (ETA) convicted of a number of terrorist offences committed between 1982 and 1987. She was sentenced in respect of these offences to terms of imprisonment amounting to over 3000 years and began serving her sentence in 1989.[146] She was informed in 2000 that 'the legal and chronological links between the offences of which she had been convicted made it possible to group them together' and that 'the maximum term to be served … in respect of all her prison sentences combined at thirty years'.[147] Her release date was subsequently fixed as 27 June 2017. In 2008, the applicant requested that the '3,282 days' remission to which she was entitled for the work she had done since 1987' be taken into account and deducted from the sentence of thirty years in line with established practice. This would have led to her being released in 2008. This application was rejected on the basis of a new practice, set by the Spanish Supreme Court in 2006 and known as the 'Parot doctrine', which meant that 'sentence adjustments and remissions were no longer to be applied to the maximum term of imprisonment of thirty years, but successively to each of the sentences imposed'. This meant that the applicant would now be released on 27 June 2017.[148] The applicant alleged that the retroactive application of the Parot doctrine resulted in an extension of her detention by almost nine years, in violation of Article 7 ECHR.[149]

The ECtHR discussed, first, the distinction between the imposition of a penalty and matters relating to its enforcement, but noted that 'measures taken by the legislature, the administrative authorities or the courts after the final sentence has been imposed or while the sentence is being served may result in the redefinition or modification of the scope of the "penalty" imposed by the trial court'. In such cases, these measures will 'fall within the scope of the prohibition of the retroactive application of penalties enshrined in Article 7 § 1 *in fine* of the Convention'.[150] It explained this approach by noting that the contracting states would otherwise be able to circumvent the guarantee in Article 7(1) ECHR by retroactively defining the scope of the penalty, thereby depriving

[145] *Achour v France* [GC] App no 67335/01, ECHR 2006-IV, para 44.
[146] *Del Río Prada v Spain* [GC] App no 42750/09, ECHR 2013, para 12.
[147] ibid para 14.
[148] ibid para 17.
[149] ibid para 56.
[150] ibid para 89.

the provision of 'useful effect' for those whose sentences were changed '*ex post facto* to their disadvantage'.[151]

In determining whether a measure was to be considered to constitute a penalty for the purposes of Article 7(1) ECHR, the ECtHR was principally influenced by the impact of the measure on the sentence. In the case at issue, the measure allowed for 'a substantial reduction' of the fixed-term sentence itself. The ECtHR was also swayed by the extent of (judicial or executive) discretion in granting the measure and by the fact that the remission of the sentence did not involve any discretion—it was essentially automatic.[152] This led the ECtHR to conclude that 'the new approach to the application of remissions of sentence for work done in detention introduced by the "Parot doctrine"' could not be regarded 'as a measure relating solely to the execution of the penalty' but instead 'led to the redefinition of the scope of the "penalty" imposed on the applicant by the trial court'. This led it to conclude both that Article 7 ECHR was applicable and that it had been violated by the retrospective application of the 'Parot doctrine'.[153] This case demonstrates clearly the difficulties in maintaining the distinction between the sentence and the manner of its enforcement.

e) *Penalties and Punishment*

A penalty will be considered punitive in nature and thus to constitute *punishment* if it is imposed as a response to a criminal offence and it is not classed as treatment.[154] If a measure is classed as criminal or punitive in national law, then Article 7(1) ECHR clearly applies. Measures imposed following an acquittal might nevertheless be considered to constitute punishment.[155] Of the criteria developed by the ECtHR, the most important is 'the nature and purpose of the measure in question'.[156] The principal criterion for determining whether a penalty is punitive is whether it was imposed *for* a criminal offence.

[151] ibid para 89.

[152] For discussion see E Maes, 'Del Río Prada v Spain and the Execution of a Penalty under Article 7: Shifting Conception of Punishment?' (2017) 5 *European Human Rights Law Review* 443, 451–52.

[153] *Del Río Prada v Spain* [GC] App no 42750/09, ECHR 2013, paras 110 and 118.

[154] In this regard, it is notable that there is no reference to punishment in the text of Art 7(1) ECHR. The provision is entitled 'No Punishment without Law' but this heading was added later with the purpose of 'facilitat[ing] the comprehension of the text' and was not to be understood as an interpretation of the text of the provision itself. See para 114 of the Explanatory Report–ETS 155–Human Rights (Protocol No 11): 'The inclusion of such headings should not be understood as an interpretation of the Articles themselves or as having any legal effect.'

[155] *GIEM SRL and Others v Italy* [GC] App nos 1828/06, 34163/07, and 19029/11, 28 June 2018.

[156] ibid para 211, citing *Welch v UK*, 9 Feb 1995, Series A no 307-A, para 28; *Jamil v France*, 8 June 1995, Series A no 317-B, para 31; *Kafkaris v Cyprus* [GC] App no 21906/04, ECHR 2008-I, para 142; *M v Germany* App no 19359/04, ECHR 2009-VI, para 120; *Del Río Prada v Spain* [GC] App no 42750/09, ECHR 2013, para 82; *Société Oxygène Plus v France* (dec) App no 76959/11, 17 May 2016, para 47.

This is particularly relevant for the 'twin-track' system of sentences and measures found in many European countries.[157] Although measures imposed in addition to a sentence are often understood as preventative (rather than punitive) in nature, they are nevertheless likely to constitute punishment for the purposes of Article 7(1) ECHR if they are imposed as a response to the commission of a criminal offence. This has given rise to problems, as we have seen, in those cases in which the authorities have subsequently extended the detention of offenders beyond the sentence imposed by the trial court on the grounds of dangerousness. The subsequent imposition of a measure indicates that a more severe punishment has been retrospectively imposed and, as we have seen, the response to this has been to argue that these subsequent measures are no longer punitive in nature but rather constitute treatment orders.[158]

Judgments such as *Ilnseher* are clearly problematic. In the words of Hart:

> the prisoner who after serving a three-year sentence is told that his punishment is over but that a seven year period of preventative detention awaits him and that this is a 'measure' of social protection, not a punishment, might think he was being tormented by a barren piece of conceptualism—though he might not express himself in that way.[159]

Such cases, though, are unlikely to be seen in the future, precisely because of legislative attempts to avoid such problems by providing for open-ended or indefinite sentences or measures.

Perhaps more interesting, therefore, is the question whether sentencing provisions which provide for the indefinite detention of an offender are compatible with legality. In such cases the problem is not one of retrospectivity and thus complaints are likely to be framed in terms of Article 5(1) ECHR or perhaps Article 3 ECHR rather than Article 7(1) ECHR.[160] It is questionable, however, whether the imposition of an indefinite sentence imposed with a short

[157] It is important to stress that this is in no sense a criticism of the twin-track system of punishment and measures per se. The idea that those found culpable of committing an offence, but whose mental illness has contributed to its commission, should first be treated, in order to establish whether it is even necessary that the offender serve the sentence seems both lawful and sensible. Nevertheless, the punishment which can be imposed is defined by the individual's culpability for the offence. Once the sentence has been served, any further 'treatment' can only be imposed in line with the (non-criminal law) rules governing the treatment of individuals against their will.

[158] Notably *Ilnseher v Germany* [GC] App nos 10211/12 and 27505/14, 4 Dec 2018.

[159] HLA Hart, 'Punishment and the Elimination of Responsibility' in Hart, *Punishment and Responsibility* (n 35) 166–67.

[160] See eg *James, Wells, and Lee v UK* App nos 25119/09, 57715/09, and 57877/09, 18 Sept 2012 (in one case a punishment part of nine months was imposed; the applicant was still in prison some nine years later).

tariff or a comparatively short sentence combined with some sort of indefinite measure is compatible with the requirement inherent in Article 7(1) ECHR that a penalty be certain and foreseeable and imposed for the criminal offence rather than for other reasons.

2. Non-Retrospectivity, Certainty, and Foreseeability of the Penalty

Legality requires that criminal offences be clearly and prospectively defined, but does it place similar constraints on punishment? Do individuals have the right to know, prior to the commission of the offence, the sentence which is likely to be imposed? The overview of the case law on legality suggests that, in the context of the guarantee in the first sentence of Article 7(1) ECHR, the ECtHR relies principally on a determination of whether laws are sufficiently accessible and foreseeable. This approach is clearly connected to an understanding of the importance of criminal laws as a priori notice provisions. It might be argued that legality only demands that an accused is able to determine, prior to the commission of the offence, whether their behaviour is criminal.[161] This would call into question the need for the accused to be aware of, or able to establish, prior to the commission of the offence, the sentence likely to be imposed in event of a conviction.

This interpretation of the legality requirement would, however, have considerable consequences for the effectiveness of the prohibition on retrospectivity. Changes to sentencing laws after the commission of the offence and before the sentencing decision would not be viewed as problematic, even if they resulted in the imposition of a more severe sentence. If the authorities were permitted to impose any punishment on the offender, this would call into question the sense of restrictions imposed by legality in the context of the definition of the offence. It is unsurprising, therefore, that the ECtHR has held that legality also demands that the sentence be prospectively defined.[162] According to the ECtHR, an individual must be able to ascertain 'the penalty he faces on that

[161] Hall notes that 'apologists of retroactivity' tend to 'ridicule the notion that the lawbreaker is entitled to notice of the possible penalty he may incur', arguing that 'experience and observation have amply demonstrated that sanctions do not deter, and that it is a vestige of a rationalistic age to believe that the would-be offender will weigh the advantage of his crime against the evil of his possible punishment', see Hall, 'Nulla Poena' (n 11) 172.

[162] *Rohlena v Czech Republic* [GC], no 59552/08, ECHR 2015, para 52, citing *Kononov v Latvia* [GC] App no 36376/04, ECHR 2010, para 198: 'it is primarily for the national authorities, notably the courts, to resolve problems of interpretation of domestic legislation ... the Court's powers of review must be greater when the Convention right itself, Article 7 in the present case, requires that there was a legal basis for a conviction and sentence. Article 7 § 1 requires the Court to examine whether there was a contemporaneous legal basis for the applicant's conviction and, in particular, it must satisfy itself that the result reached by the relevant domestic courts was compatible with Article 7 of the Convention. To accord a lesser power of review to this Court would render Article 7 devoid of purpose.'

account'.[163] The guarantee prohibiting the imposition of a heavier penalty will be violated if there was no legal basis for the penalty imposed, if the penalty was applied to an offence committed before the provision came into operation, or if the penalty was applied to the detriment of the convicted person in a way which was not reasonably foreseeable.[164]

a) The Legal Basis for the Penalty and the Prohibition on the Retrospective Imposition of a Heavier Penalty

Legality demands that the sentence be set out in law.[165] This means that the sentence to be imposed must be in force at the time of the commission of the offence. This would appear to be the least controversial aspect of legality at the sentencing stage. Article 7(1) ECHR prohibits the retrospective application of a more severe sentence than would have been available at the time when the offence was committed. Sentencing laws which are enacted after the commission of an offence cannot be relied upon at sentencing to the detriment of the offender.[166] If sentencing provisions, which come into force after the commission of an offence are more severe than those applicable at the time of the commission of the offence, then their application will violate Article 7(1) ECHR. According to the ECtHR: 'Article 7 para 1 of the Convention embodies generally the principle that only the law can define a crime and prescribe a penalty and prohibits in particular the retrospective application of the criminal law where it is to an accused's disadvantage.'[167] These principles are well illustrated by the case of *Jamil*, in which sentencing provisions were applied which came into force after the commission of the offence. The new sentencing provision allowed for the imposition of a maximum sentence of twenty-four months' as opposed to four months' imprisonment, which was the maximum sentence available at the time of the commission of the offence. This resulted in an extension of the applicant's (suspended) prison sentence by twenty months. The

[163] *Del Río Prada v Spain* [GC] App no 42750/09, ECHR 2013, para 79, citing *Cantoni v France* [GC], 15 Nov 1996, Reports 1996-V, para 29 and *Kafkaris v Cyprus* [GC] App no 21906/04, ECHR 2008-I, para 140.

[164] See DJ Harris and others, *Harris, O'Boyle and Warbrick: Law of the Convention on Human Rights* (Oxford: OUP 2018) 338. *Jorgic v Germany* App no 74613/01, ECHR 2007-III, para 140; *Cantoni v France* [GC], 15 Nov 1996, Reports 1996-V, para 35; *Achour v France* [GC] App no 67335/01, ECHR 2006-IV, para 54.

[165] *Del Río Prada v Spain* [GC] App no 42750/09, ECHR 2013, para 79. See too S Trechsel and M Jean-Richard, 'Art 1' in S Trechsel and M Pieth (eds), *Schweizerisches Strafgesetzbuch: Praxiskommentar* (3rd edn, Zurich: Dike 2018) N 2.

[166] *Achour v France* [GC] App no 67335/01, ECHR 2006-IV.

[167] *G v France* App no 15312/89, 27 Sept 1995, para 24, citing *Kokkinakis v Greece*, 25 May 1993, Series A no 260-A, para 52.

ECtHR held unanimously—and unsurprisingly—that this constituted a violation of Article 7(1) ECHR.[168]

The prohibition on the retrospective application of sentences also gives rise to questions about whether factors can be taken into account in the sentencing decision, which the sentencing judge would not have been entitled to consider at the time of the commission of the offence. This issue is well illustrated by the consideration of recidivist sentencing provisions. If sentencing provisions are altered, for instance, in order to allow previous convictions to be taken into account, is the sentencing judge entitled to rely on these? It is clear that if the law only came into force after the commission of the second offence, then the application of such provisions would be considered more severe and thus would be prohibited by Article 7(1) ECHR.

The situation is more complicated in those cases in which the law was not in force at the time of the commission of the first offence but subsequently came into force before the commission of the second offence.[169] This was the situation in the case of *Achour*. The applicant had been convicted of drugs offences and had served his sentence. Following his release, he was convicted of committing further offences. Between the two convictions the statutory definition of 'recidivism' was amended. Under the legislation in force at the time of his first conviction, the applicant would not have been considered a recidivist. According to the legislation which came into force before the applicant's conviction for the second offence, the applicant was to be treated as a recidivist and sentenced more severely.

Here the ECtHR refused to find a violation of Article 7(1) ECHR, holding that:

> there is no doubt that the applicant could have foreseen that by committing a further offence before 13 July 1996, the date on which the statutory ten-year period expired, he ran the risk of being convicted as a recidivist and of receiving a prison sentence and/or a fine that was liable to be doubled. He was thus able to foresee the legal consequences of his actions and to adapt his conduct accordingly.[170]

168 *Jamil v France*, 8 June 1995, Series A no 317-B, para 34.

169 See eg *Achour v France* [GC] App no 67335/01, ECHR 2006-IV, paras 17–18; see also *Kokkinakis v Greece*, 25 May 1993, Series A no 260-A, para 40; *Cantoni v France* [GC], 15 Nov 1996, Reports 1996-V, para 34; *Streletz, Kessler and Krenz v Germany* [GC] App nos 34044/96, 35532/97, and 44801/98, ECHR 2001-II, para 82.

170 *Achour v France* [GC] App no 67335/01, ECHR 2006-IV, para 53.

It also held that 'a law may still satisfy the requirement of "foreseeability" where the person concerned has to take appropriate legal advice to assess, to a degree that is reasonable in the circumstances, the consequences which a given action may entail'.[171] Consequently, it held that 'the sentence imposed on the applicant, who was found guilty and deemed to be a recidivist in the proceedings in issue, was applicable at the time when the second offence was committed, pursuant to a "law" which was accessible and foreseeable as to its effect'.[172] The ECtHR couches this issue in terms of 'foreseeability'—in the potential for the accused to discern, in advance, the sentence which is likely to be imposed in the event of conviction. Equally, though, it is clear that the need for clearly defined laws is of essential importance in preventing arbitrariness by ensuring that the boundaries of the involvement of state authorities are sufficiently clearly defined.[173]

In *Alimujac*,[174] the applicant argued that at the time of the commission of the criminal offence the maximum sentence for deception was five years' imprisonment. The provision did not mention any aggravating circumstances. The applicant was sentenced to a total of twenty years' imprisonment.[175] The ECtHR was willing to consider the possibility that the case law had developed to such an extent as to allow the imposition of a higher sentence. In the case at issue, though, the Supreme Court ruling that a person who had committed the criminal offence of deception was to be sentenced on as many counts as the number of injured parties had been made some time after the applicant had committed the offence. In addition, the ECtHR noted that the government had not provided 'any prior, relevant domestic case-law to the effect that a person convicted of deception ... could be sentenced on as many counts as the number of injured parties, thereby multiplying the maximum penalty to a term of imprisonment superior to five years'. This led the ECtHR to conclude that, 'at the time he committed the offence, the applicant could not reasonably foresee that he would be found guilty of 57,923 counts of deception, even if he were to seek legal advice'.[176] The ECtHR held that in sentencing the applicant to twenty years' imprisonment, 'the criminal law was extensively and unforeseeably construed' to his detriment and had violated Article 7 since a heavier penalty was

[171] ibid para 54.
[172] ibid para 60.
[173] M Pérez Manzano, JA Lascuraín Sánchez, and M Mínguez Rosique, *Multilevel Protection of the Principle of Legality in Criminal Law* (Springer: Cham 2018) 50, discussing this distinction in the context of the difference between the subjective right to foreseeability employed by the ECtHR and the right to certainty as propagated by the Spanish Supreme Court.
[174] *Alimucaj v Albania* App no 20134/05, 7 Feb 2012, paras 155–62.
[175] ibid para 155.
[176] ibid para 157.

imposed on the applicant than the one applicable at the time of the commission of the criminal offence.[177]

The prohibition on the retrospective application of sentences necessarily gives rise, however, to questions about the extent of the information to be provided about the sentence which is likely to be imposed. The suggestion in the case law of the ECtHR is that it is sufficient if the punishment falls within the limits set by the sentencing provision.[178] In cases, such as *Jamil*, in which the sentence imposed was clearly more severe than the maximum sentence available at the time of the commission of the offence, the issue is relatively unproblematic. In many cases, however, the situation will be less clear. Questions arise in particular in relation to establishing just how detailed sentencing provisions ought to be. In some jurisdictions, the maximum and minimum sentences are set out together with the definition of the offence in the criminal code. This provides an indication of the sentence which might be imposed—albeit one which is by no means precise. In other jurisdictions, including in many common law jurisdictions, it is less common for maximum and minimum sentences to be included together with the definition of the offence. In addition, most systems provide for criminal offences, such as manslaughter or theft, which are very broad and cover such a wide range of circumstances as to necessitate considerable sentencing discretion on the part of the judge. This also calls into question the potential for the sentence to be clearly defined in advance. If the law provides for broad sentencing discretion, there will be little scope for control through legality.

b) The Foreseeability of the Penalty

The ECtHR seems to apply the same requirements on accessibility and foreseeability as in the context of the first sentence of the provision. In *Camilleri*, the law provided for different sentences for an offence depending on whether the case was tried before the Criminal Court (six months to ten years) or the Court of Magistrates (four years to life).[179] The applicant complained that the determination of the 'punishment bracket' was only foreseeable after the Attorney General had determined the court in which he was to be tried.[180] The ECtHR agreed that the determination of the trial court was dependent on the prosecutor's discretion and this made it impossible for the applicant

177 ibid paras 161–62.

178 *Coëme and Others v Belgium* App nos 32492/96, 32547/96, 32548/96, 33209/96, and 33210/96, ECHR 2000-VII, para 145 and *Achour v France* [GC] App no 67335/01, ECHR 2006-IV, para 43.

179 *Camilleri v Malta* App no 4293/10, 22 Jan 2013, para 40.

180 ibid para 41.

to know the penalty likely to be imposed, even with the assistance of legal advice. In finding a violation of Article 7(1) ECHR, the ECtHR was particularly concerned by the fact that the provisions imposed different minimum penalties. This meant that the sentencing judge was essentially bound in the choice of minimum sentence by the prosecutor's decision.[181] This procedural arrangement might also be viewed as constituting an unacceptable interference with the judicial responsibility for the determination of the sentence.[182]

In *Kafkaris*, the applicant had been convicted in 1989 of three counts of murder and sentenced to life imprisonment in accordance with a mandatory sentencing provision. Prison regulations stated that where imprisonment was for life, remission of the sentence would be calculated as if the imprisonment were for twenty years and that such prisoners could be granted remission of one-quarter of such a sentence on the grounds of good conduct. There was some discussion at trial as to whether a life sentence carried a sentence of imprisonment for the rest of the offender's life or whether it rather constituted a sentence of a period of twenty years as suggested by the prison regulations. The sentencing court held that imprisonment for life meant imprisonment for the remainder of the convicted person's life and thus that it was 'pointless to consider whether the sentences will run concurrently or whether they will be served consecutively'.[183] On admission to prison, however, the applicant was given written notice by the prison authorities—in line with the prison regulations—that the date for his release, assuming good conduct, was 16 July 2002.[184] The prison regulations were subsequently ruled unconstitutional and ultra vires. The applicant was not released in 2002.

The ECtHR did not accept the Cypriot government's argument that the regulations stating that life imprisonment was to be determined as twenty years' imprisonment concerned solely the enforcement of a penalty, holding instead that the distinction between the scope of a life sentence and the manner of its execution was not immediately apparent.[185] It held that the matter at issue was not one of retrospectivity but was essentially one of the 'quality of law':

[181] ibid paras 43–45.

[182] See the partly dissenting opinion of Judge Kalaydjieva, attached to the judgment in *Camilleri v Malta* App no 4293/10, 22 Jan 2013; and for discussion F Meyer, *Systematischer Kommentar zur Strafprozessordnung, Vol X: EMRK* (5th edn, Cologne: Carl Heymanns Verlag 2019) 738. This is discussed further in Ch 5.

[183] *Kafkaris v Cyprus* [GC] App no 21906/04, ECHR 2008-I, para 15.

[184] ibid para 16.

[185] The provisions on remission were not viewed as falling within Art 7.

> at the time the applicant committed the offence, the relevant Cypriot law taken as a whole was not formulated with sufficient precision as to enable the applicant to discern, even with appropriate advice, to a degree that was reasonable in the circumstances, the scope of the penalty of life imprisonment and the manner of its execution.[186]

This was criticized by Judge Loucaides in his dissenting opinion in *Kafkaris*, in which he noted that the judgement represented the first time that the quality of law argument had been considered in the context of Article 7 ECHR of the Convention, 'with reference more particularly to the second sentence of the first paragraph'.[187] He noted that the aim of Article 7 ECHR was to prevent abuse by the state and to prohibit the retrospective effect of criminal legislation. In this case, the ECtHR, however, had expressly held that 'there had been no retrospective imposition of a heavier penalty'. He noted that:

> assuming that before the applicant embarked on the premeditated murder of the victim and his two children, he had asked a lawyer about the sentence applicable at the time of the commission of the crime, he would have received advice to the effect that the Criminal Code punished this crime with life imprisonment, and if he had wanted to know more about the manner of the execution of this sentence in terms of prison regulations or practice

this would also have been possible.[188] This draws attention to a potentially important distinction between legality at the point of attribution of criminal liability and its role in the context of the definition of the punishment.

More recently, in *Del Río Prada*, the ECtHR continued to frame the issue in terms of foreseeability, holding that its task was to

> examine whether the applicant could have foreseen at the time of her conviction, and also when she was notified of the decision to combine the sentences and set a maximum term of imprisonment—if need be, after taking appropriate legal advice—that the penalty imposed might turn into thirty years of actual imprisonment, with no reduction for the remissions of sentence for work done in detention.

186 *Kafkaris v Cyprus* [GC] App no 21906/04, ECHR 2008-I, para 150.
187 ibid; the dissenting opinion is attached to the judgment.
188 ibid.

The ECtHR held that this was not the case and thus that there had been a violation of Article 7 ECHR.[189] The test here is, ostensibly, whether the applicant could have foreseen that the penalty at issue might be imposed. The reference to the assistance of a lawyer makes it clear that this is to ensure that penalties are suitably clear at the time they are imposed to prevent subsequent arbitrary imposition of (more severe) punishment.

c) The Importance of Setting a Maximum Sentence

Does Article 7(1) ECHR require member states to clearly stipulate the maximum sentence which can be imposed as a response to the criminal offence? In *Gestur Jónsson and Ragnar Halldór Hall*, the applicants complained about the 'lack of a specific stipulation of the maximum amount of fines' in Icelandic law.[190] The applicants were both lawyers who had requested that they be recused from their responsibility as defence counsel at trial. This request was refused, but the lawyers nevertheless failed to appear for the accused at trial. They were then convicted *in absentia* of contempt of court and fined €6200. The ECtHR held that 'the mere fact that a provision of domestic law does not stipulate the maximum amount which may be imposed in the form of a fine does not, as such, run counter to the requirements of Article 7 of the Convention'.[191] It held that while the fines imposed were 'substantially higher than fines which had previously been imposed' under the section, 'the present case was the first of its kind and one in which the Supreme Court considered that the nature and gravity of the applicants' actions warranted the imposition of fines which were higher than imposed in other prior cases with different facts'. This led the ECtHR to conclude that 'the amount of the fines in question was consistent with the essence of the offence and could have been reasonably foreseen by the applicants'.[192]

This seems extremely problematic. The lack of a maximum sentence here leaves considerable scope for arbitrariness and must be considered incompatible with the requirement of legal certainty. The case was appealed to the Grand Chamber which held, following the application of the Engel criteria, that the fines were not criminal in nature and thus that Article 7(1) ECHR was not relevant.[193] In their dissenting opinion, Judges Sicilianos, Ravarani, and Serghides

[189] *Del Río Prada v Spain* [GC] App no 42750/09, ECHR 2013, paras 117–18.

[190] *Gestur Jónsson and Ragnar Halldór Hall v Iceland* App nos 68273/14 and 68271/14, 3 Oct 2018; the case was referred to the Grand Chamber.

[191] ibid para 94.

[192] ibid.

[193] *Gestur Jónsson and Ragnar Halldór Hall v Iceland* [GC] App nos 68273/14 and 68271/1422 Dec 2020, paras 112–13.

challenged this finding, noting that, '[b]y holding that Article 6 is inapplicable, the Grand Chamber avoided addressing the real issue of interest in this case, namely the question of compliance with the requirements of Article 7 of the Convention, and more specifically the legality of the penalty imposed on the applicants in the absence of an explicit statutory ceiling'.[194]

In her concurring opinion, Judge Turković suggested that while criminal offences, 'however clearly defined, would inevitably require judicial interpretation and elucidation' the same was 'not true with regard to determination of the maximum sentence'. In this context, 'greater clarity and precision are both possible and achievable; in fact, the maximum penalty can be laid down in law with absolute clarity'. The failure to outline a maximum sentence is difficult to reconcile with the guarantee in the second sentence of Article 7(1) ECHR. As Judge Turković writes, only by clearly defining a 'maximum penalty can the authorities comply with the requirements of lex praevia, prohibiting retroactive application of the more stringent law and determining which provision was the more lenient one'.[195]

This issue is of considerable importance in practice, not least because it calls into question the compatibility of indeterminate sentences (or punitive measures) with the requirement that the maximum punishment be clearly set out in law and thus with Article 7(1) ECHR.

d) Conclusions

The case law of the ECtHR leaves many questions unanswered. It might be argued that the more detailed sentencing laws are, the more scope there will be for review of the compatibility of the sentence with the legality principle. This applies to both the maximum and minimum sentences available and with regard to the sentencing factors which the judge is permitted to consider in setting the sentence. In systems in which the sentencing judge is afforded considerable discretion in setting the sentence as a result of broad sentencing provisions or in assessing the importance of sentencing factors, there will be little scope for review of the compatibility of the sentence with the legality principle. It is important to note, however, that too much detail in sentencing laws might impinge (unacceptably) on judicial discretion and the ability of the judiciary to guard against arbitrariness and thus interfere in itself with the aims of legality.[196] In this sense, legality is designed to protect against arbitrariness rather

194 Dissenting opinion of Judges Sicilianos, Ravarani, and Serghides, para 23. See also the concurring opinion of Judge Turković.

195 Citing *Del Río Prada v Spain* [GC] App no 42750/09, ECHR 2013, paras 112 and 114.

196 The role of the judge is discussed in detail in Ch 5.

than provide an offender with complete clarity as to the sentence, which will be imposed if they commit an offence. The focus must be on ensuring that only a sentence which was available to the sentencing judge at the relevant time can be imposed. The imposition of a sentence other than that set out in law will violate Article 7(1) ECHR.

3. Punishment as a Response to the Commission of a Criminal Offence

The overview of the case law of the ECtHR demonstrates that legality as guaranteed by Article 7(1) ECHR is not just relevant at the point of attribution of criminal liability, but also constrains the state in its imposition of punishment. Inherent in this notion of legality is, as we have seen, the requirement that wrongdoing had occurred in the form of an act or omission clearly defined as criminal in nature, which can be attributed to a culpable offender. It is not enough, though, merely to say that there must be a legal basis for the criminal offence and for the punishment. Legality places constraints on the process of criminalization in that it requires that offenders be held to account for what they have done and not who they are.[197] In addition, it limits the punishment which can be imposed, in that it insists on a causal relationship between the criminal offence and the punishment; punishment must be imposed as a response to the criminal behaviour and not for other reasons. The ECtHR has emphasized the relationship between the two guarantees in Article 7(1) ECHR. It has noted that it would be 'inconsistent, on the one hand to require a foreseeable and accessible legal basis and on the other to allow a person to be considered "guilty" and to "punish" him' even though he was unable to ascertain the extent of the criminal law because of an error which could not be attributed to him.[198] Just as punishment cannot be imposed following an acquittal without violating legality, so too is the imposition of a more severe sentence for reasons unconnected to an offender's blameworthiness for the criminal offence at issue impossible to reconcile with legality.

It should come as little surprise that this focus on blameworthiness for specific conduct is clearly set out in most statutory sentencing provisions. The Swiss judge, for instance, is required to establish the appropriate sentence

[197] *GIEM SRL and Others v Italy* [GC] App nos 1828/06, 34163/07, and 19029/11, 28 June 2018. See *Achour v France* [GC] App no 67335/01, ECHR 2006-IV and the concurring opinion of Judge Zupančič, attached to the judgment: '*A priori*, the word "*act*" is something *in rem*. No legislature may say: "You will be punished if you *are* a drug addict." It may say, of course: "You will be punished if you commit an *act* of drug taking."' See also Feuerbach's definition of the legality principle, which draws attention to the importance of the relationship between the punishment and the criminal behaviour, Feuerbach, *Lehrbuch* (n 46) 12, 19.

[198] *GIEM SRL and Others v Italy* [GC] App nos 1828/06, 34163/07, and 19029/11, 28 June 2018, para 242.

by examining the blameworthiness (*Verschulden*) of the offender for the offence.[199] Relevant factors in this assessment include: 'the seriousness of the harm or danger to the relevant legal interest, the reprehensibility of the conduct, the motives and aims of the offender and the extent to which the offender, in view of personal and external factors, could have avoided causing the danger or harm.'[200] In determining the sentence, the court is also obliged to consider the offender's life prior to the criminal offence, their personal circumstances, and the effect which the sentence will have on their life.[201] Similarly, in England and Wales, the focus is principally on liability for the offence: the courts must, in considering the 'seriousness of any offence', take into account 'the offender's culpability in committing the offence' and any harm which the offence caused, was intended to cause, or might foreseeably have caused.[202]

The importance of ensuring that punishment is imposed as a response to a violation of the criminal law is well established in sentencing theory.[203] It is acknowledged that it would be incompatible with the conception of criminal law as based on blameworthiness for individual acts, for the character or lifestyle of the accused to be considered independently of, or detached from, the matter of the criminal offence at issue at the sentencing stage.[204] The extent of an offender's blameworthiness, and thus the sentence to be imposed, is to be determined with regard to the prohibited conduct and not by making some kind of general assessment of the offender's character or the manner in which the offender conducts their life.[205] It is notable that this discussion is typically

199 Art 47(1) Swiss Criminal Code.

200 Art 47(2) CC.

201 ibid.

202 See Sentencing Act 2020, s 63.

203 It is important to keep in mind that at various points in time reliance on character has been more pronounced. Schmidt, writing in the 1930s, suggested that 'the guilt of the offender increased in relation to the extent of his dangerousness and the anti-social nature of his character', E Schmidt, 'Zur Theorie des Unbestimmten Strafurteils' (1931) 45 *Schweizerische Zeitschrift für Strafrecht* 227: '*Die Schuld ist umso grosser, je gefährlicher der Täter ist, je unsozialer sein Charakter uns erscheint*'); OA Germann, *Das Verbrechen im Neuen Strafrecht* (Zurich: Schulthess 1942) 58: 'Der Vorwurf gegenüber dem Täter' sei '*um so eher begründet und um so schwerer, je mehr der Willensentschluss ... seinem ganzen Wesen und Charakter entspricht*' ('the more the offender's decisions reflected his whole being and character', the more the offender's blame was to be considered 'reasonable and serious'). In a case from the early 1970s, for instance, the High Court of the Canton of Zurich held that 'the accused's guilt for the manner in which he conducted his life' was on balance 'more serious than his guilt in the context of the crime committed', ZR 70/1971, Nr 8, 27 at 29: '*Verschuldensmässig eher noch schwerer als das Tatvorgehen wiegt indessen die Lebensführungsschuld des Angeklagten.*'

204 H Wiprächtiger and S Keller, 'Art 47' in MA Niggli and H Wiprächtiger (eds), *Basler Kommentar: Strafrecht I* (4th edn, Basel: Helbing & Lichtenhahn 2019) N 123; D Jositsch, G Ege, and C Schwarzenegger, *Strafrecht II: Strafen und Massnahmen* (9th edn, Zurich: Schulthess 2018) 111.

205 S Trechsel and M Thommen, 'Art 47' in S Trechsel and M Pieth (eds), *Schweizerisches Strafgesetzbuch: Praxiskommentar* (3rd edn, Zurich: Dike 2018) N 7: '*im Gegensatz zu einer allgemeinen Lebensführungsschuld geht es nicht um eine generelle Abrechnung mit der Person des Täters, sondern um das Mass seiner Verantwortung für bestimmt umschriebenes Verhalten.*' See also eg A von Hirsch, 'Proportionate Sentences: A Desert Perspective' in A von Hirsch, A Ashworth, and J Roberts (eds),

conducted without consideration of the importance of legality or restraints on the state in the process of the imposition of punishment.

Despite this consensus that a person should be sentenced for their conduct rather than their character, it is quite common for factors which are not directly linked to an offender's blameworthiness for the commission of the offence to be taken into consideration at the sentencing stage. A number of important sentencing practices seem difficult to reconcile with the requirement that the sentence be imposed on an offender in response to the criminal conduct rather than their 'bad' character. These include the practice of imposing aggravated sentences on offenders who have prior convictions or who refuse to confess or plead guilty. If, as will be argued, these factors do not affect the blameworthiness of the offender for the commission of the criminal offence, then it seems likely that they are incompatible with the requirement of legality. Legality prohibits the imposition of criminal liability on a person for status or character, but it also prohibits the imposition of a higher sentence on a person on the grounds of character (such as recalcitrance) as opposed to reasons directly connected to the commission of the offence. Sentencing practices which rely on factors that have little to do with the blameworthiness of the offender for the offence at issue, to justify the imposition of a more severe sentence, are difficult to reconcile with the legality principle.

The consideration of legality has also been neglected in the context of treatment of the diminished culpability of an offender at sentencing. This reflects a failure to come to terms with the importance of the concept of subjective attribution or culpability at the level of the attribution of criminal liability. The Article 7(1) ECHR case law suggests, however, that the failure to take proper account of the extent of the diminished culpability of an offender in establishing their blameworthiness for the conduct at issue is incompatible with the culpability requirement inherent in the legality principle.

The examples chosen here—previous convictions, confessions, and diminished culpability—are intended to be illustrative rather than exhaustive. Each issue will be analysed by considering the nature of the practice in the case law of the courts before turning to examine the justification for the practice and the relevance of the legality principle as set out in Article 7(1) ECHR.

Principled Sentencing: Readings on Theory and Policy (Oxford: Hart Publishing 2009) 115, 116: 'the emphasis is on what the offender should fairly receive for his crime.'

IV. Legality and Sentencing Practice

A. Previous Convictions

1. Previous Convictions as an Aggravating Factor in Practice

Previous convictions are of 'extraordinary importance' in sentencing practice.[206] In many jurisdictions, they do not just play a 'central role' at sentencing,[207] but also precipitate the automatic imposition of a more severe sentence.[208] If it is accepted not just that punishment is contingent on the commission of a criminal offence, but also that the punishment must be imposed for that offence, it is questionable why the fact that an offender has previous convictions should be considered of relevance to the determination of the offender's blameworthiness for the commission of the most recent offence.[209] Here there seems to be some tension between the consideration of previous convictions on the one hand and the principle that the sentence should be based on liability for specific criminal conduct on the other.[210] In order to consider this issue in more detail, it is useful to have regard to the case law of the courts and to the reasons provided for sentence enhancements in such cases.

In Switzerland, previous convictions will result 'in principle' in the imposition of a more severe sentence.[211] This enhancement can be hugely significant. In one case, for instance, the SFSC endorsed an increase of 50% (from twenty-four months to thirty-six months) on the grounds of persistent reoffending.[212] The Swiss courts will consider not just previous convictions incurred in Switzerland, but also those imposed by foreign courts for offences committed abroad.[213] Previous convictions for some serious offences committed by the

[206] See Wiprächtiger and Keller, 'Art 47' (n 204) N 100: 'eine ausserordentlich wichtige Rolle'; P Albrecht, 'Die Strafzumessung im Spannungsfeld von Theorie und Praxis' [1991] *Schweizerische Zeitschrift für Strafrecht* 45, 53; BGE 121 IV 49, 62, E 2d; BGE 121 IV 3, 5, E 1b; BGer 6B_538/2007, 2 June 2008, E 3.2.3.1.

[207] BGer 6B_954/2009, 14 Jan 2010, E 2.2: '*Das Vorleben und insbesondere die Vorstrafen haben einen zentralen Stellenwert bei der Strafzumessung*'. See too G Schäfer, GM Sander, and G van Gemmeren, *Praxis der Strafzumessung* (6th edn, Munich: Beck 2017) 650.

[208] See eg BGE 136 IV 1, 2, E 2.6.2; see also H Mathys, *Leitfaden Strafzumessung* (2nd edn, Basel: Helbing & Lichtenhahn 2019) 121: '*Die Rechtsprechung bedeutet, dass eine Vorstrafe grundsätzlich automatisch zu einer Straferhöhung führt*.'

[209] See H Schultz, *Einführung in den Allgemeinen Teil des Strafrechts*, vol II (Bern: Stämpfli 1982) 84; Fletcher, *Rethinking Criminal Law* (n 5) 460–66; see too M Killias and others, *Grundriss des Allgemeinen Teils des Schweizerischen Gesetzbuchs* (Bern: Stämpfli 2009) 196.

[210] See also Trechsel and Thommen, 'Art 47' (n 205) N 20: '*Bei der Berücksichtigung dieser Strafzumessungstatsache ist wegen ihrer Ambivalenz grösste Zurückhaltung geboten*.'

[211] BGE 136 IV 1, 2, E 2.6.2.

[212] See eg BGer 6B_510/2015, 25 Aug 2015 (theft).

[213] For a comprehensive overview see Wiprächtiger and Keller, 'Art 47' (n 204) N100.

offender while a minor may also be taken into account.[214] Prior to an amendment to the Swiss Criminal Code, the courts were even permitted to consider previous convictions which had been expunged from the offender's criminal record.[215] This was explained by reference to the fact that these convictions could be of use to the judge in assessing the personal history of the offender and selecting the appropriate type of sentence, length of the sentence, and the determination of whether the sentence should be suspended.[216] Following an amendment to the criminal code, this practice was altered and the sentencing judge was expressly directed to ignore spent convictions on the basis that the person had been deemed to have served their time for that offence and to have been reintegrated into society.[217] Previous convictions are viewed conceptually as an aggravating factor.[218] First-time offenders will not benefit from having a clear record precisely because the absence of previous convictions is to be expected. The lack of previous convictions is considered to be a neutral rather than a mitigating factor and will not lead to a reduction of the sentence.[219]

The relevance of previous convictions is generally explained by reference to the fact that by reoffending the offender demonstrated a failure to come to terms with the importance of acting lawfully. The fact, for instance, that an individual had been convicted on multiple occasions for the same offence and had in addition reoffended during the current proceedings was said to demonstrate the offender's indifference to the importance of obeying the law and justified the imposition of a more severe sentence.[220] The significance of previous convictions is determined with regard to their severity and the time which has

[214] BGE 135 IV 87, 96, E 6: '*Das Obergericht durfte demnach bei der Anordnung der Massnahme auf das die Jugendstrafen berücksichtigende Gutachten abstellen. Es hätte die Vorstrafen überdies bei der Strafzumessung in Rechnung stellen sollen. Dieser Strafzumessungsfehler führt—für sich genommen—nicht zur Aufhebung des angefochtenen Urteils, zumal das Bundesgericht nicht über die Begehren der Partei hinausgehen darf.*

[215] See eg BGE 121 IV 3, 9, E 1c. According to Art 369 para 7, spent convictions may no longer be used against the person concerned, see eg BGer 6B_83/2009, 30 June 2009, E 4.4.

[216] BGE 121 IV 3, 4, E 1.

[217] Botschaft of 21 Sept 1998, BBl 1999 2167: '*Die Entfernungsfristen [sind] so bemessen ... , dass zwischen den staatlichen Verfolgungsinteressen und dem Bedürfnis nach vollständiger Rehabilitation eines Straffälligen ein Ausgleich geschaffen wird. Es lässt sich nicht rechtfertigen, dem Täter auch Jahrzehnte nach Verbüssung der Strafe noch von Staats wegen einer Straftat vorzuhalten [...].*'

[218] See BGE 136 IV 1, 3 and for discussion F Bommer, 'Die Strafrechtliche Rechtsprechung des Bundesgerichts im Jahr 2010' (2015) 151 *Zeitschrift des Bernischen Juristenvereins* 350, 354f.

[219] Mathys, *Leitfaden* (n 208) 150; '*Die Straffreiheit darf ausnahmsweise in die Beurteilung der Täterpersönlichkeit einbezogen werden, wenn sie auf eine aussergewöhnliche Gesetzestreue hinweist. Eine Solche ist wegen der Gefahr ungleicher Behandlung nicht leichthin anzunehmen*'; see BGE 136 IV 1, 2, E 2.6.

[220] BGer 6B_681/2013, 26 May 2014, E 1.3.5: '*Der Beschwerdeführer ist mehrfach einschlägig vorbestraft und hat während laufender Strafuntersuchungen weiter delinquiert. Die zahlreichen einschlägigen Vorstrafen zeugen zweifelsohne von einer Gleichgültigkeit gegenüber Rechtsnormen, was nach der Rechtsprechung straferhöhend zu gewichten ist.*'

elapsed since the offences were committed: the less serious or older they are, the less significance ought to be attributed to them by the courts.[221] The courts seldom make any attempt, however, to explain *why* previous convictions increase the blameworthiness of the offender for the current offence. In the academic literature, it is sometimes suggested that previous convictions might be said to increase the blameworthiness of the offender for the current offence.[222] This argument has on occasion, however, been expressly rejected by the SFSC. In one five-bench decision, for instance, it held that 'previous convictions constitute one of a number of characteristics relating to the offender and do not increase his or her blameworthiness for the offence at issue'.[223]

In England and Wales, meanwhile, the courts are obliged in 'considering the seriousness of an offence ("the current offence") committed by an offender who has one or more previous convictions' to treat 'as an aggravating factor each relevant previous conviction that it considers can reasonably be so treated, having regard in particular to—(a) the nature of the offence to which the conviction relates and its relevance to the current offence, and (b) the time that has elapsed since the conviction'.[224] This makes it clear that recent and relevant convictions 'should be regarded as an aggravating factor which should increase the severity of the sentence'.[225] This provision differs materially from the earlier provision, which directed the sentencing court 'in considering the seriousness of any offence' to take into account 'any previous convictions of the offender or any failure of his to respond to previous sentences'.[226] Even more dramatic is the departure from the text of the original version of the provision which stated that '[a]n offence shall not be regarded as more serious for the purposes of any provision of this Part by reason of any previous convictions of the offender or any failure of his to respond to previous sentences'.[227]

This demonstrates that, in England and Wales, the relationship between previous convictions and the current offence was completely revised in the space of just thirteen years. While, initially, previous convictions were deemed not to go to the seriousness of the current offence, just a few years later judges were

221 See eg BGE 121 IV 10.

222 See eg Jositsch, Ege, and Schwarzenegger, *Strafrecht II* (n 204) 112; see also Wiprächtiger and Keller, 'Art 47' (n 204) N 137.

223 BGer 6B_105/2015, 13 Jan 2016, E 1.3.2: '*Vorstrafen stellen eines von mehreren täterbezogenen Merkmalen dar und steigern das konkrete Tatverschulden nicht*.'

224 Sentencing Act 2020, s 65(1) and (2). For discussion see E Baker and A Ashworth, The Role of Previous Convictions in England and Wales' in JV Roberts and A von Hirsch (eds), *Previous Convictions at Sentencing* (Oxford: Hart Publishing 2010) 193.

225 Sentencing Act 2020, s 65(2).

226 Criminal Justice Act 1991, s 29(1) as amended by Criminal Justice Act 1993.

227 ibid.

directed that a prior record was to be considered relevant in determining the seriousness of the current offence. In view of the fact that the courts are obliged by law to take into account 'relevant and recent previous convictions', it is unsurprising that there is little discussion in the case law as to the nature of the relationship between previous convictions and the seriousness of the current offence. Instead, the discussion has focused on the definition of similar as opposed to different offences[228] and to extent of the interval between offences.[229] According to Baker and Ashworth: 'Attribution of significant weight to convictions of a qualitatively distinct kind or to ones that have grown stale runs counter to accepted sentencing culture.'[230]

Sentencing practice in Switzerland and England and Wales is similar in that previous convictions are frequently taken into consideration at the sentencing stage and will often result in the imposition of a more severe sentence. In both jurisdictions, previous convictions are likely to be of particular importance if they concern recent offences which are similar to the current offence. The extent to which the courts seek to situate this practice within a principled approach to sentencing, in the sense of explaining why the consideration of previous convictions is compatible with the principles governing the attribution of criminal liability, differs somewhat. In England and Wales, the detailed statutory direction leaves no room for the courts to question the relationship between the previous convictions and the seriousness of the current offence as this is essentially set out in law. In Switzerland, the sentencing provision states that the consideration of previous convictions is to take place in the context of the determination of the blameworthiness of the offender for the current offence. In spite of this however, the SFSC has on occasion, in treating previous convictions as aggravating factors, denied altogether the relationship between the blameworthiness of the accused for the current offence and previous convictions.

2. Justifying the Resort to Previous Convictions in Criminal Law Theory

It is useful, before examining the relationship between the reliance on previous convictions and legality, to distinguish the various justifications for the practice of considering previous convictions in assessing the appropriate sentence for the current offence in sentencing theory. First, it might simply be argued that the commission of two (or more) criminal offences justifies a more severe

[228] See eg *R v Kelly* [1999] 2 Cr App R (S) 176 (robbery and GBH with intent).
[229] See eg *R v Turner* [2000] 2 Cr App R (S) 472 (thirty-year interval).
[230] Baker and Ashworth, 'The Role of Previous Convictions' (n 224) 193.

punishment than the commission of one. In view of the fact, however, that the prior act has already been determined and punished, to consider it again would obviously constitute a violation of the prohibition on double jeopardy.[231] It is thus unsurprising that this type of interpretation is pretty much universally rejected.[232]

Second, it might be argued that the aggravated sentence is imposed not for offence-related matters per se, but rather as a response to the defiance shown by the offender to established authority. This rebellion essentially constitutes an 'an additional wrong'.[233] It would in theory be possible to create a specific criminal offence of failing to heed earlier warnings as a basis for punishing defiant offenders. This, though, gives rise to the further problem of whether this could possibly be reconciled with 'the basic premises of a society based upon formally defined offences. In a society of free and responsible adults, organized to live by the rule of formal authority, the defiant offender is punished according to what he or she does, not according to the implied threat of further disobedience.'[234]

Third, some defend the practice simply on the grounds that every sentence contains a reminder that the offender ought to abstain from committing criminal offences in the future and thus an offender cannot complain if they are subject to a more severe sentence for failing to heed this warning.[235] A person who reoffends is recalcitrant and lacking insight. The new crime demonstrates the indifference or even the 'hostility' of the offender towards the law. Reoffenders are aware of the damage caused by their behaviour and are aware of the social disapproval.[236] This type of argument gives rise to a number of further questions, though, not least whether it is the 'repetition per se that should earn additional punishment, or repetition coupled (somehow) with the further factors of relevance and recency'.[237] More problematic is the fact that this type of argument does not attempt to justify the relationship between prior convictions and blameworthiness of the offender for the current offence. Just because the

[231] See further C Byrne Hessick and A Hessick, 'Double Jeopardy as a Limit on Punishment' (2011) 97 *Cornell Law Review* 45.

[232] For discussion (and criticism) of theories which attempt to justify the sentence enhancement on the ground of an increased *Handlungs- oder Erfolgsunrecht* see PJ Schmidt, *Probleme der Rückfallkriminalität* (Diss. Göttingen 1974) 164ff.

[233] See eg Fletcher, *Rethinking Criminal Law* (n 5) 467.

[234] ibid 464.

[235] See eg G Arzt, 'Revolution in der Sackgasse' (1994) 12 *Recht* 141 N 53: '*In jeder Verurteilung steckt die Mahnung zu künftiger Abstinenz von Straftaten.*'

[236] Mathys, *Leitfaden* (n 208) 121: '*Denn wer ungeachtet früherer Verurteilungen wiederum straffällig wird, erscheint als unbelehrbar und als uneinsichtig. Aus seiner neuen Delinquenz darf auf eine Gleichgültigkeit oder gar eine Rechtsfeindlichkeit geschlossen werden.*'

[237] E Baker and A Ashworth, 'The Role of Previous Convictions' (n 224) 197.

offender was aware that reoffending might lead to a higher sentence does not serve as a sufficient justification for the practice. Although fair warning is an important part of just punishment, it is only one component; in the words of Tomlin: 'Fair warning of injustice does not make it just.'[238]

Finally, some have tried to demonstrate that prior convictions increase the blameworthiness of the offender for the current offence.[239] The assumption that prior offences increase an offender's culpability for the current offence is questionable.[240] Fletcher is deeply sceptical about the claim that 'recidivism renders the actor personally more culpable for the same act of wrongdoing'.[241] Similarly, Stratenwerth suggests that it is essentially impossible to reconcile the practice of increasing the severity of the sentence based on previous convictions with the principle that the sentence should reflect the offender's blameworthiness for the offence committed.[242] He argues that this relationship is exceptionally difficult to make out and simply cannot be sustained in the form of a general rule.[243]

The relationship between prior convictions and the blameworthiness of the offender for the current offence is problematic. This has led some to suggest it would be more honest to admit that the practice of considering previous convictions as an aggravating factor has less to do with determining the appropriate sentence in view of the offender's blameworthiness and more to do with preventing the commission of future criminal offences.[244] As Fletcher notes:

> [I]f the argument were that recidivists were particularly dangerous and punishment ought to be inflicted in proportion to the offender's dangerousness, we could at least try to argue against the proposition on ethical grounds. There might be some data that one could use to argue that some recidivists are no more dangerous than comparable categories of persons never punished. But

[238] P Tomlin, 'Extending the Golden Thread? Criminalisation and the Presumption of Innocence' (2013) 21 *Journal of Political Philosophy* 44, 58.

[239] See eg A von Hirsch, *Doing Justice: The Choice of Punishments* (New York, NY: Hill & Wang 1976) 84–88. For discussion see M Tonry, 'The Questionable Relevance of Previous Convictions' in JV Roberts and A von Hirsch, *Previous Convictions at Sentencing* (Oxford: Hart Publishing 2010) 210. See also Jositsch, Ege, and Schwarzenegger, *Strafrecht II* (n 204) 112: '*[Vorstrafen] dürften allerdings nur unter dem Gesichtspunkt der Tatschuld, d.h. nur unter engen Voraussetzungen, zu einer Erhöhung der Strafe führen.*'

[240] See eg Trechsel and Thommen, 'Art 47' (n 205) N 30.

[241] Fletcher, *Rethinking Criminal Law* (n 5) 466.

[242] See G Stratenwerth and F Bommer, *Schweizerisches Strafrecht: Allgemeiner Teil II* (3rd edn, Bern: Stämpfli 2020) 202: '*Die Begründung, weshalb es den Täter belasten soll, wenn er trotz der in früheren Sanktionen oder Strafverfahren liegenden Warnung erneut delinquiert, ist ebenso schlicht wie problematisch.*'

[243] ibid 202. See also Trechsel and Thommen, 'Art 47' (n 205) N 30.

[244] Stratenwerth and Bommer, *Schweizerisches Strafrecht: Allgemeiner Teil II* (n 242) 203.

> this is precisely the type of unethical, repressive use of governmental power that [the desert theorist] seeks to avoid.[245]

This all seems to support the contention that '[t]he contemporary pressure to consider prior convictions in setting the level of the offense and of punishment reflects a theory of social protection'.[246] This, though, gives rise to real concerns about the compatibility of the sentencing practice with legality.

3. Previous Convictions and Legality

The overview of the various theories justifying the consideration of previous convictions as an aggravating factor emphasizes, in particular, the difficulties of explaining why the fact that a person has offended in the past is of relevance to determining their blameworthiness for the current offence. It is important to stress here, though, that the insistence on compliance with legality does not necessarily imply support for any particular theory of punishment. It is not the *aim* of punishment (such as deterrence or retribution), which is at issue here, but the *reason* for the imposition of punishment (blameworthiness for specific criminal conduct), irrespective of what the punishment is designed to achieve.[247]

As we have seen, legality constrains the state by preventing it from imposing punishment in the absence of a conviction and by extension imposing a more severe punishment for reasons unconnected to the offender's blameworthiness for the offence, such as (bad) character. If a more severe sentence is imposed for reasons not pertaining to the offender's blameworthiness for the offence, such as their continued indifference to obeying the law, this is incompatible with legality. In such cases, the aggravated sentence seems to be based on notions such as 'social protection' or some abstract notion of 'social dangerousness', which represent precisely the type of arbitrary concepts that legality is designed to address. The consideration of previous convictions as an aggravating factor seems impossible to reconcile with the legality principle, precisely because in such cases the offender is being punished for reasons unconnected to his or her blameworthiness for the offence at issue.[248]

[245] Fletcher, *Rethinking Criminal* Law (n 5) 460.

[246] ibid 466.

[247] The issues are discussed in more detail in Ch 6.

[248] In addition, allowing punishment to be imposed for factors not pertaining to the criminal offence at issue might give rise to concerns that sentencing principles are being used to circumvent the burden of proof requirement in violation of the presumption of innocence.

It is notable that these issues have received virtually no attention in the case law of the ECtHR. In *Blockhin v Russia*, the applicant, a twelve-year-old boy, was detained in a 'temporary detention centre for juvenile offenders' despite the fact that criminal proceedings had not been instituted against him. The Russian government argued that the detention had been for the purposes of education but the ECtHR was not convinced, noting that the reasons provided for the detention correlated with the aims of 'criminal punishment', and held that the detention violated Article 5 ECHR.[249] The ECtHR noted that '[p]rocessing a child offender through the criminal-justice system on the sole basis of his status of being a juvenile delinquent, which lacks legal definition, cannot be considered compatible with due process and the principle of legality'.[250] This reflects clearly the act requirement: punishment can only be imposed in response to a the commission of a criminal offence; punishing someone for who they 'are' (ie a juvenile delinquent) is incompatible with legality.[251]

In *Achour*, in which the applicant complained about the application of recidivist sentencing laws, the Grand Chamber restricted its review in the case to determining whether 'at the time when an accused person performed the act which led to his being prosecuted and convicted there was in force a legal provision which made that act punishable, and that the punishment imposed did not exceed the limits fixed by that provision'.[252] It held that the 'sentence imposed on the applicant, who was found guilty and deemed to be a recidivist in the proceedings in issue, was applicable at the time when the second offence was committed, pursuant to a "law" which was accessible and foreseeable as to its effect'.[253]

In its decision, it drew attention to the distinction between someone being a recidivist on the one hand and a person committing acts of recidivism on the other, noting that: 'Recidivism, which is defined by law, is an aggravating factor—*in personam* and not *in rem*, since it is linked to the offender's conduct—in relation to the second offence, warranting a harsher sentence, where appropriate, for the recidivist'.[254] Here, the ECtHR seems to be making 'an exception regarding the *ad hominem* principle (the applicant *being* a multi-recidivist) in view of the proven *in rem* series of acts for which the defendant

[249] *Blokhin v Russia* [GC] App no 47512/06, 23 Mar 2016, para 171.
[250] ibid para 196.
[251] See also *Robinson v California* 370 US 660 (1962), in which a Californian statute was deemed unconstitutional because it made the fact of being a drug addict (status), rather than the act of drug taking, a criminal offence.
[252] *Achour v France* [GC] App no 67335/01, ECHR 2006-IV, paras 43 and 46.
[253] ibid para 70.
[254] ibid para 46, see also the concurring opinion of Judge Zupančič.

had been convicted'.[255] In the words of Judge Zupančič: 'ascribing a particular status to an individual in the criminal-justice system may simply be a consequence of the commission of a series of acts by that individual.'[256] The suggestion is that the punishment is being imposed for 'bad acts' as opposed to 'bad character'. It is questionable, though, whether this distinction is capable of being maintained in the context of previous convictions, particularly in view of the fact that the 'bad acts' in question, ie the prior offences, have already been the subject of prior criminal proceedings. The prior offences are separate from the 'new bad acts'. This means that essentially the only justification for the aggravated sentence is the offender's status as a recidivist. The consideration of prior offences as an aggravating factor is nothing other than the imposition of a more severe sentence, which is not justified by reference to the commission of the current offence. Any sentencing enhancement on these grounds is simply incompatible with the legality principle.

The lack of discussion in the case law of the ECtHR can perhaps be explained by the widespread acceptance across Europe of such sentencing practices. In *Achour*, for instance, the applicant expressly accepted that 'increasing the sentences applicable to recidivists was justified by the greater danger they posed on account of their persistence despite warnings from the courts'.[257] This, though, simply underlines the clear tension between the widely accepted justification for the practice of imposing aggravated sentences for previous convictions on the one hand and legality on the other.

B. Confessions and Guilty Pleas

1. Confessions, Guilty Pleas, and the Role of Remorse

Confessions and guilty pleas are well established in both theory and practice as of relevance to the determination of the sentence. Traditionally, they were taken as evidence of remorse, which was seen as justifying the mitigation of punishment.[258] In more recent times, there has been recognition of the fact that the judicial assessment of remorse is a complex task and that judges vary dramatically in their opinion on both the manner in which remorse should be

[255] See the concurring opinion of Judge Zupančič in *Blokhin v Russia* App no 47512/06, 23 Mar 2016, attached to the judgment.

[256] ibid.

[257] *Achour v France* [GC] App no 67335/01, ECHR 2006-IV, para 37.

[258] See eg S Bibas, *The Machinery of Criminal Justice* (New York, NY: OUP 2012).

assessed and its relevance at sentencing.[259] For our purposes, all three concepts (lack of remorse, failure to confess, failure to plead guilty) are similar in that they seem *prima facie* to have little to do with the offender's blameworthiness for the offence at issue.[260] It is difficult to see how acceptance of responsibility after the commission of the offence could influence the blameworthiness of the offender for acts or omissions which have already taken place. This in turn draws attention to the potential for tension to arise between the consideration of confessions or guilty pleas at sentencing and legality. It is useful here to distinguish between the practice of treating confessions as an aggravating factor and their consideration in mitigation.

2. Aggravated Sentences for a Failure to Express Remorse, Confess, or Plead Guilty in Practice

Legality restricts the state in its imposition of punishment in that it prohibits the imposition of a more severe sentence on an offender based on matters which are not connected to the commission of the offence at issue. The practice of considering a lack of remorse or a failure to confess as an aggravating factor is particularly problematic, precisely because it gives rise to concerns that the offender is being punished more severely for factors which have more to do with their recalcitrant character, than with their blameworthiness for the commission of the offence at issue.

The SFSC has endorsed, in a number of cases, the imposition of a more severe sentence on the grounds that the offender persistently failed to admit the offence. It has held that the courts are entitled to consider a lack of remorse or the failure to accept responsibility for a criminal offence as an aggravating factor.[261] In addition, it has noted that while an individual is entitled to remain silent or to contest or deny the charges,[262] this does not mean that the courts are prohibited from considering such conduct in relation to the assessment of the

[259] R Zhong and others, 'So You're Sorry? The Role of Remorse in Criminal Law' (2014) 42 *Journal of American Academy of Psychiatry and the Law* 39. This recognition is also in evidence in the attempts to structure judicial discretion in the Sentencing Guidelines of England and Wales, see H Maslen and JV Roberts, 'Remorse and Sentencing' in A Ashworth and JV Roberts (eds), *Sentencing Guidelines: Exploring the English Model* (Oxford: OUP 2013) 122.

[260] See eg Trechsel and Thommen, 'Art 47' (n 205) N 24: '*Auf die Tatschuld als Hauptzumessungsfaktor hat das notwendig nachfolgende Geständnis denklogisch nämlich keinen Einfluss.*'

[261] See BGer 6B_521/2019, 23 Oct 2019, E 1.7: '*Gemäss bundesgerichtlicher Rechtsprechung kann ein hartnäckiges Bestreiten auf fehlende Einsicht und Reue hinweisen und straferhöhend gewertet werden*'; BGer 6B_452/2009, 8 Sept 2009, E 1.5; BGer 6B_858/2008, 20 May 2009, E 4.3.3: '*Ein hartnäckiges Bestreiten der Tatvorwürfe kann unter gewissen Umständen als fehlende Einsicht und Reue ausgelegt werden und sogar straferhöhend berücksichtigt werden*'; BGer 6B_765/2015, 3 Feb 2016 E 6.3.4; BGer 6B_1032/2017, 1 June 2018, E 6.4.2; BGE 113 IV 56, 57, E 4c.

[262] BGE 113 IV 56.

'offender's character' for the purposes of the determination of the sentence.[263] Even the most cursory consideration of the case law highlights the problem here. In one case involving an 'undisputed homicide', the SFSC held that, taking into account the interests of the victim, it was not objectionable for the conduct of the offender, who throughout the whole proceedings refused to accept responsibility and failed to show any compassion for the victim's family, to be regarded as constituting an aggravating factor.[264] In another case, it referred to the fact that the offender's refusal throughout the proceedings to accept responsibility and his 'absurd statements', such as his claim that he had become a Belgian national by buying identity documents from a Moroccan person on the street, justified an increase of the sentence.[265] The focus of the courts in treating the failure to confess as an aggravating factor is very much on the character of the offender.

In England and Wales, a lack of remorse is not mentioned in the sentencing guidelines as a factor which will serve to increase the seriousness of the offence.[266] There are nevertheless indications that it will on occasion constitute an aggravating factor. In *R v Harrison*, for instance, in which the Court of Appeal refused the application for leave to appeal, it noted (without objection) that the trial judge had taken the offender's lack of remorse into account at sentencing.[267] Similarly, in *R v Riddel*, the Court of Appeal, in upholding the appeal and reducing the appellant's sentence, did not expressly criticize the trial judge's reliance on the defendant's lack of remorse and continued denial of responsibility in determining the sentence.[268]

[263] ibid E 4.b: '*Dies bedeutet nicht, dass ein entsprechendes Verhalten bei der Beurteilung der Täterpersönlichkeit im Rahmen der Strafzumessung nicht berücksichtigt werden dürfte.*'

[264] BGer 6B_401/2007, 8 Nov 2007, E 9.3.3: '*Das angefochtene Urteil verstösst auch in diesem Punkt nicht gegen Bundesrecht. Es ist gerade auch im Falle eines an sich unbestrittenen Tötungsdelikts mit Rücksicht auf die Opferinteressen nicht zu beanstanden, das Verhalten eines Täters, der sich während des gesamten Verfahrens ausgesprochen uneinsichtig verhielt und gegenüber dem Opfer und dessen Familie kein echtes Mitgefühl zeigte, straferhöhend zu berücksichtigen*'; see also BGer 6B_414/2009, 21 July 2009.

[265] BGer 6B_858/2008, 20 May 2009, E 4.3.3: '*Es ist vorliegend nicht zu beanstanden, das Verhalten des Täters, der sich während des gesamten Verfahrens uneinsichtig verhielt und teilweise absurde Ausführungen machte (wie beispielsweise die Behauptung, anlässlich eines Spaziergangs von einem Marokkaner Papiere gekauft zu haben und deshalb der Ansicht gewesen zu sein, dadurch die belgische Staatsbürgerschaft erworben zu haben) straferhöhend zu berücksichtigen*'; see also BGer 6B_742/2007, 10 Jan 2008, E 2; BGer 6B_401/2007, 8 Nov 2007, E 9.3.2.

[266] <https://www.sentencingcouncil.org.uk/overarching-guides/crown-court/item/general-guideline-overarching-principles/> (accessed 15 Apr 2021).

[267] *R v Harrison* [2012] EWCA Crim 2750, [2013] 1 Cr App R 15; In the Canadian case *R v Hawkins*, 2011 Carswell NS 41 (NSCA) the Nova Scotia Court of Appeal held that the emphasis on lack of remorse by the appellant as an aggravating factor constituted an error of law. A lack of remorse is expressly set out as an aggravating factor in sentencing guidelines in the State of Delaware: *Benchbook of the Delaware Sentencing Accountability Commission.*

[268] *R v Riddel* [2017] EWCA Crim 413, [2017] 2 Cr App R 3.

In both jurisdictions, the decision to consider the lack of remorse as an aggravating factor seems to be inextricably linked to a moral judgment on the (bad) character of the offender.

3. Refusal to Mitigate the Sentence Despite the Existence of a Confession, Guilty Plea, or Expression of Remorse

In view of the fact that legality serves as a constraint by requiring that the maximum punishment to be imposed is that defined by the offender's blameworthiness for the offence, sentence reductions in return for guilty pleas or confessions might be considered entirely unproblematic. It might be argued that mitigation of the sentence is simply not relevant from a human rights perspective, as the individual is not adversely affected but instead profits from the practice. This fails to consider, however, the potential for the refusal to mitigate the sentence on grounds relating to the character of the offender to result in the imposition of a higher sentence than would have been imposed in the context solely of the individual's blameworthiness for the offence. In this regard, some have argued that the distinction between the imposition of a more severe sentence for a lack of confession or guilty plea and the refusal to grant a sentence reduction on the grounds of a lack of remorse or a confession merely 'places semantics over reality' and ignores the fact that 'the *effect* of the discount is to penalize those who plead not guilty more severely'.[269]

The problem from the perspective of legality is not that a person who refuses to confess receives a more severe sentence than a person who chooses to confess.[270] The problem is rather tied to the reasons for the decision to refuse to mitigate the sentence. If the refusal to mitigate the sentence, despite the existence of a confession or guilty plea, is based on the recalcitrance of the offender, then this might give rise to the suspicion once again that 'bad character' rather than blameworthiness for the offence at issue is at the forefront of the sentencing decision. This might indicate that a more severe sentence is being imposed on the offender than that which would be justified as a response to blameworthiness for the offence. This focuses attention on the importance of the reasons provided for the practice of granting sentence reductions for confessions or guilty pleas.

[269] See eg M Bargaric and J Brebner, 'The Solution to the Dilemma Presented by the Guilty Plea Discount: The Qualified Guilty Plea—I'm Pleading Guilty Only because of the Discount' (2002) 30 *International Journal of the Sociology of Law* 51, 58.

[270] This is essentially an argument from prescriptive equality. For broader consideration of equality at sentencing see Ch 4.

In Switzerland, the SFSC has consistently held that a confession, in itself, will not automatically lead to a sentence reduction but that a reduction of the sentence may be appropriate providing that the confession reflects 'the offender's acceptance of responsibility and his or her remorse'.[271] A sentence reduction granted in the absence of (genuine) acceptance of responsibility and remorse is incompatible with federal law.[272] There is an obvious problem here, in that by providing sentence reductions for confessions, the courts are increasing the likelihood of confessions being provided for reasons not connected with remorse. It is impossible to overlook the circularity of this situation: sentence reductions are provided for genuine confessions; concerns about the genuineness of the confession arise because of the possibility that the purpose of the confession was to ensure a sentence reduction. In practice, the courts are faced with considerable, if not insurmountable, difficulties in establishing whether in confessing the offender is showing genuine remorse or whether the confession is in fact being instrumentalized for the purposes of achieving a sentence reduction.[273]

These are familiar problems for sentencing judges. In the words of one US judge, questioned in a study on sentencing:

> If you give too much consideration to it [remorse] then you are a sitting duck, I suppose, for sham protestations of remorse and breast beating, and buckets of tears and appeals of sympathy. And you have got to watch out for that and part of the sentencing process is inevitably making a value judgment on the genuineness of the appeals you receive, both from the defendant, expressions of contrition or remorse, and from the people who write in for him. And I have no doubt that some are more genuine than others, but you have got to

[271] See BGE 118 IV 342, 349 E 2d; BGE 121 IV 202, 204, E 2d; BGer 6B_974/2009, 18 Feb 2010, E 5.4: '*Geständnisse können grundsätzlich strafmindernd berücksichtigt werden, namentlich wenn sie Ausdruck von Einsicht und Reue des Täters sind.*' See also BGer 6B_584/2009, 28 Jan 2010, E 2.5 where the court held that contrary to the argument of the appellant, there was no confession available which was based essentially on acceptance and remorse: '*Entgegen den Ausführungen des Beschwerdegegners liegt kein eigentliches auf Reue und Einsicht basierendes Geständnis vor.*'

[272] See eg BGer 6B_426/2010, 22 July 2010, E 1.6, in which the lower instance had reduced the sentence by six months solely on the basis that the accused had confessed, even though it had found that he had not demonstrated 'genuine acceptance of responsibility and remorse'. The SFSC upheld the prosecution appeal on the grounds that in these circumstances there was no reason to grant a sentence reduction and that the decision to do so violated federal law. But see BGer 6B_294/2010, 15 July 2010, E 3.3.4, where the Federal Court failed to take issue with the fact that the lower instance provided a substantial sentence reduction on the basis of 'the confessions of the appellant, his cooperation during the investigation and his subsequent genuine acceptance of responsibility and remorse', which suggests that the confession was considered to be separate from the issue of remorse.

[273] See eg BGer 6S.186/2003, 22 Jan 2004, E 5.7.3, where the court noted without irony: '*Auch Geständnisse sind nicht immer und ausschliesslich Ausdruck von „Reue". Sie können namentlich (auch) in der Hoffnung auf eine mildere Strafe erfolgen.*'

> do the best you can to evaluate those. To the extent that I feel I am able to distinguish between genuinely repentant and the defiant defendant, I will give it some consideration.[274]

The Swiss courts have attempted to establish various criteria according to which the genuineness of the reasons underpinning the confession can be assessed. Confessions which are 'thorough',[275] which are made by the accused on their own initiative,[276] or which extend beyond the evidence which the prosecuting or investigating authorities have gathered against the accused are more likely to be interpreted by the courts as a sign of 'genuine' remorse. The fact, for instance, that an accused confessed to offences which the prosecutor would have been unable to prove he had committed, led the court to conclude that the accused gave the impression of a person who had 'turned over a new leaf', and was interpreted as clear evidence of acceptance of responsibility and remorse.[277] There are suggestions in the case law that partial confessions, on the other hand, will not serve as indicators of genuine remorse. The fact that the accused had 'had trouble making a partial confession' and even then, had 'only confessed to the extent absolutely necessary' led the court to conclude that 'the issue of a sentence reduction based on a confession did not even arise'.[278] In another case, the SFSC held that the lower instance was entitled to refuse to interpret the accused's partial confession, delivered bit by bit and after he had initially denied all the charges, as evidence of remorse.[279] Equally, delay in confessing is likely to be interpreted as evidence of a lack of genuineness. In one case, reference was made to the fact that the offender had not shown 'particular remorse' and that 'after initially denying the charge, his confession was made only hesitantly'.[280] Confessions which are made late on in the proceedings, meanwhile, are likely to be rejected altogether.[281]

[274] See S Wheeler, *Sitting in Judgment: The Sentencing of White-Collar Criminals* (New Haven, CT: Yale University Press 1988) 117.

[275] BGE 118 IV 342, 349, E 2d; BGer 6B_570/2010, 24 Aug 2010, E 2.

[276] BGer 6B_373/2009, 22 Sept 2009, E 3.1.1.

[277] BGE 121 IV 202, 206, E 2cc f.

[278] BGer 6B_1027/2009, 18 Feb 2010, E 4.2.3: judgment of the High Court of Zurich, referred to in the subsequent judgment of the Federal Court: '*Da er bereits mit einem teilweisen Geständnis Mühe bekundet und nur soviel wie notwendig zugegeben habe, steht eine Strafzumessungsrelevante Anrechnung des Geständnisses nicht zur Diskussion.*'

[279] BGer 6P.10/2003, 3 Apr 2003, E 5.2.1.

[280] BGer 6B_463/2010, 29 July 2010, E 2.2.

[281] BGer 6B_507/2008, 26 Nov 2008, E 6.2: '*Nicht zu seinen Gunsten berücksichtigt haben sie das erst spät erfolgte Geständnis*'; BGer 6B_452/2009, 8 Sept 2009, E 1.5: '*Die Vorinstanz musste das Geständnis nicht als „echte Reue" werten, weil dieses nahezu sieben Jahren nach Verfahrenseinleitung erfolgte.*'

It is questionable whether factors such as the point in the proceedings at which the confession is made can be regarded as reliable indicators of the genuineness of the confession or remorse. In particular, it is doubtful whether an accused person's conduct during the criminal proceedings can provide any insight into the sincerity of their claim of remorse.[282] By placing considerable emphasis on an early confession and refusing to consider the possibility that an accused may acquire remorse over time, the courts seem to be less interested in the issue of establishing remorse and more with encouraging accused persons to confess early in order to prevent the need for costly, contested proceedings.

Indeed, in several cases the SFSC has held not just that the decision to contest the charge may be regarded as evidence in itself of a lack of remorse,[283] but also that it may be appropriate to refuse to grant a sentence reduction if the confession did not facilitate the investigation.[284] There is an unambiguous movement, here, away from considering the extent of the confession in order to ascertain the genuineness of the offender's remorse or acceptance of responsibility and towards determining whether it was instrumental in facilitating the criminal investigation and proceedings. In subsequent cases, the SFSC has accepted as legitimate the refusal of sentence reductions on grounds such as that the confession, made at a late stage in the proceedings, 'only served to marginally facilitate the investigation and thus did not amount to an *active contribution* to the detection of the criminal offences';[285] that the 'willingness of the appellant to confess and cooperate dwindled in the course of the proceedings';[286] or even that the appellant failed to cooperate in the investigation as evidenced 'by the fact that she initially asserted her right to remain silent'.[287]

[282] See also BH Ward, 'Sentencing Without Remorse' (2006) 38 *Loyola University of Chicago Law Journal* 131, 151.

[283] BGer 6B_708/2009, 14 Dec 2010, E 3; BGer 6B_701/2009, 14 Dec 2009, E 2: '*Vielmehr konnte die Vorinstanz ohne Verletzung vom Bundesrecht aufgrund der Bestreitungen der Beschwerdeführerin und ihrem Verhalten an der Gerichtsverhandlung auf deren fehlende Einsicht und Reue schliessen.*'

[284] BGer 6S.531/2006, 24 Jan 2007, E 3.6.3: '*Ein Verzicht auf Strafminderung kann sich demgegenüber aufdrängen, wenn das Geständnis die Strafverfolgung nicht erleichtert hat, namentlich weil der Täter nur aufgrund einer erdrückenden Beweislage oder gar erst nach Ausfällung des erstinstanzlichen Urteils geständig geworden ist*'; see also BGer 6B_974/2009, 18 Feb 2010, E 5.4; BGer 6S.531/2006, 24 Jan 2007, E 3.6.3 (reference(s) omitted).

[285] BGer 6B_507/2008, 26 Nov 2008, E 6.2: '*Nicht zu seinen Gunsten berücksichtigt haben sie das erst spät erfolgte Geständnis, welches die Strafuntersuchung nur unwesentlich erleichtert habe und daher nicht als aktiver Beitrag zur Aufdeckung der Straftaten aufgefasst werden könne.*'

[286] BGer 6B_297/2009, 14 Aug 2009, E 4.3: '*Die abnehmende Geständnis- und Kooperationsbereitschaft im Laufe des Verfahrens berechtige zu keiner Strafreduktion.*'

[287] BGer 6B_521/2008, 26 Nov 2008, E 6.4: '*Die kantonalen Instanzen nehmen einleuchtend an, von einem kooperativen Verhalten und einem aktiven Beitrag der Beschwerdeführerin zur Aufdeckung der Straftaten könne nicht die Rede sein. Dies ist angesichts des Umstands, dass die Beschwerdeführerin zunächst die Aussage verweigert hat und alle relevanten Unterlagen bereits in den Konkursakten vorhanden gewesen sind, nicht zu beanstanden.*'

The reasoning in such cases is difficult to reconcile with the principle that confessions must be based on remorse and suggests endorsement of sentence reductions as a reward for the purposes of crime control.[288]

In England and Wales, the court is obliged in considering the sentence to be imposed on an offender who has pleaded guilty, to take into account both 'the stage in the proceedings for the offence at which the offender indicated his intention to plead guilty', and 'the circumstances in which this indication was given'.[289] Judicial discretion in the context of plea-based sentencing reductions is structured by a formal sentencing guideline.[290] Here, the focus is clearly on efficiency concerns; the sentencing reduction follows a 'purely practical rationale'.[291] According to the sentencing guidelines: 'The purpose of this guideline is to encourage those who are going to plead guilty to do so as early in the court process as possible. Nothing in the guideline should be used to put pressure on a defendant to plead guilty.' The sentence reduction in these cases is justified on the basis that an acceptance of guilt 'normally reduces the impact of the crime upon victims', 'saves victims and witnesses from having to testify', and 'is in the public interest in that it saves public time and money on investigations and trials'.[292] 'In order to maximise the above benefits and to provide an incentive to those who are guilty to indicate a guilty plea as early as possible, this guideline makes a clear distinction between a reduction in the sentence available at the first stage of the proceedings and a reduction in the sentence available at a later stage of the proceedings.'[293]

The extent of the reduction is clearly indicated in the guidelines: 'where a guilty plea is indicated at the first stage of the proceedings a reduction of one third should be made.' As a general rule, after the first stage of the proceedings,

[288] In this context it is interesting to consider parallels with tax law provisions which provide for sentence reductions or even for the sentence to be revoked altogether if the offender confesses their involvement in tax offences to the relevant authorities, before the authorities have become aware of the offences. This practice has little to do with rewarding acceptance of responsibility or remorse and is orientated rather towards encouraging the payment of taxes owed. See A Donatsch and M Frei, 'Allgemeine Strafmilderungs- und Strafbefreiungsgründe im Steuerstrafrecht' [2010] *Steuer Revue* 12, 15; M Betschart, 'Erstaunliches, Ungereimtes und Gesetzgeberisches Versehen im Neuen Bundesgesetz über die Einführung der Straflosen Selbstanzeige' [2009] *Steuer Revue* 519, 527.

[289] Sentencing Act 2020, s 73(2).

[290] For consideration of remorse in the context of these guidelines see Maslen and Roberts, 'Remorse' (n 259) 122.

[291] See D Cole and JV Roberts, '*R v FHL*: What's the Point in Pleading Guilty?' (2018) 44 *Criminal Reports* 44.

[292] See also earlier cases such as *R v Johnston & Tremayne* [1970] 4 CCC 64 and *R v DeHaan* (1967) 52 Cr App R 25. Sentencing Council, Reduction in Sentence for a Guilty Plea, effective from 1 June 2017, 4; JV Roberts and B Bradford, 'Sentence Reduction for a Guilty Plea in England and Wales: Exploring New Trends' (2015) 12 *Journal of Empirical Legal Studies* 187 suggesting 'plea-based discounts are more modest than reported by previous researchers'.

[293] ibid.

the reduction 'should be decreased from one-quarter to a maximum of one-tenth on the first day of the trial having regard to the time when the guilty plea is first indicated to the court relative to the process of the case and trial date'. The reduction 'should normally be decreased further, even to zero, if the guilty plea is entered during trial'.[294] These general rules are subject to exceptions and the courts retain some discretion for determining the extent of the reduction. Other factors such as 'admissions at interview, co-operation with the investigation and demonstrations of remorse should not be taken into account in determining the level of reduction. Rather, they should be considered separately and prior to any guilty plea reduction, as potential mitigating factors.'[295] Early admissions may attract a reduction 'on the basis there is no attempt to "play the system" and wait until the evidence is disclosed'.[296]

In Switzerland and in England and Wales, sentence discounts are available for offenders who choose to admit their guilt. The overview provides little support for the suggestion that the refusal to grant a sentence reduction in these cases is based principally on moral judgments on the character of the offender. In England and Wales there is an overt focus on guilty pleas as a means of improving efficiency and crime control. Such concerns are also evident in the sentencing practice in Switzerland in which there seems to have been a movement away from seeing confessions as evidence of remorse and towards consideration of their role in facilitating the investigation.

4. Justifications for the Importance of Remorse in Sentencing Theory

The normative significance of remorse is the subject of considerable debate in sentencing theory. Retributivist theories encounter considerable difficulties in explaining why remorse should affect an offender's blameworthiness for the seriousness of the offence.[297] If the aim of the sentence is to punish an offender for the criminal offence committed, then the severity of the punishment ought to be linked solely to the blameworthiness of the offender for the offence. Nothing that an offender does after the commission of the offence has the potential to impact on this.[298] Some have tried to address such concerns by

294 Sentencing Council, Reduction in Sentence for a Guilty Plea, D.

295 *R v Price (George)* [2018] EWCA Crim 1784.

296 See L Harris, 'Comment on R v Price' (2019) 1 *Sentencing News* 3: 'It is trite that a guilty plea is merely a transaction between defendant and state; gone are the days when it would indicate remorse.'

297 See eg JG Murphy, 'Well Excuse Me!—Remorse, Apology, and Criminal Sentencing' (2006) 38 *Arizona State Law Journal* 371.

298 See RA Lippke, 'Response to Tudor: Remorse-based Sentence Reductions in Theory and Practice' (2008) 2 *Criminal Law and Philosophy* 259; RA Duff, *Punishment, Communication and Community* (Oxford: OUP 2001) 121. But see H Maslen, *Remorse, Penal Theory and Sentencing* (Oxford: Hart Publishing 2015).

arguing that a person's behaviour after the commission of the offence might be relevant insofar as it provides insight into the person's attitude to the offence itself;[299] or by arguing that by expressing remorse and accepting responsibility the offender is less culpable (at the time of sentencing) than an unremorseful offender.[300] Consequentialist accounts are better able to explain the importance of remorse in that it might be argued that a person who shows remorse does not need to be punished as much to achieve the same result as someone who has not (yet) come to terms with their offence. The problem here, though, is that remorse is a 'weak predictor of desistance'.[301]

The practice of treating a lack of remorse as an aggravating factor is generally viewed with more scepticism than the reliance on remorse in mitigation.[302] This is sometimes explained with reference to the importance of upholding the right of an accused person to refuse to actively cooperate with the authorities within the context of criminal proceedings.[303] Such arguments, though, simply draw attention to the broader issue that there may be a whole host of reasons for the decision not to confess or plead guilty. The biggest problem lies in explaining why a lack of remorse justifies the imposition of a more severe sentence.[304] This underlines the difficulties of establishing a connection between the reasons for the decision not to confess and the blameworthiness of the individual for the offence. Such concerns also underpin the decision to refuse to mitigate the sentence in the absence of remorse.

The problems associated with establishing the normative significance of remorse apply in criminal law theory in relation to both the mitigation and aggravation of the sentence.

This poses problems for theorists who argue in favour of the consideration of remorse in mitigation but reject its role as an aggravating factor.[305]

[299] See Wiprächtiger and Keller, 'Art 47' (n 204) N 168; G Arzt, 'Geständnisbereitschaft und Strafrechtssystem' (1992) 110 *Schweizerische Zeitschrift für Strafrecht* 233, 238.

[300] For a defence of this type of argument see SK Tudor, 'Why Should Remorse be a Mitigating Factor in Sentencing?' (2008) 2 *Criminal Law and Philosophy* 241.

[301] Maslen and Roberts, 'Remorse' (n 259) 125, citing M Cox, 'Remorse and Reparation: "To double business bound"' in M Cox (ed), *Remorse and Reparation* (London: Jessica Kingsley 1998).

[302] See too Stratenwerth and Bommer, *Schweizerisches Strafrecht, Allgemeiner Teil II* (n 242) 207. *State v Shreves*, 60 P.3d 991, 996 (Mont 2002) (court should not have considered accused's refusal to admit guilt as a sentencing factor); *State v Ramires*, 37 P.3d 343, 352 (Wash Ct App 2002) (trial court's consideration of accused's lack of remorse in giving accused a harsher sentence deemed improper). See eg Tudor, 'Why Should Remorse be a Mitigating Factor' (n 300) 256–57.

[303] Jositsch, Ege, and Schwarzenegger, *Strafrecht II* (n 204) 117–18; Stratenwerth and Bommer, *Schweizerisches Strafrecht, Allgemeiner Teil II* (n 242) 208. See also eg *State v Hardwick*, 905 P.2d 1384, 1391 (Ariz Ct App 1995) (sentencing court's reliance on defendant's lack of remorse violated the privilege against self-incrimination).

[304] Stratenwerth and Bommer, *Schweizerisches Strafrecht, Allgemeiner Teil II* (n 242) 208.

[305] See too J Peterson, 'A Review of Hannah Maslen: Remorse Penal Theory and Sentence' (2019) 13 *Criminal Law and Philosophy* 667, 671, who notes: 'It's also striking that Maslen assumes that lack of

Consideration of the importance of legality explains the asymmetric nature of the appeal to remorse at sentencing: legality prohibits the aggravation of a sentence on the grounds of a lack of remorse or a failure to confess; sentence reductions on the other hand are unproblematic.

5. Confessions, Guilty Pleas, and Legality

Legality requires that punishment be imposed in response to an offender's blameworthiness for the conduct defined in law as criminal. In this sense, it marks the maximum punishment which can be imposed for a criminal offence. Treating a lack of remorse or the failure to confess or plead guilty as an aggravating factor is incompatible with this requirement as it implies that a person is to be punished more severely for reasons not connected to their blameworthiness for specified wrongdoing, but rather for their recalcitrant character. This is impossible to reconcile with the requirement of legality in Article 7(1) ECHR precisely because legality prohibits the imposition of (more severe) punishment for reasons not connected to the offender's blameworthiness for the offence. This has not been discussed in the case law of the ECtHR.

The limiting nature of legality as a human right prevents the imposition of a more severe sentence on the grounds of factors not pertaining to the offence at issue. As a rule, legality will not prevent, however, the mitigation of the sentence. This means that the practice of mitigating the sentence of an offender who has confessed or pled guilty will not interfere with legality. In considering whether a refusal of mitigation might be said to interfere with legality, it is important to distinguish between a neutral baseline sentence, which an unremorseful offender would receive, and an aggravated sentence, a higher sentence than the baseline sentence, to be imposed on an offender who shows a lack of remorse.[306] Sentencing discounts benefit those who plead guilty but do not (necessarily) penalize those who elect to have their case heard in contested proceedings. This suggests that the refusal of a sentence reduction should be considered neutral: 'the fact that a more lenient sentence is imposed upon a contrite defendant does not establish a corollary that those who elect to stand trial are penalised.'[307]

remorse in the face of censure should not count as an aggravating factor at sentencing. This seems odd on the responsive censure account.'

[306] See eg Tudor, 'Why Should Remorse be a Mitigating Factor' (n 300) 256–57, arguing that a lack of remorse can either aggravate the baseline sentence or have no effect on the baseline sentence and that both are compatible with the remorse principle.

[307] *United States v White*, 869 F 2d. 822, 826 (5th Cir).

A refusal to grant a sentence reduction might interfere with legality if the refusal of mitigation is based solely on an offender's bad character. The overview of the sentencing practice suggests, though, that this is not usually the case. A whole host of reasons explain the practice of providing sentence reductions in such cases. The case law of the courts might thus be criticized as somewhat arbitrary, but it does not appear to be incompatible with legality. In this sense, attempts to structure judicial discretion by way of sentencing guidelines such as those in England and Wales are to be welcomed.

This examination of the relationship between confessions and legality explains the asymmetrical nature of the constraints on the sentencing exercise, whereby remorse may serve to mitigate but not aggravate a sentence.[308] This also explains more generally why concerns such as prevention, rehabilitation, and re-socialization, where relevant, may only serve to justify the mitigation, not the aggravation, of the sentence.[309]

C. Diminished Culpability

1. Legality, Culpability, and Blameworthiness

Culpability is inherent in legality as guaranteed by Article 7(1) ECHR. Legality demands that only those who can be held accountable for their actions, who are deemed 'culpable', can be punished.[310] The definition of 'culpability' in the case law of Article 7(1) ECHR is, as we have seen, unclear. The requirement seems, at the very least, to prohibit the imposition of liability and punishment on those deemed to be 'criminally insane' or whose conduct was based on an unavoidable (and thus excusable) error of law. This gives rise to questions about the relevance of legality in cases in which the culpability of an individual is considered to be diminished, but not entirely negated. Legality does not say anything about the appropriate sentence, beyond the fact that the maximum punishment which can be imposed is marked by the offender's culpability for the commission of the criminal offence. In this regard, it is important to stress

[308] JV Roberts, 'Aggravating and Mitigating Factors at Sentencing: Towards Greater Consistency of Application' [2008] *Criminal Law Review* 264. Roberts notes that the situation is unclear and that it would be 'useful to clarify the asymmetry of effect whereby remorse mitigates but its absence may not aggravate'.

[309] See eg Stratenwerth and Bommer, *Schweizerisches Strafrecht, Allgemeiner Teil II* (n 242) 213: '*Einigkeit besteht nunmehr über das uneingeschränkte Verbot, die schuldangemessene Strafe aus Gründen der Prävention zu überschreiten*.'

[310] See Trechsel, Noll, and Pieth, *Schweizerisches Strafrecht* (n 5) 142. See also *GIEM SRL and Others v Italy* [GC] App nos 1828/06, 34163/07, and 19029/11, 28 June 2018; *AP, MP and TP v Switzerland*, 29 Aug 1997, Reports 1997-V.

that the determination of an offender's blameworthiness (*Verschulden*) differs substantially from consideration of their culpability (*Schuld*). A host of factors are relevant in the determination of blameworthiness, including the personal circumstances of the offender, which are irrelevant to the issue of culpability.[311] It is important to stress that these factors can only serve to mitigate the sentence, precisely because the maximum sentence is defined by the offender's culpability for the offence. This means that an offender can only be punished if they are culpable and then only to the extent of this culpability. With this in mind, it is useful to examine the sentencing practice in this area.

2. Diminished Culpability in Sentencing Practice

In Switzerland, the sentencing judge is obliged to reduce the sentence in all cases in which an offender's culpability is considered to be diminished. There is symmetry, here, between the substantive criminal law and sentencing law. In all situations in which an offender's culpability is considered relevant, including in the context of insanity, necessity, and unavoidable (excusable) errors of law,[312] the sentencing judge is provided with wide discretion to determine the impact of the reduced culpability of the individual on the sentence. In particular, the judge is not bound by any mandatory minimum sentences set out in the sentencing framework.[313]

Consideration of the case law of the courts regarding the sentencing of those whose culpability is diminished because of their partial inability to appreciate the wrongfulness of the act and to act accordingly provides a useful basis for illustrating the issues here. In the context of insanity, the Swiss Criminal Code makes it clear that only those who were capable of both appreciating the wrongful nature of their act and acting accordingly are to be punished.[314] Equally, a person who was only partially able at the time of the commission of the offence to appreciate the wrongfulness of their conduct and to act accordingly is entitled to a reduction of the sentence that would have otherwise been imposed.[315] Unsurprisingly, in view of the statutory framework, it is uncontested in the case law that an offender who is only partially culpable for the offence must receive a lesser sentence than that which would have been imposed

[311] See eg the reference in Art 47(1) CC to the obligation on the judge to take into account 'the previous conduct and the personal circumstances of the offender as well as the effect that the sentence is likely to have on his or her life'.
[312] See Trechsel, Noll, and Pieth, *Schweizerisches Strafrecht* (n 5) 142–63.
[313] Art 48(a) of the Swiss Criminal Code.
[314] Art 19(1) of the Swiss Criminal Code.
[315] Art 19(2) of the Swiss Criminal Code.

had they been deemed fully culpable[316] and that the judge is not bound by any mandatory minimum sentencing provisions.[317]

Prior to a controversial judgment in 2010, the case law of the courts made it clear that the central aspect in determining the extent of the sentence reduction was the degree of the reduced culpability of the offender (and the impact of this on the offence committed). This meant that other issues, such as the seriousness of the offence, were not relevant to this determination.[318] In addition, it was settled that the sentencing judge was to proceed by considering first the sentence that would have been imposed had the offender been fully culpable and then reducing this accordingly in order to reflect the offender's diminished culpability. The judge was to determine whether the diminished culpability was 'low', 'medium', or 'high' and to reduce the sentence that would have been imposed in event of full culpability by 25%, 50%, or 70% respectively.[319]

In 2010, the SFSC radically altered its approach. It held that the diminished culpability of an offender was generally afforded too much importance and that it was just 'one of several factors' which might suggest lesser culpability (*ein geringerer Schuldvorwurf*) on the part of the accused.[320] Other factors which the SFSC suggested might similarly reduce the 'culpability' of the accused included *dolus eventualis*.[321] This equation of subjective aspects of the offence (intention) with matters of culpability is unfortunate and at odds with the Swiss theory on the attribution of criminal liability, which insists on a clear separation of the element of the offence and the issues of unlawfulness and culpability.

The SFSC held that the sentencing judge was still obliged to ascertain the extent of the offender's diminished culpability and the extent to which this impacted on their culpability for the offence committed (*Tatverschulden*). In a crucial shift, however, the judge was then expected to take this into

[316] See eg BGer 6B_585/2008, 19 June 2009, E 3.5; see too BGE 118 IV 1, 4, E 2.

[317] According to Art 48a para 1 of the Criminal Code, the sentencing judge is not bound by the minimum sentence set out in law if they decide it necessary to reduce the sentence (*Strafmilderung*). According to Art 111 StGB the minimum sentence to be imposed in a case involving intentional homicide is five years' imprisonment.

[318] See eg BGE 134 IV 132, 136, E 6.1: 'The reduced culpability of the offender is to be considered in the context of determination of the sentence, irrespective of the seriousness of the offence, in its entirety'; '*Die Verminderung der Schuldfähigkeit ist bei der Strafzumessung ungeachtet der Schwere der Tat im ganzen Ausmass der Verminderung zu berücksichtigen*.'

[319] ibid.

[320] BGE 136 IV 55, 50, E 5.6.

[321] ibid: '*Bei der Frage, in welchem Umfang die Einschränkung der Schuldfähigkeit die Verschuldensbewertung beeinflusst, gilt es vor Augen zu halten, dass die verminderte Schuldfähigkeit im Sinne von Art. 19 Abs. 2 StGB (bzw. aArt. 11 StGB) eines von mehreren Kriterien sein kann, wenn auch—je nach Grad der Verminderung—von wesentlichem Gewicht. So trifft etwa denjenigen ein geringerer Schuldvorwurf, dem lediglich eventualvorsätzliches Handeln anzulasten ist*.'

account in determining 'the overall culpability of the offender for the offence' (*Gesamtverschulden*). The judge was then to consider, in a next step, matters such as offender-related sentencing components (*Täterkomponeneten*).[322]

The sentencing judge was still obliged to take into account the diminished culpability of the offender in mitigation, but the approach did not allow for the sentence to be reduced in proportion to the offender's reduced culpability. The result of this approach is that the sentence reduction afforded for the diminished culpability of the offender is not deducted from the full sentence which would have been imposed had the offender been deemed fully culpable. The consequences of this issue are well illustrated by the case under consideration in 2010.

In that case, the mother of a small child has been convicted of killing her daughter by omission for failing to intervene to protect the child. The trial judge determined that the mother was only partially culpable for her behaviour and considered this reduced culpability to justify a 50% reduction of the sentence. The trial judge held that had the offender been fully culpable, he would have imposed a sentence of twelve years; in view of the offender's reduced culpability this was to be reduced to six years' imprisonment. Following the successful appeal of the prosecution, the case was sent back to the sentencing court, which held that when the culpability of the offender was just one factor to be considered, a sentence of eight years was to be imposed. The sentence imposed on the offender (in line with the new method) was two years longer than that imposed in line with the previous case law which provided for the sentence reduction for diminished culpability to be deducted from the sentence which would otherwise have been imposed.

In England and Wales, the fact that the culpability principle is considerably less well established at the point of attribution of liability means that its relevance at sentencing is also less well developed. According to the sentencing guideline, the judge is to reach a provisional sentence by evaluating the 'seriousness' of the offence which is to be determined with reference to the 'culpability of the offender' and the 'harm caused by the offending'.[323] Culpability is to be 'assessed with reference to the offender's role, level of intention and/or premeditation and the extent and sophistication of planning'. This makes it clear that this notion of 'culpability' is not equivalent to the principle of subjective attribution or *Schuld*. In a second step, the judge is to consider mitigating

[322] BGE 136 IV 55, 62, E 5.7.

[323] Sentencing guideline: overarching principles, step 1, available at <https://www.sentencingcouncil.org.uk/overarching-guides/crown-court/item/general-guideline-overarching-principles/> (accessed 15 Apr 2021).

or aggravating factors. Mitigating factors include 'limited awareness or understanding of the offence'. If the 'offender had genuinely failed to understand or appreciate the seriousness of the offence, the sentence may be reduced from that which would have applied if the offender had understood the full extent of the offence and the likely harm that would be caused'. Other factors include the fact that the offender's involvement was caused by coercion, intimidation, or exploitation.[324]

A specific guideline applies in those cases in which an offender lacks capacity to understand the full extent of the offending. In such cases, there is recognition that 'the culpability of an offender may be reduced if an offender was at the time of the offence suffering from an impairment or disorder (or combination of impairments or disorders)'.[325] The sentencing judge is directed to 'make an initial assessment of culpability in accordance with any relevant offence-specific guideline, and should then consider whether culpability was reduced by reason of the impairment or disorder'.[326] Culpability will only be reduced if there is 'sufficient connection between the offender's impairment or disorder and the offending behaviour'.[327] The sentencing judge has considerable discretion and must assess, taking into account any expert evidence, whether the impairment or disorder is relevant to the issue of culpability.[328] The judge is required to state whether the offender's culpability was reduced and 'the reasons for and extent of that reduction'.[329]

Special provisions apply in the context of murder (intentional killing), where the partial defence of diminished responsibility is available. This is necessary because of the mandatory life sentence which is to be imposed in response to a conviction for murder. A successful plea of diminished responsibility will lead to a reduction of the charge from homicide to manslaughter, thereby providing the judge with discretion to determine the appropriate sentence.[330] In order to successfully lead a defence of diminished responsibility, the accused must have been 'suffering from an abnormality of mental functioning' which 'arose from a recognised medical condition', substantially impaired the accused's 'ability to

[324] ibid step 2.

[325] Sentencing offenders with mental disorders, developmental disorders, or neurological impairments, <https://www.sentencingcouncil.org.uk/overarching-guides/crown-court/item/sentencing-offenders-with-mental-disorders-developmental-disorders-or-neurological-impairments/>, step 9 (accessed 15 Apr 2021).

[326] ibid step 10.

[327] ibid step 11.

[328] ibid steps 12–13.

[329] ibid step 14.

[330] For detailed consideration see L Kennefick, 'Introducing a New Diminished Responsibility Defence for England and Wales' (2011) 74 *Modern Law Review* 750.

understand the nature of his or her conduct', to 'form rational judgment', or to 'exercise self-control', thus providing 'an explanation' for the acts and omissions of the accused 'in doing or being party to the killing'.[331]

In sentencing an accused who was convicted of manslaughter by reason of diminished responsibility, the court is first required to determine the level of the responsibility of the offender as 'high, medium or lower'.[332] This is to be determined principally with regard to the 'extent to which the offender's responsibility was diminished by the mental disorder at the time of the offence'. The court must then use the corresponding starting point within the category range as set out in the guidelines. For medium responsibility, for instance, the category range is between ten and twenty-five years' custody and the starting point is fifteen years' custody.[333] From this starting point, the court should consider those factors which increase or reduce seriousness in order to adjust the sentence upwards or downwards. In a third step, the court is required to consider the dangerousness of the offender and determine whether it is appropriate to impose a life sentence or an extended sentence. The fourth step involves consideration of possible mental health disposals, while the fifth directs the court to consider factors that may warrant an adjustment to the sentence noting that '[c]ases of manslaughter by reason of diminished responsibility vary considerably on the facts of the offence and on the circumstances of the offender'.

3. Diminished Culpability and Legality

If it is accepted that punishment can only be imposed on those who are culpable, then it must also be accepted that a person whose culpability is reduced must be punished less than a person who was fully culpable. Otherwise, the culpability of the offender would not be properly taken into consideration. The failure to grant a reduction of the sentence in cases of diminished culpability would be incompatible with the culpability principle[334] and thus with legality as guaranteed by Article 7(1) ECHR. For the same reason, legality also acts as a constraint on the nature of the reduction, to the extent that the punishment of a person whose culpability was diminished must be reduced in proportion to their diminished culpability for the offence.

[331] Homicide Act 1957, s 2(1), as inserted by s 53 of the Coroners and Justice Act.

[332] See manslaughter by reason of diminished responsibility, sentencing council guideline; the guidelines are available at <https://www.sentencingcouncil.org.uk> (accessed 15 Apr 2021).

[333] High: fifteen–forty years' custody, starting point twenty-four years' custody; lower: three–twelve years' custody, starting point seven years' custody.

[334] S Trechsel and M Jean-Richard, 'Art 19' in S Trechsel and M Pieth (eds), *Schweizersiches Strafgesetzbuch* (3rd edn, Zurich: Dike 2017) N 16: '*Verzicht auf Herabsetzung der Strafe bei verminderter Schuldfähigkeit ist mit einem Schuldstrafrecht nicht vereinbar*.'

This reasoning can best be illustrated by way of example: three people (A, B, and C) are convicted of an offence for which the appropriate sentence is five years of imprisonment. All sentencing factors are identical with the exception of the culpability of the offender. Offender A is fully culpable. The culpability of offender B is somewhat diminished. The culpability of offender C is significantly diminished. A ought to receive a sentence of five years' imprisonment. Legality prohibits the imposition of the sentence of five years' imprisonment on both B and C. Both must receive a lesser sentence than the sentence that would have been imposed were they fully culpable in order to ensure that their culpability was properly taken into account. For the same reason, legality prohibits imposition of the same sentence on B and C. This means that the sentence of C must be less than that of B. Legality demands not just mitigation of the punishment of someone whose culpability is diminished, but also mitigation in proportion to the reduced culpability of the offender.

The overview of the practice of the Swiss courts demonstrates that there is clear symmetry between consideration of culpability at the point of attribution of liability and in the context of the imposition of punishment. Sentence reductions are available for reduced culpability in all situations in which the total lack of culpability of the individual would result in an acquittal. The examination of the practice of the courts in the context of diminished responsibility because of impairment or disorder demonstrates that the earlier approach of the courts took proper account of culpability and might be described as a model approach to upholding culpability and legality. The current approach following the 2010 judgment of the SFSC is unprincipled, fails to insist that culpability be taken sufficiently into consideration, and violates the principle of legality. This judgment is also disappointing because the previous case law of the SFSC represented an approach which could have served well as a model for the consideration of diminished responsibility at sentencing, in that it took account of the need to distinguish degrees of diminished responsibility, while clearly structuring judicial discretion in this regard.

The situation in England and Wales is considerably less clear, not least because there is limited recognition of the importance of separating the issue of culpability from the subjective elements of the offence. The sentencing of those convicted of manslaughter by reason of diminished responsibility might be viewed as problematic, particularly in those cases in which the diminished responsibility leads to a characterization of the offender's culpability as 'lower'. Here the court is directed to reach a sentence within the category range of three–twelve years. This gives rise to the questions regarding the procedure in those cases in which the offender's culpability would suggest an appropriate sentence of less than three years.

There is little discussion in the case law of the ECtHR on the position as regards diminished culpability. In view of the contested scope of the culpability principle in the various European jurisdictions,[335] it is perhaps unsurprising that the ECtHR has been rather reticent in its attempt to separate culpability from the subjective aspects of criminal liability (intention etc).[336] Nevertheless, consideration of the issue suggests that this is an area that poses reals problems from the perspective of legality.

V. Conclusions: What Role for Legality at the Sentencing Stage?

The importance of legality is well established in the context of the attribution of liability. Its role in restricting the imposition of punishment has received considerably less attention. This might be a reflection of the tendency to see the role of the judge in the sentencing process as essentially guided by 'extra-legal moral intuitions',[337] rather than as constrained by political or constitutional rights in the context of the imposition of state punishment. This is evident too in theories on punishment which do not distinguish between 'private punishment' and 'state punishment'[338] or which resort to analogies between the between the role of the sentencing judge and that of parents in disciplining their children.[339] As Thorburn has argued, however, such analogies between criminal punishment and the parental discipline of children are 'misleading', 'for there are dynamics at work in state-citizen relationships that do not exist in the

335 Such concerns might be understood to underpin the dissenting opinion of Judges Spano and Lemmens, attached to the judgment in *GIEM SRL and Others v Italy* [GC] App nos 1828/06, 34163/07, and 19029/11, 28 June 2018.

336 See the criticism of Judge Pinto de Albuquerque in his partly dissenting, partly concurring opinion in *GIEM SRL and Others v Italy* [GC] App nos 1828/06, 34163/07, and 19029/11, 28 June 2018, para 61.

337 M Thorburn, 'Proportionate Sentencing and the Rule of Law' in L Zedner and JV Roberts (eds), *Principles and Values in Criminal Law and Criminal Justice* (Oxford: OUP 2012) 276.

338 See eg Hart, *Punishment and Responsibility* (n 35) 1: 'It is very common for one estranged spouse to punish the other, for example, by preventing him or her from spending time with his or her children, fully intending that this should be a terrible experience. I know of no reason to think that such punishment is "sub-standard or secondary" as compared with, say, imprisonment by the courts'; see also N MacCormick and D Garland, 'Sovereign States and Vengeful Victims: The Problem of the Right to Punish' in A Ashworth and M Wasik (eds), *Fundamentals of Sentencing Theory* (Oxford: OUP 1998) 23; A Bottoms, 'Five Puzzles in von Hirsch's Theory of Punishment' in A Ashworth and M Wasik (eds), *Fundamentals of Sentencing Theory* (Oxford: OUP 1998) 55.

339 For detailed consideration of this issue see Thorburn, 'Proportionate Sentencing' (n 337) 276–78.

parent-child relationship'.[340] The normative grounds for the jurisdiction of the state and parents to 'punish' are quite different and this suggests that the 'scope of that jurisdiction' will likely differ too.[341] The tendency to focus on the aims of punishment rather than the reasons for the imposition of punishment is symptomatic of the failure to come to terms with the understanding of sentencing in its political context.

Legality demands that criminal offences be clearly defined and prohibits the attribution of liability or the imposition of punishment on the grounds of status or character. It also implies causality between the attribution of liability and the imposition of punishment in that punishment is only to be imposed for the offence and only to the extent of the offender's culpability for that offence. In this sense, it limits the maximum sentence which can be imposed and defines this as the punishment which can be imposed in response to an offender's blameworthiness for the offence. It prohibits the aggravation of the sentence on grounds not connected to the culpability for the criminal offence but crucially does not prevent a sentence being mitigated for other reasons. This understanding of punishment, which places the relationship between the state and the individual at the heart of the sentencing exercise, explains the asymmetry between aggravating and mitigating factors, which are often difficult to explain on other accounts of punishment.

The overview of the case law on Article 7(1) ECHR demonstrates that legality places the same constraints on the state in the context of the attribution of criminal liability and the imposition of punishment. There must be symmetry between the constraints on the attribution of liability and those on the imposition of punishment. It makes little sense to insist on strict rules regulating the state authorities in imposing liability for clearly defined acts or omissions if similar restrictions are not in place at the sentencing stage. Respect for legality at sentencing must be regarded as central to ensuring the coherence of the criminal law.

[340] ibid 277.
[341] ibid 278.

3
Proportionality

I. Proportionality: Rationale and Restraint

One of the principal difficulties at sentencing is the determination of the appropriate sentence. In this regard, it is common for reference to be made to the idea that 'the punishment should fit the crime'.[1] This is often referred to in sentencing theory, particularly in the context of just deserts theory, as a matter of proportionality.[2] Just punishment is said to be punishment which is 'in proportion to the seriousness of the offence'.[3] In view of this, it is unsurprising that proportionality is often associated with, or even 'inextricably linked' to,[4] retributive theories of punishment.[5] This is well illustrated by the statement of Judge Scalia in the US Supreme Court case *Ewing v California* that the Eighth Amendment did not contain any guarantee against disproportionate sentences because proportionality was 'inherently a concept tied to the penological goal of retribution' and the Constitution did not 'mandate adoption of any one penological theory'.[6] This view seems incorrect, though, because it fails to distinguish between proportionality in the relationship between the sentence and the seriousness of the offence on the one hand and the proportionality of a state's interference with the rights of an individual in the context of the imposition of punishment on the other.

[1] See eg J Feinberg, *Doing and Deserving: Essays in the Theory of Responsibility* (Princeton, NJ: Princeton University Press 1974) 118: 'the degree of disapproval expressed by the punishment should "fit" the crime ... in the ... sense that the more serious crimes should receive stronger disapproval than the less serious ones.'

[2] See notably A von Hirsch, 'Proportionality in the Philosophy of Punishment' (1992) 16 *Crime and Justice* 55; A von Hirsch, *Doing Justice: The Choice of Punishments* (Report of the Committee for the Study of Incarceration) (New York, NY: Hill & Wang 1976). See too S Trechsel, P Noll, and M Pieth, *Schweizersiches Strafrecht, Allgemeiner Teil I: Allgemeine Voraussetzungen der Strafbarkeit* (7th edn, Zurich: Schulthess, 2017) 18.

[3] See the White Paper, *Crime, Justice and Protecting the Public* (London: Home Office 1990) para 2.4.

[4] A Ristroph, 'Proportionality as a Principle of Limited Government' (2005) 55 *Duke Law Journal* 263, 266.

[5] Y Lee, 'Why Proportionality Matters' (2012) 160 *University of Pennsylvania Law Review* 1835, 1836. See eg A von Hirsch and A Ashworth, *Proportionate Sentencing: Exploring the Principles* (Oxford: OUP 2005) 1, who use the terms 'deserved' and 'proportionate' interchangeably.

[6] *Ewing v California*, 538 US 11, 31 (2003) Scalia J concurring.

Sentencing and Human Rights. Sarah J Summers, Oxford University Press. © Sarah J Summers 2022.
DOI: 10.1093/oso/9780192870384.003.0003

The state's obligation to impose punishment necessarily impinges on the human rights of those subjected to the punishment.[7] Proportionality acts as a constraint on the state's power to punish individuals by restricting the extent to which it is entitled to interfere with an individual's human rights and fundamental freedoms.[8] In settling conflicts between the public interest in punishment and the fundamental rights of individuals, the state is obliged to act in a rational and non-arbitrary manner.[9] This is achieved in constitutional democracies by way of recourse to the principle of proportionality.[10] In this sense, the proportionality principle emerges from the nature of constitutional or human rights themselves,[11] at least to the extent that these rights can be considered to constitute, in Alexy's terminology, 'principles' rather than 'rules'.[12] Interferences with such rights must be proportionate to the aim legitimately pursued.[13]

The state is responsible for attributing blame and imposing punishment, but this power is not absolute. Just as the state is only permitted to impose punishment on a culpable individual for behaviour which has been clearly declared as criminal,[14] so too are there restrictions on the extent and nature of punishment which can be imposed. Such limitations apply 'whether the state is punishing to exact retribution, to deter, to incapacitate, or (as is most often the case) to pursue some amalgam of ill-defined and possibly conflicting purposes'.[15] In this sense, proportionality, while compatible with many of the

[7] On the obligation of the state to impose liability and punish individuals R Roth, 'Libres Propos sur la Subsidiarité du Droit Pénal' in A Auer and others (eds), *Aux Confins du Droit. Essais en l'Honneur du Professeur Charles-Albert Morand* (Basel: Helbing & Lichtenhahn 2001) 429, 437; M Delmas-Marty, 'Le Paradoxe Pénal' in M Delmas-Marty and C Lucas de Leyssac (eds), *Libertés et Droits Fondamentaux* (Paris: Seuil 1996) 368, 368.

[8] R Kannai, 'Proportionality in Sentencing: Constitutional or Criminal Issue' (2005) 9 *Canadian Criminal Law Review* 315.

[9] See B Schlink, 'Proportionality (1)' in M Rosenfeld and A Sajó (eds), *The Oxford Handbook of Comparative Constitutional Law* (Oxford: OUP 2012) 730.

[10] A Barak, 'Proportionality (2)' in M Rosenfeld and A Sajó (eds), *The Oxford Handbook of Comparative Constitutional Law* (Oxford: OUP 2012) 741.

[11] See the judgment of the German Federal Constitutional Court: BVerGE 19, 342 (348); 65, 1 (44).

[12] R Alexy, *A Theory of Constitutional Rights* (Oxford: OUP 2002) 66 and at 48 distinguishing between principles ('optimization requirements' that 'can be satisfied to varying degrees', where 'the appropriate degree of satisfaction depends not only on what is factually possible but also on what is legally possible') and rules ('norms which are always fulfilled or not').

[13] There is not complete agreement regarding the definition of proportionality, or perhaps more accurately the classification of its constituent parts, see eg Barak, 'Proportionality (2)' (n 10) 742 who identifies four elements of proportionality: 'proper purpose, rational connection, necessity, and proportionality in the narrow sense, that is, balance' but notes that there is some disagreement as to that taxonomy, notably in that some 'do not consider a proper purpose to be part of proportionality; others link the consideration of proper purpose to that of rational connection'.

[14] See further discussion in Ch 2.

[15] Ristroph, 'Proportionality' (n 4) 266.

theories justifying the imposition of punishment, is not contingent on any particular theory.[16]

As we shall see, the European Court of Human Rights (ECtHR) has adopted an understanding of proportionality which demands that state action follow a legitimate aim, which is strictly necessary, and which meets the requirements of subsidiarity and proportionality in the narrow sense of balance. In the determination of whether punishment constitutes a disproportionate interference with individual rights, the issue of proportionality between the punishment and the offender's culpability will often be of relevance. This chapter will begin by considering the ECtHR's approach to proportionality at sentencing by considering its application in the context of the prohibition on torture and inhuman and degrading punishment, the right to freedom and security of person, in relation to the rights to private life and freedom of expression and assembly, and in the context of the right to protection of property. This will provide the basis for (re)examining the importance of the human rights account of proportionality in practice.

II. Proportionality at Sentencing and the European Convention on Human Rights

A. Introduction

Unlike many national constitutions[17] or the EU Charter of Fundamental Rights which directs that '[t]he severity of penalties must not be disproportionate to the criminal offence',[18] the ECHR does not contain any express provisions on proportionality at sentencing. Indeed, the Strasbourg authorities have generally adopted a cautious approach to complaints concerning criminal sentences. The ECtHR has appeared reluctant to assume responsibility for determining the proportionality of criminal sentences, noting that 'matters of appropriate

[16] RS Frase, 'Excessive Prison Sentences, Punishment Goals, and the Eighth Amendment: "Proportionality" Relative to What?' (2005) 89 *Minnesota Law Review* 571, 607–9 discussing 'retributive proportionality' and 'utilitarian proportionality'; Ristroph, 'Proportionality' (n 4) 271.

[17] See eg Art 12 para 3 of the Cypriot Constitution: 'the law must not provide for a penalty that is disproportionate to the gravity of the offence.'

[18] Art 49(3) of the Charter of Fundamental Rights of the EU, 2012/C 326/02. See further L Mancano, *The European Union and Deprivation of Liberty: A Legislative and Judicial Analysis from the Perspective of the Individual* (Oxford: Hart Publishing 2019).

sentencing largely fall outside the scope of the Convention'.[19] It has held that it is not its role to decide 'the appropriate term of detention applicable to a particular offence or to pronounce on the appropriate length of detention or other sentence which should be served by a person after conviction by a competent court'.[20] This reflects, perhaps, the well-rehearsed difficulties in establishing the aim(s) of punishment. The role of the ECtHR is limited to determining whether the sentence imposed is so disproportionate as to violate one of the rights set out in the Convention. The approach of the ECtHR to proportionality at sentencing is thus best examined by looking at its case law in relation to the alleged violation of each human rights norm.

In the context of Article 3 ECHR, the ECtHR has declared that certain sentences will be incompatible with the provision, irrespective of the severity of the crime. In addition, it has held that the imposition of sentences deemed 'grossly disproportionate' to the offence at issue will violate the prohibition on inhuman and degrading punishment. Article 5 ECHR allows for consideration of whether a deprivation of liberty is arbitrary, but as we shall see, there is little scope for consideration of the proportionality of sentences of imprisonment. In relation to interferences with the rights and freedoms set out in Articles 8, 10, and 11 ECHR, the ECtHR has insisted that the sentence imposed must be proportionate to the aim pursued. In these cases, the ECtHR compares the gravity of the offence with the severity of the sentence in order to determine the legitimacy of the interference with the fundamental right. Finally, the ECtHR has reviewed the proportionality of fines and other criminal 'penalties' in the context of Article 1 of Protocol No 1 to the ECHR. Before considering the nature of the ECtHR's proportionality examination, it is necessary first to engage with the ECtHR's case law in relation to each of the distinct guarantees.

B. Proportionality and the Prohibition on Inhuman and Degrading Punishment in Article 3 ECHR

1. Introduction

There is no mention of proportionality in the text of Article 3 ECHR, which dictates that 'no one shall be subjected to torture or inhuman or degrading treatment or punishment'. In its case law on the guarantee, the ECtHR has

[19] See eg *Vinter and Others v UK* App nos 66069/09, 130/10, and 3896/10, 17 Jan 2012, para 89; *Léger v France* App no 19324/02, 11 Apr 2006, para 72. *Léger* was referred to the GC but was struck out following the death of the applicant and the applicant's lawyer some four weeks later.

[20] *Vinter and Others v UK* [GC] App nos 66069/09, 130/10, and 3896/10, ECHR 2013-III, para 105.

articulated—sometimes clearly, sometimes more ambiguously—the importance of proportionality concerns in relation to the sentence.[21] The importance of proportionality in this context is not especially surprising, particularly if one subscribes to the view expressed by the South African Constitutional Court in *S v Dodo* that '[t]he concept of proportionality goes to the heart of the inquiry as to whether punishment is cruel, inhuman or degrading, particularly where . . . it is almost exclusively the length of time for which an offender is sentenced that is at issue'.[22]

Notwithstanding the fact that 'issues relating to just and proportionate punishment are the subject of rational debate and civilised disagreement' and thus that national authorities are best placed to determine the 'appropriate length of prison sentences for particular crimes',[23] there are clear indications in the case law of the Strasbourg authorities that 'excessive sentences' may give rise to a violation of Article 3 ECHR. The obligation on states to impose criminal law and attribute punishment[24] in order to protect the public[25] gives rise to a corresponding obligation to ensure that the punishment imposed is not excessive. In this regard, though, it is clear that unlike 'treatment', 'punishment' will necessarily involve some degree of hardship.[26] The ECtHR has noted that 'a person may be humiliated by the mere fact of being criminally convicted' and, more relevantly in the context of Article 3 ECHR, might be 'humiliated not simply by his conviction but by the execution of the punishment which is imposed on him'.[27] The ECtHR has stated that it does not consider the punitive nature of sentences per se to be problematic, noting in the context of life

[21] In this chapter the focus will be on the sentence itself rather than the enforcement of the sentence, although this distinction is not always easy to establish or maintain.

[22] *S v Dodo* 2001 SA 382 (CC) 403–4, para [37] cited by and A Ashworth and D van Zyl Smit, 'Disproportionate Sentences as Human Rights Violations' (2004) 67 Modern Law Review 541, 546. See also J Callenwert, 'L'Article 3 de la Convention Européenne: Une Norme Relativement Absolue ou Absolument Relative?', in*Liber Amicorum Marc-André Eissen* (Brussels: Bryulant 1995) 13–38.

[23] See eg *Vinter and Others v UK* [GC] App nos 66069/09, and 130/10 and 3896/10, ECHR 2013-III, para 106; *Kafkaris v Cyprus* [GC] App no 21906/04, ECHR 2008-I, para 97.

[24] See eg *MC v Bulgaria* App no 39272/98, ECHR 2003-XII.

[25] See eg *T v UK* [GC] App no 24724/94, 16 Dec 1999, para 97 citing *A v UK*, 23 Sept 1998, Reports 1998-VI, 2699, para 22; *Osman v UK*, 28 Oct 1998, Reports 1998-VIII, 3159, para 115. See on the 'sword' and 'shield' functions of the criminal law, inter alia, F Tulkens, 'The Paradoxical Relationship between Criminal Law and Human Rights' (2011) 9 *Journal of International Criminal Justice* 577; R Roth,'Libres Propos sur la Subsidiarité du Droit Pénal' in A Auer and others (eds), *Aux Confins du Droit: Essais en l'Honneur du Professeur Charles-Albert Morand* (Basel: Helbing & Lichtenhahn 2001) 429, 437; Y Cartuyvels, 'Les Droits de l'Homme, Frein ou Amplificateur de Criminalisation?' in H Dumont, F Ost, and S Van Drooghenbroeck (eds), *La Responsabilité, Face Cachée des Droits de l'Homme* (Brussels, Bruylant 2005) 391, 439.

[26] N Mavronicola, 'Crime, Punishment and Article 3 ECHR: Puzzles and Prospects of Applying an Absolute Right in a Penal Context' (2015) 15 *Human Rights Law Review* 721, 721, who cautions against the assimilation of punishment and the notion of treatment, arguing that this might lead to 'the particular conceptual issues which arise in relation to punishment' being ignored.

[27] *Tyrer v UK*, 25 Apr 1978, Series A no 26, para 30.

sentences 'that the punitive element inherent in the tariff approach' does not in itself give rise to a breach of Article 3 ECHR.[28] It has referred to the 'suffering inherent in imprisonment' and has suggested that other 'aggravating' circumstances will have to be identified in order to 'warrant the conclusion that the applicant underwent an exceptional ordeal capable of constituting treatment contrary to Article 3'.[29] In order for punishment to be considered 'inhuman' or 'degrading', 'the suffering or humiliation involved must go beyond that inevitable element of suffering or humiliation connected with a given form of legitimate treatment or punishment'.[30] This means that states are obliged to ensure that a person is not subjected to 'distress or hardship exceeding the unavoidable level of suffering inherent' in punishment.[31] It also means that illegitimate punishment can only be determined by reference to whether it goes beyond punishment which might be regarded as legitimate.[32]

It is important here to distinguish punishment which by its very nature constitutes a violation of Article 3 ECHR from punishment which appears *prima facie* compatible with Article 3 ECHR, but which nevertheless may be considered in the particular context to be excessively harsh. The ECtHR has determined some sentences, as we shall see, to be by their nature incompatible with Article 3 ECHR. It has repeatedly stressed that Article 3 ECHR prohibits in absolute terms torture and inhuman or degrading punishment.[33] This means that 'the nature of any offence allegedly committed by the applicant is . . . irrelevant for the purposes of Article 3'.[34] If the sentence at issue meets the Article 3 ECHR threshold of inhuman and degrading punishment, then it will be incompatible with the requirement of just punishment in a democratic society.

While this rules out any balancing or consideration of the crime committed in determining whether the Article 3 ECHR threshold has been respected, it does not exclude the possibility that a sentence which does not reach the Article 3 ECHR threshold may nevertheless violate the provision if imposed for a minor offence.[35] In this sense, proportionality considerations which

[28] *T v UK* [GC] App no 24724/94, 16 Dec 1999, para 97; *Hussain v UK* [GC], 21 Feb 1996, Reports 1996-I, para 53.

[29] *Léger v France* App no 19324/02, 11 Apr 2006, para 94.

[30] *A v UK*, 23 Sept 1998, Reports 1998-VI, 2699, para 127.

[31] *Kafkaris v Cyprus* [GC] App no 21906/04, ECHR 2008-I, para 96.

[32] For criticism see Mavronicola, 'Crime, Punishment and Article 3 ECHR' (n 26) 727.

[33] *Saadi v Italy* [GC] App no 37201/06, ECHR 2008-II, para 127.

[34] ibid.

[35] See also S Palmer, 'A Wrong Turning: Article 3 ECHR and Proportionality' (2006) 65 *Cambridge Law Journal* 438, 439 discussing confusion between the relativity requirement in Art 3 ECHR and proportionality.

balance the 'gravity of the offence and the severity of the sentence'[36] could well be of relevance in the Article 3 ECHR context.

2. Sentences which are Incompatible with Article 3 ECHR

a) *Judicial Corporal Punishment*

The 'absolute' nature of Article 3 ECHR means that any interference with 'human dignity' or 'physical integrity' for the purposes of punishment must not amount to inhuman or degrading treatment.[37] This means that the seriousness of the crime cannot be employed as a means of mitigating punishment which reaches the Article 3 ECHR threshold.[38] There is no room in this context for the seriousness of the offence to be afforded any weight in balancing the interference (the sentence) and the aim of that interference (punishment of crime).

This is well illustrated by the position of ECtHR in the context of judicial corporal punishment. The imposition of a sentence of judicial corporal punishment has been held by the ECtHR to be categorically prohibited by Article 3 ECHR. In *Tyrer*, a schoolboy who had assaulted a schoolmate was sentenced to 'birching', which was then carried out in a police station: he was held by two policemen while a third gave him three strokes of the birch on his bare bottom.[39] The ECtHR ruled that the sentence violated Article 3 ECHR in that it was to be considered degrading punishment. It held that 'in most if not all cases this may be one of the effects of judicial punishment, involving as it does unwilling subjection to the demands of the penal system' and that 'it would be absurd to hold that judicial punishment generally, by reason of its usual and perhaps almost inevitable element of humiliation, is "degrading" within the meaning of Article 3'.[40] In this regard it held that 'Article 3, by expressly prohibiting "inhuman" and "degrading" punishment, implies that there is a distinction between such punishment and punishment in general'.[41] This assessment was necessarily 'relative' in that it depended on 'all the circumstances of the case and, in particular,

[36] See eg that employed by the US Supreme Court in *Graham v Florida*, 560 US 48 (2010).

[37] *Tyrer v UK*, 25 Apr 1978, Series A no 26, para 33: one of the main purposes of Art 3 is to protect a 'person's dignity and physical integrity'; *Bouyid v Belgium* [GC] App no 23380/09, ECHR 2015-V, para 81: 'the prohibition of torture or human and degrading treatment or punishment is a value of civilisation closely bound up with respect for human dignity.' See also *Pretty v UK* App no 2346/02, ECHR 2003-III, para 65; *Vinter and Others v UK* [GC] App nos 66069/09, and 130/10 and 3896/10, ECHR 2013, para 113; *VC v Slovakia* App no 18968/07, ECHR 2011-V, para 105.

[38] *Al Saadoon v UK* App no 61498/08, ECHR 2010, para 122; *Saadi v Italy* [GC] App no 37210/06, ECHR 2008-II, para 127.

[39] *Tyrer v UK*, 25 Apr 1978, Series A no 26.

[40] ibid.

[41] ibid para 30.

on the nature and context of the punishment itself and the manner and method of its execution'.[42]

The determination of the compatibility of the punishment with Article 3 ECHR was not to be measured empirically and, in this regard, it was irrelevant whether the punishment could be characterized as serving a legitimate purpose. The ECtHR was not convinced by argument that judicial corporal punishment was legitimate because public opinion was supportive of the practice, holding that:

> even assuming that local public opinion can have an incidence on the interpretation of the concept of "degrading punishment" appearing in Article 3, the Court does not regard it as established that judicial corporal punishment is not considered degrading by those members of the Manx population who favour its retention: it might well be that one of the reasons why they view the penalty as an effective deterrent is precisely the element of degradation which it involves. As regards their belief that judicial corporal punishment deters criminals, it must be pointed out that a punishment does not lose its degrading character just because it is believed to be, or actually is, an effective deterrent or aid to crime control. Above all, as the Court must emphasise, it is never permissible to have recourse to punishments which are contrary to Article 3, whatever their deterrent effect may be.[43]

In its consideration of whether the applicant's punishment was to be considered degrading within the meaning of Article 3 ECHR, the ECtHR noted that the 'very nature of judicial corporal punishment is that it involves one human being inflicting physical violence on another human being' and further that it had to be characterized as 'institutional violence'.[44] It held that while 'the applicant did not suffer any severe or long-lasting physical effects, his punishment—whereby he was treated as an object in the power of the authorities—constituted an assault on precisely that which it is one of the main purposes of Article 3 to protect, namely a person's dignity and physical integrity'. The ECtHR was not moved by the argument that the judicial corporal punishment had been imposed on the applicant for an offence of violence, nor that it was an alternative to imprisonment, noting that 'the fact that one penalty may be preferable to, or have less adverse effects or be less serious than, another

[42] ibid.
[43] ibid para 31.
[44] ibid para 33.

penalty does not of itself mean that the first penalty is not "degrading" within the meaning of Article 3'.[45] Consequently, the ECtHR held that the applicant had been subjected to punishment which was to be considered as degrading within the meaning of Article 3 ECHR.[46]

These arguments are framed by the ECtHR in terms of addressing an assault on individual integrity. The effect of the punishment on the individual's dignity and physical integrity is so severe as to render it unacceptable in every case, irrespective of the offence committed and irrespective of the aim of the punishment. The argument might also be expressed in terms of proportionality: The seriousness of the interference in the rights of the individual is such that it could never be justified, irrespective of the purpose which it seeks to meet—in this case punishment for the commission of an offence—and irrespective of the seriousness of the offence committed. In this sense judicial corporal punishment will be disproportionate in every case, irrespective of the offence at issue. To paraphrase the Canadian Supreme Court in *Bedford*: the connection between the draconian impact of the law and its object are 'entirely outside the norms accepted in our free and democratic society'.[47]

b) *The Death Penalty*

The ECtHR's strict approach to judicial corporal punishment led to something of an anomaly in its case law in that while such sentences were prohibited, the death penalty was initially not deemed to violate Article 3 ECHR. The early case law on the compatibility of the death penalty with Article 3 ECHR was complicated by the fact that capital punishment was expressly 'permitted under certain conditions' by Article 2(1) ECHR.[48] According to this provision: 'Everyone's right to life shall be protected by law. No one shall be deprived of his life intentionally save in the execution of a sentence of a court following his conviction of a crime for which this penalty is provided by law.' In *Soering*, the ECtHR resisted arguments that 'evolving standards in Western Europe regarding the existence and use of the death penalty required that the death penalty should now be considered as an inhuman and degrading punishment

[45] ibid para 34.

[46] See also *Jabari v Turkey* App no 40035/98, ECHR 2000-VIII in which the ECtHR held in finding a violation of Art 3 ECHR simply that there was a real risk of ill-treatment (stoning to death, flogging, whipping) were the applicant to be expelled to Iran. Neither the nature of the crime (adultery) committed by the applicant nor the proportionality between the crime and the sentence was considered by the ECtHR.

[47] *Canada (Attorney General) v Bedford*, 2013 3 SCR 1101, 2013 SCC 72, para 120.

[48] *Soering v UK*, 7 July 1989, Series A no 161, para 101.

within the meaning of Article 3', noting that the Convention had to be 'read as a whole' and that Article 3 was to be construed in harmony with the provisions of Article 2.[49] This led the ECtHR to conclude that 'Article 3 evidently cannot have been intended by the drafters of the Convention to include a general prohibition of the death penalty since that would nullify the clear wording of Article 2'. Consequently, Article 3 ECHR could not be 'interpreted as generally prohibiting the death penalty'.[50]

Although the imposition of the death penalty as a sentence was not deemed to give rise to a violation of Article 3 ECHR per se, the ECtHR held that the circumstances surrounding the imposition of the death penalty could give rise to a violation of Article 3 ECHR. In *Soering*, it noted that the 'death row phenomenon' could itself give rise to a violation of Article 3 ECHR:

> Although it is not for this Court to prejudge issues of criminal responsibility and appropriate sentence, the applicant's youth at the time of the offence and his then mental state, on the psychiatric evidence as it stands, are therefore to be taken into consideration as contributory factors tending, in this case, to bring the treatment on death row within the terms of Article 3.[51]

In finding a violation of Article 3 ECHR, it held that:

> in the Court's view, having regard to the very long period of time spent on death row in such extreme conditions, with the ever present and mounting anguish of awaiting execution of the death penalty, and to the personal circumstances of the applicant, especially his age and mental state at the time of the offence, the applicant's extradition to the United States would expose him to a real risk of treatment going beyond the threshold set by Article 3.[52]

In this case, the ECtHR focuses principally on the potential for long periods of time spent on death row to cause such anguish as to result in the punishment

[49] ibid para 103.
[50] ibid.
[51] ibid para 109; the applicant was eighteen years old and questions were raised as to his mental capacity at the time of the commission of the offence.
[52] ibid para 111. Similarly in *Öcalan* the ECtHR held that 'the manner in which the death penalty is imposed or executed, the personal circumstances of the condemned person and a disproportionality to the gravity of the crime committed, as well as the conditions of detention awaiting execution, are examples of factors capable of bringing the treatment or punishment received by the condemned person within the proscription under Article 3', *Öcalan v Turkey* [GC] App no 46221/99, ECHR 2005-IV, para 168; see also *Soering v UK*, 7 July 1989, Series A no 161, para 104; *Kirkwood v UK* (dec) [1984] 37 DR 158.

meeting the Article 3 ECHR threshold.[53] Reference to the age and mental state of the accused at the time of the commission of the offence (rather than at the time of the imposition of the punishment), however, seems to suggest that the ECtHR is also employing a type of culpability test. The suggestion is that subjecting those who were mentally ill or who committed crimes while they were children or young adults to the death penalty is to fail to sufficiently take into account their diminished blameworthiness when compared with those who had full capacity or who were adults at the time of the commission of the offence.[54]

In *Jabari*, the applicant had committed adultery and left Iran before criminal proceedings could be instigated against her. She noted that according to the established case law of the Iranian courts, 'stoning to death, flogging and whipping' were the penalties prescribed by Iranian law for the offence of adultery.[55] The ECtHR, in finding that Article 3 ECHR would be violated were she to be deported to Iran, held that it was 'not persuaded that the situation in the applicant's country of origin has evolved to the extent that adulterous behaviour is no longer considered a reprehensible affront to Islamic law' and 'that punishment of adultery by stoning still remains on the statute book and may be resorted to by the authorities'.[56] Her deportation to Iran would thus give rise to a violation of Article 3 ECHR. Similarly, in *Bader and Kanbor v Sweden*, the ECtHR held that Article 3 ECHR prevented the applicants, who were charged with complicity in a murder and who risked being executed if they returned, being deported to Syria.[57]

The case law of the ECtHR has changed in line with political developments in Europe. The regulation of the death penalty in Europe has developed considerably since the creation of the Convention. The trend away from the imposition of capital sentences in Europe was clearly illustrated by the entry into force of Protocol 6 to the Convention on the abolition of the death penalty in

[53] See also *Öcalan v Turkey* [GC] App no 46221/99, ECHR 2005-IV, where the ECtHR concluded that the imposition of the death penalty on the applicant following an unfair trial violated Art 3 ECHR in a similar manner, at paras 169–75: 'to impose a death sentence on a person after an unfair trial is to subject that person wrongfully to the fear that he will be executed. The fear and uncertainty as to the future generated by a sentence of death, in circumstances where there exists a real possibility that the sentence will be enforced, must give rise to a significant degree of anguish. Such anguish cannot be dissociated from the unfairness of the proceedings underlying the sentence which, given that human life is at stake, becomes unlawful under the Convention.'

[54] See similar arguments by the USSC in eg *Graham v Florida*, 560 US 46, 130 S Ct 2011 at 2022: 'when compared to an adult murderer, a juvenile offender who did not kill or intend to kill has a twice diminished moral culpability.'

[55] *Jabari v Turkey* App no 40035/98, ECHR 2000-VIII, para 34.

[56] ibid para 41.

[57] *Bader and Kanbor v Sweden* App no 13284/04, ECHR 2005-XI.

1985.[58] All but one of the 47 Member States of the Council of Europe ratified this Protocol.[59] In 2003, a second protocol entered into force concerning the abolition of the death penalty in all circumstances. Only two states have so far failed to sign the Protocol.[60] These developments have led to a corresponding change in the approach of the ECtHR to the imposition of the death penalty in the context of Article 3 ECHR, as is well illustrated by the judgment in *Al-Saadoon and Mufdhi v the United Kingdom*.[61]

In this case, the applicants, who were both Iraqi nationals accused of involvement in the murder of British soldiers, argued that their transfer by the UK authorities into Iraqi custody put them at real risk of execution by hanging. The ECtHR noted that the Grand Chamber in *Öcalan* had not excluded the possibility 'that Article 2 had already been amended so as to remove the exception permitting the death penalty'.[62] It held that the fact that almost all the contracting states had ratified the Protocol on the abolition of the death penalty in all circumstances combined with the fact that states had consistently observed in practice 'the moratorium on capital punishment' were 'strongly indicative that Article 2 has been amended so as to prohibit the death penalty in all circumstances'. Consequently, it held that it did not 'consider that the wording of the second sentence of Article 2 § 1 continues to act as a bar to its interpreting the words "inhuman or degrading treatment or punishment" in Article 3 as including the death penalty'.[63]

In reaching its conclusion, the ECtHR noted that Article 3 ECHR prohibited torture and inhuman or degrading treatment or punishment in 'absolute terms' as one of the 'fundamental values of democratic societies'. In view of this, the prohibition on torture or degrading treatment or punishment was absolute, 'irrespective of the victim's conduct, the nature of any offence allegedly committed by the applicant is therefore irrelevant for the purposes of Article 3 ECHR'.[64] This clearly indicates that there is no room in the context of capital

[58] As amended by Protocol No 11 (ETS No 155).

[59] Russia signed Protocol No 6 in 1997 but has not (yet) ratified it.

[60] Russia and Azerbaijan. Armenia signed the Protocol in 2006 but has not (yet) ratified it.

[61] *Al-Saadoon and Mufdhi v UK* App no 61498/08, ECHR 2010-II, para 120.

[62] ibid para 120, referring to *Öcalan v Turkey* [GC] App no 46221/99, ECHR 2005-IV.

[63] *Al-Saadoon and Mufdhi v UK* App no 61498/08, ECHR 2010-II. It noted too that both Art 2 and Art 1 of Protocol No 13 prohibited the extradition or deportation of an individual to another state where there were substantial grounds for believing that they would face a real risk of being subjected to the death penalty, citing *Hakizimana v Sweden* (dec) App no 37913/05, 27 Mar 2008; *SR v Sweden* (dec) App no 62806/00, 23 Apr 2002; *Ismaili v Germany* (dec) App no 58128/00, 15 Mar 2001; *Bader and Kanbor v Sweden* App no 13284/04, ECHR 2005-XI, para 42; *Kaboulov v Ukraine* App no 41015/04, 19 Nov 2009, para 99.

[64] *Al-Saadoon and Mufdhi v UK* App no 61498/08, ECHR 2010-II, para 122 citing *Saadi v Italy* [GC] App no 37201/06, ECHR 2008-II, para 127.

sentences for the seriousness of the crime to be taken into account in balancing the severity of the ill-treatment against the seriousness of the crime committed. If the punishment imposed violates Article 3 ECHR, then this will be the case irrespective of the crime committed.

The ECtHR has confirmed in a number of more recent cases that the deportation of individuals to a retentionist country in the absence of a guarantee that the death penalty will not be imposed, will violate Article 3 ECHR. In *Al Nashiri*, a Saudi Arabian national of Yemeni descent complained that he had first been held at a Central Intelligence Agency (CIA) 'black site' in Poland before being transferred to the United States Guantanamo Bay Naval Base in Cuba on suspicion of having committed terrorist acts. The decision to transfer the applicant, despite the existence of real grounds for believing that he would be subjected to the death penalty, violated Article 3 ECHR.[65] Similarly, in another case, the applicant complained that his deportation to China would put him at a substantial risk of being convicted and sentenced to death. The ECtHR held that his forcible return to China would violate Article 3 ECHR. The Russian authorities were obliged by Article 3 ECHR to ensure that the applicant was not exposed to a real risk of being sentenced to death.[66]

It is notable, here, that the while the ECtHR ruled in these cases that the imposition of the death penalty would in itself violate Article 3 ECHR, it refrained from actually expressing the finding of a violation of the provision in these terms. Instead, it held that the 'psychological suffering' inflicted on the applicants by being exposed to the threat of capital punishment constituted inhuman punishment in the sense of Article 3 ECHR. In *Al-Saldoon*, for instance, it held that the applicants had been subjected 'to the fear of execution by the Iraqi authorities ... causing the applicants psychological suffering' which amounted to inhuman treatment.[67] The ECtHR's focus on the 'psychological suffering' imposed on the applicant facing the death penalty, rather than the penalty itself, has called into question, as we shall see, the compatibility of other sentences, notably the sentence of life imprisonment, with Article 3 ECHR.

Exposing an individual to the death penalty will give rise in every case to a violation of Article 3 ECHR irrespective of the nature of the crime that the individual has committed. The interference with the individual right to bodily integrity in such cases is—although the ECtHR does not refer expressly to proportionality—disproportionate to the public interest in punishing

65 *Al-Nashiri v Poland* App no 28761/11, 24 July 2014.
66 *AL (XW) v Russia* App no 44095/14, 29 Oct 2015.
67 *Al-Saadoon and Mufdhi v UK* App no 61498/08, ECHR 2010-II, para 144.

individuals for crimes committed. This must be seen as representing a clear rejection of *lex talionis*, of the idea that the punishment imposed on the offender should be the same in kind or in degree as that employed by the offender on his victim. In the words of Lord Justice Laws: 'The destruction of a life may be accepted in some special circumstances, such as self-defence or just war; but retributive punishment is never enough to justify it.'[68] Even for the most serious of crimes—such as murder—the death penalty will never be justified.

c) 'Irreducible' Life Sentences (Life Sentences without the Possibility of Release)

The ECtHR has repeatedly held that the imposition of a life sentence on an adult offender[69] is not prohibited by Article 3 ECHR.[70] Equally, Article 3 ECHR does not prevent life sentences being served in full.[71] This is despite the fact that 'although such sentences are based on imprisonment, which is generally considered a tolerable infliction of pain, they present an indefinite term of imprisonment, taking to the extreme the traditional issues of incarceration'.[72]

In its more recent case law, the Grand Chamber has confirmed, though, that the imposition of a 'whole life' sentence without the 'possibility of release' will violate Article 3 ECHR.[73] Indications that such sentences might not be compatible with human rights principles were visible in the chamber judgments in *Vinter and Others* and *Harkins and Edwards*.[74] In these cases, the ECtHR

[68] *R (Wellington) v Secretary of State for the Home Department* [2007] EWHC 1109 (Admin).

[69] See eg *López Elorza v Spain* App no 30614/15, 12 Dec 2017, para 97: 'It is well established . . . that the imposition of life imprisonment on an adult offender is not in itself prohibited by or incompatible with Article 3 ECHR.' This suggests that the ECtHR might view the imposition of life sentences on children differently. See though the UN Convention on the Rights of the Child which only prohibits the imposition of a life sentence on a child if there is no possibility of release: Convention on the Rights of the Child, New York, 20 Nov 1989, UNTS vol 1577, 3, entry into force 2 Sept 1990; Art 37(a): 'No child shall be subjected to torture or other cruel, inhuman or degrading treatment or punishment. Neither capital punishment nor life imprisonment without possibility of release shall be imposed for offences committed by persons below eighteen years of age.' See also the judgments of the US Supreme Court in *Graham v Florida*, 560 US 48 (2010) and *Miller v Alabama* 567 US 460 (2012), holding that the imposition of a sentence of life imprisonment without parole in cases concerning juveniles constitutes cruel and unusual punishment.

[70] *Vinter and Others v UK* [GC] App nos 66069/09, 130/10, and 3896/10, ECHR 2013-III, para 106; *Kafkaris v Cyprus* [GC] App no 21906/04, ECHR 2008-I, para 97; see, among many authorities, *Kotälla v Netherlands* (dec) App no 7994/77, 6 May 1978, 14 (DR) 238; *Bamber v UK* App no 13183/87 (dec), 14 Dec 1988, 59 DR 235; *Sawoniuk v UK* (dec) App no 63716/00, ECHR 2001-VI. See also F Meyer, *Systematischer Kommentar zur Strafprozessordnung: Band X EMRK* (5th edn, Cologne: Carl Heymanns Verlag 2019) 277.

[71] See eg *López Elorza v Spain* App no 30614/15, 12 Dec 2017, para 98: Art 3 ECHR does not prohibit life sentences from being 'served in their entirety'.

[72] For a thought-provoking take on the regulation of life imprisonment at the ICC see D Marchesi, 'Imprisonment for Life at the International Criminal Court' (2018) 14 *Utrecht Law Review* 97.

[73] *Vinter and Others v UK* [GC] App nos 66069/09, 130/10, and 3896/10, ECHR 2013-III.

[74] *Harkins and Edwards v UK* App nos 9146/07 and 32650/07, 17 Jan 2012; *Vinter and Others v UK* App nos 66069/09, 130/10, and 3896/10, 17 Jan 2012; see also *Nivette v France* (dec) App no 44190/98, ECHR 2001-VII; *Stanford v UK* (dec) App no 73299/01, 12 Dec 2002; *Wynne v UK* (dec) App no 67385/01, 22 May 2003; *Kafkaris v Cyprus* [GC] App no 21906/04, ECHR 2008-I, para 98.

held that 'a sentence of life imprisonment without the possibility of parole' was not '*per se* incompatible with the Convention, although the trend in Europe is clearly against such sentences'.[75] Instead, it applied a dual test holding that a life sentence would only violate Article 3 ECHR if: '(i) ... the applicant's continued imprisonment can no longer be justified on any legitimate penological grounds; and (ii) ... the sentence is irreducible *de facto* and *de iure*'.[76]

This test is extremely difficult to understand: if the imprisonment cannot be justified on legitimate penological grounds then it might be assumed that it would be considered arbitrary and thus disproportionate, thereby making any examination of the second element superfluous.[77] Notwithstanding the clumsy formulation, the point which the ECtHR appeared to be making, here, was that the offender's imprisonment might at some point become so detached from the reasons justifying the sentencing at the time when it was imposed as to become incompatible with their Article 3 ECHR rights, but that this would not occur at the moment of the imposition of the sentence.

None of the applicants had been able to show either than their sentence did not serve any penological purpose or that they would not be able to apply for clemency. The applicant Vinter had only served three years of his life sentence for a 'particularly brutal and callous murder' and the ECtHR was satisfied that the incarceration served 'the legitimate penological purposes of punishment and deterrence'. Although the other applicants, Bamber and Moore, had served twenty-six and sixteen years in prison respectively, the ECtHR was persuaded that their continued incarceration also served the purposes of 'punishment and deterrence'.[78] The applicants Harkins and Edwards meanwhile were contesting their extradition to the USA and had not yet served any of their sentence.[79]

Vinter and Others was referred to the Grand Chamber and its judgment marked a dramatic change of approach. The Grand Chamber held that irreducible life sentences were essentially incompatible per se with Article 3 ECHR, holding that it was 'axiomatic that a prisoner cannot be detained unless there are legitimate penological grounds for that detention'.[80] It referred to those grounds as including 'punishment, deterrence, public protection and rehabilitation' and held that while many of the grounds would be 'present at the time when a life sentence is imposed', 'the balance between these justifications for

[75] *Harkins and Edwards v UK* App nos 9146/07 and 32650/07, 17 Jan 2012, para 138.
[76] ibid para 135.
[77] See, for criticism of the pointless suffering test of the USSC, Lee, 'Why Proportionality Matters' (n 5) 1845.
[78] *Vinter and Others v UK* App nos 66069/09, 130/10, and 3896/10, 17 Jan 2012, para 95.
[79] *Harkins and Edwards v UK* App nos 9146/07 and 32650/07, 17 Jan 2012, para 142.
[80] *Vinter and Others v UK* [GC] App nos 66069/09, 130/10, 3896/10, ECHR 2013-III, para 111.

detention is not necessarily static and may shift in the course of the sentence'.[81] This meant that 'the primary justification for detention at the start of the sentence may not be so after a lengthy period into the service of the sentence'. Only 'a review of the justification for continued detention at an appropriate point in the sentence' would allow for these 'factors or shifts' to be 'properly evaluated'.[82] Consequently, in order for life sentences to be compatible with Article 3 ECHR there had to be a possibility of review and a corresponding prospect of release. Crucially, it held that where domestic law did not 'provide any mechanism or possibility for review of a whole life sentence, the incompatibility with Article 3 on this ground already arises at the moment of the imposition of the whole life sentence and not at a later stage of incarceration'.[83] The ECtHR judgment did not receive unanimous approval. Judge Villiger, dissenting, queried whether the arbitrariness could really arise already at the moment of the imposition of the sentence.[84]

The argument here might be that although the imposition of an irreducible life sentence follows a legitimate aim (retribution, deterrence etc) at sentencing, it is very probable that with time the sentence will lose its connection to that initial aim. The direct connection between the purpose of the law and the impugned effect on the individual is so likely to be severed as to call into question the reasonableness of the interference. Here it might be argued that the ECtHR is concerned with arbitrariness[85] and the potential for disproportionality to arise on the grounds of a lack of rational connection between purpose and interference.[86] The likelihood of detention following the imposition of an irreducible life sentence becoming arbitrary at some point was so high as to result in such sentences being deemed incompatible with Article 3 ECHR from the moment of the imposition of the sentence. Perhaps more plausibly, the approach might be understood as linked to the hopelessness which is connected with the imposition of such a sentence. This explains why the sentence itself is

[81] ibid.

[82] ibid.

[83] ibid para 122.

[84] See his dissenting opinion which is attached to the judgment in *Vinter and Others v UK* [GC] App nos 66069/09, 130/10, and 3896/10, ECHR 2013-III, para 122.

[85] See H Stewart, 'Bedford and the Structure of Section 7' (2015) 60 *McGill Law Journal* 575 discussing the relationship between arbitrariness and gross disproportionality (and overbreadth); *R v Labaye* [2005] 3 SCR 728, 2005 SCC 80, para 123.

[86] In the sense that the means adopted by the law limiting the constitutional right are not capable of advancing the realization of its proper purpose. This requirement of 'rational connection' is one of the four requirements of proportionality in the broader sense—see Barak, 'Proportionality (2)' (n 10) 743. 'This idea [gross disproportionality] is captured by the hypothetical of a law with the purpose of keeping the streets clean that imposes a sentence of life imprisonment for spitting on the sidewalk.'

problematic at the point of its imposition and not just the enforcement of the sentence at some future point in time.

The Grand Chamber refers to the fact that the review mechanism must exist at the moment of the imposition of the life sentence and explains this by reference to the fact that '[a] whole life prisoner is entitled to know, at the outset of his sentence, what he must do to be considered for release and under what conditions, including when a review of his sentence will take place or may be sought'.[87] Consequently, where domestic law did not provide any mechanism or possibility for review of a whole-life sentence, the incompatibility with Article 3 on this ground already arose at 'the moment of the imposition of the whole-life sentence and not at a later stage of incarceration'.[88] The problem highlighted by Strasbourg is that even if the purposes of the sentence were no longer fulfilled, there would be no way for the accused to seek a review of the sentence. The problem thus seemed very much to lie in the mandatory nature of the sentence.

The ECtHR has also connected the prospect of release to the potential for rehabilitation: 'Even those who commit the most abhorrent and egregious acts nevertheless retain their essential humanity and carry within themselves the capacity to change, to deny them the experience of hope [of being released] would be to deny a fundamental aspect of their humanity.'[89] The connection is clear: if a person is not to be released, there seems to be little point in making any efforts towards rehabilitation. In *Murray*, it held that 'life prisoners should thus be detained under such conditions, and be provided with such treatment that they are given a realistic opportunity to rehabilitate themselves in order to have a hope of release'.[90] This approach has led some commentators to go so far as to suggest that there might be a 'right to the opportunity to rehabilitate oneself' in the Convention.[91] Although, in *Murray*, the Grand Chamber seemed to suggest that the Convention did not 'guarantee as such a right to rehabilitation', it did note that states were under an obligation to provide offenders with the opportunity to rehabilitate themselves.[92] The justification of the importance of providing an offender with the prospect of release is closely connected

[87] *Vinter and Others* [GC] App nos 66069/09, 130/10, and 3896/10, ECHR 2013-III, para 122. See also *Trablesi v Belgium* App no 140/10, ECHR 2014-IV: 'objective, pre-established criteria'.

[88] *López Elorza v Spain* App no 30614/15, 12 Dec 2017, para 100 citing *Vinter and Others v UK* [GC] App nos 66069/09, 130/10, and 3896/10, ECHR 2013-III, para 122.

[89] See eg *Matiošaitis and Others v Lithuania* App nos 22662/13, 51059/1, 58823/13, 59692/13, 60115/13, and 69425/13, 23 May 2017.

[90] *Murray v Netherlands* [GC] App no 10511/10, ECHR 2016, para 112.

[91] D van Zyl Smit, P Weatherby, and S Creighton, 'Whole Life Sentences and the Tide of European Human Rights Jurisprudence: What Is to Be Done?' (2014) 14 *Human Rights Law Review* 59.

[92] *Murray v Netherlands* [GC] App no 10511/10, ECHR 2016, para 103: 'Notwithstanding the fact that the Convention does not guarantee, as such, a right to rehabilitation ... Life prisoners are to be provided with an opportunity to rehabilitate themselves'; 'The obligation to offer a possibility of rehabilitation is

to notions of human dignity and the prospect of release as an entitlement of humanity.[93]

Of crucial importance is the determination of the point in time at which this review should take place, not least because of the suggestion inherent in this line of reasoning that Article 3 ECHR essentially restricts the length of the punitive part of a life sentence. The ECtHR noted that 'the comparative and international law materials ... showed clear support for the institution of a dedicated mechanism guaranteeing a review no later than twenty-five years after the imposition of a life sentence, with further periodic review thereafter'.[94] Subsequently, in *TP and AT*, the ECtHR did not directly respond to the government's characterization of the 25-year period set out in *Vinter and Others* as a 'general indication rather than a clear standard set in all Council of Europe member states',[95] noting that although the states enjoyed a margin of appreciation in the area of criminal justice and sentencing, that it was 'axiomatic that the said margin of appreciation cannot be unlimited'.[96]

to be seen as an obligation of means, not one of result ... it entails a positive obligation to secure prison regimes to life prisoners which are compatible with the aim of rehabilitation.'

[93] For a useful consideration of Art 3 ECHR in the context of punishment see Mavronicola, 'Crime, Punishment and Article 3 ECHR' (n 26); see also N Mavronicola, 'Inhuman and Degrading Punishment, Dignity and the Limits of Retribution' (2014) 77 *Modern Law Review* 292; N Mavronicola, *Torture, Inhumanity and Degradation under Article 3 of the ECHR: Absolute Rights and Absolute Wrongs* (Oxford: Hart Publishing 2021).

[94] *Murray v Netherlands* [GC] App no 10511/10, ECHR 2016, para 120; see too *Harakchiev and Tolumov* App nos 15018/11 and 61199/12, ECHR 2014-III, para 246; *TP and AT v Hungary* App nos 37871/14 and 73986/14, 4 Oct 2016, para 41 (forty years before the applicant could apply for release—violation); *Murray v Netherlands* [GC] App no 10511/10, ECHR 2016, para 99. In the earlier case of *Bodein v France* App no 40014/10, 13 Nov 2014, the opportunity to apply for parole after a period of twenty-six years was deemed acceptable.

[95] In England and Wales, the minimum term for those convicted of murder and who are not to be subjected to a whole life order is set out in law. Here a number of rigid starting points are defined: thirty years, twenty-five years, or twelve years, see Sentencing Act 2020, Sch 21. The regulation of indefinite sentences of imprisonment is frankly bewildering. Padfield notes that while the Court of Appeal referred to 'four situations in which the sentence of imprisonment for life arises for consideration', there may currently be people in prison 'serving 11 different forms of indeterminate sentence'. See N Padfield, 'Justifying Indefinite Detention: On What Grounds? [2016] *Criminal Law Review* 797, 798 referring to *Saunders* [2013] EWCA Crim 1027, [5]; [2014] 1 Cr App R (S) 45, 258. Despite the judgment in *Vinter*, the Court of Appeal continued to maintain that such sentences were compatible with the ECHR, see eg *Attorney General's Reference (No. 69 of 2013) (Newell and McLoughlin)* [2014] EWCA 188; 1 WLR 3964; [2014] Cr App R (S) 40, 321. In *Hutchinson v UK* [GC] App no 57592/08, ECHR 2017 the ECtHR accepted that the (very limited) possibility of review (essentially a compassionate release scheme) was such as to meet the requirements of the Convention. This judgment was referred to as 'the great review and release swindle' and subject to considerable criticism from academics in the United Kingdom, but it was nevertheless subsequently upheld by the Grand Chamber. S Foster, 'The Great Review and Release Swindle: The European Court, Whole Life Sentences and the Possibility of Review and Release' (2015) 20 *Coventry Law Journal* 53.

[96] *TP and AT v Hungary* App nos 37871/14 and 73986/14, 4 Oct 2016, para 44: forty years was considered to be too long.

Much of the case law post *Vinter and Others* has concerned the extent of the *Vinter* review and the possibility of release.[97] The ECtHR has suggested that this type of review differs from that undertaken by the sentencing judge: 'the need for independent judges to determine whether a whole life order may be imposed is quite separate from the need for such whole life orders to be reviewed at a later stage so as to ensure that they remain justified on legitimate penological grounds.'[98] This makes it clear that the procedural requirements of Article 6(1) ECHR do not have to be fulfilled. Less understandable is the suggestion of the ECtHR that the *Vinter* review can be executive or judicial in nature.[99] This seems absolutely at odds with the ECtHR's own established principles on the review of detention.[100] There is no reason why the procedural requirements applicable to a *Vinter* review should be different from those applicable to a post-tariff review. This means that the standard criteria for a procedural review of detention developed in the Article 5(4) ECHR case law must also be met in the context of the *Vinter* review.[101]

The ECtHR has held the review must be such as to offer a real prospect of release. In *Vinter and Others*, the ECtHR noted that release from a whole life sentence was only possible if the prisoner was terminally ill or physically incapacitated. The ECtHR was sceptical as to whether 'compassionate release' could even be considered to constitute release at all. In any event, the review was deemed insufficient as it did not provide for consideration of whether the applicant's continued incarceration was still justified, 'either because the requirements of punishment and deterrence have not yet entirely been fulfilled or because the applicant's continued detention is justified by reason of his dangerousness'.[102] Reviews based on compassionate grounds such as ill-health,

97 See eg L Graham, 'From Vinter to Hutchinson and Back Again' (2018) 3 *European Human Rights Law Review* 258, 260.

98 *Vinter and Others v UK* [GC] App nos 66069/09, 130/10, and 3896/10, ECHR 2013-III para 124.

99 *Murray v Netherlands* [GC] App no 10511/10, ECHR 2016, para 99: 'It is for the States to decide—and not for the Court to prescribe—what form (executive or juridical) that review should take', citing *Vinter and Others v UK* [GC] App nos 66069/09, 130/10, and 3896/10, ECHR 2013-III paras 104 and 120.

100 For detailed consideration of this point see van Zyl Smit, Weatherby, and Creighton, 'Whole Life Sentences' (n 91) 71ff.

101 ibid 79.

102 *Vinter and Others v UK* [GC] App nos 66069/09, 130/10, and 3896/10, ECHR 2013-III, para 127. In *Hutchinson v UK*, the UK government managed to convince the ECtHR—to the surprise of many UK commentators—that the Home Secretary's power of compassionate release properly understood actually required consideration of the continued penological justification of the sentence. For criticism see Graham, 'From Vinter to Hutchinson' (n 97) 258; M Pettigrew, 'A Vinter Retreat in Europe: Returning to the Issue of Whole-Life Sentences in Strasbourg' (2017) 8 *New Journal of European Criminal Law* 128; A Beetham, 'Whole Life Orders and Article 3' (2017) 81 *Journal of Criminal Law* 236; J Bild, 'The Whole Life Sentence in England and Wales' (2015) 74 *Cambridge Law Journal* 1; N Hart, 'Whole Life Sentences in the UK: Volte-Face at the European Court of Human Rights?' (2015) 74 *Cambridge Law Journal* 205.

incapacity, old age,[103] or following a presidential pardon, which did not clearly allow the prisoner to establish the criteria to be met in order to be released,[104] will not satisfy the demands of Article 3 ECHR. Similarly, US legislation on release from a life sentence and presidential pardons were not compatible with Article 3 ECHR because the procedures did not constitute

> a review mechanism requiring national authorities to ascertain, on the basis of objective, pre-established criteria of which the prisoner had precise cognisance at the time of the imposition of the life sentence, whether, while serving his sentence, the prisoner has changed and progressed to such an extent that continued detention can no longer be justified on legitimate penological grounds.[105]

The position of the ECtHR can be summed up in the following terms. Whole life sentences or life sentences without the possibility of parole are incompatible with Article 3 ECHR. Life sentences are compatible with Article 3 ECHR, but the punitive part of a life sentence can only constitute a maximum of around twenty-five years. Any detention beyond this period will only be justified on the grounds of public protection. The imposition of a life sentence without the possibility of parole is unacceptable because it is based either on the view that the punitive part of the sentence can legitimately be longer than twenty-five years or on the idea that it is possible to establish with certainty that a person will pose a danger to the public for the rest of their life. Neither assumption is compatible with Article 3 ECHR. By capping the punitive part of a life sentence at twenty-five years, the ECtHR essentially prohibits the imposition of a mandatory minimum sentence of imprisonment for life without parole.

3. Gross Disproportionality between the Sentence and the Offence

Any interference with human dignity for the purposes of punishment which does not constitute a violation of Article 3 ECHR per se may nevertheless violate Article 3 ECHR if it is considered severely disproportionate to the seriousness of the crime committed. Excessively severe sentences might give rise to a violation of Article 3 ECHR. In a series of decisions from the 1970s, the European Commission on Human Rights held that 'exceptionally harsh punishment for a trivial offence might raise a question under Article 3'.[106]

[103] *Murray v Netherlands* [GC] App no 10511/10, ECHR 2016, para 99.
[104] See *Matiošaitis and Others v Lithuania* App nos 22662/13, 51059/1, 58823/13, 59692/13, 60115/13, and 69425/13, 23 May 2017.
[105] *Trabelsi v Belgium* App no 140/10, ECHR 2014-IV, para 137.
[106] *X v UK* (dec) [1973] 43 Coll 160; *X v Germany* (dec) App no 7057/75 [1976], 6 DR 127.

Examples of complaints considered by the Commission include the imposition of a sentence of four years for arson,[107] a sentence of eight years' imprisonment imposed on a woman for attempting to poison her husband,[108] and the imposition of a sentence of five years' imprisonment following a conviction for robbery.[109] All of these cases were ruled inadmissible on the basis that there was no evidence that the sentences were in fact disproportionate. While these decisions are relatively unsurprising in that few would consider any of the sentences to be *prima facie* disproportionate,[110] they are nevertheless interesting, in that they demonstrate a willingness on the part of the Strasbourg authorities to read a requirement of proportionality between the sentence and the offence into Article 3 ECHR. The ECtHR's case law suggests, however, that the ECtHR will only rarely be prepared to intervene in sentencing decisions on the express grounds of proportionality between the sentence and the offence. In more recent times, as we shall see, the ECtHR, drawing on the case law of other courts, has begun to develop its own notion of gross disproportionality.

a) Life Sentences and Indeterminate Sentences of Imprisonment

In its judgment in *Weeks*, the ECtHR acknowledged the potential for excessively long sentences to interfere with Article 3 ECHR. The applicant had been convicted at the age of seventeen of armed robbery and was sentenced to life imprisonment, in the case at issue essentially an indeterminate sentence, which the ECtHR referred to as 'the severest sentence known to English law (save in cases of treason and certain forms of piracy)'.[111] He had entered a pet shop carrying a starting pistol loaded with blank cartridges and stolen 35 pence, which was later found on the shop floor. The ECtHR noted that '[w]hat otherwise would appear a "terrible" sentence in relation to these pathetic circumstances was seen by the trial judge and the appeal court as appropriate in the light of the purpose intended to be achieved'.[112] It cited approvingly the opinion of the Court of Appeal that 'when the factors to which reference has

[107] *X v UK* (dec) App no 5871/72 [1974] 1 DR 54: 'There is no indication that the sentence of four years' imprisonment imposed on the applicant could possibly fall within the ambit of Art 3 of the Convention which prohibits torture or inhuman or degrading treatment or punishment and the applicant does not allege that it does so. Moreover the Convention does not provide as such any general right to call into question the length of a sentence imposed by a competent court', at para 4.

[108] *X v Germany* (dec) App no 7057/75 [1976] 6 DR 127.

[109] *X v UK* (dec) [1973] 43 Coll 160.

[110] See also L Kurki, 'International Standards for Sentencing and Punishment' in M Tonry and RS Frase (eds), *Sentences and Sanctions in Western Countries* (Oxford: OUP 2001) 362: 'Most would agree that these sentences appear not to be grossly disproportionate to the offenses.'

[111] *Weeks v UK*, 2 Mar 1987, Series A no 114, para 46. The sentence at that time allowed the Home Secretary to release the applicant when he was no longer deemed to pose a risk to the public

[112] ibid.

been made are considered it will be seen that this is really in mercy to the boy and will perhaps enable him to be released much sooner than if a long term of imprisonment had been imposed, which was the only other alternative'.[113] Here, the ECtHR appears to have been particularly influenced by the fact that the trial judge had chosen the sentence precisely because he considered it to be the less severe sentence than the alternative (a long determinate sentence of imprisonment), noting that the sentencing judges 'were hoping for, though could not predict, an early release back into the community'.[114] This demonstrated not just that the sentencing judge had had discretion in choosing the sentence, but also that he had carefully weighed up the issues and imposed what he considered to be the less severe of the sentences available. It is questionable, though, whether the fact that the judge was able to choose between two (bad) sentences is sufficient to ensure that the judge had sufficient discretion to guard against the imposition of arbitrary punishment. To paraphrase the judgment of the ECtHR in *Tyrer*, the fact one penalty is preferable to another penalty does not necessarily imply that the first penalty is compatible with Article 3 ECHR.[115]

The principal factor for the ECtHR in its determination that the sentence was not to be characterized as disproportionate to the offence was the fact that it was not a life sentence 'in the ordinary sense'. It had been imposed in part for the purposes of public protection, because, in the words of the trial judge, the applicant was 'a very dangerous young man'. It held that taking into consideration the applicant's 'age at the time and to the particular facts of the offence he committed . . . , if it had not been for the specific reasons advanced for the sentence imposed, one could have serious doubts as to its compatibility with Article 3 of the Convention, which prohibits, *inter alia*, inhuman punishment'.[116] The ECtHR does not expand on this statement, nor does it mention proportionality or explain why Article 3 ECHR would have been violated. It seems likely, however, that the concerns are essentially those expressed by Judge De Meyer in his dissenting opinion.

Judge De Meyer noted that:

> Life imprisonment in its ordinary sense would indeed have been a punishment too 'terrible' for a somewhat aggressive young man of seventeen, guilty of robbing—after menacing his victim with a starting pistol loaded with

[113] ibid citing Lord Justice Salmon in the Court of Appeal.
[114] ibid para 47.
[115] *Tyrer v UK*, 25 Apr 1978, Series A no 26, para 34.
[116] *Weeks v UK*, 2 Mar 1987, Series A no 114, para 46.

> blank cartridges—a sum of 35 old pence, which he did not even take away. It would have exceeded any reasonable relationship of proportionality with what actually happened. It would have been what the Eighth Amendment to the Constitution of the United States of America calls 'cruel and unusual punishment', and what Article 3 of the European Convention on Human Rights terms 'inhuman punishment'.[117]

The sentence was not deemed disproportionate or inhuman in *Weeks* because it was not an ordinary life sentence but rather an indeterminate sentence, which allowed for the offender to be released as soon as he was deemed to no longer pose a danger to the public. It is noticeable, however, that the accused did not know how long he would be imprisoned for and the possibilities for review and release at that time were not well developed.[118] Indeed, in this regard it seems particularly relevant that the decision on release was not to be made by a judge, let alone the trial judge.

The ECtHR seemed in *Weeks* to draw attention to the various aims of long sentences of imprisonment and to the potential for the balance of this to change with time. It has subsequently confirmed this position in relation to both children and adults. In *Hussain*, for instance, it held that in the case of

> young persons convicted of serious crimes, the corresponding sentence undoubtedly contains a punitive element ... to reflect the requirements of retribution and deterrence. However, an indeterminate term of detention for a convicted young person, which may be as long as that person's life, can only be justified by considerations based on the need to protect the public.[119]

Similar issues arose in the cases of *T v United Kingdom* and *V v United Kingdom*, in which the applicants, who at the age of ten had abducted and brutally killed a two-year-old child, complained that the sentences imposed on them were 'severely disproportionate'.[120] They were sentenced to 'detention at Her Majesty's Pleasure'—essentially a life sentence—and the tariff (the minimum period to be served) had been set at fifteen years. The ECtHR held that it did

[117] Dissenting opinion of Judge De Meyer annexed to the judgment in *Weeks v UK*, 2 Mar 1987, Series A no 114, para 2.

[118] For development of law on this see *James, Wells, and Lee v UK* App nos 25119/09, 57715/09, and 57877/09, 18 Sept 2012.

[119] *Hussain v UK* [GC], 21 Feb 1996, Reports 1996-I, para 53.

[120] *T v UK* [GC] App no 24724/94, 16 Dec 1999, para 92; *V v UK* [GC] App no 24888/94, ECHR 1999-IX, para 93.

> not consider that the punitive element inherent in the tariff approach itself gives rise to a breach of Article 3, or that the Convention prohibits States from subjecting a child or young person convicted of a serious crime to an indeterminate sentence allowing for the offender's continued detention or recall to detention following release where necessary for the protection of the public.[121]

It held that taking into account all the circumstances of the case 'including the applicant's age and his conditions of detention, a period of punitive detention of this length cannot be said to amount to inhuman or degrading treatment'.[122]

These judgments represent a clear endorsement of the tariff system and the characterization of life sentences as comprising both a punishment part and a subsequent primarily preventive element, which serves the purpose of public protection. The reasoning of the ECtHR also suggests that in the context of long indeterminate sentences or life sentences, after a certain amount of time has elapsed, the aims of the sentence can no longer be characterized as solely retributive. The ECtHR held that such sentences are compatible with Article 3 ECHR,[123] and that states may continue to detain prisoners sentenced to life 'for as long as they remain dangerous'.[124] Crucially, though, as soon as the sentence is considered to serve primarily preventative as opposed to retributive aims, the offender must have the opportunity to demonstrate that they are able to be reintegrated into society. Otherwise, the sentence would have to be characterized as arbitrary. The ECtHR has expressed this notion in the following terms: 'The mere fact that such prisoners may have already served a long period of imprisonment does not weaken the State's positive obligation to protect the public; States may fulfil that obligation by continuing to detain such life sentenced prisoners for as long as they remain dangerous',[125] providing there is 'both a prospect of release and a possibility of review'.[126]

It is notable that in these cases the Strasbourg authorities only engaged in a rudimentary examination of whether the sentence was proportionate to the offence and the relevance of such issues for Article 3 ECHR. In this sense, the chamber judgments in the cases of *Vinter and Others* and *Harkins and*

[121] *T v UK* [GC] App no 24724/94, 16 Dec 1999, para 97; *V v UK* [GC] App no 24888/94, ECHR 1999-IX, para 98.

[122] *T v UK* [GC] App no 24724/94, 16 Dec 1999, para 98; *V v UK* [GC] App no 24888/94, ECHR 1999-IX, para 99.

[123] *Vinter and Others v UK* [GC] App nos 66069/09, 130/10, and 3896/10, ECHR 2013-III, para 10.

[124] ibid para 108; *Maiorano and Others v Italy* App no 28634/06, 15 Dec 2009, para 108; *Choreftakis and Choreftaki v Greece* App no 46846/08, 17 Jan 2012, para 45.

[125] *Vinter and Others v UK* [GC] App nos 66069/09, 130/10, and 3896/10, ECHR 2013-III, para 108.

[126] ibid para 110.

Edwards seemed to mark a change of approach. Both cases concerned applicants who were facing life sentences without the possibility of release. In *Vinter and Others*, the applicants had been convicted of murder and subjected to whole life orders,[127] while in *Harkins and Edwards*, the applicants complained about their extradition to the USA, where they faced sentences of life imprisonment without parole. In these cases, the ECtHR introduced the concept of gross disproportionality for the first time in the context of Article 3 ECHR. In both cases, the ECtHR held that it was 'necessary to consider first whether a grossly disproportionate sentence imposed by a Contracting State would violate Article 3 and second, at what point in the course of a life or other very long sentence an Article 3 issue might arise'.[128] This underscores the fact that the ECtHR's understanding of a grossly disproportionate sentence was quite distinct from other claims about the incompatibility of life sentences with Article 3 ECHR.[129]

With regard to gross disproportionality, it referred to the fact that the UK government had accepted that an extradition could violate Article 3 ECHR 'if the applicant faced a grossly disproportionate sentence in the receiving State'[130] and also that 'a particular sentence could violate Article 3 if it were wholly unjustified or grossly disproportionate to the gravity of the crime'.[131] It also referred to the fact that the review of the comparative materials demonstrated that gross disproportionality was 'a widely accepted and applied test for determining when a sentence will amount to inhuman or degrading punishment, or equivalent constitutional norms'.[132] This led it to conclude that 'a grossly disproportionate sentence could amount to ill-treatment contrary to Article 3 at the moment of its imposition',[133] although it qualified this by stating

[127] A whole life order indicates that the criminal offence was so serious that the offender will never be released from prison. As of 30 June 2018, there were sixty-six people serving a whole life sentence in England and Wales whose crime was so serious that they will never be released from prison. See <https://www.sentencingcouncil.org.uk/sentencing-and-the-council/types-of-sentence/life-sentences/>.

[128] *Harkins and Edwards v UK* App nos 9146/07 and 32650/07, 17 Jan 2012, para 132; *Vinter and Others v UK* App nos 66069/09, 130/10, and 3896/10, 17 Jan 2012, para 87.

[129] *Vinter and Others v UK* App nos 66069/09, 130/10, and 3896/10, 17 Jan 2012, para 93; *Harkins and Edwards v UK* App nos 9146/07 and 32650/07, 17 Jan 2012, para 138.

[130] *Harkins and Edwards v UK* App nos 9146/07 and 32650/07, 17 Jan 2012, para 133; *Vinter and Others v UK* App nos 66069/09, 130/10, and 3896/10, 17 Jan 2012, para 88.

[131] *Vinter and Others v UK* App nos 66069/09, 130/10, and 3896/10, 17 Jan 2012, para 88.

[132] ibid; *Harkins and Edwards v UK* App nos 9146/07 and 32650/07, 17 Jan 2012, para 133.

[133] *Vinter and Others v UK* App nos 66069/09, 130/10, and 3896/10, 17 Jan 2012, para 89; *Harkins and Edwards v UK* App nos 9146/07 and 32650/07, 17 Jan 2012, para 133. In *Harkins and Edwards v UK*, para 134, the ECtHR also referred expressly to specific difficulties in establishing disproportionality in removal cases, referring to the need for 'due regard to be had for the fact that sentencing practices vary greatly between states and that there will often be legitimate and reasonable differences between states as to the length of the sentences which are imposed, even for similar offences'.

that 'gross disproportionality' was a 'strict test' and endorsing the Canadian Supreme Court's opinion in *Latimer* that it would be met only on 'rare and unique occasions'.[134]

The ECtHR did not find the sentences of any of the applicants to be grossly disproportionate. In *Vinter and Others*, it noted that none of the applicants had sought to argue that their sentences were grossly disproportionate and indeed that in view of the 'gravity of the murders for which they were convicted' it could not find any indication of gross disproportionality.[135] In relation to the applicant Edwards, it held that the imposition of a discretionary sentence of life imprisonment without parole following a conviction of premeditated murder imposed by a judge after considering all relevant aggravating and mitigating factors was not grossly disproportionate.[136]

In *Willcox and Hurford v United Kingdom*, the applicants were both convicted in Thailand for drugs offences and sentenced to thirty-three and twenty-six years of imprisonment. The applicants were both transferred to the United Kingdom under the prisoner transfer scheme and sought to argue that the sentence imposed by the Thai authorities was grossly disproportionate and violated Article 3 ECHR. They argued that the sentences were 'four to five times as long as the sentences which they would likely have received had they been convicted of the same offences in the United Kingdom' and that their 'continued detention no longer served a legitimate penological purpose, having regard to the time that they had already spent in detention'.[137] The ECtHR noted that:

> different considerations arise in cases in which a Contracting State is asked to refuse extradition to a jurisdiction where a grossly disproportionate sentence might be imposed; and in cases where that same State is confronted with a request by a prisoner for transfer to serve a sentence imposed by a foreign court, that might have been considered grossly disproportionate had it been assessed in the context of a prior extradition request. In the former case, it is within the State's power to prevent the offending sentence being imposed. In

[134] *Vinter and Others v UK* App nos 66069/09, 130/10, and 3896/10, 17 Jan 2012, para 89; *Harkins and Edwards v UK* App nos 9146/07 and 32650/07, 17 Jan 2012, para 133. After conducting a review of 'comparative materials', the EctHR held that that ' "gross disproportionality" is a widely accepted and applied test for determining when a sentence will amount to inhuman or degrading punishment, or equivalent constitutional norms' but that it was a 'strict test' which would only be met on 'rare and unique' occasions. This was subsequently endorsed by the GC in *Vinter and Others v UK* [GC] App nos 66069/09, 130/10, and 3896/10, ECHR 2013-III, para 102.

[135] *Vinter and Others v UK* App nos 66069/09, 130/10, and 3896/10, 17 Jan 2012, para 95.

[136] *Harkins and Edwards v UK* App nos 9146/07 and 32650/07, 17 Jan 2012, para 142.

[137] *Willcox and Hurford v UK* (dec) App nos 43759/10 and 43771/12, 8 Jan 2013, para 72.

> the latter, the sentence has been imposed and might have to be served in harsh and degrading conditions, subject to limited early-release provisions.[138]

In considering the proportionality of the sentences, the ECtHR emphasized first that there was 'no suggestion that the sentences imposed on the applicants were outwith the range of sentences generally imposed on others convicted in Thailand for similar offences' and that the 'sentences imposed on the applicants also fall within the permitted maximum sentences applicable to equivalent convictions in England'.[139] Finally it referred to the 'vast differences in the civil, political, economic, social and cultural conditions prevailing in countries across the globe', noting that 'solutions applied in one State may not be suited to another, and it follows that a sentence cannot be deemed grossly disproportionate simply because it is more severe than the sentence which would be imposed in another State'. It concluded that the sentences imposed in Thailand, while harsher than those applicable in the United Kingdom, were 'legitimate and necessary'.[140] The affirmation of the necessity of the sentence, here, seems particularly unnecessary.

Proportionality concerns have also been raised in relation to elderly people sentenced to long prison terms. In *Sawoniuk v United Kingdom*,[141] the ECtHR had to consider the proportionality of a sentence imposed on an elderly man. The applicant, who was almost eighty years old, had been prosecuted under war crimes legislation in respect of atrocities committed during the Second World War, convicted on two counts of murder, and sentenced to life imprisonment with a tariff of five years. The ECtHR held that while 'matters of appropriate sentencing largely fall outside the scope' of the ECHR, it had 'not been excluded that an arbitrary or disproportionately lengthy sentence might in some circumstances raise issues under the Convention'.[142] The ECtHR rejected the applicant's contention that his 'advanced age' was in itself a problem, noting that:

> In the circumstances, the Court sees no basis for finding that the imposition of a sentence of imprisonment on the applicant infringes the prohibition

[138] ibid para 75.
[139] ibid para 77.
[140] ibid para 77.
[141] *Sawoniuk v UK* (dec) App no 63716/00, ECHR 2001-VI. The applicant was convicted on 1 April 1999 and died in prison in November 2005—six and a half years later. See further M Bazyler and F Tuerkheimer, *Forgotten Trials of the Holocaust* (New York, NY: New York University Press 2015) 297–99.
[142] *Sawoniuk v UK* (dec) App no 63716/00, ECHR 2001-VI, para 3, citing *V v UK* [GC], no 24888/94, ECHR 1999-IX, paras 97–101, concerning life sentences imposed on juveniles.

> contained in Article 3. Nor, given the seriousness of the offences for which the applicant was convicted, can a sentence of life imprisonment be regarded as arbitrary or disproportionate in the context of Article 5 of the Convention.[143]

b) Mandatory Sentences

The ECtHR has also considered whether the imposition of a mandatory sentence of imprisonment might be considered to be grossly disproportionate. In *Harkins and Edwards*, which was decided before the Grand Chamber judgment in *Vinter and Others*, it rejected the contention of the applicant Harkins that his sentence was grossly disproportionate. Mandatory sentences of life imprisonment without the possibility of parole were, according to the ECtHR not '*per se* incompatible with the Convention, although the trend in Europe is clearly against such sentences', but they were to be treated with particular caution:

> The vice of any mandatory sentence is that it deprives the defendant of any possibility to put any mitigating factors or special circumstances before the sentencing court. This is especially true in the case of a mandatory sentence of life imprisonment without the possibility of parole, a sentence which, in effect, condemns a defendant to spend the rest of his days in prison, irrespective of his level of culpability and irrespective of whether the sentencing court considers the sentence to be justified.[144]

Mandatory sentences of life imprisonment without the possibility of parole were 'much more likely to be grossly disproportionate than any of the other types of life sentence, especially if it requires the sentencing court to disregard mitigating factors which are generally understood as indicating a significantly lower level of culpability on the part of the defendant, such as youth or severe mental health problems'.[145]

In rejecting the applicant's contentions, it noted that although he faced a mandatory sentence of life imprisonment without parole, he was twenty years old and not a minor at the time that he committed the crime. Referring to 37(a) of the United Nations Convention on the Rights of the Child, it noted that it supported the view that the imposition of such a sentence on a child under the

[143] *Sawoniuk v UK* (dec) App no 63716/00, ECHR 2001-VI, para 3.

[144] ibid para 138 (references omitted).

[145] *Vinter and Others v UK* App nos 66069/09, 130/10, and 3896/10, 17 Jan 2012, para 93; *Harkins and Edwards v UK* App nos 9146/07 and 32650/07, 17 Jan 2012, para 138: citing *Hussain v UK* [GC], 21 Feb 1996, Reports 1996-I and *Prem Singh v UK*, 21 Feb 1996, Reports 1996-I, paras 53 and 61.

age of eighteen would be 'grossly disproportionate'. It was not persuaded, however, that an international consensus prohibited the imposition of such a sentence on a young defendant over the age of eighteen. In addition, it noted that while the applicant had been diagnosed with mental health problems, he had not been 'diagnosed with a psychiatric disorder', thus it was not of the opinion that the 'applicant possesses mitigating factors which would indicate a significantly lower level of culpability on his part'.[146]

The suggestion is that mandatory sentences which do not allow for consideration of issues which might mitigate the culpability of the accused, such as mental health issues or age, could give rise to gross disproportionality in the sense of Article 3 ECHR. This seems to be based on notions of comparative culpability in the sense that those who act with diminished culpability ought to be punished less severely than they would have been had they been deemed fully culpable. The hurdle here though is extremely high.[147]

The ECtHR confirmed its 'hands-off' approach in *Babar Ahmad*, in which the applicants complained that their extradition to the United States would violate Article 3 ECHR 'not just because their sentences would in practice be irreducible, but also because the sentences were grossly disproportionate'. They argued that the sentences which would be imposed were 'in effect, mandatory sentences which left no room for consideration of their individual cases' and that they 'risked life sentences for non-murder offences; in those circumstances, their sentences would be disproportionate because they could be imposed for non-murder offences without any real judicial discretion'.[148]

One of the applicants was charged with terror offences and faced 'two hundred and sixty-nine counts of murder and thus multiple mandatory sentences of life imprisonment without the possibility of parole'. The ECtHR held that it did not find

> a mandatory life sentence would be grossly disproportionate for such offences, particularly when the fifth applicant has not adduced any evidence of exceptional circumstances which would indicate a significantly lower level of culpability on his part. Indeed, if he is convicted of these charges, it is difficult to conceive of any mitigating factors which would lead a court to impose a lesser sentence than life imprisonment without the possibility of parole, even if it had the discretion to do so. Moreover, for the reasons it has given

146 *Harkins and Edwards v UK* App nos 9146/07 and 32650/07, 17 Jan 2012, para 139.
147 See also the discussion of culpability in Ch 2.
148 *Babar Ahmad and Others v UK* App nos 24027/07, 11949/08, 36742/08, 66911/09, and 67354/09, 10 April 2012, para 231.

> in respect of the first, third, fourth and sixth applicants, the Court considers that he has not shown that incarceration in the United States would not serve any legitimate penological purpose. Therefore, he too has failed to demonstrate that there would be a real risk of treatment reaching the threshold of Article 3 as a result of his sentence if he were extradited to the United States. Accordingly, the Court finds that there would be no violation of Article 3 in his case.[149]

In *Maričák v Slovakia*, the ECtHR had to examine the proportionality of mandatory recidivist sentencing provisions. The applicant complained that the sentence imposed on him was 'disproportionately severe' and thus violated the prohibition on inhuman punishment. He had been convicted of a third robbery during which he had

> grabbed a man from behind, had pressed his hand against the victim's eyes and face, threatened him with injury and pulled a purse from the pocket of his trousers which contained some 189 euros. The victim had suffered haematomas on the eyelids and the mobility of his neck had been restricted. He had undergone a single medical examination; his capacity to work had remained unaffected.[150]

This conviction led to the court to apply, as a result of the applicant's previous convictions, a 'three-strikes type'[151] mandatory sentencing provision, according to which the court was to 'impose a life prison term' or in certain other circumstances a sentence of twenty-five years' imprisonment. The ECtHR rejected the applicant's complaint, noting that the Slovakian court had imposed the less severe of the sentences available to it.[152] Once again, the fact that the judge chose the less severe of two excessively severe sentences does not seem sufficient to guarantee that they had sufficient discretion to guard against the imposition of an arbitrary or disproportionate sentence.[153]

149 ibid para 244.

150 *Maričák v Slovakia* (dec) App no 26621/10, 7 June 2011.

151 California's 'three strikes' sentencing law was enacted in 1994 and meant that a defendant who had one prior conviction for a serious felony was to be sentenced in respect of the new felony to state prison for twice the term otherwise provided for the crime. If the defendant was convicted of any felony and had two or more prior convictions for a serious felony, the law required the imposition of a state prison term of at least twenty-five years to life. On three strikes sentencing laws, see M Romano, 'Divining the Spirit of California's Three Strikes Law' (2010) 22 *Federal Sentencing Reporter* 171.

152 *Maričák v Slovakia* (dec) App no 26621/10, 7 June 2011.

153 The role of the judge is considered in more detail in Ch 5.

4. The Scope of the Review of Proportionate Punishment in Article 3 ECHR
The overview of the case law on Article 3 ECHR makes it clear that the provision does not encompass a right to an appropriate or 'proportionate' sentence. Consideration of the relationship between an offender's culpability for the offence and the sentence imposed might nevertheless be of relevance in determining whether a sentence is compatible with Article 3 ECHR.

The imposition of a sentence which meets the Article 3 ECHR threshold for inhuman punishment will in every case constitute a disproportionate interference with an offender's right to dignity. This is the case with regard to the death penalty, judicial corporal punishment, and 'irreducible' sentences of life imprisonment. This approach is an attractive option for the ECtHR, as it allows consideration of the compatibility of the sentence with Article 3 ECHR without requiring it to undertake an express review of the decision of the sentencing judge. In such cases there is no room for weighing up the proportionality of the severity of the sentence against an offender's blameworthiness for the offence.[154] In essence, the position of the ECtHR is that the interference with the rights of the individual weigh so heavily as to make consideration of the reasons for the imposition of the punishment superfluous.

In addition, the ECtHR's case law demonstrates that sentences which do not meet the threshold for inhuman punishment might nevertheless violate Article 3 ECHR if they are deemed to be grossly disproportionate to the offence committed. Here the case law of the ECtHR is considerably less well developed. The ECtHR has not yet found a violation of Article 3 ECHR on the grounds of 'gross disproportionality' between the offence and the sentence, but the case law indicates that there might be scope for such 'gross disproportionality' to arise in particular situations.

First, if the sentence is obviously excessive when compared to the offence at issue.[155] The importance of this type of absolute test for proportionality is obvious. A sentence of imprisonment for a minor traffic offence, for instance,

[154] J Feinberg, 'Noncomparative Justice' (1974) 83 *Philosophical Review* 297, 311: 'If beheading and disembowelment became the standard punishment for overtime parking … the penalty as applied in a given case would be unjust … even though it were uniformly applied without discrimination to all offenders. Moreover, it would be unjust even if it were the mildest penalty in the whole system of criminal law, with more serious offences punished with proportionately greater severity still.' See also Lee, 'Why Proportionality Matters' (n 5) 1843.

[155] 'The Court notes at the outset that the applicants in the instant case did not seek to argue that their sentence was, as such, grossly disproportionate to the gravity of their offences', *Matiošaitis and Others v Lithuania* App nos 22662/13, 51059/1, 58823/13, 59692/13, 60115/13, and 69425/13, 23 May 2017, para 157.

would be so disproportionate as to constitute inhuman punishment in violation of Article 3 ECHR. The ECtHR has proven reluctant to intervene on such grounds, partly because of the importance of the margin of appreciation of the contracting states, but also because the hurdle of proving that the sentence was so excessive as to constitute inhuman punishment is particularly high.

Second, the case law suggests that a sentence imposed on an individual might be considered disproportionate if the culpability of the offender has not been appropriately taken into account in the determination of the sentence. Here the ECtHR has referred in particular to young offenders and to those who were, for some other reason, deemed to be less culpable at the time of the commission of the offence.[156] The sentence is deemed to constitute an unacceptable interference with the dignity of the offender because it fails to take proper account of their reduced culpability.

Finally, the ECtHR's case law suggests that mandatory sentences which do not allow the sentencing judge to appropriately determine the actual scope of the offender's blameworthiness—taken here to include both the offender's culpability in the narrow sense and other relevant mitigating factors—might well violate the prohibition on disproportionate sentences in Article 3 ECHR. This has been discussed in particular in the context of mandatory sentences of life imprisonment but is potentially relevant in relation to the imposition of any mandatory minimum sentence. If sentencing provisions are such as to prevent the sentencing judge from fully taking into account all factors pertaining to the accused's blameworthiness, then there is clearly a risk that the judge will be unable to properly take account of the reduced blameworthiness in determining the sentence, thereby giving rise to disproportionality and a violation of the Article 3 ECHR. Consideration of such issues is again easier for the ECtHR to address as it is able to consider the disproportionality *in abstracto*—simply by referring to the existence of such mandatory provisions and the lack of scope for judicial discretion—without conducting any detailed examination of the nature of the offence and the sentence actually imposed by the domestic court.[157] Despite these indications, it is instructive that the ECtHR has not yet found a violation of Article 3 ECHR on the grounds of a lack of proportionality between punishment and offence.

[156] *Soering v UK*, 7 July 1989, Series A no 161; *Weeks v UK*, 2 Mar 1987, Series A no 114, para 46.
[157] These issues are discussed further in Ch 5.

C. Proportionality and the Right to Liberty and Security of Person in Article 5 ECHR

1. Proportionality between a Sentence of Imprisonment and the Offence

It might be assumed that the right to liberty, as guaranteed by Article 5(1) ECHR, would take on considerable importance in prohibiting the imposition of disproportionate sentences of imprisonment. Here, though, the scope of control is considerably narrower than in the context of Article 3 ECHR. There is certainly no right in Article 5(1) ECHR to an 'appropriate' or proportionate prison sentence. Further, the ECtHR has held that there is no room in the context of Article 5(1)(a) ECHR for any consideration of the proportionality of the interference with a person's right to liberty. The ECtHR has consistently held that there is no basis in Article 5(1)(a) ECHR to permit any weighing up of the proportionality of a prison sentence and the offence. Instead, 'the decision to impose a sentence of detention and the length of that sentence' are 'generally' matters for the national authorities.[158] It has held that 'matters of appropriate sentencing largely fall outside the scope of the scope of the Convention' and that it is not for the ECtHR 'to decide, for example, ... the appropriate term of detention applicable to a particular offence'.[159] In addition, it has noted that it 'is not its task, within the context of Article 5, to review the appropriateness of the original sentence';[160] or to pronounce on 'the appropriate length of detention or other sentence which should be served by a person after conviction by a competent court'.[161] The reason for this seemingly narrow approach lies in the text of the Convention.

An interference with the right to liberty is expressly permitted in certain circumstances.[162] According to Article 5(1)(a) ECHR, the right to liberty and security of person does not apply to 'the lawful detention of a person after conviction by a competent court' providing that the deprivation of liberty was 'in accordance with a procedure prescribed by law'. Either the deprivation was imposed 'after conviction by a competent court' or it was not.[163] This means that the guarantee in Article 5(1)(a) ECHR 'does not as a matter of principle, empower the Convention organs to test the conviction itself'.[164] There is no

[158] *James, Wells, and Lee v UK* App nos 25119/09, 57715/09, and 57877/09, 18 Sept 2012, para 195 (references omitted).

[159] See *Sawoniuk v UK* (dec) App no 63716/00, ECHR 2001-VI.

[160] See *Weeks v UK*, 2 Mar 1987, Series A no 114, para 5.

[161] See *T v UK* [GC] App no 24724/94, 16 Dec 1999 and *V v UK* [GC] App no 24888/94, ECHR 1999-IX.

[162] Art 5(1) ECHR.

[163] This might be the type of provision which Alexy would refer to as a rule: Alexy, *A Theory of Constitutional Rights* (n 12) 48.

[164] S Trechsel, *Human Rights in Criminal Proceedings* (Oxford: OUP 2005).

room for consideration of whether a sentence of imprisonment constitutes a disproportionate interference with the right to liberty or within that evaluation of the relationship of proportionality between the sentence imposed by the court and the offence. The exception to the prohibition against deprivation of liberty in Article 5(1)(a) ECHR is 'as a general rule not subject to the principle of proportionality'.[165]

The ECtHR has held that Article 5(1) ECHR requires both that the restrictions on liberty are lawful in the sense of being in compliance with national law and also that they are in keeping with 'the purpose of protecting the individual from arbitrariness'.[166] The ECtHR has not set out an exhaustive definition of arbitrariness, but has provided some indications[167] of the type of situation which will give rise to a finding that a deprivation of liberty was arbitrary, including those cases in which the authorities acted in bad faith or resorted to the use of deception in securing the individual's detention;[168] cases in which the order to detain the individual or the nature of the detention did not conform to the restrictions permitted by the relevant sub-paragraph of Article 5(1) ECHR;[169] and those cases in which the relationship between the ground of detention and the place and conditions of detention was not sufficiently strong.[170]

It is important to note that there are considerable differences in the interpretation of this requirement in relation to the various grounds for the deprivation of liberty. In the context of Article 5(1)(e) ECHR (deprivation of liberty of those of unsound mind), for instance, the ECtHR has read a type of subsidiarity requirement into the provision. It has held that:

[165] See J Christofferson, *Fair Balance: Proportionality, Subsidiarity and Primarity in the European Convention of Human Rights* (Leiden: Martinus Nijhoff 2009); S Trechsel, *Die Europäische Menschenrechtskonvention, ihr Schutz der Persönlichen Freiheit und die Schweizerischen Strafprozessrechte* (Bern: Stämpfli 1974).

[166] See *Bouamar v Belgium*, 29 Feb 1988, Series A no 129, para 47; *Chahal v UK*, 15 Nov 1996, Reports 1996-V, para 118; *Stafford v UK* [GC] App no 46295/99, ECHR 2002-IV, para 63; *Saadi v Italy* [GC] App no 37201/06, ECHR 2008-II, para 67; *Kafkaris v Cyprus* [GC] App no 21906/04, ECHR 2008, para 116; *A and Others v UK* [GC] App no 3455/05, ECHR 2009, para 164; *Medvedyev and Others v France* [GC] App no 3394/03, 29 March 2010, para 79; *James, Wells, and Lee v UK* App nos 25119/09, 57715/09, and 57877/09, 18 Sept 2012, para 191; *Léger v France* App no 19324/02, 11 Apr 2006, paras 72–77.

[167] Notably in *Saadi v Italy* [GC] App no 37201/06, ECHR 2008-II, para 69, *James, Wells, and Lee v UK* App nos 25119/09, 57715/09, and 57877/09, 18 Sept 2012, paras 192–95.

[168] See eg *Saadi v Italy* [GC] App no 37201/06, ECHR 2008-II, para 69; *Bozano v France*, 18 Dec 1986, Series A no 111, paras 59–60; *Čonka v Belgium* App no 51564/99, ECHR 2002-I, paras 40–42.

[169] See *O'Hara v UK* App no 37555/97, ECHR 2001-X, paras 34–35; *Bouamar v Belgium*, 29 Feb 1988, Series A no 129, paras 50 and 52; *Winterwerp v Netherlands*, 24 Oct 1979, Series A no 33, para 39; *Lukanov v Bulgaria*, 20 Mar 1997, Reports 1997-II.

[170] See eg *Aerts v Belgium*, 30 July 1998, *Reports* 1998-V, para 46; *Brand v Netherlands* App no 49902/99, 11 May 2004, para 62; *M v Germany* App no 19359/04, ECHR 2009-VI, para 128; *Grosskopf v Germany* App no 24478/03, 21 Oct 210, para 51.

> the detention of an individual is such a serious measure that it is only justified where other, less severe measures have been considered and found to be insufficient to safeguard the individual or public interest which might require that the person concerned be detained. That means that it does not suffice that the deprivation of liberty is in conformity with national law; it must also be necessary in the circumstances.[171]

The situation in the context of Article 5(1)(a) ECHR is quite different. At issue here is whether the detention of the person was lawful, not whether their conviction (or sentence) was lawful.[172] A period of detention will, in principle, be lawful if it is based on the decision of a court.[173] In this regard, the ECtHR has also referred to the fact that 'the Convention respects the principle of the finality of judgments, which itself guarantees legal certainty, a principle enshrined in the rule of law'.[174] The fact that the sentence was imposed following a conviction by a competent court provides the safeguard against arbitrariness, in that the conviction provides the rational connection between the interference (the sentence of imprisonment) and the purpose (punishment of crime). This means that 'a flawed conviction' will render 'a detention unlawful (only) if it is the result of a flagrant denial of justice'.[175] This was considered to be the case in *Ilaşcu*, in which the ECtHR held that as none of the applicants had been convicted by a 'court',[176] the sentence of imprisonment could not be 'regarded as "lawful detention" ordered "in accordance with a procedure prescribed by law"'.[177] In *Tsirlis*, the ECtHR noted that the court's findings so blatantly ignored national law as to render the detention arbitrary.[178] This all makes it clear that Article 5(1)(a) ECHR does not contain any sort of subsidiarity requirement or a principle of parsimony[179] in the context of decisions to resort to the imposition of a sentence of imprisonment. As we have seen, the ECtHR refers to the purposes of the sentence as encompassing 'punishment, deterrence, public protection and rehabilitation'.[180] The diversity in this regard poses

171 *Stanev v Bulgaria* App no 36760/06, ECHR 2012, para 143; *Witold Litwa v Poland* App no 26629/95, ECHR 2000-III, para 78.

172 *Radu v Germany* App no 20084/07, 16 May 2013, para 88.

173 *Ladent v Poland* App no 11036/03, 18 March 2008, para 45.

174 *Radu v Germany* App no 20084/07, 16 May 2013, para 117.

175 *Ilaşcu and Others v Moldova and* Russia [GC] App no 48787/99, ECHR 2004-VII, para 461; see also *Tsirlis and Kouloumpas v Greece*, 29 May 1997, Reports 1997-III, para 57.

176 The importance of the role of the court in setting the sentence is discussed in more detail in Ch 5.

177 *Ilaşcu and Others v Moldova and* Russia [GC] App no 48787/99, ECHR 2004-VII, para 461.

178 *Tsirlis and Kouloumpas v Greece*, 29 May 1997, Reports 1997-III, para 57.

179 See on this principle RE Barkow, *Prisoners of Politics: Breaking the Cycle of Mass Incarceration* (Cambridge, MA: Harvard University Press 2019).

180 *Vinter and Others v UK* [GC] App nos 66069/09, 130/10, and 3896/10, ECHR 2013-III, para 111.

difficulties for any examination of the necessity of the imposition of a prison sentence: 'the issue of effectiveness is complicated by the multiple objectives that the sentence of imprisonment is designed to achieve.'[181]

The ECtHR has held, though, that the requirement that detention not be arbitrary implies the need for a clear connection 'between the ground of detention relied upon and the detention in question'.[182] In the majority of criminal cases, this requirement will clearly be met. The offender will be deprived of their liberty following conviction for the purposes of punishment. Some issues have arisen, however, in the context of long and indeterminate sentences of imprisonment, due to the suggestion that the continuing detention is no longer based on the original reasons for the detention as set out in the sentencing decision.

2. Rational Connection between the Reasons for the Imposition of the Sentence and the Continued Detention ('*after* conviction by a competent court')

Issues concerning the connection between the ground of detention relied upon and the nature of the detention in question have been particularly evident in the context of cases involving release on licence and subsequent recall to prison.[183] In some early cases concerning indefinite prison sentences, the applicants sought to argue that the reasons given for their continued detention after a lengthy period of imprisonment and in particular the 'lack of any connection between those reasons and the punitive purpose of the initial conviction' violated Article 5 ECHR.[184] They argued that beyond 'a punitive period' the continued detention of a life prisoner had to be justified by considerations of dangerousness and public safety.[185] This has been accepted by

[181] D van Zyl Smit, *UN Handbook on Basic Principles and Promising Alternatives to Prison* (New York, NY: UN 2007) 7. Some purposes are easier to measure empirically than others. Recent empirical studies have called into question, for instance, the effectiveness of sentences of imprisonment in terms of preventing reoffending. A Dutch study on prisons and reoffending has demonstrated, for instance, that the imposition of prison sentences is not an effective way to reduce crime. See in particular many important studies by the Prison Project run by Paul Nieuwbeerta at Leiden University, including: H Wermink and others, 'The Effects of Punishment on Criminal Behavior' in C Damboeanu (ed), *Sociological Studies on Imprisonment: A European Perspective* (Bucharest: Tritonic, 2016) 115–48; H Wermink and others, 'Short-term Effects of Imprisonment Length on Recidivism in the Netherlands' (2018) 64 *Crime & Delinquency* 1057–93. Similarly, the potential or likelihood of rehabilitation might be studied rationally. In an opinion piece for *Time* magazine *Lauren-Brooke Eisen and Inimai Chettiar* of NYU Law School, for instance, suggested that '25% of prisoners (364,000 people), almost all non-violent, lower-level offenders, would be better served by alternatives to incarceration such as treatment, community service, or probation'. L-B Eisen and I Chettiar, '39% of Prisoners Should Not Be in Prison', *Time*, 9 Dec 2016, available at <https://time.com/4596081/incarceration-report/> (accessed 15 Apr 2021).

[182] *James, Wells, and Lee v UK* App nos 25119/09, 57715/09, and 57877/09, 18 Sept 2012, para 195.

[183] See eg *Van Droogenbroeck v Belgium*, 24 June 1982, Series A no 50, para 40.

[184] *Léger v France* App no 19324/02, 11 Apr 2006, para 68.

[185] ibid relying on *Stafford v UK* [GC] App no 46295/99, ECHR 2002-IV.

the ECtHR, which has held that, '[o]nce the punishment element of the sentence … has been satisfied, the grounds for the continued detention … must be considerations of risk and dangerousness', although such considerations must be 'associated with the objectives of the original sentence'. In addition, the element of dangerousness is susceptible by its very nature to change with the passage of time.[186]

Similarly, in *James, Lee, and Wells*, the ECtHR stressed that:

> in circumstances where a decision not to release or to re-detain a prisoner was based on grounds that were inconsistent with the objectives of the initial decision by the sentencing court, or on an assessment that was unreasonable in terms of those objectives, a detention that was lawful at the outset could be transformed into a deprivation of liberty that was arbitrary.[187]

In this case, it considered the relevance of mandatory sentencing provisions in the context of Article 5 ECHR and held that while restrictions on judicial discretion 'did not per se render any ensuing detention arbitrary and therefore incompatible' with Article 5 ECHR, such restrictions were nevertheless relevant in the determination of whether the applicant's detention was to be considered arbitrary.[188]

The applicants had all been sentenced to a period of imprisonment for public protection (IPP), essentially indeterminate sentences of imprisonment designed to 'protect the public from serious offenders whose crimes did not merit a life sentence'.[189] The sentence provided for a minimum term (tariff) to be set, which the offender had to serve in prison. After the expiry of this period, the offender was able to apply to the Parole Board for release. If the Parole Board was satisfied that the detention was no longer necessary for the protection of the public then the offender was to be released on supervised licence for a period of at least ten years. If release was refused, the offender had to wait one year before reapplying for release. The applicants complained that they were not able to counter the assumption that they posed a risk to the public because of the lack of availability of appropriate treatment and assessment measures. Similar issues to those arising in the context of Article 3 ECHR are visible in the ECtHR's case law on Article 5 ECHR.

[186] ibid.

[187] *James, Wells, and Lee v UK* App nos 25119/09, 57715/09, and 57877/09, 18 Sept 2012.

[188] ibid para 204.

[189] UK Government, IPP Factsheet, available at <https://www.justice.gov.uk/downloads/legislation/bills-acts/legal-aid-sentencing/ipp-factsheet.pdf> (accessed 15 Apr 2021).

The applicant James had been sentenced in September 2005 to a punishment part of two years for unlawful wounding with intent. He was released on licence in March 2008. The applicant Wells was sentenced in November 2005 to a tariff of twelve months for robbery; he was released on licence in December 2009 but recalled to custody in February 2010 and was still in prison when the ECtHR issued its judgment in September 2012.[190] The applicant Lee was sentenced in April 2005 to a tariff of nine months for criminal damage. He was released in July 2011. All three applicants spent long periods of time in prison following the expiry of the tariff. The Court of Appeal determined that the 'detention of the applicants would cease to be justified only when the stage was reached that it was no longer necessary for the protection of the public that they be confined' or following the lapse of a long period 'without a meaningful review of this question that their detention became disproportionate or arbitrary'.[191]

The ECtHR accepted that the detention was still based in the sense of Article 5(1)(a) ECHR on the 'conviction by a competent court', even after the expiry of the punishment part of the sentence, noting that there was a sufficient causal connection between the conviction and the applicant's post-tariff detention. As long as the preventative detention is in accordance with national law and provided for in the sentencing decision of the court, then it will fall to be considered as detention 'after conviction by a competent court'.[192]

The ECtHR has stressed here the importance of a legal basis for 'subsequent' or 'post-tariff' preventative detention. In the absence of a legal basis, this continued detention will no longer be based on Article 5(1)(a) ECHR.[193] In *M v Germany*, for instance, the ECtHR held that the preventive detention of the applicant beyond the ten-year sentence imposed by the sentencing court was no longer based on the conviction of the court and did not fall within Article 5(1)(a) ECHR.[194] In such cases, the question arises then whether someone is being punished twice for the same conduct.[195] The ECtHR has accepted, however, that continued detention might well fall under Article 5(1)(e) ECHR. In *Ilnseher*, for instance, the ECtHR accepted that the subsequent detention of an

[190] *James, Wells, and Lee v UK* App nos 25119/09, 57715/09, and 57877/09, 18 Sept 2012, para 73.

[191] *The Secretary of State for Justice v Brett James* [2008] EWCA Civ 30, per Lord Phillips of Worth Matravers CJ, para 72.

[192] *James, Wells, and Lee v UK* App nos 25119/09, 57715/09, and 57877/09, 18 Sept 2012, para 197. See also *Van Droogenbroeck v Belgium*, 24 June 1982, Series A no 50, paras 33–42; *Eriksen v Norway*, 27 May 1997, Reports 1997-III para 78; *M v Germany* App no 19359/04, ECHR 2009-VI, para 96; *Grosskopf v Germany* App no 24478/03, 21 Oct 2010, para 47.

[193] *M v Germany* App no 19359/04, ECHR 2009-VI, para 101.

[194] ibid para 101.

[195] See L Parein, 'Exécution des Sanctions: La Réserve de Dangerosité Met-elle en Danger le Principe *ne bis in idem*?' (2020) *Neue Zeitschrift für Kriminologie und Kriminalpolitik* 48, 57–59.

applicant following expiry of a prison sentence in a therapeutic placement was to be regarded as falling under Article 5(1)(e) ECHR, even though in doing so it seemed to accept that those suffering from abnormal personality disorders not amounting to mental illness were to be considered as 'persons of unsound mind' for the purposes of Article 5(1)(e) ECHR.[196] This broad approach seems to allow also for the preventative detention of people with 'abnormal personalities' in the absence of the commission of a crime.

Of particular importance in the context of sentencing is consideration of when the detention might be said to be or to become unlawful, at the point of imposition of the sentence or at a later stage.[197] In *James, Wells, and Lee*, the continued detention of the applicant was held to be arbitrary, but it is important to note that this conclusion was based more on the nature of the detention rather than the sentence itself. For our purposes, the ECtHR made it clear in *James, Wells, and Lee* that the initial detention and by extension the sentence of imprisonment were lawful and that it was only at some later point in time that the reasonableness of the detention could be called into question. In this sense, this case is essentially concerned with the nature of the enforcement of the sentence rather than the sentencing decision itself for the purposes of Article 5(1) ECHR.

It is questionable, though, whether the imposition of indeterminate sentences, with comparatively short punishment parts, are compatible with the requirement of Article 7(1) ECHR. Assuming a sentence is imposed for reasons which are, at least in part, punitive, the offender should be entitled to know from the outset the maximum length of the sentence. Failure to ensure clarity at the outset of the length not just of the punitive part of the sentence but the overall length of the sentence will give rise to questions about the lawfulness of the detention. In cases involving life imprisonment, the maximum sentence is life. In all other cases, legality will require that a maximum sentence is stipulated. Failure to do so gives rise to real concerns about the legal basis for the detention and in particular whether it can be said to be based on the conviction.[198] If a sentence of imprisonment is not necessary as a response to a

[196] *Ilnseher v Germany* [GC] App nos 10211/12 and 27505/14, 14 Dec 2018, para 160.

[197] *James, Wells, and Lee v UK* App nos 25119/09, 57715/09, and 57877/09, 18 Sept 2012, para 209: 'in cases concerning indeterminate sentences of imprisonment for the protection of the public, a real opportunity for rehabilitation is a necessary element of any part of the detention which is to be justified solely by reference to public protection.' These sentences have now been abolished, although this had no impact on those already sentenced. There are thus a considerable number of prisoners still in prison on account of having received an IPP sentence. For discussion see V Bettinson and G Dingwall, 'Challenging the Ongoing Injustice of Imprisonment for Public Protection: *James, Wells and Lee v The United Kingdom*' (2013) 76 *Modern Law Review* 1094.

[198] This issue is discussed in more detail in Ch 2.

particular crime, there is a danger that it is ordered not as a punishment but for other reasons such as the prevention of social dangerousness.[199]

3. The Limited Scope of Review in Article 5(1)(a) ECHR

Article 5(1)(a) ECHR expressly allows for individuals to be 'lawfully' deprived of their liberty following a conviction by a competent court. The requirement that detention be free from arbitrariness is inherent in Article 5(1)(a) ECHR and gives rise to a measure of review, as is clear in cases such as *James, Wells, and Lee*. In this sense, it might be argued that cases such as *Ilnseher* involve a circumvention of the ordinary principles governing detention and thus that detention under such circumstances ought to be classed as arbitrary.[200] Nevertheless, there is virtually no scope in the context of Article 5(1)(a) ECHR for review of the lawfulness of the sentence of imprisonment itself, provided that it is imposed by a court in accordance national law. The provision does not contain any right to a 'proportionate' sentence of imprisonment. Nor does it allow for consideration of whether a sentence of imprisonment is disproportionate to the aim followed by the imposition of a deprivation of liberty. This emphasizes the formal character of the guarantee. Here, the aim of the interference with liberty is simply punishment. Article 5(1)(a) ECHR does not allow for consideration of the purpose or necessity of that punishment.

Difficult questions arise in the context of indeterminate sentences or measures, such as the IPP sentence in *James, Wells, and Lee*, which are not imposed in the form of, or in conjunction with,[201] a sentence of *life* imprisonment. Here, real questions arise as to the lawfulness of these sentences in the sense of their connection to the criminal conviction. If a sentencing court imposes an indefinite sentence with a short punishment part, questions arise as to whether the detention after expiry of the tariff can really be regarded as still based on the criminal conviction or whether it should be understood as preventative detention. From the perspective of Article 5(1)(a) ECHR, the continued detention is still technically a deprivation of liberty 'after conviction by a competent court' as the sentencing judgment expressly allows for the imposition of the sentence. This means that although the detention might at some point become arbitrary,

[199] See MM Feeley and J Simon, 'Actuarial Justice: The Emerging New Criminal Law' in P O'Malley (ed), *Crime and the Risk Society* (New York, NY: Ashgate 1998) 449; CS Streiker, 'Foreword: The Limits of the Preventive State' (1998) 88 *Journal of Criminal Law and Criminology* 771.

[200] See for a forceful argument to this effect the dissenting opinion of Judge Albuquerque, attached to the judgment in *Ilnseher v Germany* [GC] App nos 10211/12 and 27505/14, 14 Dec 2018.

[201] In Switzerland, those who are convicted of serious criminal offences can be subjected, in addition to their sentence, to a custodial measure allowing for their indefinite detention on the basis of their dangerousness, Art 64 para 1 of the Swiss Criminal Code.

sentences such as the IPP sentence cannot be considered incompatible with Article 5(1)(a) ECHR, even though detention after the expiry of the punishment part seems to constitute detention based on social dangerousness rather than on culpability for the offence.[202] This demonstrates clearly the fact that Article 5(1)(a) ECHR does not provide any significant restraints from proportionality on the state in its imposition of punishment.

D. Proportionality and Articles 8, 10, and 11 ECHR

1. Introduction

The ECtHR's reluctance to consider sentences as violating the proportionality requirement in Article 3 ECHR and Article 5 ECHR can be contrasted with its comparative activism in relation to its assessment of the proportionality of interferences with other rights, particularly those guaranteed by Articles 8, 10, and 11 ECHR. These guarantees share a similar structure in that they first set out the right to be protected (private life, expression, assembly) before regulating the circumstances under which interferences with the rights will be considered legitimate. Restrictions on the rights are permitted in the interests of the 'prevention of disorder or crime' providing that they are prescribed in law and considered to be 'necessary in a democratic society'. This means that the reasons adduced by the national authorities to justify the interference must be both 'relevant and sufficient' and that the measure taken was 'proportionate to the legitimate aims pursued'.[203]

The ECtHR's proportionality test requires consideration of whether the aim pursued was sufficiently important to justify the interference with the right, whether the measures taken could be said to be rationally connected to the aim pursued, whether a less intrusive measure could have been used without unacceptably compromising the aim followed, and whether the impact of the infringement of the right is disproportionate to the benefit likely to be achieved by the measure.[204] In determining the proportionality of the interference with these rights and freedoms, the ECtHR has frequently held that 'the nature and

[202] It is questionable, however, whether it is compatible with the principle of legality in Art 7(1) ECHR, which states that the maximum punishment that can be imposed is that which is determined in accordance with an offender's culpability for the commission of a specific criminal offence. It is legality, though, rather than proportionality which is at issue here, see further Ch 2.

[203] *Cumpănă and Mazăre v Romania* [GC] App no 33348/96, ECHR 2004-XI, para 90 citing *Chauvy and Others v France* App no 64915/01, ECHR 2004-VI, para 70.

[204] For an interesting comparison of the ECtHR's proportionality test with that of the CJEU see *Bank Mellat (Appellant) v Her Majesty's Treasury (Respondent) (No 2)* [2013] UKSC 39 per Lord Reed, dissenting.

severity of the penalty imposed' are among the factors which are to be taken into account.[205]

2. Private Life and Proportionality

The ECtHR has on occasion suggested that the criminalization and prosecution of certain activities might violate Article 8 ECHR.[206] Even if the designation of an act or omission as criminal is recognized as legitimate, the ECtHR has also insisted that the sentence imposed must not be disproportionate to the right to private life guaranteed by Article 8 ECHR.[207] The Article 8 ECHR case law is sparse and underdeveloped, particularly when contrasted with the case law on Articles 10 and 11 ECHR. In *Laskey, Jaggard, and Brown*, for instance, the applicants argued that their sentence for assault and wounding in the course of consensual sado-masochistic activities between adults was disproportionate to the aims pursued. The ECtHR disagreed, holding that measures could not be considered disproportionate.[208]

In *Lactus v Switzerland*, the ECtHR considered whether the imposition of a sentence on an applicant for begging constituted a disproportionate interference with her Article 8 ECHR rights.[209] The applicant had been fined 500 CHF (to be replaced by five days' imprisonment in event of non-payment) in pursuance of a cantonal law criminalizing begging.[210] She was unable to pay the fine and spent five days in Champ-Dollon prison in Geneva. The ECtHR held that this constituted an interference with the applicant's right to private life, that this interference had a basis in law, and that it pursued a legitimate aim.[211]

In considering whether the punishment was necessary in a democratic society, the ECtHR noted that the provision set out a very general prohibition on begging, '*[c]elui qui aura mendié sera puni de l'amende*', and that such provisions required not just particular justification, but also that the courts were able to weigh up the various interests at issue.[212] The ECtHR indicated that the law did not seem to afford sufficient scope to allow the judges to conduct a

[205] See *Ceylan v Turkey* [GC] App no 23556/94, ECHR 1999-IV, para 37; *Tammer v Estonia* App no 41205/98, ECHR 2001-I, para 69; *Skałka v Poland* App no 43425/98, 27 May 2003, para 38.

[206] See eg in the context of Art 8 ECHR *Stubing v Germany* App no 43547/08, 12 Apr 2012, para 55. See also eg in the context of the criminalization of homosexuality *ADT v UK* App no 35765/97, 31 July 2000, paras 36–39; *Dudgeon v UK*, 22 Oct 1981 Series A no 45, para 41; *Norris v Ireland*, 26 Oct 1988, Series A no 142; *Modinos v Cyprus*, 22 Apr 1993, Series A no 259.

[207] *Laskey, Jaggard and Brown v UK* App nos 21627/93, 21628/93, and 21974/93, 19 Feb 1997, paras 47–49.

[208] ibid.

[209] *Lacatus v Switzerland* App no 14065/15, 19 Jan 2021.

[210] Art 11A de la loi pénale genevoise. *Lacatus v Switzerland* App no 14065/15, 19 Jan 2021, para 91.

[211] ibid paras 92–98.

[212] ibid para 101.

proper balancing exercise and in particular to take account of the vulnerable nature of the offender. It did not reach a conclusion on this matter, however, as it in any event found a violation of Article 8 ECHR. It noted that the applicant was extremely vulnerable, did not receive benefits, and that begging was essentially a means of survival. In addition, the sanction was significant and in view of her situation it was clear that she would not be able to pay the fine and that in her case a sentence of imprisonment was inevitable. The ECtHR noted that less restrictive measures would be likely to be just as effective and held that the punishment imposed on the applicant was not proportionate to the aim of fighting organized crime or protecting the rights of residents, business owners, or passers-by. Instead, the applicant had been punished for conduct, despite the fact that she had been in a situation in which she had no other means of survival and was essentially forced to beg in order to survive. In this context, the punishment violated Article 8 ECHR.[213]

3. Freedom of Expression and Proportionality

There is clear potential for conflict to arise between the right to freedom of expression and sentences imposed following a criminal conviction. The right to freedom of expression in Article 10 ECHR does not apply only to 'information or ideas that are favourably received or regarded as inoffensive or as a matter of indifference, but also to those that offend, shock or disturb. Such are the demands of pluralism, tolerance and broadmindedness without which there is no "democratic society"'.[214] The majority of the cases concerning alleged violations of the right to freedom of expression on account of disproportionate sentences have concerned criminal convictions for defamation or insult.[215] It is important to note here at the outset the close relationship between the issue of criminalization and the determination of the proportionality of the sentence. Restrictions on the extent of the sentence which may be imposed necessarily have the potential to call into question the legitimacy of the criminal offence itself. In *Lindon*, for instance, the Grand Chamber ruled that the criminalization of defamation cannot in itself be considered disproportionate to the aim pursued (the protection of the rights and reputation of others).[216] A number of judges, though, were not convinced and questioned 'whether it

[213] ibid 99–117.

[214] *Handyside v UK*, 7 Dec 1976, Series A no 24, para 49.

[215] Other crimes include making false accusations, privacy violations, and contempt of court.

[216] See eg *Lindon, Otchakovsky-Laurens and July v France* [GC] App nos 21279/02 and 36448/02, ECHR 2007-IV, para 59: thirteen votes to four. See also *Radio France and Others v France* App no 53984/00, ECHR 2004-II, para 40; *Lindon, Otchakovsky-Laurens and July v France* [GC] App nos 21279/02 and 36448/02, ECHR 2007-IV, para 47; *Długołęcki v Poland* App no 23806/03, 24 Feb 2009, para 47.

is still justified, in the twenty-first century, for damage to reputation through the press, media or other forms of communication to entail punishment in the criminal courts'.[217]

For now, at least,[218] the contracting states are entitled to criminalize speech and other forms of expression, but the ECtHR has increasingly placed tight limits on the nature of the penalties which they are entitled to impose. It is useful to consider the case law of the ECtHR by focusing on proportionality of the nature and extent of the penalty imposed. The ECtHR has adopted a particularly restrictive approach to the imposition of prison sentences.

a) Proportionality of Sentences of Imprisonment

The ECtHR has called into question the proportionality of the imposition of prison sentences, even if suspended or conditional in nature, for defamation or insult and frequently refers to a resolution of the Parliamentary Assembly of the Council of Europe on the abolition of prison sentences for defamation.[219] The resolution places particular emphasis on the protection of journalists, but is broad in the sense that it calls for prison sentences to be abolished for defamation offences, irrespective of whether these are committed by private persons or journalists and even if the statements or allegations are inaccurate, providing they were made in the public interest and in good faith.[220] The ECtHR has had to consider the compatibility of sentences imposed for defamation with the protections afforded by Article 10 ECHR in a number of cases.

In *Cumpănă and Mazăre*, for instance, the applicants were journalists who were charged with insult[221] and defamation[222] after writing an article suggesting that the deputy mayor and his legal advisor had unlawfully awarded local government contracts to a private company to tow and impound illegally parked vehicles. The article was accompanied by a cartoon showing a man

[217] See dissenting opinion of Rozakis, Brazta, and Tulkins attached to the judgment in *Lindon Otchakovsky-Laurens and July v France* [GC] App nos 21279/02 and 36448/02, ECHR 2007-IV: '[I]t may also be questioned whether it is still justified, in the twenty-first century, for damage to reputation through the press, media or other forms of communication to entail punishment in the criminal courts.'

[218] The Council of Europe has been advocating strongly for the decriminalization of defamation. See Resolution 1577 (2007) *Towards Decriminalisation of Defamation*, Parliamentary Assembly of the Council of Europe adopted on 4 Oct 2007.

[219] ibid.

[220] ibid para 7.

[221] Art 205 of the Romanian Criminal Code: 'Anyone who tarnishes the reputation or honour of another through words, gestures or any other means shall be liable to imprisonment for between one month and two years or to a fine', see para 55 of the GC judgment.

[222] Art 206 of the Romanian Criminal Code: 'Anyone who makes any statement or allegation in public concerning a particular person which, if true, would render that person liable to a criminal, administrative or disciplinary penalty or expose them to public opprobrium shall be liable to imprisonment for between three months and three years or to a fine', see para 55 of the GC judgment.

and a woman arm in arm, carrying a bag full of banknotes.[223] The defamation charge related to the fact that in the article the applicants had suggested that the judge was either ignorant of the law or that she had accepted bribes. The insult charge related to the cartoon and accompanying text and the suggestion that those depicted were conducting an extramarital relationship. The journalists were convicted and sentenced to three months' imprisonment for insult and seven months' imprisonment for defamation, disqualified from exercising various civil rights, disqualified from working as journalists for a year, and ordered to pay one of the victims €2033 in non-pecuniary damages.[224] They subsequently received a presidential pardon which meant that they did not have to serve the sentence of imprisonment and which resulted in their civil rights being restored.[225]

The Chamber voted by a majority of five votes to two that Article 10 ECHR had not been violated. It held that 'the applicants' conviction for insult on account of the cartoon accompanying the article, ... was based on relevant grounds, namely the protection of [the judge's] reputation and of the authority of the judiciary'[226] and that the applicants had 'overstepped the limits of acceptable criticism'.[227] In holding that the sentence was not disproportionate, it was influenced by the fact that although the penalty imposed on the applicants had been 'harsh', they had not actually had to serve their custodial sentence. It also noted that 'the penalty by which the applicants were prohibited from practising their profession had no practical consequences' in that both applicants had continued to work as journalists.[228]

The case was referred to the Grand Chamber which took a radically different approach, holding unanimously that there had been a violation of Article 10 ECHR. The ECtHR noted that 'the domestic authorities were entitled to consider it necessary to restrict the exercise of the applicants' right to freedom of expression and that the applicants' conviction for insult and defamation accordingly met a "pressing social need" '.[229] It was not convinced, however, that the conviction and sanction were proportionate to the aims pursued. It noted, referring to the chilling effect on the exercise of journalistic freedom,[230] that the court had to exercise 'the utmost caution where the measures taken or

223 *Cumpănă and Mazăre v Romania* [GC] App no 33348/96, ECHR 2004-XI, paras 20–21.
224 ibid para 37.
225 ibid para 50.
226 *Cumpănă and Mazăre v Romania* (chamber) App no 33348/96, 10 June 2003, para 56.
227 ibid para 57.
228 ibid para 59.
229 *Cumpănă and Mazăre v Romania* [GC] App no 33348/96, ECHR 2004-XI, para 110.
230 See further R O'Fathaigh, 'Article 10 and the Chilling Effect Principle' (2013) 6 European Human Rights Law Review 304.

sanctions imposed by the national authorities are such as to dissuade the press from taking part in the discussion of matters of legitimate public concern' and the sanctions imposed were 'undoubtedly very severe'.[231] It held that while 'sentencing is in principle a matter for the national courts ... the imposition of a prison sentence for a press offence will be compatible with journalists' freedom of expression as guaranteed by Article 10 of the Convention only in exceptional circumstances'.[232] It held that 'the circumstances of the instant case—a classic case of defamation of an individual in the context of a debate on a matter of legitimate public interest—present no justification whatsoever for the imposition of a prison sentence'.[233]

The ECtHR has come to the same conclusion based on analogous reasoning in a number of subsequent cases. In *Mahmudov*, for instance, the five-month sentence of imprisonment imposed on the applicants—an editor and a journalist—for insult and defamation following the publication of an article which suggested that a well-known agricultural expert and member of parliament was involved in the misappropriation of state funds for agricultural research was held to be disproportionate.[234] The ECtHR held that the courts had failed 'to provide any relevant reasons for the applicant's conviction on charges of threat of terrorism and incitement to ethnic hostility', that the gravity of the interference with the applicant's Article 10 ECHR rights was 'exacerbated by the particular severity of the penalties imposed on the applicant', and that the 'circumstances of the case disclose no justification for the imposition of a prison sentence on the applicant'.[235] Similarly, in *Sallusti*, a prison sentence imposed on the editor-in-chief of *Libero*, an Italian daily, following a conviction for publishing an article which falsely reported that a 13-year-old girl had been forced by her parents and the guardianship judge to have an abortion, was held to be disproportionate. This was deemed to be the case even though the ECtHR noted that the article was inaccurate and had seriously infringed the reputation

[231] *Cumpănă and Mazăre v Romania* [GC] App no 33348/96, ECHR 2004-XI, para 112.

[232] Referring to hate speech or incitement to violence. See eg *Feridun Yazar v Turkey* App no 42713/98, 23 Sept 2004, para 27 and *Sürek and Özdemir v Turkey* [GC] App nos 23927/94 and 24277/94, 8 July 1999, para 63.

[233] *Cumpănă and Mazăre v Romania* [GC] App no 33348/96, ECHR 2004-XI, para 116.

[234] *Mahmudov v Azerbeijan* App no 35877/04, 18 Dec 2008. See also *Fatullayev v Azerbaijan* App no 40984/07, 22 Apr 2010: chief editor of a newspaper was convicted in a first set of proceedings of publishing an article which defamed and falsely accused Azerbaijani soldiers of committing crimes in the Nagorno-Karabakh region and sentenced to thirty months' imprisonment. In a second set of proceedings, he was convicted of terrorist activities and inciting ethnic hostility for publishing an article discussing the consequences of Azerbaijan's support for an 'anti-Iranian' resolution of the United Nations and was sentenced to eight years' imprisonment for threat of terrorism and to three years' imprisonment for inciting ethnic hostility, which resulted, when taken together with earlier sentences, in a combined sentence of eight years and six months' imprisonment.

[235] *Mahmudov v Azerbeijan* App no 35877/04, 18 Dec 2008, paras 127–28.

and privacy rights of those involved.[236] It reiterated its position that there was 'no justification for the imposition of a prison sentence' and that the fact that the applicant had not actually had to serve the sentence was irrelevant.[237]

The imposition of prison sentences for speech offences may well violate Article 10 ECHR, even if those involved do not enjoy the special protection of the press.[238] In *Mariya Akekhina and Others v Russia*, the imposition of a prison sentence on the applicants was ruled to be disproportionate. The applicants were members of a punk band and had attempted to perform their song 'Punk Prayer—Virgin Mary, Drive Putin Away' from the altar of Christ the Saviour Cathedral in Moscow. They were convicted and sentenced to one year and eleven months in prison. In describing the punishment as 'very severe in relation to the actions in question', the ECtHR held that 'the applicants' actions did not disrupt any religious services, nor did they cause any injuries to people inside the cathedral or any damage to church property'.[239] The ECtHR also noted that proceedings were not instituted against the applicants on an earlier occasion for performing their song in a different church in Moscow. The ECtHR held that while a response to the applicant's action might have been warranted on account of the obligation to protect the rights of others, 'the domestic courts failed to adduce "relevant and sufficient" reasons to justify the criminal conviction and prison sentence imposed on the applicants and the sanctions were not proportionate to the legitimate aim pursued'.[240]

The ECtHR has also held in the context of those who are not journalists that in determining the proportionality of the interference, the fact that the prison sentence was suspended or conditional in nature was irrelevant. In *Marchenko v Ukraine*, the applicant, who was a teacher and the head of the school branch of a trade union, was accused of falsely accusing the head teacher of the school of abuse of office and misappropriation of funds and for organizing a protest during which the demonstrators displayed offensive placards stating that the teacher had misappropriated public funds. He was convicted of defamation

[236] *Sallusti v Italy* App no 22350/13, 7 Mar 2019, para 53.

[237] ibid para 62, 'while such an act of clemency dispenses convicted persons from having to serve their sentence, it does not expunge their conviction' citing *Cumpănă and Mazăre v Romania* [GC] App no 33348/96, ECHR 2004-XI, para 116, and *Marchenko v Ukraine* App no 4063/04, 19 Feb 2009, para 52.

[238] The ECtHR has often held that journalists acting in their 'vital role as public watchdog' enjoy particular protection under Art 10 ECHR, see eg *Goodwin v UK*, 27 March 1996, Reports 1996-II, 500, para 39, and *Bladet Tromsø and Stensaas v Norway* [GC] App no 21980/93, ECHR 1999-III, para 59: 'One factor of particular importance for the Court's determination of the present case is the vital role of "public watchdog" which the press performs in a democratic society.'

[239] *Mariya Alekhina and Others v Russia* App no 38004/12, 17 July 2018, para 215.

[240] ibid para 228.

by making false accusations[241] and sentenced to one year's imprisonment suspended for one year and a fine of 200 Ukrainian hryvnas (UAH).[242] The ECtHR was not convinced in view of the sanctions imposed—even though the prison sentence had been suspended—that the interference was proportionate to the aim pursued.[243] Repeating similar statements made in the context of journalists, it held that the case was 'a classic case of defamation of an individual in the context of a debate on a matter of public interest' and that it 'presented no justification for the imposition of a prison sentence', which would 'by its very nature, ... inevitably have a chilling effect on public discussion'.[244]

Similarly, in *Mariapori*, the imposition of a prison sentence on a tax expert acting as an expert witness for the defence in a case involving tax fraud was ruled disproportionate. While giving evidence in court, she had challenged the tax inspection report drawn up by two inspectors, arguing that they had intentionally overstated the defendant's taxable income by €500,000. She later wrote a book in which she referenced the case and stated that one of the tax inspectors had knowingly perjured herself and suggested that she was able to do so as she was married to a prosecutor. She was charged and convicted of aggravated defamation.[245] In relation to the statements made in the applicant's book, the ECtHR noted that it could be characterized as a 'polemical document or pamphlet attempting to contribute to a public debate'.[246] The ECtHR classified

[241] Art 125 para 3 of the Criminal Code: 'Defamation linked with an unfounded accusation of committing a grave offence shall be punishable by up to five years' imprisonment'.

[242] *Marchenko v Ukraine* App no 4063/04, 19 Feb 2009. The Court also ordered the applicant to pay the civil claimant UAH 1000 in non-pecuniary damages and UAH 100 in legal fees

[243] ibid para 51.

[244] ibid para 52.

[245] *Mariapori v Finland* App no 37751/07, 6 July 2010, para 24: Chapter 27, section 1, of the Penal Code, which was in force at the time when the events took place, read as follows: 'A person alleging, albeit not contrary to his or her better knowledge, that someone has committed an offence or other act which might make this person an object of contempt or might affect his or her trade or success, or who spreads a lie or a false insinuation about someone, is to be convicted of defamation and sentenced to imprisonment for at least one month and at most one year or to a fine of at least one hundred marks. If defamation is public or in a printed publication, in writing or through pictures, which the accused distributes or had distributed, the punishment is imprisonment of at least two months and at most two years or a fine of at least two hundred marks.' 25. Chapter 24 (531/2000), section 9, of the Penal Code, which was in force at the time of conviction, read as follows: 'A person who (1) spreads false information or a false insinuation about another person so that the act is conducive to causing damage or suffering to that person, or subjecting that person to contempt, or (2) makes a derogatory comment about another otherwise than in a manner referred to in subparagraph (1), shall be sentenced for defamation to a fine or to imprisonment for at most six months. Criticism that is directed at a person's activities in politics, business, public office, public position, science, art or in a comparable public position and which does not obviously overstep the limits of propriety does not constitute defamation referred to in paragraphs (1) and (2).' Chapter 24, section 10, of the Penal Code provides that if, in the defamation referred to in section 9, the offence is committed through the use of the mass media or otherwise by making the information or insinuation available to a large number of people, the offender shall be sentenced for aggravated defamation to a fine or to imprisonment for at most two years.

[246] *Mariapori v Finland* App no 37751/07, 6 July 2010, para 67.

the case again as a 'classic case of defamation of an individual in the context of a debate on an important matter of legitimate public interest, namely the actions of the tax authorities' and held that the circumstances of the case presented 'no justification whatsoever for the imposition of a prison sentence'. It noted that the fact that the prison sentence was conditional and that she did not have to spend any time in prison was irrelevant, holding that 'the criminal sanction and the accompanying obligation to pay compensation imposed on her by the national courts were manifestly disproportionate in their nature and severity, having regard to the legitimate aim pursued by the applicant's conviction for defamation'.[247]

The ECtHR noted that while sentencing was 'in principle a matter for the national courts', 'the imposition of a prison sentence for a defamation offence will be compatible with an applicant's right to freedom of expression as guaranteed by Article 10 of the Convention only in exceptional circumstances, notably where other fundamental rights have been seriously impaired, as, for example, in the case of hate speech or incitement to violence'.[248]

These cases demonstrate that the ECtHR has moved towards an understanding of the imposition of prison sentences for defamation or insult as incompatible with Article 10 ECHR, assuming there is no element of racial hatred or incitement to violence and irrespective of whether the sentence was suspended or conditional in nature. The extent of the ECtHR's proportionality analysis is somewhat restricted in that it does not engage in any detail in the consideration of the proportionality of the sentence in relation to the offence committed. As in the context of Article 3 ECHR, the ECtHR prefers to hold that the imposition of a particular type of sentence—here sentences of imprisonment—when imposed for certain crimes—notably speech crimes such as defamation or insult—will be disproportionate per se to the aim pursued.

b) Proportionality of Fines and Financial Penalties

The ECtHR's de facto prohibition on the imposition of prison sentences for defamation or insult, taken together with its reluctance to insist on the decriminalization of such offences, might lead to the assumption that it would take a more lenient approach to fines or financial penalties. In fact, this is not the case. Once again, it is useful to consider the position of journalists separately.

[247] ibid para 68.

[248] ibid para 67 citing *Cumpǎnǎ and Mazǎre v Romania* [GC] App no 33348/96, ECHR 2004-XI, para 115; *Feridun Yazar v Turkey* App no 42713/98, 23 Sept 2004, para 27; *Sürek and Özdemir v Turkey* [GC] App nos 23927/94 and 24277/94, 8 July 1999, para 63.

Even relatively minor fines imposed on journalists following convictions for defamation or insult are likely to result in a finding of a violation of Article 10 ECHR,[249] assuming that the statements are made in 'good faith',[250] in line with the principles of journalistic due diligence,[251] and do not constitute a 'gratuitous personal attack with pointlessly harmful comments'.[252]

In *Ziembinski*, the applicant, who was the editor of a newspaper, 'wrote a satirical article criticising the quail farming project endorsed by the local officials as a remedy to the problem of local unemployment'.[253] He was subsequently convicted of insult for referring to one of the officials as a 'numbskull', 'poser', and 'dim-witted official' and to two others as 'dull bosses' and sentenced to a fine of €2,630 and costs of €755. Although the local officials were not named, they were identifiable. The ECtHR held that 'the nature and severity of the penalties imposed are factors to be taken into account' in assessing the proportionality of the sentence, 'because they must not be such as to dissuade the press or others who engage in public debate from taking part in the discussion of matters of legitimate public concern'.[254] It suggested that the sentence was not proportionate, concluding that the domestic courts had not provided relevant and sufficient reasons to justify the applicant's conviction and sentence.[255] Similarly, in *Colaco Mestre*, the defamation conviction and imposition of a financial penalty (equivalent to eighty-six days of imprisonment) and damages of €3,990 on a journalist for discussing allegations of bribery of football referees was considered disproportionate. Although the reasons for the conviction were relevant (protection of reputation), they were not sufficient to permit the imposition of such sanctions.[256]

[249] See eg *Jersild v Denmark* [GC], 23 Sept 1994, Series A no 298, para 35; in *Lopes Gomes da Silva v Portugal* App no 37698/97, 28 Sept 2000, Reports 2000-X, the ECtHR noted that the fine was 'minor' but nevertheless held that 'what matters is not that the applicant was sentenced to a minor penalty, but that he was convicted at all'.

[250] See eg *Mihaiu v Romania* App no 42512/02, 4 Nov 2018 where the ECtHR was not convinced that the statements were made in good faith and found no violation of Art 10 ECHR. *Frisk and Jensen v Denmark* App no 19657/12, 5 Dec 2017: the conviction of the applicants for defamation and their sentence of ten day-fines of DKK 1,000 (totalling approximately €1,340) following a broadcast criticizing the treatment of cancer patients at the Copenhagen University Hospital was deemed justified as the allegations had been factually incorrect and had resulted in public mistrust in chemotherapy at the hospital.

[251] *Dorota Kania v Poland (no 2)* App no 44436/13, 4 Oct 2016: the imposition of a fine of €85 plus costs following a conviction for defamation was deemed proportionate because the journalist had not employed proper journalistic diligence when writing the articles in question.

[252] See eg *Katamadze v Georgia* (dec) App no 65857/01, 14 Feb 2006.

[253] *Ziembinski v Poland (no 2)* App no 1799/07, 5 July 2016.

[254] ibid para 46.

[255] ibid para 47.

[256] *Colaco Mestre and SIC v Portugal* App nos 11182/03 and 11319/03, 26 Apr 2007.

The ECtHR has also extended its approach beyond defamation and insult. In *Haldimann v Switzerland*, four journalists were convicted of privacy offences for recording the alleged malpractice of an insurance broker by way of a hidden camera.[257] The first three applicants were sentenced to twelve day-fines of CHF 350 (approximately €290), CHF 200 (approximately €160), and CHF 100 (approximately €80) respectively and the fourth applicant was given four day-fines of CHF 30. The penalties were all suspended for a probationary period of two years. The ECtHR, in considering the nature and severity of the sanction, noted that 'in some cases, a person's conviction in itself may be more important than the minor nature of the penalty imposed'. In the case at issue, 'although the pecuniary penalties of twelve day-fines for the first three applicants and four day-fines for the fourth applicant were relatively modest', it held that 'the sanction imposed by the criminal court may be liable to deter the media from expressing criticism'.[258]

Sufficiently strong reasons were found to exist for the imposition of sanctions in the cases of *Bédat v Switzerland*. In this case, a journalist had published documents in violation of provisions guaranteeing the confidentiality of the criminal investigation. Here the ECtHR held that the provisions were designed to protect the proper functioning of the judicial system and the right of the accused to a fair trial and respect for his private life. It noted that the offence of disclosing information 'covered by the secrecy of judicial investigations is punishable in all thirty Council of Europe member States whose legislation was studied in the present case'.[259] The ECtHR held that in such circumstances the sentence—a fine of CHF 4000—could not be considered to be disproportionate.[260]

The ECtHR has taken a less strict approach to fines imposed on private individuals with Article 10 ECHR. In *Janowski v Poland*, the applicant had noticed two municipal guards ordering street vendors to move on. The applicant intervened, taking issue with their actions, and in the course of the conversation, which was witnessed by several bystanders, he called the guards 'oafs' and 'dumb'. He was subsequently convicted of insulting the guards[261] and sentenced to a fine of PLZ 1,500,000—equivalent to one month's unemployment

[257] In violation of Art 179*bis* paras 1 and 2, Art 179ter para 1, and Art 179quater of the Criminal Code.
[258] *Haldimann v Switzerland* App no 21830/09, 24 Feb 2005, para 67 (references omitted).
[259] *Bédat v Switzerland* [GC] App no 56925/08, 29 Mar 2016, para 80.
[260] ibid para 81.
[261] Art 236 of the Criminal Code: 'Anyone who insults a civil servant . . . during and in connection with the carrying out of his official duties is liable to up to two years' imprisonment, to restriction of personal liberty or to a fine.'

benefit. The ECtHR held that while the applicant was a journalist, he was clearly acting as a private individual and thus the freedom of the press was not at issue. The applicant's conviction was based on the fact that he had insulted the guards—referred to by the ECtHR as an abusive and offensive verbal attack—and not due to the fact that he was critical of their actions.[262] The ECtHR consequently held that the interference was proportionate to the aim pursued.[263] A minority of the Grand Chamber disagreed. According to Judge Wildhaber, there was no 'pressing social need' for the fine as 'the applicant used only two moderately insulting words, in a spontaneous and lively discussion, to defend a position which was legally correct and in which he had no immediate personal interest, it was not "necessary in a democratic society" to fine him in order to "prevent disorder" '.[264] Nevertheless, the ECtHR's finding of a violation was based on the idea that the context was not one of public interest—not made in good faith.

In a subsequent case, *Raichenov v Bulgaria*, the applicant was convicted of insulting a high-ranking official, the deputy Prosecutor-General, and sentenced to a fine of BGN 3000 and a public reprimand. The ECtHR distinguished the facts from those in *Janowski*, noting that unlike in *Janowski*, 'where the municipal guards had been insulted in the street, while performing their policing duties, in front of numerous bystanders... the applicant's remark was made in front of a limited audience, at a meeting held behind closed doors. Thus, no press or other form of publicity was involved ... The negative impact, if any, of the applicant's words on [the victim's] reputation was therefore quite limited.'[265] It held that the applicant's sentence—a fine and a public reprimand—while being in the lower range of the possible penalties, was still a sentence under criminal law, registered in the applicant's criminal record.[266] It was not compatible with Article 10 ECHR.

When minor fines are at issue, the suggestion is that the imposition of any sentence would violate Article 10 ECHR and seems thus to call into question the legitimacy of the criminalization of the activity in the first place.

262 *Janowski v Poland* [GC] App no 25716/94, 21 Jan 1999, para 32.

263 ibid para 35.

264 ibid attached to the judgment.

265 *Raichenov v Bulgaria* App no 47579/99, 20 Apr 2006, para 48, citing *Nikula v Finland* App no 31611/96, ECHR 2002-II, para 52; *Yankov v Bulgaria* App no 39084/97, ECHR 2003-XII, paras 139 and 141; and, as an example to the contrary, *Pedersen and Baadsgaard v Denmark* [GC] App no 49017/99, ECHR 2004-XI, para 79.

266 *Raichenov v Bulgaria* App no 47579/99, 20 Apr 2006, para 51.

c) *Costs, Damages, and Ancillary Orders*

In some cases, the accused was convicted of an offence, and while the domestic courts refrained from imposing a sentence as such, it nevertheless required the accused to pay costs and damages. Even the imposition of such penalties following a conviction might well be considered disproportionate to the aims pursued. In *Brunet Lecomte and Lyon Mag*, the applicants were convicted following publication of an article insinuating that a Muslim professor had taken part in terrorist activities. The ECtHR held that the conviction and the imposition of damages amounting to €2500 were disproportionate and violated Article 10 ECHR.

In this regard it is instructive that the ECtHR considers the proportionality of sanctions imposed in the broad sense and not simply the criminal sentence. The suggestion is that the definition of punishment includes not just the criminal sentence—ie the fine—but also ancillary consequences such as the obligations to pay damages or costs. This is clearly evident in *Cumpănă and Mazăre v Romania*, where the criminal sanction and accompanying prohibitions (such as the orders disqualifying the applicants from exercising a number of civil rights) were manifestly disproportionate in their nature and severity to the legitimate aim pursued by the applicants' conviction for insult and defamation'.[267] Similarly, in *Frisk and Jansen*, in determining the 'severity of the sanction imposed' the ECtHR considered not just the sentence but also the legal costs of the other side in determining whether the sanction could be considered reasonable and proportionate in the sense of Article 10 ECHR.[268] In *Kasabova*, the ECtHR held that, in assessing the extent of the interference with the applicant's rights, it was necessary to consider not just the fines imposed on the journalist convicted of defamation but also the damages and costs awarded to the complainants.[269]

Again, the imposition of such penalties will only be proportionate if 'strong reasons' are provided. Such reasons were held to exist in *Ruokanen and Others*, where the applicants had published allegations of rape by members of a baseball team and were subsequently convicted of defamation. In holding that the order that the applicants pay damages of €80,000 to each member of the team did not violate Article 10 ECHR, the ECtHR referred to the fundamental importance of the presumption of innocence.[270]

[267] *Cumpănă and Mazăre v Romania* [GC] App no 33348/96, ECHR 2004-XI, para 120.
[268] *Frisk and Jensen v Denmark* App no 19657/12, 5 Dec 2017.
[269] *Kasabova v Bulgaria* App no 22385/03, 19 Apr 2011, para 71.
[270] *Ruokanen and Others v Finland* App no 45130/06, 6 Apr 2010.

These cases highlight that the ECtHR's understanding of punishment is closely tied to the actual interference with the applicant's rights and is thus considerably broader than the understanding of punishment in criminal theory.

4. Freedom of Assembly and Proportionality

In the context of freedom of assembly as protected by Article 11 ECHR, the ECtHR has employed a similar approach. The ECtHR will conduct a detailed assessment of penalties imposed on protestors, particularly if the protests involve matters of public interest and only result in minor disruption.[271] Penalties imposed on those taking part in lawful protests or assemblies in the absence of any indication of violence or unruliness are likely to be considered disproportionate.[272] The imposition of penalties on an individual for participation in an unauthorized protest might also be considered disproportionate.[273]

Article 11 ECHR only protects the right to 'peaceful assembly' and 'does not cover a demonstration where the organisers and participants have violent intentions'.[274] The ECtHR has stressed, however, that 'an individual does not cease to enjoy the right to freedom of peaceful assembly as a result of sporadic violence or other punishable acts committed by others in the course of a demonstration if the individual in question remains peaceful in his or her own intentions or behaviour'.[275] In addition,

> even if there is a real risk that a public demonstration might result in disorder as a result of developments outside the control of the organisers, such a demonstration does not as such fall outside the scope of paragraph 1 of Article 11, and any restriction placed thereon must be in conformity with the terms of paragraph 2 of that provision.[276]

Further, the ECtHR has held in a number of cases in which demonstrators had engaged in acts of violence, that the demonstrations in question had been within the scope of Article 11 ECHR as 'the organisers of these assemblies had

[271] See for discussion K Reid, *A Practitioner's Guide to the European Convention on Human Rights* (5th edn, London: Sweet & Maxwell 2015) 578–81.

[272] ibid 578. See eg *Galstyan v Armenia* App no 26986/03, 15 Nov 2009.

[273] See eg *Gün v Turkey* App no 8029/07, 18 June 2013, paras 77–85 (sentence of imprisonment of eighteen months for participation in a banned demonstration which had turned violent disproportionate; no evidence applicant was involved in acts of violence).

[274] *Stankov and the United Macedonian Organisation Llinden v Bulgaria* App nos 29221/95 and 29225/95, ECHR 2001-IX, para 77.

[275] See eg *Primov and Others v Russia* App no 17391/06, 12 June 2014, para 155; *Laguna Guzman v Spain* App no 41462/17, 6 Oct 2020, para 34.

[276] *Laguna Guzman v Spain* App no 41462/17, 6 Oct 2020, para 34; *Taranenko v Russia* App no 199554/05, 15 May 2014, para 66.

not expressed violent intentions and there were no grounds to believe that the assemblies were not meant to be peaceful.'[277]

In *Yaroslav Belousov v Russia*, for instance, the applicant was accused of having been involved in the 'disruption of a previously peaceful assembly engineered by the organisers to stir up political unrest'. The applicant was found guilty of participating in mass disorder and of violent acts against police officers and sentenced to 'two years and three months' imprisonment for attending an authorised public assembly, chanting anti-government slogans, and throwing an unidentified small round object which hit a police officer on the shoulder and caused him pain'.[278] Here the ECtHR engaged in a more detailed consideration of the proportionality of the sentence imposed and seemed to attach weight to the nature of the distribution of the sentences for the separate crimes. It stated that it was 'noteworthy' that the applicant had been sentenced to nine months' imprisonment for committing violence against a public official by 'throwing the yellow object', which although 'severe', was 'significantly more lenient than the partly concurrent twenty-one-month sentence for participation in mass disorder'.[279]

The ECtHR noted that there were 'a number of individuals in the crowd who contributed to the onset of clashes between the protesters and the police' and attached 'crucial' importance to the fact that 'the applicant was not found to be among those responsible for the initial acts of aggression' noting that he 'threw the yellow object at the height of the clashes, when the police were already arresting the protesters' and that the domestic courts had referred to his participation in the mass disorder as 'insignificant'. In finding a violation of Article 11 ECHR, it held that:

> Given the applicant's minor role in the assembly and his only marginal involvement in the clashes, the Court does not consider that the risks referred to by the Government—potential civil unrest, political instability and threat to public order—had any personal relation to the applicant. These reasons

[277] See eg *Gülcü v Turkey* App no 17526/10, 19 Jan 2016, para 93: 'Firstly, the Court observes that the applicant was arrested, detained on remand and subsequently convicted on the ground of having attended a demonstration and thrown stones at the security forces during that demonstration. The Court reiterates in this regard that in a number of cases where demonstrators had engaged in acts of violence, it held that the demonstrations in question had been within the scope of Article 11 of the Convention but that the interferences with the right guaranteed by Article 11 of the Convention were justified for the prevention of disorder or crime and for the protection of the rights and freedoms of others.'

[278] *Yaroslav Belousov v Russia* App nos 2653/13 and 60980/14, 4 Oct 2016, para 177.

[279] ibid.

> could not therefore justify the sentence of two years and three months, which was, moreover, served in full.[280]

The ECtHR noted too that:

> the applicant's criminal conviction, and especially the severity of his sentence, could not but have had the effect of discouraging him and other opposition supporters, as well as the public at large, from attending demonstrations and, more generally, from participating in open political debate. The chilling effect of his sanction was further amplified by the large-scale proceedings in this case which attracted widespread media coverage.[281]

It concluded that 'in view of the severity of the sanction imposed on the applicant his criminal conviction was a measure grossly disproportionate to the legitimate aims of preventing disorder and crime and the protection of the rights and freedoms of others'.[282] Here the ECtHR conducts a detailed comparative examination of the sentence imposed in relation to each of the charges and uses this to justify its finding that the longer sentence was disproportionate.

In *Gülcü v Turkey*, the ECtHR held that there had been a violation of Article 11 ECHR on account of a disproportionate sentence imposed on the applicant for attending a demonstration and throwing stones at the security forces.[283] The demonstration was held to protest the show of support for Abdullah Öcalan and was attended by 3000 people. The demonstrators refused to obey the police warnings and request to disperse and as a result the police forcibly intervened using truncheons, water, and tear gas.[284] The applicant was convicted and sentenced to a total of seven years and six months of imprisonment. For the offences of membership of an illegal organization, he was sentenced to four years and two months of imprisonment; for the offence of disseminating propaganda in support of a terrorist organization he was sentenced to a total of six months and twenty days; for the offence of resisting the orders of the security forces he was sentenced to two years, nine months, and ten days' imprisonment. Once again the ECtHR considered the proportionality of each of the sentences imposed and held that they were all, including the sentence imposed

[280] ibid para 180.
[281] ibid para 181.
[282] ibid para 182.
[283] See *Gülcü v Turkey* App no 17526/10, 19 Jan 2016, paras 91–97.
[284] ibid para 8.

for acts of violence against the police, disproportionate.[285] It noted that photographic evidence showed that the applicant 'threw stones at the security forces and was thus involved in an act of violence' and that 'when individuals are involved in such acts the State authorities enjoy a wider margin of appreciation when examining the need for an interference with freedom of assembly'.[286] Consequently, 'the imposition of a sanction for such a reprehensible act' was 'compatible with the guarantees of Article 11 of the Convention'.[287] In spite of this, however, the ECtHR held that it could not 'overlook the harshness of the sentence imposed on the applicant ... that is to say, two years, nine months and ten days' imprisonment'. Taking into account the circumstances of the case and in particular the applicant's age, the ECtHR concluded that 'the applicant's punishment for throwing stones at the police officers during the demonstration was not proportionate to the legitimate aims pursued'.[288]

These cases demonstrate both the considerable protection afforded to 'political' protest and a clear willingness of the ECtHR to consider sentences imposed for participating in protests, even those which turn violent, as disproportionate and as violating the guarantees set out in Article 11 ECHR.

5. Conclusion

In the context of the rights guaranteed by Articles 8, 10, and 11 ECHR, the ECtHR has demonstrated willingness, notwithstanding its repeated statements to the effect that sentencing is a matter for the national authorities, to engage in detailed consideration of the proportionality of the sentence when compared to the interference with the rights. Here, the ECtHR has been prepared to assess the domestic court's reasoning in detail, engaging, for instance, in a comparison of the relative severity of sentences imposed for different offences[289] and considering in detail the severity of the financial penalties imposed.

The scope of the ECtHR's proportionality review in this context differs significantly from that in relation to Article 3 ECHR and Article 5 ECHR. The reason for this is connected to limits on the criminalization of acts or omissions, which interfere with the rights to privacy, expression, or assembly. The fact that states are entitled to enact criminal legislation which interferes with

[285] Contrast *Osmani and Others v The Former Yugoslav Republic of Macedonia* (dec) App no 50841/99, ECHR 2001-X; *Protopapa v Turkey* App no 16084/90, 24 Feb 2009, paras 104–12; *Primov and Others v Russia* App no 17391/06, 12 June 2014, paras 156–63.

[286] *Gülcü v Turkey* App no 17526/10, 19 Jan 2016, para 116, citing *Sürek v Turkey (no 1)* [GC] App no 26682/95, ECHR 1999-IV, para 61.

[287] *Gülcü v Turkey* App no 17526/10, 19 Jan 2016.

[288] ibid.

[289] *Yaroslav Belousov v Russia* App nos 2653/13 and 60980/14, 4 Oct 2016, para 182.

these rights (such as in the context of speech offences), does not mean that the imposition of penalties will automatically be considered compatible with the provisions. In these cases, the aim of the imposition of penalties will have to be weighed up against the extent of the interference in the right.

E. Proportionality and the Protection of Property in Article 1 of Protocol 1 ECHR

The imposition of a disproportionate fine may give rise to questions of compatibility with the right to the protection of property. According to Article 1 of Protocol No 1 ECHR: 'Every natural or legal person is entitled to the peaceful enjoyment of his possessions. No one shall be deprived of his possessions except in the public interest and subject to the conditions provided for by law and by the general principles of international law.' According to the second paragraph, the guarantee is not to impair 'the right of a State to enforce such laws as it deems necessary to control the use of property in accordance with the general interest or to secure the payment of taxes or other contributions or penalties'.

The provision thus contains three distinct rules: the right to peaceful enjoyment of one's possessions; the possibility for a person to be 'deprived' of their 'possessions' under certain circumstances, namely in the 'public interest and subject to the conditions provided for by law'; and, in the second paragraph, the rule that the contracting states are entitled to control the use of property in accordance with the general interest or to secure the payment of penalties.

There is no express mention of the proportionality. The ECtHR has held, however, that the second and third rules must be construed in light of the general principle set out in the first rule.[290] This means, inter alia, that there must be 'a reasonable relationship of proportionality between the means employed and the aim sought to be realised'.[291] The need to 'ascertain whether a fair balance has been struck between the demands of the general interest of the community and the requirements of the protection of the individual's fundamental rights becomes relevant only once it has been established that the impugned interference satisfied the requirement of lawfulness and was not arbitrary'.[292]

[290] *Konstantin Stefanov v Bulgaria* App no 35399/05, 27 Oct 2015, para 53.

[291] *Phillips v UK* App no 41087/98, ECHR 2001-VII, para 51; *Allan Jacobsson v Sweden (no 1)*, 25 Oct 1989, Series A no 163, para 55; *Balsamo v San Marino* App nos 20319/17 and 21414/17, 8 Oct 2019, para 81.

[292] *Varvara v Italy* App no 17475/09, 29 Oct 2013, para 84.

The guarantee thus requires that any interference with property is 'lawful', follows a legitimate public interest, and is proportionate to that aim.

Criminal fines are 'penalties' for the purposes of the Convention and thus fall within the scope of the third rule, according to which the right to the peaceful enjoyment of possessions shall not impair the state's right to control the use of property to secure the payment of penalties. Less clear is whether a fine is to be considered as an interference with the right to the peaceful enjoyment of one's possessions. This issue has seldom been considered by the ECtHR, but in *Konstantin Stefanov*, the ECtHR held that a fine did in fact constitute an 'interference' with the applicant's 'possessions'.[293]

The case involved a lawyer who had been appointed as one of two legal aid counsel in a case involving the defence of an individual charged with aggravated theft. The applicant was nominated by the Bar to represent the accused and was informed that he was obliged to act as defence counsel and that the failure to appear at court would result in disciplinary action and civil liability. In addition, the applicant was informed that the criminal court was obliged to set the applicant's fees at 'an amount not lower than the minimum provided for' in the relevant laws and that if the court failed to do so, then the lawyer was to refuse to provide legal representation or risk a disciplinary sanction under Bar Council laws.

At the beginning of the hearing, the applicant requested that the court comply with the relevant provisions concerning his fees. The presiding judge refused to determine the minimum fees at that point in the proceedings and warned the applicant that he would fine him if he refused to act as counsel. The applicant refused to act for the accused and left the courtroom. He was subsequently fined BGN 500 (approximately €260), which was equivalent to around four months of the minimum wage in Bulgaria at the time.[294] The ECtHR held that the 'possession' which formed the object of the applicant's complaint was 'a sum of money, that is to say the EUR 260 which was imposed as a fine on the applicant' and noted that the fine constituted 'an interference with the applicant's right to peaceful enjoyment of possessions'.[295] In addition, it held that the fine constituted a 'penalty' within the meaning of the Convention and fell with the scope of the second paragraph of the guarantee.[296]

[293] See also *Valico SRL v Italy* (dec) App no 70074/01, Reports 2006-III 'the imposition of a fine will in principle constitute interference with the right guaranteed by the first paragraph of Article 1 of Protocol No. 1 as it deprives the person concerned of an item of property, namely the sum that has to be paid.' There is similarly little considered in the USSC case law: see *Timbs v Indiana*, 586 US ___ (2019), 139 S Ct 682 (2019) on the 'excessive fines' clause.

[294] *Konstantin Stefanov v Bulgaria* App no 35399/05, 27 Oct 2015, paras 8–14.

[295] ibid para 57.

[296] ibid para 58.

This case suggests, therefore, that a fine is to be understood as constituting an interference with property rights and thus as falling within the scope of protection of Article 1 of Protocol No 1 ECHR. The approach reflects the broad definition of the notion of 'possession', which is perhaps better reflected in the reference in the French version of the Convention to '*bien*', in that it encompasses 'a wide range of proprietorial interests'.[297]

The ECtHR has developed an extensive jurisprudence on other penalties, notably confiscation and asset forfeiture orders. In *Phillips*, for instance, the applicant had been convicted of drug offences and sentenced to nine years' imprisonment. In addition, the judge imposed a confiscation order requiring that he (re)pay £91,400, deemed to constitute assets obtained through his criminal activities. In the event of failure to pay this amount, the applicant was to serve a sentence of two years' imprisonment. The applicant took issue with the statutory assumption that all property held by him 'within the preceding six years represented the proceeds of drug trafficking'. This, he claimed, was 'unduly extensive' and interfered with his rights under Article 1 of Protocol No 1'.[298] The ECtHR held that the £91,400 represented a possession and that the confiscation order amounted to an interference with the applicant's peaceful enjoyment of his possessions in the sense of Article 1 of Protocol No 1. The order was also a 'penalty' for the purposes of the ECHR and thus fell within the scope of the second paragraph of Article 1 of Protocol No 1.

Some have criticized the approach of the ECtHR in *Konstantin Stefanov* as unprincipled[299] on the basis that it is questionable whether the financial loss suffered by a person when he pays a sum in order to comply with a fine can be compared to 'the "expropriation" of a determinate "possession"', as was the case in *Phillips*.[300] In the United Kingdom, however, confiscation orders, unlike forfeiture orders,[301] are not directed towards a particular asset. They are essentially an order to pay a sum of money enforced as if it were a fine.[302]

Assuming that a fine is to be considered to constitute an interference with a possession, then it is clear that the interference must be both lawful and

[297] See D Harris and others, *Harris, O'Boyle, and Warbrick: Law of the European Convention on Human Rights* (4th edn, Oxford: OUP 2018) 656–57. Harris suggests that the 'essential characteristic is the acquired economic value of the individual interest'.

[298] *Phillips v UK* App no 41087/98, ECHR 2001-VII, para 48.

[299] L Lavrynsen, 'Don't Open the Floodgates: Fines and Article 1 Protocol 1' Strasbourg Observers Blog, available at: <https://strasbourgobservers.com/2015/11/09/dont-open-the-floodgates-fines-and-article-1-protocol-1/> (accessed 15 Apr 2021).

[300] ibid.

[301] Forfeiture orders are directed towards particular assets and deprive the defendants of title to the assets.

[302] <https://www.cps.gov.uk/legal-guidance/confiscation-and-ancillary-orders-pre-poca-proceeds-crime-guidance> (accessed 15 Apr 2021).

proportionate. The ECtHR has held that the 'requisite balance will not be struck where the person concerned bears an individual and excessive burden'; thus 'a financial liability arising out of a fine may undermine the guarantee afforded by that provision if it places an excessive burden on the person or fundamentally interferes with his or her financial position'.[303] Equally, the ECtHR has frequently stressed that decisions on appropriate penalties, taxes, and contributions 'commonly involve the appreciation of political, economic and social questions' and 'that the margin of appreciation of the Contracting States in those areas is a wide one'.[304]

In the sentencing context, the lawfulness of the punishment will generally be guaranteed by the lawfulness of the criminal judgment. In *Natsvlishvili and Togonidze v Georgia*, for instance, the ECtHR held that 'lawfulness and appropriateness of those criminal sanctions of a pecuniary nature cannot thus be dissociated from the issue of the fairness of the plea bargain itself'.[305] Similarly, in *Öztürk*, in which the applicant complained that a confiscation order imposed following conviction violated his property rights, the ECtHR held that 'the measure complained of by the applicant was an incidental effect of his conviction' which had been found to have been in breach of Article 10 ECHR and thus that it was unnecessary to consider the complaint separately.[306]

In *Konstantin Stefanov*, the ECtHR held that the fine was 'lawful' in the sense of sufficiently 'accessible, precise and foreseeable'.[307] It held that it was not its role 'to interpret and define the precise meaning of national law' and that 'domestic legislation could not in any case provide for every eventuality and the level of precision required depends to a considerable degree on the content of the instrument in question, the field it is designed to cover and the number and status of those to whom it is addressed'. In the circumstances of the case, and in particular in view of fact that the applicant was a lawyer, the application of the law was not considered to be 'arbitrary' and that the applicant had been 'fined lawfully, that is to say on the basis of an accessible, clear and foreseeable legal provision'.[308] It is interesting here that the Court relied on its case law in the context of Article 10 ECHR and Article 6(1) ECHR, rather than on Article

303 *Konstantiv Stefanov v Bulgaria* App no 35399/05, 27 Oct 2015, para 55.

304 ibid para 56, citing *Gasus Dosier- und Fördertechnik GmbH v Netherlands*, 23 Feb 1995, Series A no 306-B, para 60. See also, in relation to fiscal policy, *Baláž v Slovakia* (dec) App no 60243/00, 16 Sept 2003; *Konstantin Stefanov v Bulgaria* App no 35399/05, 27 Oct 2015.

305 *Natsvlishvili and Togonidze v Georgia* App no 9043/05, 29 Apr 2014, para 110.

306 *Öztürk v Turkey* App no 22479/93, 28 Sept 1999, para 76.

307 ibid para 54.

308 ibid para 63.

7(1) ECHR.[309] Much of the case law is concerned with the determination of whether a confiscation measure constitutes a criminal sanction or penalty. Here the same criteria are applied as have been developed in the context of Articles 6 and 7 ECHR.[310] In those cases in which the measures are deemed not to be criminal in nature, the requirement of legality is guaranteed by Article 1 of Protocol No 1.[311] In cases in which the confiscation order is considered to be criminal in nature, it might be assumed that the guarantee of lawfulness in Article 7 ECHR applies.

In assessing the proportionality of the fine, the ECtHR held that a 'fair balance' was to be 'struck between the demands of the general interest of the community and the requirements of the protection of the individual's fundamental rights' and that the 'requisite balance will not be struck where the person concerned bears an individual and excessive burden' .[312]

In the case at issue, it held that the law 'pursued the legitimate aim of ensuring the smooth operation of the justice system' and then went on to consider whether 'a "fair balance" was struck between the demands of the general interest and the requirements of the protection of the applicant's fundamental rights'.[313] In this regard, it noted that the issue of whether the conduct leading to an interference with the 'smooth functioning of the justice system' should be punished by a financial sanction with a deterrent effect, such as the fine in the present case, comes within the margin of appreciation of the State' and that 'the margin is a wide one', precisely because such issues involve 'the appreciation of political, economic and social questions which the Convention leaves within the competence of the Contracting States'.[314]

The ECtHR noted that the applicant had been able to take advantage of a procedural guarantee in the form of a judicial review of the decision to impose the fine and that there was 'nothing to show that the decision-making process resulting in the fine complained of was unfair or arbitrary'.[315] In addition, it

[309] *Nejdet Şahin and Perihan Şahin v Turkey* [GC] App no 13279/05, 20 Oct 2011, para 50; *Rekvényi v Hungary* [GC] App no 25390/94, ECHR 1999-III, para 34. See also *Hashman and Harrup v UK* [GC] App no 25594/94, ECHR 1999-VIII, para 31.

[310] See in particular the criteria developed in *Engel and Others v Netherlands*, 8 June 1976, Series A no 22, para 81 and for further consideration Ch 2.

[311] There must be a legal basis in national law for the interference and the interference must be compatible with 'the rule of law' which the ECtHR has held 'presupposes that the rules of domestic law must be sufficiently precise and foreseeable' and that the law provides 'a measure of legal protection against arbitrariness', *Dimitrovi v Bulgaria* App no 12655/09, 3 Mar 2015, para 45 citing *Hentrich v France*, 22 Sept 1994, Series A no 296-A, para 42, and *Beyeler v Italy* [GC] App no 33202/96, ECHR 2000-I, para 109; see *Zlínsat, spol s ro v Bulgaria* App no 57785/00, 15 June 2006.

[312] *Konstantiv Stefanov v Bulgaria* App no 35399/05, 27 Oct 2015, para 55.

[313] ibid paras 64–65.

[314] ibid para 56.

[315] ibid para 66.

held that 'although the fine imposed on the applicant was in the maximum possible amount under the relevant legal provision, it is neither prohibitive, nor oppressive or otherwise disproportionate'.[316] Consequently, the ECtHR held that the authorities had 'struck a fair balance between, on the one hand, the general interest and, on the other, respect for the applicant's right to property. The interference did not, therefore, impose an excessive burden on the applicant.'[317]

Similarly, in *Phillips*, the ECtHR noted that the confiscation order procedure aimed to assist in the 'fight against the scourge of drug trafficking' and thus that 'the making of a confiscation order operates in the way of a deterrent to those considering engaging in drug trafficking, and also to deprive a person of profits received from drug trafficking and to remove the value of the proceeds from possible future use in the drugs trade'.[318] It noted that while the 'sum payable under the confiscation order was considerable, namely GBP 91,400', 'it corresponded to the amount which the Crown Court judge found the applicant to have benefited from through drug trafficking over the preceding six years and was a sum which he was able to realise from the assets in his possession'. In addition, the ECtHR attached weight to the fact that 'the procedure followed in the making of the order was fair and respected the rights of the defence.' This led it to conclude that, '[a]gainst this background, and given the importance of the aim pursued, the Court does not consider that the interference suffered by the applicant with the peaceful enjoyment of his possessions was disproportionate'.[319]

The proportionality assessment in Article 1 of Protocol No 1 ECHR involves consideration of whether the fine constitutes a disproportionate inference in the applicant's right to peaceful enjoyment of property. This will be the case if it places an 'excessive burden on the person or fundamentally interferes with his or her financial position'. The issue of proportionality between the offence and fine is of relevance in this regard in marking the extent of an offender's liability. This is clearly evident in *Phillips* in the reference to the fact that the confiscation order corresponded to the amount which the applicant had benefited from drug trafficking. This can be contrasted with the US case *State of New Jersey v Bennie Anderson*, involving a defendant who had worked for Jersey City for forty years, was convicted of accepting a $300 bribe, and sentenced to a two-year probationary term, with five months of home confinement, and a

316 ibid para 67.
317 ibid paras 69–70.
318 ibid para 52.
319 ibid para 35.

fine of $3,000.[320] In addition, the court ordered the forfeiture of the defendant's entire pension, as was provided for in law. The appeal court upheld this order, noting that the forfeiture order was punitive in nature and thus subject to constitutional constraints but that it was not excessive as it was proportionate to the 'gravity' of the defendant's crime. The forfeiture of the pension was proportionate to the defendant's betrayal of the public trust by accepting the bribe. This narrow focus on proportionality between the offence and the sentence can be contrasted with the approach of the ECtHR, which instead examines the relationship between the sentence and the applicant's right to property.[321]

III. Human Rights and Disproportionate Punishment

Proportionality is afforded considerable relevance in sentencing theory and is frequently referred to in terms of fairness or justice.[322] The idea here is that the sentence which is imposed ought to fit the crime. This works both ways: a sentence which is too lenient might be considered to be just as problematic as a sentence which is too severe. In the human rights context, it might be assumed that the focus would be skewed in favour of undue severity. Proportionality might be expected to act as a more important constraint on unduly severe sentences rather than on those deemed too lenient. The overview of the importance of proportionality in the human rights case law seems to cast doubt both on the relevance of proportionality as a constraint in practice and on the assumption that it acts primarily to prevent the imposition of disproportionately severe sentences. In this regard it is instructive that the only cases in which the ECtHR has found a violation of the proportionality requirement in Article 3 ECHR have involved sentences which were considered unduly lenient due to a 'manifest disproportion' between the offence committed and the sanction.[323]

[320] *State of New Jersey v Bennie Anderson*, ___ NJ Super ___, 2020 WL 1502170 (App Div Mar 30, 2020). The New Jersey Supreme Court has granted certification in the case.

[321] *Banfield v UK* (dec) App no 6223/04, ECHR 2005-XI; *Apostolakis v Greece* App no 39574/07, 22 Oct 2009; *Azinas v Cyprus* App no 56679/00, 20 June 2002, para 45: in which the application of similar laws was deemed to have 'upset to his detriment the balance that must be struck between the protection of the individual's right of property and public interest requirements'. See also *Azinas v Cyprus* [GC] App no 56679/00, ECHR 2004-III.

[322] See eg von Hirsch, *Doing Justice* (n 2). See too the approach of the USSC, which has held that the notion that punishment for an offence is 'graduated and proportioned' to the offence is a 'precept of justice' and thus embodied in a ban on cruel and unusual punishments. *Kennedy v Louisiana*, 554 US 407 (2008); *Weems v US*, 217 US 349 (1910).

[323] See eg *Ali and Ayşe Duran v Turkey* App no 42942/02, 8 Apr 2008 paras 65–67; *Kasap and Others* App no 8656/10, 14 Jan 2014, para 59; *A v Croatia* App no 55164/08, 14 Oct 2010, para 66 (referring to 'excessively light punishments'); *Nikolova and Velichova v Bulgaria* App no 7888/03, 20 Dec 2007, para 62.

The overview of the case law of the ECtHR demonstrates that the Convention does not set out any right to an appropriate or proportionate sentence, but rather prohibits the imposition of punishment which is deemed to constitute a disproportionate interference with the human rights of the offender.[324] The issue of balance between the offence and the sentence will only be of relevance in the context of the determination of whether the punishment can be considered proportionate to the individual right.

The case law suggests that proportionality will only serve as a constraint in relation to interferences with substantive rights, such as those to freedom of expression or assembly. These provisions provide individuals with rights to behave in certain ways and thus the ECtHR's review extends to consideration of whether interferences with such rights were necessary in a democratic society. This provides the ECtHR with some scope to consider whether the interference with the right to freedom of expression (such as by way of the criminalization of defamation) was proportionate to the aim pursued (such as the protection of rights and reputation of others). Just as the criminalization has the scope to interfere with, or have a chilling effect on, the exercise of such rights, so too does the imposition of disproportionate penalties. The human rights principles thus act to restrict both the type of sentences which can be imposed and the extent of the sentence.

There is little scope for any broader type of review of the proportionality of sentences. In relation to Article 3 ECHR, the review is necessarily limited by the fact that any disproportionality must be so severe as to reach the threshold for inhuman and degrading punishment. As we have seen, though, the ECtHR has yet to find a sentence to be so grossly excessive as to violate the prohibition on inhuman punishment in Article 3 ECHR. There is even less scope in the context of Article 5(1) ECHR for consideration of whether a sentence of imprisonment was proportionate to aims followed by the deprivation of liberty. The ECtHR has consistently refused to subject sentences of imprisonment to any sort of proportionality analysis based on Article 5(1) ECHR because the lawfulness of punishment is considered to be guaranteed by the lawfulness of the judgment of the sentencing court. In particular, it has refused to enter into any discussion about the proper aims of punishment, preferring, as we have seen, to refer somewhat nebulously to 'penological purposes', such as 'punishment, deterrence, public protection and rehabilitation'.[325]

[324] See also Ashworth and van Zyl Smit, 'Disproportionate Sentences' (n 22) 560.
[325] *Vinter and Others v UK* [GC] App nos 66069/09, 130/10, and 3896/10, ECHR 2013-III, para 111.

Some have argued that it 'is illogical for the Court to apply a stricter subsidiarity and proportionality principle to sanctions imposed under Articles 8–11 than to those under Article 5'.[326] The overview of the case law demonstrates that the reason for this is not that 'crime and punishment are incommensurable',[327] but rather because the legitimate aim pursued in sentencing an individual is not 'proportionate punishment' but simply 'lawful' punishment, defined in the sense of Article 7(1) ECHR as a sentence imposed on a culpable individual for clearly defined criminal conduct. This all suggests that proportionality has limited scope to act as a restraint on the state in its imposition of punishment.

[326] S Snacken and D van Zyl Smit, 'European Penology and Penal Policy-Making' in T Daems, D van Zyl Smith, and S Snacken (eds), *European Penology?* (Oxford: Hart Publishing 2017) 3, 11.

[327] Lee, 'Why Proportionality Matters' (n 5) 1844. See also HLA Hart, *Punishment and Responsibility: Essays in the Philosophy of Law* (J Gardner, 2nd edn, Oxford: OUP 2008) 233.

4

Equality and Non-Discrimination

I. Equality, Certainty, and Justice

Equality famously requires that people who are alike should be treated alike, while those who are unalike should be treated unalike.[1] It is 'at once the most appealing and the most threatening of ideas', giving rise to the promise that everyone will be treated the same, while at the same time leading to the worry that the very fact of treating some people the same will lead to some people being treated wrongly.[2] Equality has particular resonance in the sentencing context.[3] In this regard, it is common for equality to be equated with consistency of outcome: 'Equal justice requires identity of outcome in cases that are relevantly identical ... Consistency in the punishment of offences against the criminal law is a reflection of the notion of equal justice and is a fundamental element in any rational and fair system of criminal justice.'[4] Many of the most important and widely discussed sentencing reforms of the twentieth century, such as the development of the US Federal Sentencing Guidelines, were driven by attempts to promote consistency of outcome by reducing bias and disparity.[5]

Concerns about the lack of equality or 'disparity' at sentencing were viewed partly as a consequence of too much judicial discretion,[6] but also as a result of what was considered to be an overly narrow focus on individual justice: 'individualized justice is prima facie at war with such concepts, at least as fundamental, as equality, objectivity, and consistency in the law.'[7] Such arguments

[1] See notably Aristotle, *Nicomachean Ethics* (WD Ross tr, L Brown ed, Oxford: OUP 2009) Book V, v 3. On the connection between these two propositions see T Honoré, 'Social Justice' (1962) 8 *McGill Law Journal* 77, 83.

[2] CJ Peters, 'Equality Revisited' (1997) 110 *Harvard Law Review* 1210, 1211.

[3] See eg HLA Hart, *Punishment and Responsibility: Essays in the Philosophy of 0Law* (J Gardner, 2nd edn, Oxford: OUP 2008) 80: 'the idea of justice' requires 'treating morally like cases alike and morally different ones differently'. WJ Stuntz, 'Unequal Justice' (2008) 121 *Harvard Law Review* 1969, 1976; M Tonry, *Sentencing Matters* (New York, NY: OUP 1996).

[4] *Green v Queen* [2011] HCA 49 (High Court of Australia).

[5] For discussion see A Alschuler, 'The Failure of Sentencing Guidelines: A Plea for Less Aggregation' (1991) 58 *University of Chicago Law Review* 901.

[6] ibid. 'The vices of unconstrained discretion go beyond idiosyncrasy, caprice, and strategic behaviour to invidious discrimination on the basis of race, class, gender, and the like.'

[7] ME Frankel, *Criminal Sentences: Law Without Order* (New York, NY: Hill & Wang 1972) 5–11. For discussion see Tonry, *Sentencing Matters* (n 3) 6 and 9; RA Bierschbach and S Bibas, 'What's Wrong

Sentencing and Human Rights. Sarah J Summers, Oxford University Press. © Sarah J Summers 2022.
DOI: 10.1093/oso/9780192870384.003.0004

point to tension between equality and justice or rights.[8] This conception of the relationship between justice and equality, however, is by no means universally accepted. Some have argued that prescriptive equality is essentially tautological, 'an empty vessel with no substantive moral content of its own'.[9] Others have suggested that even if equality is non-tautological, it must be said to suffer from 'logical emptiness'.[10] On such accounts, equality, far from being the source of all rights,[11] lacks any independent normative force: 'the work of prescriptive "equality" is almost always performed entirely by some nonegalitarian norm.'[12] This means that while equality is a necessary product of some notion of 'nonegalitarian justice', treating people equally will not necessarily mean treating them rightly.[13] This calls into question any attempt to juxtapose rights and equality, precisely because 'entitlements people mistakenly attribute to the idea of equality all derive from external substantive rights'.[14]

Of central significance, here, is consideration of the scope and normative content of equality. This is particularly important in the sentencing context not least because of the tendency to rely on prescriptive equality as a justification for sentencing reform. Is equality or 'consistency' of fundamental importance at sentencing and, if so, what is it that ought to be consistent? Can equality be said to be in conflict with some idea of individualized justice? In order to consider these issues, this chapter begins by considering the right to equality and non-discrimination in the European Convention on Human Rights (ECHR). Article 1 ECHR requires that the rights protected by the Convention be applied equally, while Article 14 ECHR sets out a distinct right to non-discrimination. An examination of the relationship between the notion of equality inherent in the individual articles and the right to non-discrimination suggests that Article 14 ECHR is principally concerned with preventing arbitrariness in

with Sentencing Equality?' (2016) 102 *Virginia Law Review* 1447, 1459; J Bowers, 'What's Wrong with Sentencing Equality? Sentencing Legality: A Response to Professors Bierschbach and Bibas' (2016) 102 *Virginia Law Review Online* 120, 125 referring to (and criticizing) the 'conventional wisdom that mandatory sentencing regimes developed as compromises between progressives (intent on reigning in racial, ethnic, and class discrimination) and conservatives (intent on reigning in lenient judges)'.

[8] D Phillips, *Equality, Justice and Rectification* (New York, NY: Academic Press 1979) 70–75.

[9] Notably P Westen, 'The Empty Idea of Equality' (1982) 95 *Harvard Law Review* 537 arguing against the idea that equality might be said to exist as a prescriptive norm.

[10] See Peters, 'Equality Revisited' (n 2) 1212: 'The fullest nontautological claim of the egalitarian comes down to this: sometimes a person should be treated wrongly simply because another, identically situated person has been treated wrongly.'

[11] J Rawls, *Justice as Fairness* (1958) 67 *Philosophy Review* 164, 165f; R Dworkin, *Taking Rights Seriously* (Cambridge, MA: Harvard University Press 1977) 273f; and for criticism of this position HLA Hart, 'Between Utility and Rights' (1989) 79 *Columbia Law Review* 828, 845f.

[12] Peters, 'Equality Revisited' (n 2) 1228.

[13] ibid 1213.

[14] Westen, 'The Empty Idea of Equality' (n 9) 542.

the application of the individual substantive rights. Discrimination at sentencing has the potential to impact on the right to a fair trial, the right to respect for human dignity, and the prohibition on arbitrary detention. Each of these is considered in turn. This analysis provides the basis for revisiting some important issues in sentencing theory and practice, including the potential for persistent disparity to emerge at sentencing, which has little to do with the sentencing decision itself and the role of sentencing guidelines.

II. Equality, Non-Discrimination, and Article 14 ECHR

A. The Scope of the Protection in Article 14 ECHR

The close relationship between equality and the individual substantive rights guaranteed by the Convention is evident in Article 1 ECHR, Article 14 ECHR, and Article 1 of Protocol No 12 to the ECHR.[15] Article 1 ECHR states that the contracting parties are to 'secure to everyone within their jurisdiction the rights and freedoms defined in Section I of this Convention',[16] while Article 14 ECHR guarantees that the rights and freedoms of the Convention are to be secured 'without discrimination on any ground such as sex, race, colour, language, religion, political or other opinion, national or social origin, association with a national minority, property, birth or other status'. Article 14 ECHR can only be invoked together with one of the substantive rights. In this sense, it is said to 'complement' the other substantive provisions of the Convention and the Protocols but does not have any 'independent existence'.[17] This has led some to argue that the prohibition on discrimination is narrower than similar provisions in other instruments,[18] in that it does not set out an independent provision on non-discrimination.[19]

[15] Protocol No 12 to the ECHR was adopted on 26 June 2000 and came into force on 1 April 2005, ETS No 177. According to Art 1: 'The enjoyment of any right set forth by law shall be secured without discrimination on any ground such as sex, race, colour, language, religion, political or other opinion, national or social origin, association with a national minority, property, birth or other status.' It is telling that many contracting states, including the UK, Germany, France, and Switzerland, have not (yet) ratified it.

[16] This commitment to the guarantee of equality as a fundamental human right is set out in Art 1 of the Universal Declaration on Human Rights (UDHR): 'All human beings are born free and equal in dignity and rights.'

[17] *Khamtokhu and Aksenchik v Russia* [GC] App no 60367/08, ECHR 2017, para 53. See also Small who describes the right as 'parasitic', J Small, 'Structure and Substance: Developing a Practical and Effective Prohibition on Discrimination under the Convention on Human Rights' (2003) 6 *European Journal of Discrimination and the Law* 45, 47.

[18] See eg Art 26 of the International Covenant on Civil and Political Rights (ICCPR).

[19] Recognition of the importance of a stronger equality guarantee led to the adoption of Protocol No 12 to the ECHR which sets out a general non-discrimination clause in Art 1. For detailed discussion see

If all of the rights in the Convention are in any case to be applied equally to all people, then the guarantee in Article 14 ECHR does not seem to provide any additional or distinct protection beyond that which is already set out in or implied by the individual substantive rights.[20] As Gerards notes:

> To be justiciable before the Court, a difference in treatment must always relate to a substantive Convention right. However, since the Convention right can usually also be invoked on its own and almost any difference in treatment can be dealt with in that context, discrimination complaints often do not add very much to the other allegations made.[21]

This position finds some express support in the case law. In *Airey*, for instance, the ECtHR stated unambiguously that Article 14 ECHR did not enjoy any 'independent existence' but simply constituted 'one particular element (non-discrimination) of each of the rights safeguarded by the Convention'.[22]

The apparent redundancy of Article 14 ECHR is compounded by the obvious relationship between discrimination and arbitrariness.[23] Article 14 ECHR will be violated if there is a 'difference in the treatment of persons in analogous or relevantly similar situations' which is discriminatory in that it has 'no objective and reasonable justification, in other words, if it does not pursue a legitimate aim or if there is not a reasonable relationship of proportionality between the means employed and the aim sought to be realised'.[24] Article 14

eg S Besson, 'Evolutions in Non-Discrimination Law within the ECHR and the ESC Systems: "It Takes Two to Tango in the Council of Europe"' (2012) 60 *American Journal of Comparative Law* 147.

[20] See also RK Fullinwider, *The Reverse Discrimination Controversy: A Moral and Legal Analysis* (Totowa, NJ: Rowman and Littlefield 1980) 223, who makes the same point in the context of the US Fourteenth Amendment: '[A]n explicit rule of constitutional equality, such as the equal protection clause of the Fourteenth Amendment, does not add anything distinct from or independent of the other rights (to liberty, security, due process etc.) already enumerated in or implied in other provisions of the constitution. Since these other constitutional rights apply to all citizens, their form already entails their equal application. The explicit principle of constitutional equality serves only a rhetorical purpose, reminding us of the nature of other constitutional principles.'

[21] J Gerards, 'The Discrimination Grounds of Article 14 of the European Convention on Human Rights' (2013) 13 *Human Rights Law Review* 99, 100.

[22] *Airey v Ireland*, 9 Oct 1997, Series A no 32, para 30 citing *Marckx v Belgium*, 13 June 1979, Series A no 31, para 32

[23] See also R Reed and J Murdoch, *Human Rights Law in Scotland* (4th edn, West Sussex: Bloomsbury 2017) who note that 'the classic example given of unreasonable behaviour, in the *Wednesbury* case, was of discrimination'.

[24] *Khamtokhu and Aksenchik v Russia* [GC] App no 60367/08, ECHR 2017, para 64. In the context of the determination of whether there are objective justifications for *prima facie* discriminatory treatment, the contracting states enjoy a certain margin of appreciation, see *Gaygusuz v Austria*, 16 Sept 1996, Reports 1996-IV, para 42. More recently, the ECtHR has begun to consider the relevance

ECHR does not prohibit distinctions in treatment which are 'founded on an objective assessment of essentially different factual circumstances and which, being based on the public interest, strike a fair balance between the protection of the interests of the community and respect for the rights and freedoms safeguarded by the Convention'.[25] Equally, though, any type of arbitrariness in the application of the right is likely to result in a violation of the substantive right.

There are two aspects of the scope of protection, which might call into question a reading of the Article 14 ECHR as essentially superfluous and which call for further consideration. First, the ECtHR has held that Article 14 ECHR may be violated even if there has not been a violation of the substantive right. This suggests that Article 14 ECHR may well afford protection beyond that provided by the individual right at issue. Second, the protection against discrimination might differ from broader notions of 'equality', in that it might afford extra protection to certain categories of person. The ECtHR has noted not just that differences in treatment aimed at ensuring 'substantive equality' may be justified under Article 14 ECHR,[26] but also that the contracting states are under a positive obligation to take measures to eradicate certain types of discrimination.[27] In these situations, the failure to take such measures may constitute in itself discriminatory treatment.[28] Before considering the specific importance of Article 14 ECHR at sentencing, it is important to investigate these issues in more detail.

1. The 'Autonomous' Character of Article 14 ECHR

The ECtHR has repeatedly held that the right in Article 14 ECHR is 'autonomous' in nature in that it does not presuppose a violation of the substantive

of a common European consensus, see eg *Khamtokhu and Aksenchik v Russia* [GC] App no 60367/08, ECHR 2017, para 79; *Schwizgebel v Switzerland* App no 25762/07, 10 June 2010, paras 79–80; *Dickson v United Kingdom* [GC] App no 44362/04, ECHR 2007-V, para 81; *Fretté v France* App no 36515/97, ECHR 2002-I, para 40; *Petrovic v Austria*, 27 Mar 1998, *Reports* 1998-II, para 38; *Biao v Denmark* [GC] App no 38590/10, ECHR 2016, paras 131–33.

[25] *GMB and KM v Switzerland* (dec) App no 36797/97, 27 Sept 2001.

[26] *Khamtokhu and Aksenchik v Russia* [GC] App no 60367/08, ECHR 2017, para 86; see also *Alexandru Enache v Romania* App no 16986/12, 3 Oct 2017, para 77. *Ēcis v Latvia* App no 12879/09, 10 Jan 2019, para 84: 'providing for the distinctive needs of women prisoners, particularly in relation to maternity, in order to accomplish substantial gender equality should not be regarded as discriminatory.'

[27] *Kafkaris v Cyprus* [GC] App no 21906/04, ECHR 2008, para 161 referring to 'cases where a person or group is treated, without proper justification, less favourably than another, even though the more favourable treatment is not called for by the Convention' and citing *Abdulaziz, Cabales and Balkandali v UK*, 28 May 1985, Series A no 94, para 82.

[28] In the context of domestic violence for instance, which is recognized as a form of discrimination against women, the failure of the contracting state to ensure effective investigation and prosecution of complaints gave rise to a violation of Art 14 ECHR in conjunction with Arts 2 and 3 ECHR, see eg *Opuz v Turkey* App no 33401/02, 9 June 2009, ECHR 2009, para 184.

right.[29] Although the guarantee only applies to the rights and freedoms in the Convention and the Protocols, the ECtHR has held that Article 14 ECHR is engaged if the facts of the case fall 'within the ambit' of one of the substantive provisions of the ECHR or its Protocols.[30] This means that '[a] measure which in itself is in conformity with the requirements of the Article enshrining the right or freedom in question may however infringe the Article when read in conjunction with Article 14, for the reason that it is of a discriminatory nature'.[31] This seems to imply support for an understanding of 'equality' or 'non-discrimination', which affords it some substantive, normative content beyond that protected by the relevant individual right.

In many cases, the reasoning in support of a finding of a violation of Article 14 ECHR will mirror the reasoning that a substantive right was violated.[32] More instructive are those cases in which the ECtHR has found a violation of Article 14 ECHR in the absence of a violation of the substantive right or freedom. In *Clift*, for instance, the applicant had been sentenced to eighteen years' imprisonment for serious crimes. Under the legislative regime applicable at the time, he became eligible for release on parole on 13 March 2002 and was entitled to release on 18 March 2005. On 25 March 2002 the Parole Board recommended that he be released on parole.[33] According to the relevant legislation, 'the final decision on early release in cases involving prisoners serving determinate sentences (ie fixed-term sentences) of more than fifteen years' imprisonment lay with the Secretary of State'.[34] The position differed from that regarding prisoners serving determinate sentences of less than fifteen years and for prisoners serving indeterminate (ie life) sentences. In those cases, the approval of the Secretary of State was not required. The Secretary of State subsequently rejected the recommendation of the Parole Board and concluded that the applicant's release 'would present an unacceptable risk to the public'. The applicant was not released.[35]

The ECtHR found a violation of Article 14 taken together with Article 5 ECHR. Its reasoning can be summarized as follows: first, although Article 5

[29] *Fretté v France* App no 36515/97, ECHR 2002-I; *Zarb Adami v Malta* App no 17209/02, ECHR 2006-VIII—Judge Bratza, dissenting.

[30] See eg *Clift v UK* App no 7205/07, 13 July 2010, para 41; *Kafkaris v Cyprus* [GC] App no 21906/04, ECHR 2008, para 159; *Case 'relating to certain aspects of the laws on the use of languages in education in Belgium' v Belgium*, 23 July 1968, Series A no 6, para 9.

[31] *Khamtokhu and Aksenchik v Russia* [GC] App no 60367/08, ECHR 2017, para 53.

[32] See eg *Munteanu v The Republic of Moldova* App no 34168/11, 26 May 2020, para 75: the authorities did not properly discharge their positive obligation to prevent the real and immediate threat of domestic violence against the applicants.

[33] *Clift v UK* App no 7205/07, 13 July 2010, paras 6–8.

[34] ibid para 8.

[35] ibid para 8.

ECHR does not guarantee a right to be automatically released on parole, if procedures relating to the release of prisoners operate in a discriminatory manner, this will raise an issue under Article 5 ECHR together with Article 14 ECHR.[36] Second, the protection conferred by Article 14 ECHR 'is not limited to different treatment based on characteristics which are personal in the sense that they are innate or inherent', but also applies to different treatment of different categories of prisoner depending on the sentences imposed.[37] Third, the applicant was in an analogous position to long-term prisoners serving less than fifteen years and life prisoners. Finally, the early release scheme to which the applicant was subject[38] lacked objective justification and violated Article 5 ECHR taken together with Article 14 ECHR.

This reasoning is instructive as it calls into question the role of Article 14 ECHR. The ECtHR begins by noting that Article 5 ECHR does not guarantee any automatic right to parole, thereby suggesting that it is necessary to consider the case under the ambit of Article 14 ECHR. The contracting states are not required under Article 5(1) ECHR to establish an early release scheme, but if they do so, it must be applied in a non-arbitrary manner.

The suggestion here is that there could be no argument that Article 5(1) ECHR had been violated. The applicant was detained 'in accordance with a procedure prescribed by law after conviction by a competent court' in the sense of Article 5(1)(a) ECHR.[39] The applicant's conviction thus provided the legal basis for the applicant's detention for the full length of the sentence imposed by the trial court. Nevertheless, it is important to note too that the law of England and Wales provided for an early release scheme. Here the question is whether the operation of the scheme in the case at issue was 'in accordance with the law' and the consequences of this for the compatibility of the applicant's detention with Article 5(1) ECHR. The ECtHR seems to allude to this state of affairs in holding that if parole provisions were applied 'differently to prisoners depending on the length of their sentences, there is a risk that, unless the difference in treatment is objectively justified, it will run counter to the very purpose of Article 5, namely to protect the individual from arbitrary detention'.[40] In this sense, it might be argued that the applicant's continued detention after the

[36] ibid para 42.
[37] ibid para 59.
[38] In that it entitled those serving long-term determinate sentences of less than fifteen years and those serving indeterminate sentences to be released upon a positive recommendation of the Parole Board but required those serving long-term determinate sentences of fifteen years or more to secure in addition the approval of the Secretary of State.
[39] See similarly *Webster v UK* (dec) App no 12118/86, 4 Mar 1987.
[40] *Clift v UK* App no 7205/07, 13 July 2010, paras 62–63.

decision of the Parole Board 'lacked objective justification' and was thus unlawful in the sense of Article 5(1) ECHR. This, though, calls into question the necessity of reliance on additional equality or non-discrimination principles.

Similarly, in *Qing*, the applicant, a Chinese national living in Portugal, complained about the fact that she had been detained on remand, alleging that the detention was both arbitrary and discriminatory.[41] The ECtHR considered the issue under both Article 5(1) ECHR and Article 14 ECHR. In holding that Article 5(1) ECHR had not been violated, it reasoned that the applicant's 'arrest and detention were based on relevant and sufficient grounds' in that 'there was a risk of the applicant absconding, obstructing the investigation or continuing criminal activity'.[42] Similarly, in finding that Article 14 ECHR had been upheld, it noted that domestic courts' analysis of the lawfulness of her arrest and detention 'was based on relevant factors and cannot be seen as arbitrary or discriminatory'.[43] Had the ECtHR found that the applicant had only been held on remand as a consequence of the fact that she was a foreign national, then it is clear that this would have been arbitrary and would also have resulted in a violation of Article 5(1) ECHR.

In *DG v Ireland*, the applicant, who was a minor in need of special care, complained that his detention in a young offender's institute—even though he had neither been charged with, nor convicted of, committing a crime—was arbitrary and discriminatory. The ECtHR found a violation of Article 5(1) ECHR but held that no separate issue arose under Article 14 ECHR. It noted that the applicant's complaint that the treatment was discriminatory as compared to other minors raised 'the same issue which lies at the heart of the Article 5 complaint in respect of which the Court has found a violation of the Convention'.[44]

It should come as little surprise that there are very few cases in which the ECtHR has found a violation of Article 14 ECHR while simultaneously holding that there was no violation of the substantive right in question. One recent exception is the case of *Makuchyan and Minasyan v Azerbaijan and Hungary*.[45] In this case, Mr Makuchyan and the nephew of Mr Minasyan, GM, took part as members of the Armenian military in a NATO-sponsored programme in Hungary. During the course, a member of the Azerbaijani military, RS, murdered Mr Minasyan's nephew, GM, while he was asleep by decapitating him with an axe. He also tried to break into Mr Makuchyan's room but was stopped

[41] *Qing v Portugal* App no 69861/11, 5 Nov 2015.
[42] ibid para 49.
[43] ibid para 89.
[44] *DG v Ireland* App no 39474/98, ECHR 2002-II, para 115.
[45] *Makuchyan and Minasyan v Azerbaijan and Hungary* App no 17247/13, 26 May 2020.

by the Hungarian police. He was tried in Hungary and found 'guilty of the exceptionally cruel and premeditated murder of GM and of preparation for murder of the first applicant'. The Hungarian court also found the crimes to have been 'committed with vile motives and exclusively because of the Armenian nationality of the victims'.[46] In 2006, the applicant was sentenced to life imprisonment with a punishment part of thirty years. In 2012, he was transferred to Azerbaijan, in accordance with the Council of Europe Convention on the Transfer of Sentenced Persons, to serve the rest of his sentence. On arrival, he was informed that he was to be released immediately 'on the basis of a presidential pardon that had been issued on the same day'. In addition, he was 'promoted to the rank of major by the Minister of the Defence during the course of a public ceremony' and 'provided use of a flat belonging to the State housing fund and ... awarded eight years of salary arrears'.[47]

The ECtHR held that there had been a violation of the procedural limb of Article 2 ECHR but stopped short of finding a violation of the substantive aspect of the right to life. It held that in deciding to pardon RS, promote him to the rank of major, and award him eight years of salary arrears and the use of a flat, 'Azerbaijan must be considered to have demonstrated its "approval" and "endorsement" of RS's conduct'.[48] It held, however, that 'it has not been convincingly demonstrated that Azerbaijan had "clearly and unequivocally" "acknowledged" and "adopted" "as its own" RS's deplorable acts, thus assuming, as such, responsibility for his actual killing of GM and the preparations for the murder of the first applicant'.[49]

In considering the violation of Article 14 ECHR, the ECtHR held that the complaint was linked to the one examined above under Article 2 ECHR, but it did not consider the nature of the relationship between the two provisions.[50] The applicants complained that the actions taken by the Azerbaijani authorities, 'including pardoning RS' were in the words of the Parliamentary Assembly to be classified as 'a reward for the [the victim's] murder, motivated by nationalist hate' and constituted the 'glorification of a crime on political grounds'.[51] The ECtHR held that the actions of the Azerbaijani authorities to be considered included not just the pardon, but also the 'hero's welcome accorded to him, the various benefits granted to him, and the unquestionable approval of his actions

[46] ibid para 15.
[47] ibid para 20f.
[48] ibid para 117.
[49] ibid para 118.
[50] ibid para 200.
[51] ibid para 203.

expressed by high-ranking officials and by Azerbaijani society as a whole'. It concluded that Azerbaijan had not managed to 'refute the overwhelming body of evidence submitted by the applicants indicating that the various measures leading to RS's virtual impunity, coupled with the glorification of his extremely cruel hate crime, had a causal link to the Armenian ethnicity of his victims' and thus were racially motivated and discriminatory.[52]

The fact that the Azerbaijani authorities praised RS as a hero and role model suggests that they tolerated and glorified his conduct. The conclusion of the ECtHR in the context of Article 14 ECHR that the actions of the authorities constituted the glorification of a hate crime are difficult to reconcile with its finding that the authorities' behaviour did not trigger state responsibility in the sense of Article 11 of the ILC Draft Articles on State Responsibility.[53] The pardon was not just discriminatory; it was also unjust in the sense that it called into question the sanctity of life in violation of Article 2 ECHR. This case suggests that the autonomous notion of Article 14 ECHR might be invoked in those cases in which the ECHR is unwilling to directly condemn the substantive injustice at issue. In any event, the case law provides only limited support for an understanding of equality, which goes beyond the protection inherent in the substantive provisions of the Convention, except for those cases in which the contracting states have opted to offer protection that exceeds the minimum guarantees established by the Convention.[54]

2. Discriminatory v Disparate Treatment

The prohibition on discrimination in Article 14 ECHR might differ from a more general obligation to apply all rights equally if it is restricted to particular types of unequal treatment, which are considered to be a priori problematic, such as discrimination on the grounds of race.[55] In this sense, it might offer protection beyond that implied by the violation of the substantive article by signalling that some types of inequality deserve particular condemnation. In *Aghdgomelashvili and Japaridze*, for instance, the ECtHR held that, in the

[52] ibid para 220.

[53] See too the dissenting opinion of Judge Pinto de Albuquerque who described the ECtHR's decision on the substantive aspect of Art 2 ECHR as 'beyond my comprehension', attached to the judgment at para 8.

[54] See *Fretté v France* App no 36515/97, ECHR 2002-I and dissenting opinion attached to the judgment.

[55] Discrimination based on race is clearly prohibited by Art 14 ECHR, see eg *Moldovan and Others v Romania (No 2)*, 41138/98 64320/01, 12 July 2015, para 139. The ECtHR has stressed, referring to the Declarations of the Vienna and Strasbourg Summits of the Council of Europe, that 'in today's multicultural European societies, the eradication of racism has become a common priority goal for all Contracting States', *Sander v UK* App no 34129/96, 9 May 2000, para 23.

course of a search of the offices of an LGBT NGO, police officers had 'wilfully humiliated and debased the applicants' by resorting to hate speech and subjecting the applicants to unnecessary strip searches in the NGO office toilets.[56] The ECtHR noted that:

> treating violence and brutality with discriminatory intent, irrespective of whether they are perpetrated by State agents or private individuals, on an equal footing with cases that have no such overtones would be to turn a blind eye to the specific nature of acts that are particularly destructive of fundamental rights. A failure to make a distinction in the way situations that are essentially different are handled may constitute unjustified treatment irreconcilable with Article 14 of the Convention.[57]

The ECtHR concluded that 'the wholly inappropriate conduct of the police officers during the search [of the office] ... was motivated by homophobic and/or transphobic hatred and must necessarily have aroused in the applicants feelings of fear, anguish and insecurity which were not compatible with respect for their human dignity'. This led the ECtHR to conclude that the 'conduct reached the threshold of severity within the meaning of Article 3 taken in conjunction with Article 14 of the Convention' and violated the substantive limb of Article 3 ECHR.[58]

In *Munteanu*, the ECtHR noted that the authorities' actions did not constitute 'a simple failure or delay in dealing with violence against the first applicant, but in fact condonation of that violence, reflecting a discriminatory attitude towards her as a woman' and resulted in a violation of Article 14 in addition to Article 3 ECHR.[59] Similarly, in *Lakatošová and Lakatoš*, the failure of the criminal court to address the racist motives of the offender led to a violation of both Article 2 and Article 14 ECHR.[60] The ECtHR has also held that:

[56] *Aghdgomelashvili and Japaridze v Georgia* App no 7224/11, 8 Oct 2020.
[57] ibid para 44.
[58] ibid paras 49–50.
[59] *Munteanu v The Republic of Moldova* App no 34168/11, 26 May 2020, para 75.
[60] Referring to the fact that 'the adequacy of the action taken by the authorities dealing with the investigation and prosecution in this case was impaired to an extent that is irreconcilable with the State's obligation in this field to conduct vigorous investigations, having regard to the need to continuously reassert society's condemnation of racism in order to maintain the confidence of minorities in the ability of the authorities to protect them from the threat of racist violence', citing *Koky and Others v Slovakia* App no 13624/03, 12 June 2012, para 239; *Amadayev v Russia* App no 18114/06, 3 July 2014, para 81, and *Balázs v Hungary* App no 15529/12, 20 Oct 2015, para 52. See also *Virabyan v Armenia* App no 40094/05, 2 Dec 2012, para 224: the Court therefore concludes that the authorities failed in their duty under Art 14 of the Convention taken in conjunction with Art 3 to take all possible steps to investigate whether or not discrimination may have played a role in the applicant's ill-treatment.

> there could be said to be an emerging international consensus among the Contracting States of the Council of Europe recognising the special needs of minorities and an obligation to protect their security, identity and lifestyle, not only for the purpose of safeguarding the interests of the minorities themselves but to preserve a cultural diversity of value to the whole community.[61]

The ECtHR's approach to discrimination can be characterized as focused on formal conceptions of equality in the sense of determining the reasonableness of any justification for the difference in treatment, although there are some indications that the ECtHR is beginning to recognize a more substantive understanding of equality.[62] Similarly, it has recognized that *prima facie* discrimination under Article 14 ECHR might be acceptable and indeed necessary to 'correct factual inequalities' and that affirmative action measures will be legitimate providing that they can be considered necessary to address factual inequality.[63]

The case law offers little support, however, for a restrictive interpretation of Article 14 ECHR as focused on particularly problematic types of discrimination. The ECtHR has held that 'discrimination means treating differently, without an objective and reasonable justification, persons in relevantly similar situations'.[64] The focus in this regard is very much on the nature of the justification, rather than on whether two people can be said to be in a similar position.[65] The ECtHR has suggested that discriminatory treatment is not synonymous with disparate treatment:

> Article 14 does not forbid every difference in treatment in the exercise of the rights and freedoms recognised by the Convention. It safeguards persons who are in analogous or relevantly similar positions against discriminatory differences in treatment that have as their basis or reason a personal characteristic ('status') by which persons or a group of persons are distinguishable from each other.[66]

[61] *Chapman v UK* [GC] App no 27238/95, ECHR 2001-I, paras 93–94; *DH and Others v Czech Republic* [GC] App no 57325/00, ECHR 2007-IV, para 181.

[62] See eg R O'Connell, 'Cinderella Comes to the Ball: Article 14 and the Right to Non-Discrimination in the ECHR' (2009) 29 *Legal Studies* 211, 212.

[63] See eg *Stec and Others v UK* [GC] App nos 65731/01 and 65900/01, ECHR 2006-VI, para 66.

[64] *DH and Others v Czech Republic* [GC] App no 57325/00, ECHR 2007-IV, para 175.

[65] See also *AL (Serbia) v Secretary of State for the Home Department* [2008] 1 WLR 1434, para 25 per Baroness Hale of Richmond: 'unless there are obvious relevant differences between the two situations, it is better to concentrate on the reasons for the difference in treatment and whether they amount to an objective and reasonable justifications.'

[66] *Kafkaris v Cyprus* [GC] App no 21906/04, ECHR 2008, para 160, citing *Kjeldsen, Busk Madsen and Pedersen v Denmark*, 7 Dec 1976, Series A no 23, para 56 and *Thlimmenos v Greece* [GC] App no 34369/97, ECHR 2000-IV, paras 40–49.

This makes it clear that not every basis for different treatment will fall within the scope of Article 14 ECHR.

Article 14 ECHR sets out a list of prohibited grounds of discrimination including, but not limited to, sex, race, colour, language, religion, political or other opinion, national or social origin, association with a national minority, property, birth, or other status. The reference to 'other status', or '*toute autre situation*', in the French version of the ECHR makes it clear that this list is not exhaustive.[67] The ECtHR has suggested in a number of judgments that the difference in treatment must be based on 'a personal characteristic ("status") by which persons or groups of persons are distinguishable from each other'.[68] Prohibited grounds of discrimination which fall within this understanding of the provision and which have been held to fall within Article 14 ECHR include age[69] and physical disability.[70] In a number of cases, however, the ECtHR has held that Article 14 ECHR is applicable in the context of differences in treatment, which are patently not based on 'personal characteristics'.[71] These include distinctions based on military rank,[72] disparate treatment of prisoners based on the length of their sentences,[73] and immigration status.[74]

Grounds which have been determined to fall outside the scope of Article 14 ECHR include differences based on geographical location. In *Magee*, the applicant complained that suspects arrested in England and Wales under prevention of terrorism legislation were entitled to have immediate access to legal counsel, whereas this was not the case in Northern Ireland.[75] The ECtHR noted that 'in the constituent parts of the United Kingdom there is not always a uniform approach to legislation in particular areas. Whether or not an individual can assert a right derived from legislation may accordingly depend on the

[67] See also F Edel, *The Prohibition of Discrimination under the European Convention on Human Rights* (Strasbourg: Council of Europe Publishing 2010) 86. See also *Rasmussen v Denmark*, 28 Nov 1984, Series A no 87, para 34.

[68] *Kjeldsen, Busk Madsen and Pedersen v Denmark*, 7 Dec 1976, Series A no 23, para 56.

[69] See eg *Schwizgebel v Switzerland* App no 25762/07, ECHR 2010, para 85 and *Nelson v UK* (dec) App no 11077/84, 13 Oct 1986.

[70] *Glor v Switzerland* App no 13444/04, ECHR 2009, para 80.

[71] For detailed consideration see Gerards, 'The Discrimination Grounds' (n 21) 107ff.

[72] *Engel and Others v Netherlands*, 8 June 1976, Series A no 22, para 72.

[73] *Clift v UK* App no 7205/07, 13 July 2010, para 62. In *Gerger v Turkey* App no 24919/94, 8 July 1999, para 69 in which convicted terrorists were not entitled to parole until they had served three-quarters of their sentence, unlike prisoners sentenced for ordinary criminal offences, the ECtHR held that 'the distinction [was] made not between different groups of people, but between different types of offence, according to the legislature's view of their gravity'; see also *Kafkaris v Cyprus* [GC] App no 21906/04, ECHR 2008, para 165, in which the Court did not accept that a prisoner serving a life sentence was in an 'analogous or relevantly similar position to other prisoners who were not serving life sentences, given the nature of a life sentence'.

[74] See eg *Bah v UK* App no 56328/07, ECHR 2011-VI.

[75] *Magee v UK* App no 28135/95, 6 June 2000, para 48.

geographical reach of the legislation at issue and the individual's location at the time.' It held that:

> in so far as there exists a difference in treatment of detained suspects ... that difference is not to be explained in terms of personal characteristics, such as national origin or association with a national minority, but on the geographical location where the individual is arrested and detained. This permits legislation to take account of regional differences and characteristics of an objective and reasonable nature. In the present case, such a difference does not amount to discriminatory treatment within the meaning of Article 14 of the Convention.[76]

Similarly, in *Nelson*, the applicant complained that he was subject to discriminatory treatment, as children sentenced in England were entitled to remission whereas those sentenced in Scotland were not.[77] The European Commission on Human Rights held that the complaint essentially concerned 'differences in the penal legislation of two regional jurisdictions within the United Kingdom' and that 'any difference in treatment concerning release on remission which results from these regional differences' was not related in any way to the personal status of the applicant. Consequently, it held that 'the application did not fall within any of the grounds specified in Article 14'.[78] In more recent cases, on the other hand, the ECtHR has held place of residence to be relevant. In *Carlson*, for instance, it found that place of residence constituted an element of personal status in a case involving pension entitlements.[79] Similarly, in *Aleksandr Aleksandrov v Russia*, the applicant's place of residence was deemed to constitute an aspect of 'personal status'.[80]

It is difficult to establish from these cases which grounds will be considered discriminatory and the reasons for this classification.[81] The ECtHR has certainly extended the scope of the provision beyond the immutable personal status cases and has applied Article 14 ECHR in cases in which the status at issue seems legal rather than personal. The case law is too inconsistent and incoherent, however, to constitute support for the argument that the scope of protection is focused principally on propagating a prohibition on discrimination

[76] ibid para 50.
[77] *Nelson v UK* (dec) App no 11077/84, 13 Oct 1986.
[78] ibid.
[79] *Carson and Others v UK* App no 42184/05, ECHR 2010-II.
[80] *Aleksandr Aleksandrov v Russia* App no 14431/06, 27 Mar 2018, para 25.
[81] Gerards, 'The Discrimination Grounds' (n 21) 106ff.

in those cases in which the unequal treatment is based on reasons which are a priori problematic such as race or gender.[82]

3. Non-Discrimination as the Equal Application of Rights

This all suggests that the freedom from discrimination in Article 14 ECHR does not go beyond the Article 1 ECHR guarantee that the various rights in the Convention are to be applied equally to all people. In particular, there is little evidence of any sort of right to prescriptive equality. In view of this, the consideration of the specific relevance of equality or non-discrimination in the sentencing context will approach the subject by looking at the nature of the interference, namely at the discrimination inherent in the arbitrary approach to the individual substantive right,[83] rather than at the nature of the discrimination itself. Of particular importance in the case law are the issues of sex, gender, and racial discrimination.

B. Discriminatory Sentences: Sex, Gender, and Racial Discrimination

1. Discriminatory Sentences and Article 6(1) ECHR

Judgments that rely on discriminatory reasoning will violate the right to a reasoned judgment as guaranteed by Article 6(1) ECHR. It is important to note at the outset that this does not imply that Article 6(1) ECHR encompasses any sort of right to a 'reasonable' judgment:[84] 'the Court will not, in principle, contest the factual and legal findings of the domestic courts, unless their decisions appear arbitrary or manifestly unreasonable.'[85] The right in Article 6(1) ECHR is to a 'reasoned' judgment in the sense of a judgment free from arbitrariness. Discriminatory reasoning by its very nature lacks objective justification and thus reliance on such reasoning is likely to lead to the judgment being classed as arbitrary.[86] The ECtHR has nevertheless chosen to consider this issue by relying on Article 14 ECHR. It has held that if a judgment of a domestic court 'introduces a difference in treatment exclusively based on one of the criteria

[82] See eg S Besson, 'Gender Discrimination under EU and ECHR Law: Never the Twain Shall Meet?' (2008) 8 *Human Rights Law Review* 647, 649.

[83] MP Foran, 'Discrimination as an Individual Wrong' (2019) 39 *Oxford Journal of Legal Studies* 901.

[84] S Trechsel, *Human Rights in Criminal Proceedings* (Oxford: OUP 2005) 106.

[85] See eg *Navalnyy and Ofitserov v Russia* App nos 46632/13 and 28671/14, 23 Feb 2016, para 101.

[86] On the relationship between the obligation to provide reasons and the protection against arbitrariness see *Dulaurans v France* App no 34553/97, 21 Mar 2000 and for discussion, see Trechsel, *Human Rights in Criminal Proceedings* (n 84) 106.

enumerated in Article 14, the State is under an obligation to justify that difference in treatment'.[87] In the absence of such justification, there will be a violation of Article 14 ECHR taken together with Article 6(1) ECHR.

In *Paraskeva Todorova*, the ECtHR held that the refusal to suspend the applicant's sentence was based on her Roma ethnicity and was thus discriminatory and undermined her right to a fair trial.[88] In refusing to suspend the sentence, the judge had stated that:

> The decision to impose an effective sentence of imprisonment in this case arises from the legal obligation for the court (Article 66 of the Penal Code) to determine whether suspension of the sentence's execution is compatible with the objectives of the penal sanction. The court considers that this is not the case in this case, especially as there is a feeling of impunity, especially among members of minority groups, for whom a conditional sentence is not a conviction (this concerns general prevention). Moreover, this conclusion is equally valid with regard to special prevention—the execution of the sentence imposed will prevent [the applicant] from committing other criminal offenses and [will enable her] to correct her behaviour and to rehabilitate herself.[89]

In its judgment, the ECtHR noted that the court of first instance had been obliged to consider whether the objectives of general and specific prevention could be achieved without the need to enforce the sentence. In considering the issue of general prevention, it had referred to a 'widespread sentiment of impunity in society, highlighting in particular the extent of this phenomenon in the case of minority groups, "for whom a suspended sentence is not a conviction"'.[90] The ECtHR accepted that 'in assessing the deterring effect of a sentence vis-à-vis other members of society, a court may have to take into consideration phenomena of a more or less general nature, such as, for example, the situation of crime in the country, the perception by the general public of this or that type of crime, or the possible existence of a social climate of insecurity'. It

[87] *Paraskeva Todorova v Bulgaria* App no 37193/07, 25 Mar 2010, para 36, citing *Schuler-Zgraggen v Switzerland*, 24 June 1993, Series A No 263, para 67; *Moldovan and Others v Romania (No 2)* App nos 41138/98 and 64320/01, ECHR 2005-VII, paras 139 and 140; *Navalnyy and Ofitserov v Russia* App nos 46632/13 and 28671/14, 23 Feb 2016, para 101; *Van Kück v Germany* App no 35968/97, ECHR 2003-VII, paras 46–47; *Khamidov v Russia* App no 72118/01, ECHR 2007-XII, para 170; *Berhani v Albania* App no 847/05, 27 May 2010, paras 50–56; *Ajdarić v Croatia* App no 20883/09, 13 Dec 2011, paras 47–52; *Anđelković v Serbia* App no 1401/08, 9 Apr 2013, paras 26–29.

[88] *Paraskeva Todorova v Bulgaria* App no 37193/07, 25 Mar 2010, para 46.

[89] ibid para 10.

[90] ibid para 38.

stressed, however, that such observations had to 'rest on a certain factual basis'. In the case at issue, this was not the case. The domestic courts had not sought to underpin their argument with arguments or facts.[91] The ECtHR held that it was not convinced that the applicant's ethnicity was only of subsidiary importance in the court's assessment, noting that the court had expressly referred to the applicant's Roma origin and its comments on the 'feeling of imputing in society' was focused on minority groups and thus on the applicant herself.[92] This led the ECtHR to conclude that this statement 'taken together with the applicant's ethnic affiliation, was likely to inspire the public, as well as the applicant, with the sentiment that the court was seeking to impose, in this case, an exemplary sentence for the Roma community, by condemning to an effective sentence a person belonging to the same minority group'.[93]

Judgments which contain discriminatory reasoning in relation to the determination of the sentence will necessarily be arbitrary and will violate the right to a fair trial and the prohibition on discrimination.

2. Discriminatory Sentences and Article 3 ECHR

It might be argued that some types of discriminatory reasoning in the sentencing judgment are such as to meet the threshold for degrading treatment in the sense of Article 3 ECHR taken alone or together with Article 14 ECHR. In some early decisions, the European Commission on Human Rights suggested that the resort to some types of discrimination, notably based on race, might be such as to amount to degrading treatment contrary to Article 3 ECHR.[94] In the *East African Asians* case, the Commission noted that 'discrimination based on race could, in certain circumstances, of itself amount to degrading treatment within the meaning of Article 3 of the Convention'.[95] It distinguished the particular problem of racism, noting that it was 'generally recognised' that 'special importance should be attached to discrimination based on race' and that 'publicly to single out a group of persons for differential treatment on the basis of race might, in certain circumstances, constitute a special form of affront to human dignity'. Crucially, it held that 'differential treatment of a group of persons on the basis of race might therefore be capable of constituting degrading

[91] ibid para 39.
[92] ibid para 40.
[93] ibid para 40.
[94] *East African Asians v United Kingdom* App nos 4403/70–4419/70, 4422/70, 4423/70, 4434/70, 4443/70, 4476/70–4478/70, 4501/70, and 4526/70–4530/70 (joined), Report of 14 Dec 1973 (1994) DR 78-A, para 207.
[95] ibid.

treatment when differential treatment on some other ground would raise no such questions'.[96] Similarly, in *Aghdgomelashvili and Japaridze*, the fact that the inappropriate conduct of the police was motivated by homophobic and/or transphobic hatred was central to the ECtHR's finding that it was incompatible with respect for their human dignity and as such met the threshold of severity within the meaning of Article 3 ECHR.[97]

This type of reasoning suggests support for an understanding of equality in Article 3 ECHR as concerned with the prohibition of certain grounds of discrimination (particularly those which relate to innate or immutable personal characteristics) which are a priori suspect.[98] It is conceivable that a judgment which relied on discriminatory reasoning in the imposition or aggravation of a sentence might be considered to reach the threshold for the purposes of Article 3 ECHR.[99]

3. Discriminatory Sentences and Articles 5(1) and 7(1) ECHR

The imposition of a discriminatory sentence is likely to violate Article 7(1) ECHR. Article 7(1) ECHR prohibits punishment without law. Read in the light of Article 1 ECHR and Article 14 ECHR this must be understood to demand that punishment must be applied in a non-arbitrary fashion and free from discrimination.

Discriminatory sentences of imprisonment might also violate the right to freedom from arbitrary detention as guaranteed by Article 5(1)(a) ECHR.[100] The fact that the deprivation of liberty was sanctioned by a court following a conviction in criminal proceedings provides a *prima facie* basis for the legitimacy of the detention and thus the punishment. The ECtHR is reluctant to consider the appropriateness of the sentence for the criminal offence at issue.[101] Consideration of the compliance of a sentence with Article 5(1) ECHR will generally be restricted to those cases in which the applicant alleges that the

[96] ibid citing admissibility decision in the Group 1 (East African Asians I) cases *Samji Maji Patel (4403/70) and Others (twenty-five applications) v UK* (1971) Coll 36, 92 at 117.

[97] *Aghdgomelashvili and Japaridze v Georgia* App no 7224/11, 8 Oct 2020, para 49.

[98] Besson, 'Gender Discrimination' (n 82) 653.

[99] See in the context of Art 8 ECHR, *Sutherland v UK* (dec) App no 25186/94, 21 May 1996.

[100] Art 5(1)(a) ECHR expressly provides for deprivation of liberty following conviction by a competent court. On the specific issues concerning life sentences see Ch 3.

[101] See *Khamtokhu and Aksenchik v Russia* [GC] App no 60367/08, ECHR 2017, para 55: 'matters of appropriate sentencing fall in principle outside the scope of the Convention, it not being its role to decide, for example, what is the appropriate term of detention applicable to a particular offence' citing *Vinter and Others v UK* [GC] App nos 66069/09, 130/10, and 3896/10, ECHR 2013, para 105; *Sawoniuk v UK* (dec) App no 63716/00, ECHR 2001-VI; *T v UK* [GC] App no 24724/94, 16 Dec 1999, para 117; *V v UK* [GC] App no 24888/94, ECHR 1999-IX, para 118.

sentence was clearly arbitrary.[102] There is a clear connection, though, between arbitrariness and discriminatory detention.

Sentencing provisions, which introduce different rules for different people, or which are applied differently to different people, will, in the absence of clear and valid reasons for the unequal treatment, give rise to suspicions of arbitrariness. The ECtHR has confirmed that sentencing policies on imprisonment, which appear 'to affect individuals in a discriminatory fashion', may raise issues under Article 5(1) ECHR read in conjunction with Article 14 ECHR.[103] As we shall see, these cases are often considered in the context of the Article 14 ECHR prohibition on discrimination taken together with Article 5(1) ECHR rather than solely under the Article 5(1) ECHR prohibition on arbitrary detention. It is important to stress that the problem here does not just involve the enforcement of the sentence, but also goes to the legitimacy of the sentence decision itself.

In *Aleksandr Aleksandrov*, the applicant had been convicted of assaulting a police officer and sentenced to one year of imprisonment. The trial court explained its decision to impose a custodial sentence on the following grounds:

> When sentencing the defendant, Mr Aleksandrov, the court takes into account the nature and degree of the social danger of the offence, all the circumstances of the case, and the information regarding the defendant's personality: [he] has never incurred any criminal or administrative liability, he is not registered [as a drug addict or as a person suffering from psychotic disorders], he was given positive references by his neighbours and employers, [and] his military resignation has been annulled because of a kidney disease. The court accepts the above-mentioned circumstances as mitigating the defendant's guilt; however, it does not find any grounds for sentencing [him] to probation or imposing a fine on him, given the particular circumstances in which the offence was committed and the fact that [he] does not have a permanent place of residence in Moscow or in the Moscow Region.[104]

The applicant complained that he had been discriminated against as the court had refused to consider a non-custodial disposal purely on the grounds that he did not have a permanent residence in Moscow or the Moscow region.

[102] See further Ch 3. See also disproportionate punishment for ill-treatment, *Nikolova and Velichkova v Bulgaria* App no 7888/03, 20 Dec 2007, para 61; *Okkalı v Turkey* App no 52067/99, ECHR 2006-XII para 73; *Derman v Turkey* App no 21789/02, 31 May 2011, para 28.

[103] *Nelson v UK* (dec) App no 11077/84, 13 Oct 1986.

[104] *Aleksandr Aleksandrov v Russia* App no 14431/06, 27 Mar 2018, para 5.

The ECtHR held that 'place of residence constitutes an aspect of personal status for the purposes of Article 14 ECHR' and that 'in so far as the applicant's place of residence was explicitly mentioned as a factor in the sentencing decision, it introduced a difference of treatment based on this ground between the applicant and other offenders convicted of similar offences and eligible for sentence of probation or a fine'.[105] It concluded that the difference in treatment was not 'capable of being objectively and reasonably justified' and thus violated Article 14 ECHR in conjunction with Article 5 ECHR.[106]

In a number of cases, the Strasbourg authorities have had to consider complaints that the sentences imposed violated the prohibition on gender discrimination. In *P*, the applicant had been convicted of a number of property and motoring offences and sentenced to three months' custodial detention in a young offender's institution. He complained that under English law, the law provided that boys but not girls of fourteen years of age could be sentenced to a period of up to four months' imprisonment in a young offender's institution.[107] He argued that had he been a girl, he could not have been imprisoned and thus that he had been 'treated in a manner different from a comparable female offender'. The case was settled after the United Kingdom agreed to pay the applicant compensation and costs and to abolish the possibility of custodial detention in respect of fourteen-year-old boys.[108]

More recently, in *Khamtokhu and Aksenchik*, the Grand Chamber had to consider the case of two applicants, both men, who had been sentenced to life imprisonment. The applicants complained that they had been exposed to discriminatory treatment solely on account of their sex in violation of Article 14 ECHR, taken together with Article 5 ECHR.[109] Russian law expressly prohibited the imposition of a sentence of life imprisonment on female offenders. This meant that they had been treated less favourably than similarly situated female offenders. The ECtHR agreed that the applicants were 'in an analogous situation to all other offenders who had been convicted of the same or comparable offences'[110] and noted that 'differences based on sex require particularly serious reasons by way of justification'.[111] In this regard, it has frequently referred

[105] ibid para 25.
[106] ibid para 30.
[107] *P v UK* (dec) App no 15397/89, 8 Jan 1992.
[108] ibid.
[109] *Khamtokhu and Aksenchik v Russia* [GC] App no 60367/08, ECHR 2017, para 54.
[110] ibid paras 67–68.
[111] ibid para 78 citing *Konstantin Markin v Russia* [GC] App no 30078/06, 22 Mar 2012, para 127; *X and Others v Austria* [GC] App no 19010/07, ECHR 2013-II, para 99; *Vallianatos and Others v Greece* [GC] App nos 29381/09 and 32684/09, ECHR 2013-VI, para 77; *Hämäläinen v Finland* [GC] App no 37359/09, ECHR 2014, para 109.

to the fact that the 'advancement of the equality of the sexes' is a 'major goal in the member States of the Council of Europe' and that 'very weighty reasons would have to be put forward before such a difference of treatment could be regarded as compatible with the Convention'.[112] It has also held on numerous occasions that 'references to traditions, general assumptions or prevailing social attitudes in a particular country are insufficient justification for a difference in treatment on grounds of sex'.[113]

In the case at issue, the Grand Chamber refused to find a violation of Article 14 ECHR. It held that the 'public interest underlying the exemption of female offenders from life imprisonment' justified the difference in treatment. In reaching this conclusion it referred to: 'the needs of women for protection against gender-based violence, abuse and sexual harassment in the prison environment'; 'the needs for protection of pregnancy and motherhood'; and data provided by the Russian government which showed a 'considerable difference between the total number of male and female prison inmates' and the 'relatively small number of persons sentenced to life imprisonment'.[114] One judge went even further, referring in his concurring opinion to the fact that 'female offenders typically do not pose the same security problem that men do, and the danger of recidivism is less' and that the 'same period of imprisonment for a woman is more painful than for a man, perhaps because, typically, a woman is deprived of the possibility of giving birth to a child, and in particular raising a child'.[115] He also stated:

> This may sound like a simple gender stereotype, although many people would argue that there are biological differences and specificities of the female brain. But in a society where women are expected to have children and are raised in a social environment in which they are conditioned to believe that their happiness comes from having children they will suffer from the lack of fulfilment of this socially imposed expectation.[116]

Unsurprisingly, the judgment provoked considerable controversy. Critics complained that the Grand Chamber had failed to recognize that the harm

112 *Schuler-Zgraggen v Switzerland* [GC], 24 June 1993, Series A no 263, para 67; see too *Abdulaziz, Cabales and Balkandali v UK*, 28 May 1985, Series A no 94, para 78

113 *Konstantin Markin v Russia* [GC] App no 30078/06, 22 Mar 2012, para 127. See also *Ünal Tekeli v Turkey* App no 29865/96, ECHR 2004, para 63: states are prohibited from 'imposing traditions that derive from the man's primordial role and the woman's secondary role in the family'.

114 *Khamtokhu and Aksenchik v Russia* [GC] App no 60367/08, ECHR 2017, para 82.

115 Concurring opinion of Judge Sajo, annexed to the judgment. References omitted.

116 ibid.

of stereotyping is 'that it justifies and reinforces discrimination: stereotypes anchor structural inequality'.[117] In his dissenting opinion, Judge Pinto de Albuquerque warned of the dangers of perpetuating 'age-old prejudices regarding the nature or role of women in society',[118] arguing that, 'an unjustified differentiation between men and women, in the sense that it is not based on an actual factual disadvantage but on a preconceived idea of the supposed weaknesses of the latter as compared with the former, would have the effect not of reducing inequalities but perpetuating, or even exacerbating them'.[119] The case is definitely not an example of affirmative action, of treating women differently in order to prevent discrimination. Rather, it might be characterized as preoccupied with the position of female offenders in Russia, rather than the position of the applicants.

The ECtHR was said to have been caught between the proverbial rock and a hard place.[120] Were it to have found a violation of Article 14 ECHR, the Russian authorities would have been forced to adopt one of two strategies in order to ensure compliance with the Convention: abolish life sentences for all prisoners or abolish the exemption on life sentences for female offenders. The ECtHR refused to insist on the abolition of life imprisonment.[121] Equally, though, it was unwilling to 'criticise the Russian legislature for having established, in a way which reflects the evolution of society in that sphere, the exemption of certain groups of offenders from life imprisonment. Such an exemption represents, all things considered, social progress in penological matters.'[122]

[117] See eg the case comment 'Non Discrimination and Life Imprisonment' (2017) *European Human Rights Law Review* 318: '[T]his case and the deep division amongst the judges demonstrated that questions of non-discrimination in relation to life imprisonment are rather controversial leading the Court to rely on stereotypes against female, juvenile and elder offenders for the sake of preventing life imprisonment for these groups'; N Padfield, 'Advancing Human Rights: Levelling Up or Levelling Down?' [2017] *Criminal Law Review* 423; see on stereotypes A Timmer, 'Judging Stereotypes: What the European Court of Human Rights Can Borrow from American and Canadian Equal Protection Law' (2015) 63 *American Journal of Comparative Law* 239, 251.

[118] Dissenting opinion of Judge Pinto de Albuquerque, annexed to the judgment, para 8. The judgment was confirmed by ten votes to seven.

[119] Annexed to the judgment, para 11, referring to Art 5 of the CEDAW which obliges the states parties to take all appropriate measures: 'to modify the social and cultural patterns of conduct of men and women, with a view to achieving the elimination of prejudices and customary and all other practices which are based on the idea of the inferiority or the superiority of either of the sexes or on stereotyped roles for men and women'.

[120] M Vannier, 'Caught between a Rock and a Hard Place-Human Rights, Life Imprisonment and Gender Stereotyping: A Critical Analysis of Khamtokhu and Aksenchik v Russia (2017)' in S Walklate and others (eds), *Emerald Handbook on Feminism, Criminology and Social Change* (Bingley: Emerald Publishing 2020).

[121] *Khamtokhu and Aksenchik v Russia* [GC] App no 60367/08, ECHR 2017, para 86: 'The Court is unable to discern an intentional trend in favour of abolishing life imprisonment or, on the contrary, confirming positive support for it.'

[122] ibid para 86.

This case demonstrates clearly the problems of the focus on equality rather than on the injustice inherent in the violation of the substantive right. It involves precisely the type of case identified by Peters as the only 'kind of case in which prescriptive equality ever matters', namely the case in which it 'purports to tell us something we would not already do under some conception of nonegalitarian justice. This is the case in which a person already has been treated wrongly—unjustly—and we must decide whether, because of that fact, to treat another similar person unjustly.'[123]

In the case at issue, it was the female offenders (and not the male offenders) that were 'wrongly' treated. In this sense, it is important to stress that '[w]rong treatment need not mean detrimental treatment, and indeed most egalitarian claims advocate treating people better than they are otherwise entitled to be treated'.[124] The women were afforded (unjust) preferential treatment.[125] The decision to spare female offenders from life imprisonment/capital punishment might be seen as morally correct—something hinted at in the judgment and concurring opinions—in that women prisoners do not deserve to be subject to life imprisonment or capital punishment, but the criteria for making it were wrong. Women were only spared because of their sex. Accordingly, their treatment was 'wrong'. Prescriptive equality demands that male offenders also be treated 'wrongly'. The implementation of prescriptive equality requires 'for its operation the treatment of a person according to the same irrelevant criterion (or according to the same incorrect balancing of criteria) that has been applied in the unjust treatment of an identically situated person'.[126] As we have seen, though, Article 14 ECHR does not set out any notion of prescriptive equality.

This judgment can best be understood if we accept that the ECtHR was unwilling to go beyond the scope of protection in Article 5(1) ECHR. The ECtHR noted that the offenders had been 'found guilty of particularly serious crimes punishable with imprisonment for life'.[127] In addition it held that 'the outcome of the applicants' trials was decided on the specific facts of their cases and their sentences were the product of individualised application of criminal law by the trial court whose discretion in the choice of appropriate sentence was not curtailed on account of the requirements prescribed in paragraph 2 of Article 57

123 Peters, 'Equality Revisited' (n 2) 1263.
124 ibid 1212.
125 *Ēcis v Latvia* App no 12879/09, 10 Jan 2019, para 93: the applicant complained that male and female prisoners who had been convicted of the same crimes and given the same term of imprisonment were treated differently when serving their sentences: Here the ECtHR held that 'a blanket ban for men to leave the prison, even for attending a funeral of a family member', was not 'conducive to the goal of ensuring that the distinctive needs of women prisoners are taken into account'.
126 Peters, 'Equality Revisited' (n 2) 1250.
127 *Khamtokhu and Aksenchik v Russia* [GC] App no 60367/08, ECHR 2017, para 67.

of the Criminal Code'. This led it to conclude that 'in view of the penological objectives of the protection of society and general and individual deterrence, the life sentences imposed on the applicants do not appear arbitrary or unreasonable'.[128] The case illustrates the limits of the suggestion that the guarantee in Article 14 ECHR has any independent normative force.

The ECtHR also considered the issue of discrimination on the grounds of age in *Khamtokhu and Aksenchik* as the applicants also complained that they were treated less favourably than other men aged under eighteen and over sixty-five who had convicted of similar or comparable crimes. Males under the age of eighteen or over the age of sixty-five, like all women, could not be sentenced to life imprisonment. The ECtHR held that there were good reasons for the difference in treatment of adult and juvenile offenders in the context of life imprisonment, noting that the exemption of juvenile offenders from life imprisonment was accepted by the legal systems of the majority of the contracting states and was in line with the Recommendation of the Committee on the Rights of the Child to abolish all forms of life imprisonment for offences committed by persons below the age of eighteen and with the UN General Assembly's Resolution inviting the states to consider repealing all forms of life imprisonment for such persons. It held that the purpose of the difference in treatment was 'to facilitate the rehabilitation of juvenile delinquents' and that 'when young offenders are held accountable for their deeds, however serious, this must be done with due regard for their presumed immaturity, both mental and emotional, as well as the greater malleability of their personality and their capacity for rehabilitation and reformation'.

This reasoning was in line with earlier case law of the Strasbourg authorities to the effect that the 'penal law of a State Party obviously cannot be expected to treat child and adult offenders in the same way', not least because 'persons sentenced at such an early age may change greatly in the course of their sentence and that flexibility is an important prerequisite in the rules governing their detention'. This meant that legislation allowing considerable discretion in deciding the type of institution to which child offenders should be sent and allowing release on licence at all stages of the sentence were acceptable and that 'any difference in treatment finds objective and reasonable justification in the different considerations which apply in the sentencing of children'.[129]

The exemption of those aged sixty-five or over from being sentenced to life imprisonment was held by the ECtHR to be reasonable and objectively

[128] ibid para 76.
[129] *Nelson v UK* (dec) App no 11077/84, 13 Oct 1986.

justified. It held that the '[r]educibility of a life sentence carries even greater weight for elderly offenders in order not to become a mere illusory possibility' and that by 'limiting the imposition of life sentences through providing for a maximum age limit, the Russian legislature used one among several methods at its disposal for securing a prospect of release for a reasonable number of prisoners and thus acted within its margin of appreciation in line with Convention standards'.[130] Discriminatory sentences of imprisonment will likely give rise to a violation of Article 5 ECHR without the need to refer to Article 14 ECHR.

C. Conclusion: Equality and Justice

The discussion of the normative scope of equality as protected by the ECHR is of fundamental importance in the sentencing context. Neither the right to equality in Article 1 ECHR nor the prohibition on discrimination as set out in Article 14 ECHR implies a right to 'prescriptive equality'. Rather the guarantees embody the requirement that every person must be treated in the manner required by the substantive individual right.[131] This means that notions of individualized justice are not, in the words of Judge Frankel, 'at war' with 'equality, objectivity and consistency in the law',[132] but rather that equality and indeed certainty can best be achieved by ensuring that each individual case is decided correctly on its merits. This is of considerable importance in the sentencing context.

Any sentence imposed must be free from arbitrariness in the sense that only relevant criteria are to be considered in establishing the punishment. In each individual case, the sentencing authority must determine the sentence, without employing discriminatory reasoning. The resort to discriminatory reasoning is likely to result in the characterization of the judgment and the punishment as arbitrary in violation of Article 6(1) ECHR, Article 7(1) ECHR, and in the context of sentences of imprisonment Article 5(1)(a) ECHR. In addition, sentences which rely on discriminatory reasoning may have the potential to reach the Article 3 ECHR threshold. Crucially, in each case, the manner in which other people have been treated (in the past) is not relevant to this determination. The focus of the sentencing judge must be on establishing the appropriate sentence

130 Cf *Sawoniuk v UK* (dec) App no 63716/00, ECHR 2001-VI, discussed further in Ch 3.

131 See also Peters, 'Equality Revisited' (n 2) 1264: 'My argument against prescriptive equality has really been an argument in favor of making every decision on its own merits, of treating people the way justice dictates that they be treated, regardless of how someone else has been treated in the past.'

132 Frankel, *Criminal Sentences* (n 7) 5.

in the case at issue and without reliance on any discriminatory criteria. With this in mind, it is useful to revisit some issues in sentencing practice and theory.

III. Equality and Certainty in Sentencing Practice

A. 'Disparity' as Discrimination?

1. Disparity in Individual Cases

To what extent might the imposition of different sentences for similar conduct and levels of culpability be said to give rise to discrimination? The problem of disparity at sentencing is perhaps best illustrated by the treatment of those convicted of the same offence in the same case. The fact that two offenders were convicted of the same offence does not of course imply that they must receive the same sentence. It is possible and indeed likely that their culpability for the offence will vary. Nevertheless, such cases focus attention on the reasons for sentence disparity.

In one case considered by the Swiss Federal Supreme Court (SFSC), for instance, two offenders (A and B) were convicted of drugs offences and money laundering. A was sentenced to six years, B to four and a half years of imprisonment. B accepted the judgment, while A appealed. On appeal, the High Court upheld the conviction, but reduced A's sentence to four and a half years' imprisonment. It held that although a sentence of six years of imprisonment seemed appropriate, when compared to the sentence imposed on B, it was too high. The prosecution appealed against this judgment. The SFSC upheld the appeal, holding that there was no right to be treated in the same way as someone who had been treated wrongly.[133] In view of the fact that the High Court had determined that a sentence of six years would be appropriate, there was no reason for not imposing this sentence on A.[134] The fact that the sentence imposed on B was too lenient did not mean that the sentence imposed on A was unduly severe. In other words, the wrongful treatment of B did not provide A with a right also to be treated wrongly.

It might be argued here that there is no discriminatory treatment, no personal characteristic (such as gender or race) on which the differential treatment

[133] BGE 134 IV 191, 194, E 3.3 (*kein Anspruch auf "Gleichbehandlung im Unrecht*). On this issue see notably P Tschannen, 'Die Gleichheit im Unrecht: Gerichtsstrafe im Grundrechtskleid' (2011) 112 *Schweizerisches Zentralblatt für Staats- und Verwaltungsrecht* 57; A Auer, 'L'Égalité dans l'Illégalité' (1978) 79 *Schweizerisches Zentralblatt für Staats- und Verwaltungsrecht* 281.

[134] BGE 134 IV 191, 195, E 3.4.

is based. There is no evidence here to suggest that the disparity is based on any sort of 'personal characteristic' of those involved or any of the other various factors accepted by the ECtHR.[135] Even assuming, though, that this type of situation could be classed as one involving discrimination, the judgment of the SFSC seems to be in line with the ECtHR's reasoning in *Khamtokhu and Aksenchik*.[136] Neither the prohibition on discrimination nor the requirement that rights be applied equally provides an individual the right to be treated in the same way as someone who has been treated wrongly. This has considerable implications in the context of sentencing disparity.

2. Disparity between Groups of Offenders

It might be argued that if punishment as a practice disproportionately impacts on groups of offenders, the punishment should be understood as discriminatory.[137] In this sense, issues involving discrimination might arise even if the individual sentence is appropriate in the sense that it reflects an offender's culpability for distinct criminal conduct. The issue, here, is not the application of discriminatory criteria as such, but rather that despite the application of appropriate, non-discriminatory criteria at sentencing, disparity arises which is seen as evidence of 'societal and criminal justice unfairness'.[138] In the USA, for instance 'racial disparity' at sentencing as measured by disproportionate minority confinement is 'substantial and persistent'.[139] The question, here, is whether such problems can be addressed at the sentencing stage.

Frase considers in detail the issue of disproportionate racial impact in the USA with reference to the state of Minnesota and notes that the 'sources of racially disparate inmate populations in other states and in the federal system are probably similar' to those discussed in the context of Minnesota. In one study on racial disparity, he found that 'most of the racial disparity found at the final stage of processing—in the state's prison and jail populations—was already present at the first measurable stage—arrest'.[140] Other factors which he refers to as contributing to 'racial disproportionality after the point of arrest' include prior convictions, statutes imposing mandatory prison sentences (often connected to the issue of prior convictions), the likelihood of pleading

[135] See the discussion in what follows.
[136] *Khamtokhu and Aksenchik v Russia* [GC] App no 60367/08, ECHR 2017.
[137] M Tonry, *Malign Neglect: Race, Crime and Punishment in America* (New York, NY: OUP 1995) 127.
[138] See discussion in RS Frase, *Just Sentencing* (New York, NY: OUP 2013) 210.
[139] ibid.
[140] ibid 213, citing RS Frase, 'What Explains Persistent Racial Disproportionality in Minnesota's Prison and Jail Populations?' in M Tonry (ed), *Crime and Justice: A Review of Research*, vol 38 (Chicago, IL: University of Chicago Press 2009).

guilty (pointing to effective assistance of counsel), and socio-economic deprivation and lack of opportunity.[141] He notes that there is 'little evidence of racial disparity in sentencing decisions by Minnesota judges'.[142]

This suggests that disparity, or even discrimination, which is not based on the application of discriminatory criteria at sentencing, cannot be 'healed' at the sentencing stage. Discriminatory practices in the context of the investigation of crime—such as stop and search or arrest issues—need to be tackled at that stage. The use of evidence collected in a discriminatory fashion will call into question the fairness of the proceedings and thus the lawfulness of the conviction itself. Similarly, issues involving fair access to justice and appropriate legal support to enable defendants to participate effectively can only be remedied by improving access to criminal legal aid. Once again, it is the fairness of the proceedings which is at issue here. In addition, it is noticeable that the sentencing practices identified by Frase as particularly problematic in the context of disparity—notably the treatment of previous conviction as an aggravating factor and the imposition of mandatory sentences—are also problematic from the perspective of legality and proportionality.

B. Sentencing Guidelines and Frameworks

The discussion of disparity and discrimination illustrates the limits of sentencing proposals, which are based on promoting some abstract notion of consistency between cases. It is not consistency of outcome between cases, but rather freedom from arbitrariness in each individual case, which must be guaranteed. Sentencing guidelines could be of use in this sense by assisting the judge in reaching the appropriate sentence in the case at issue.[143] Equally, they could play an important role in guaranteeing legality at sentencing by providing prior indication of the sentence likely to be imposed.

Sentencing guidelines have something of a chequered past. Perhaps the most famous and controversial example is that of the US Federal Sentencing Guidelines, which have been described as 'one of the greatest failures at law

141 Frase, *Just Sentencing* (n 138) 216.

142 ibid.

143 See also N Padfield, 'Exploring the Sentencing Guidelines' in A Ashworth and JV Roberts (eds), *Sentencing Guidelines: Exploring the English Model* (Oxford: OUP 2013) 31: 'So let me make clear from the outset that I am wholly convinced of the need for guidelines: they are important not only for the public but also for judges. They are a useful tool, providing some reassurance that the sentence is "approximately right"'.

reform in US history'.[144] The focus of these guidelines was principally on equalizing outputs by ensuring that offenders receive similar sentences for similar offences.[145] The US Sentencing Commission was directed to seek to achieve 'certainty and fairness' by eliminating 'unwarranted disparity' among sentences for 'similar defendants committing similar offences'.[146] These guidelines had the knock-on effect of increasing punitiveness[147] and were criticized for being too rigid and harsh.[148] In addition, the focus of the guidelines was very much on reining in activist judges. Frankel famously referred to the 'unchecked powers of the untutored judge'[149] and there can be little doubt that the guidelines seemed to display considerable distrust of judges and for the potential for arbitrary judicial discretion.[150]

The reason for the failure of the US Federal Sentencing Guidelines might be said to lie in their overt focus on consistency of outcome and the resulting restriction of judicial discretion.[151] Some other guidelines, notably the Minnesota guidelines and a series of sentencing guidelines based on the Minnesota model,[152] are generally regarded as having been more 'successful' and as constituting 'rare bright spots within a larger picture of desolation'.[153] From the perspective of the ECHR, it is clear that the sentencing judge must have sufficient discretion to enable determination of an offender's culpability for the conduct at issue. Any focus on consistency of outcome (in the sense of standardizing sentences for various offences) which does not allow for sufficient consideration of similarity or difference in each individual case (particularly in the context of the offender's culpability) will be difficult to reconcile

144 ML Miller and RF Wright, 'Your Cheatin' Heart(land): The Long Search for Administrative Sentencing Justice' (1999) 2 *Buffalo Criminal Law Review* 723, 726.

145 See eg Bierschbach and Bibas, 'What's Wrong with Sentencing Equality?' (n 7) 1450.

146 S Rep No 225, 98th Cong, 1st Sess 52, 56 (1984) discussed by L Adelman and J Dietrich, 'Marvin Frankel's Mistakes and the Need to Rethink Federal Sentencing' (2008) 13 *Berkeley Journal of Criminal Law* 239, 240.

147 Tonry, *Sentencing Matters* (n 3) 14.

148 M Tonry, 'The Success of Judge Frankel's Sentencing Commission' (1993) 64 *University of Colorado Law Review* 713, 716; K Stith and SY Koh, 'The Politics of Sentencing Reform: The Legislative History of the Federal Sentencing Guidelines' (1993) 28 *Wake Forest Law Review* 223, 284.

149 Frankel, *Criminal Sentences* (n 7) 41.

150 Adelman and Dietrich, 'Marvin Frankel's Mistakes' (n 146) 242. For discussion of the role of the judge at the sentencing stage see Ch 5.

151 Judicial discretion might be seen as central not just to the determination of the individual culpability of offenders but also as allowing for community-based approaches to sanctions as opposed to more centralized hierarchical structures, see eg Bierschbach and Bibas, 'What's Wrong with Sentencing Equality?' (n 7) 1454. See also C Spohn, *How do Judges Decide?: The Search for Fairness and Justice in Punishment* (Thousand Oaks, CA: Sage 2009) 140 distinguishing between warranted and unwarranted disparity.

152 See further Frase, *Just Sentencing* (n 138).

153 KR Reitz, 'Comparing Sentencing Guidelines: Do US Systems Have Anything Worthwhile to Offer England and Wales?' in A Ashworth and JV Roberts (eds), *Sentencing Guidelines: Exploring the English Model* (Oxford: OUP 2013) 183.

with the legality principle. Reitz suggests that the emerging consensus is that 'consistency of outcome is not what is wanted from a sentencing system, but consistency of analysis as applied in individual cases'.[154]

Judicial discretion is of essential importance to ensuring the imposition of sentences which are free from arbitrariness.[155] In this regard, judges have particular responsibility for distinguishing between disparity, in the sense of a difference in treatment 'which does not necessarily result from intentional bias or prejudice'[156] and discrimination in the sense of the 'differential treatment of individuals based on irrelevant criteria such as race, gender or social class'.[157] Only by providing the sentencing judge with sufficient room to manoeuvre will it be possible to distinguish between disparity and unlawful discrimination. In this regard, it is notable that the ECtHR has referred to the importance of 'adequate and appropriate judicial supervision' of legislative schemes which might be considered discriminatory.[158] This clearly implies recognition of the importance of the potential for judicial decision-making in this regard. Restricting the potential for judicial evaluation of all relevant circumstances by enacting strict sentencing guidelines could clearly prevent the identification and eradication of discriminatory sentencing practices.[159]

C. Criminal Deportation Orders

One sentencing practice which does give rise to questions regarding compliance with the prohibition on discrimination is the resort to deportation as a

[154] See Reitz, 'Comparing Sentencing Guidelines' (n 153) 192. In this sense it is noticeable that the Sentencing Council for England and Wales created in 2010 refers to its role in producing sentencing guidelines as focused on promoting a 'clear, fair and consistent approach to sentencing' <https://www.sentencingcouncil.org.uk/sentencing-and-the-council/about-the-sentencing-council/our-criteria-for-developing-or-revising-guidelines/> (accessed 5 Apr 2021). On developments in England and Wales, see JV Roberts, 'Sentencing Guidelines and Judicial Discretion: Evolution of Duty of Courts to Comply in England and Wales' (2011) 51 British Journal of Criminology 997. See also Padfield, 'Exploring the Sentencing Guidelines' (n 143) 32 referring to consistency as a 'slippery concept'. See A Ashworth and JV Roberts, 'The Origins and Nature of the Sentencing Guidelines in England and Wales' in A Ashworth and JV Roberts (eds), *Sentencing Guidelines: Exploring the English Model* (Oxford: OUP 2013) 1.

[155] This is discussed in detail in Ch 5.

[156] Spohn, *How do Judges Decide?* (n 151) 140.

[157] ibid 129. See too Bierschbach and Bibas, 'What's Wrong with Sentencing Equality?' (n 7) 1455: 'Sentencing equality could borrow the conceptual tiers of equal-protection scrutiny: Racial, ethnic, religious, and fundamental-rights discrimination would face strict scrutiny and virtually always be unconstitutional, whereas geographic and jurisdictional variations would be least troubling and merit deference on any rational basis.'

[158] See eg *Sidabras and Dziautas v Lithuania* App nos 55480/00 and 59330/00, ECHR 2004-VIII, para 59.

[159] This is considered in detail in Ch 5.

means of punishment. It is common for offenders who are not citizens of the country in which they committed an offence to be subjected to a deportation order in addition, or sometimes as an alternative,[160] to another sentence, such as a sentence of imprisonment. In this regard, non-citizens are treated differently from citizens solely on the grounds of their nationality. This issue is complicated by the considerable differences in the nature and characterization of deportation orders, as we shall see, in the various contracting states. It is nevertheless interesting to consider the compatibility of such orders with Article 14 ECHR. Before considering whether such orders are discriminatory in nature, it is essential to consider whether they fall within the scope of one of the articles to the Convention. It might be argued that Article 6(1) ECHR and Article 7(1) ECHR are applicable. This will only be the case, though, if the deportation order is classified as criminal (rather than say administrative) in nature and thus said to constitute punishment.

1. Deportation Orders as Criminal Penalties?

The determination of whether a deportation order is a criminal sanction follows the general criteria for establishing whether the proceedings involve the determination of a 'criminal charge' for the purposes of Article 6(1) ECHR and have resulted in the imposition of a penalty in the sense of Article 7(1) ECHR. In *Maaouia*, the applicant was sentenced to six years' imprisonment for armed robbery and assault. Following his release from prison, the Interior Minister issued an order that he be deported.[161] The ECtHR held that 'in general, exclusion orders are not classified as criminal within the member States of the Council of Europe'. It noted that 'such orders, which in most States may also be made by the administrative authorities, constitute a special preventive measure for the purposes of immigration control and do not concern the determination of a criminal charge against the applicant for the purposes of Article 6'. This led it to conclude that the 'fact that they are imposed in the context of criminal proceedings cannot alter their essentially preventive nature'.[162]

The ECtHR reached a different conclusion in *Gurguchiani*, in which the applicant, who was a foreign national living in Spain, received a sentence of eighteen months' imprisonment for attempted burglary. The Spanish Criminal Code provided the criminal court with two options in prescribing the enforcement of the sentence: either the convicted person could be imprisoned

[160] See eg *Gurguchiani v Spain* App no 16012/06, 15 Dec 2009.
[161] *Maaouia v France* [GC] App no 39652/98, ECHR 2000-X, paras 9–11.
[162] ibid para 39.

and not deported or alternatively they could be deported and prohibited from re-entering the country for between three and ten years, instead of going to prison.[163] Initially, the trial court opted to impose a sentence of imprisonment. Following the introduction of a new law in 2013, however, the appeal court held that the applicant should be deported and prevented from entering Spain for a period of ten years instead of serving the sentence.

The ECtHR held that there had been a violation of Article 7(1) ECHR, as a more severe sentence had been imposed on the applicant than that which had originally been provided for in respect of the offence for which he was convicted. In the ECtHR's view, the replacement of the applicant's prison sentence by his deportation and his exclusion from Spain for ten years meant that he had not just been given a new sentence, but had been given a sentence that was harsher than the sentence provided for by law at the time of the commission of the offence.[164] Of particular importance here is the ECtHR's ruling that the case did not concern an administrative removal order, but a criminal deportation order which constituted punishment for the purposes of Article 7(1) ECHR and which was imposed in 'the determination of a criminal charge' for the purposes of Article 6(1) ECHR.[165]

In this regard, the characterization of the measure in domestic law and the manner in which it is implemented, takes on considerable importance. A brief comparison of the law in Switzerland and the law in England and Wales demonstrates the implications of this characterization. In Switzerland, the trial judge is obliged to order the deportation of a foreign offender for a period of between five and fifteen years if the offender has committed a crime which is listed in law as a relevant offence,[166] irrespective of the sentence actually imposed.[167] The judge may only refrain from imposing a mandatory deportation order in two situations: first, if the offender has successfully argued an exculpatory defence of self-defence or necessity;[168] or second, if the expulsion would cause

[163] *Gurguchiani v Spain* App no 16012/06, 15 Dec 2009, para 32.
[164] ibid para 44.
[165] ibid paras 47–48.
[166] Including, inter alia, intentional homicide; serious assault, female genital mutilation, abandonment, endangering life, aggravated embezzlement, aggravated theft, robbery, fraud for commercial gain, computer fraud for commercial gain, misuse of a cheque card or credit card for commercial gain, aggravated extortion, profiteering for commercial gain, handling stolen goods for commercial gain, theft in conjunction with unlawful entry; fraud related to social insurance or social assistance, unlawful claims for social insurance or social assistance benefits; fraud, fraud in relation to administrative services and charges or tax fraud, misappropriation of taxes deducted at source or any other offence related to public charges that carries a maximum penalty of a one-year custodial sentence or more; indecent assault, rape, encouraging prostitution, pornography, arson, genocide, crimes against humanity, violations of Art 116 para 3 or Art 118 para 3 of the Foreign Nationals Act of 16 Dec 2005; violation of Arts 19 para 2 or 20 para 2 of the Misuse of Drugs Act of 3 Oct 1951.
[167] Art 66a(1) of the Swiss Criminal Code.
[168] Art 66a(3) of the Swiss Criminal Code.

serious personal hardship to the foreign national concerned.[169] This second exception applies principally to foreign nationals who were born or who grew up in Switzerland.[170] The deportation order is set out in the Criminal Code and described as an 'other measure'. It is imposed by the trial judge following the criminal conviction. In view of this, there can be little doubt that such an order is to be classed as a penalty for the purposes of Article 7 ECHR and that it is imposed within the context of proceedings involving the determination of a criminal charge in the sense of Article 6(1) ECHR.

Deportation in England and Wales is within the statutory power of the Home Secretary.[171] According to the United Kingdom Borders Act 2007, foreign criminals who are sentenced to a period of imprisonment of at least twelve months are, subject to a number of exceptions,[172] to be subject to an automatic deportation order.[173] It might be argued that these measures are to be considered administrative in nature, that they do not constitute penalties for the purposes of Article 7(1) ECHR, and thus that they fall outwith the scope of Article 6(1) and Article 14 ECHR.

2. Deportation Orders as Discrimination on the Grounds of Nationality

Assuming that a deportation order falls within the scope of Article 6(1) and Article 7(1) ECHR, it is necessary to consider whether the different treatment of national and foreign offenders is such as to violate Article 14 ECHR. This requires consideration of whether a person 'in a relevantly similar situation' has been 'treated differently' without 'objective and reasonable' justification.

All offenders might be said to be in a similar situation in the context of the state's entitlement to impose punishment for a criminal offence. The punishment imposed on a foreign offender who is subjected to a deportation order is more severe than that imposed on a national offender, because the punishment is made up of both the sentence for the offence and the deportation order. This is underlined by the ECtHR's classification in *Gurguchiani v Spain* of the deportation order as a more severe penalty than an eighteen-month sentence of imprisonment.[174] This different treatment is based solely

169 Art 66a(2) of the Swiss Criminal Code.

170 See though *MM v Switzerland* App no 59006/18, 8 Dec 2020: expulsion of an applicant who was born in Switzerland for a period of five years.

171 For a useful overview of the issue see T McGuiness and H Wilkins, 'Deportation of Foreign Offenders', House of Commons Briefing Paper No 8062, 31 Dec 2019.

172 See UK Borders Act 2007, s 33.

173 See UK Borders Act 2007, s 32.

174 *Gurguchiani v Spain* App no 16012/06, 15 Dec 2009.

on account of the nationality of the accused. This gives rise to the question whether it is legitimate to punish foreign offenders more severely solely because of their nationality.

Different treatment based solely on the grounds of nationality will be deemed to fall foul of the prohibition on discrimination unless 'very weighty reasons' can be provided to justify the disparate treatment.[175] The refusal of legal aid to a foreign national seeking to establish the paternity of her child, on the grounds that she did not have a residence permit;[176] the exclusion of a foreign national from employment or social security benefit, despite the fact that he satisfied all the criteria;[177] and the refusal of family benefits because the mother was a foreign national[178] were all situations in which weighty reasons were not deemed to exist.[179]

In *Rangelov*, the applicant complained that foreign nationals in prison were refused access to rehabilitative programs and thus treated differently in relation to prisoners of national origin in a similar situation. This meant that the applicant was 'denied a chance to fulfil essential preconditions for the domestic courts to conclude that the execution of the preventive detention order against him could be suspended and probation be granted'.[180] The ECtHR noted that the refusal to allow foreign nationals who were due to be expelled to take part in 'social therapy' was based on the fact that 'the therapists were considered not being in a position to prepare those prisoners for a life without offences in a country the living conditions of which were not sufficiently known to them.'[181] In addition, the 'refusal to grant relaxations in the conditions of detention to foreign nationals against whom a final expulsion order has been made appears to be to prevent them from absconding prior to having served their term of imprisonment and to secure the execution of the expulsion order afterwards'. The ECtHR held that the measures aimed to ensure enforcement of the decisions of the criminal courts and to ensure that the therapies offered were appropriate.[182] In determining whether the difference in treatment could be

[175] *Luczak v Poland* App no 77782/01, 27 Nov 2007, para 52; *Rangelov v Germany* App no 5123/07, 22 Mar 2012, para 102.

[176] *Anakomba Yula v Belgium* App no 45413/07, 10 Mar 2009.

[177] *Gaygusuz v Austria*, 16 Sept 1996, Reports 1996-IV.

[178] *Weller v Hungry* App no 44399/05, 31 Mar 2009.

[179] For detailed consideration of these cases see K Reid, *A Practitioner's Guide to the European Convention on Human Rights* (6th edn, London, Sweet and Maxwell 2019) 488–89.

[180] *Rangelov v Germany* App no 5123/07, 22 Mar 2012.

[181] ibid para 101.

[182] ibid para 101.

considered proportionate to aims pursued, the ECtHR noted that the refusal to 'grant the applicant measures usually considered as important in order to obtain a suspension of the preventive detention order on probation were not compensated by offers of a different therapy or any other measures adapted to his situation'.[183] The ECtHR concluded that the difference in treatment of the applicant lacked 'objective justification' and violated Article 14 in conjunction with Article 5 ECHR.[184]

In *Moustaquim v Belgium*, the applicant complained about a violation of Article 14 taken together with Article 8 ECHR on the grounds of nationality with regard to juvenile delinquents of two categories: 'those who possessed Belgian nationality, since they could not be deported; and those who were citizens of another member State of the European Communities, as a criminal conviction was not sufficient to render them liable to deportation'.[185] The ECtHR held that 'the applicant cannot be compared to Belgian juvenile delinquents. The latter have a right of abode in their own country and cannot be expelled from it; this is confirmed by Article 3 of Protocol No. 4 (P4-3).' In addition, it held that with regard to 'the preferential treatment given to nationals of the other member States of the Communities, there is objective and reasonable justification for it as Belgium belongs, together with those States, to a special legal order'.[186] Here, though, the issue is considerably different in that it involves a right to remain in a country based on Article 8(1) ECHR rather than the imposition of more severe punishment.

Should the lack of citizenship be regarded as a reasonable ground for punishing a person more severely? Almost certainly not.[187] This conclusion is underscored by considering the issue from the perspective of Article 7(1) ECHR (read in the light of Article 1 ECHR). Article 7(1) ECHR prohibits the imposition of punishment without law and is expressly designed to prevent arbitrariness. This means not just that criminal laws and sentencing provisions must be applicable to all individuals equally, but also that the imposition of a more severe sentence on an individual for reasons not connected to a person's liability for the criminal offence at issue is incompatible with the guarantee of legality.

183 ibid para 102.
184 ibid paras 104–5.
185 *Moustaquim v Belgium*, 18 Feb 1991, Series A no 193, para 48.
186 ibid para 49.
187 *Paraskeva Todorova v Bulgaria* App no 37193/07, 25 Mar 2010.

IV. Equality, Non-Discrimination, and Sentencing Disparity

The punishment which a state is entitled to impose is restricted by the right to equality, inherent in all human rights guarantees, and the prohibition on discrimination. Equality demands freedom from arbitrariness in the application of fundamental rights. It embodies the requirement that each case must be decided correctly on its merits. This understanding of equality should not be confused with any sort of 'prescriptive equality',[188] which entitles everyone to be treated in a certain way simply because another person has been treated in that way. In particular, an offender has no right to be treated in the same manner as others who have been treated 'wrongly'.

The scope of equality focuses attention on the importance of the role of the judge and the much-discussed relationship between judicial discretion and consistency. In the words of Tonry, anyone with an interest in making sentencing more consistent, 'whether in the name of justice, efficiency, effectiveness, or economy' must 'confront the antipodean twins of discretion and disparity. Someone must in every case decide what to do.'[189] This debate is often framed as a balancing exercise whereby the importance of judicial discretion is weighed up against the importance of certainty, consistency, or what Hart describes as 'the somewhat hazy requirement that like cases be treated alike'.[190] This is often taken to mean that 'similarly situated people who commit similar crimes should receive similar penalties'.[191] As we have seen,[192] though, there is no right to consistency in this sense. Disparity—like equality—is simply

[188] In the sense of Peters, 'Equality Revisited' (n 2) 1223: 'the bare fact that a person has been treated in a certain way is a reason in itself for treating another, identically positioned person in an identical way'; see also CJ Peters, 'Foolish Consistency: On Equality, Integrity, and Justice in Stare Decisis' (1996) 105 *Yale Law Journal* 2031; J Raz, *The Morality of Freedom* (Oxford: OUP 1988) 225.

[189] Tonry, *Sentencing Matters* (n 3) 177.

[190] Hart, *Punishment and Responsibility* (n 3) 24.

[191] See eg S Roach Anleu, R Brewer, K Mac, 'Locating the Judge within Sentencing Research' (2017) 6 *International Journal for Crime, Justice and Social Democracy* 46, 48: 'Consistency is an important principle of justice', citing A Ashworth, 'Departures from the Sentencing Guidelines' (2012) *Criminal Law Review* 81; C Tata, 'The Struggle for Sentencing Reform' in A Ashworth and JV Roberts (eds), *Sentencing Guidelines: Exploring the English Model* (Oxford: OUP 2013). On the difficulties of definition: R Dworkin, *Law's Empire* (Harvard, MT: Harvard University Press 1986) 185, 219: 'Is integrity only consistency (deciding like cases alike) under a prouder name? That depends on what we mean by consistency or like cases.' Dworkin argues that integrity requires judges decide cases not so much consistent with previous cases but with an overarching theory of justice. Moreover, integrity demands that cases should not (in theory or in practice) be treated differently unless that difference can be justified with reference to the axioms of that pure theory.

[192] See further Ch 5.

an 'empty category that can be filled only by reference to some standard [of nonegalitarian justice]'.[193]

The right to equality inherent in human rights and to non-discrimination demands that each decision be taken on its own merits in the manner that justice demands and irrespective of the manner in which other people have been treated in the past.[194] Essentially, equality demands freedom from arbitrariness in the application of human rights. The discretion of the judge is of central importance to guaranteeing freedom from arbitrariness and upholding substantive human rights, such as freedom from inhuman and degrading treatment. Individualized justice, far from being at odds with principles such as consistency, is in fact the only way of ensuring the imposition of non-arbitrary punishment in each individual case.

193 Tonry, *Sentencing Matters* (n 3) 186. Here the words of Joni Mitchell come to mind: 'Just before our love got lost you said, I am as constant as a northern star And I said, "Constantly in the darkness, Where's that at? If you want me I'll be in the bar"'. A Case of You, Blue, Reprise 1971.

194 See Peters, 'Equality Revisited' (n 2) 1264.

5

Judicial Imposition of Punishment

I. The Imposition of Punishment as a Judicial Exercise

The state is restricted in the imposition of punishment by the requirements of legality, equality, and the obligation to refrain from infringing certain important human rights. It is important to consider, too, restrictions on the authority responsible for setting the sentence. The imposition of punishment, like the determination of guilt or innocence, is usually understood as a judicial exercise.[1] The importance of the judge lies at the heart of procedural fairness, which demands that individuals have the right of access to court in the determination of a criminal charge.[2] The responsibility of the judge for the imposition of punishment is also of central importance, though, to the characterization of the sentence itself (and not just the manner of its imposition) as lawful or just.

Judicial responsibility for the imposition of punishment is closely related to the principle of legality as guaranteed by Article 7(1) ECHR, in the sense that adherence to legality implies acceptance of the separation of powers in the context of state punishment. This is usually discussed in the context of the importance of the legality principle as a check on judicial powers and its role in preventing judicial arbitrariness and activism.[3] Laws must be sufficiently

[1] G Stratenwerth and F Bommer, *Allgemeiner Teil II: Strafen und Massnahmen* (3rd edn, Bern: Stämpfli 2020) 180: '*Es ist Sache des Gerichts, innerhalb des Strafrahmens ... die im Einzelfall angemessene Strafe zu finden*'; *Art 47(1) SCC: 'the court shall determine the sentence.'* J Steyn, 'The Weakest and Least Dangerous Department of Government' [1997] *Public Law* 84, 93: 'Sentencing for any crime is a judicial function'; S McDonald, 'Involuntary Detention and the Separation of Judicial Power' (2007) 35 *Federal Law Review* 25, 27: 'Because the function of punishment for criminal guilt is seen as exclusively judicial, the imposition of detention which in substance amounts to punishment cannot be imposed by the Parliament or the executive in a system operating under a strict separation of powers' citing, inter alia, *Waterside Workers' Federation of Australia v JW Alexander Ltd* (1918) 25 CLR 434, 444 (Griffith CJ); *Federal Commissioner of Taxation v Munro* (1926) 38 CLR 153, 175 (Isaacs J).

[2] See S Trechsel, *Human Rights in Criminal Proceedings* (Oxford: OUP 2005) 46. See also *Cuscani v UK* App no 32771/96, 24 Sept 2002, para 39: 'the ultimate guardian of the fairness of the proceedings was the trial judge.'

[3] See F Dwarris, *A General Treatise on Statutes* (Albany, NY: W Gould 1873) 247: 'A penal law then, shall not be extended by construction. The law of England does not allow of constructive offenses, or of arbitrary punishments. No man incurs a penalty unless the act which subjects him to it, is clearly both within the spirit and the letter of the statute imposing such penalty. "If these rules are violated," said Best, CJ in the case of *Fletcher v Lord Sondes* [3 Bingham 580], "the fate of accused persons is decided by the arbitrary discretion of judges, and not by the express authority of the laws!"', discussed by J Hall, 'Nulla Poena Sine Lege' (1937) 47 *Yale Law Journal* 165, 179.

Sentencing and Human Rights. Sarah J Summers, Oxford University Press. © Sarah J Summers 2022.
DOI: 10.1093/oso/9780192870384.003.0005

clearly defined in order to prevent arbitrary judicial discretion or overreach. Equally, though, judges play an important role in preventing the arbitrary exercise of executive, and possibly also legislative, power in the imposition of punishment. In the words of O Dálaigh CJ:

> The degree of punishment which a particular citizen is to undergo for an offence is a matter vitally affecting his liberty; and it is inconceivable to my mind that a Constitution which is broadly based on the separation of powers ... could have intended to place in the hands of the Executive the power to select the punishment to be undergone by citizens. It would not be wrong to characterise such a system of government as one of arbitrary power. In my opinion, the selection of the punishment is an integral part of the administration of justice and, as such, cannot be committed to the hands of the Executive.[4]

If there is consensus that the rule of law is dependent on some form of adjudication,[5] the extent and nature of the judicial power to interpret the law is nevertheless very much disputed.[6] On one account, judges have particular responsibility as the 'guardians of legality' for ensuring fidelity to the rule of law.[7] On the other, they are simply the 'mouth that produces the words of the law'.[8] Further, there can be little doubt that the rule of law is a contested

[4] *Deaton* 1963 IR 170, at 182–83. See also D Manderson and N Sharp, 'Mandatory Sentences and The Constitution: Discretion, Responsibility, and Judicial Process' (2000) 22 *Sydney Law Review* 585, 604.

[5] For discussion of the idea that 'legal positivists deep down, want law without judges' see D Dyzenhaus, 'The Very Idea of a Judge' (2010) 60 *University of Toronto Law Journal* 61, 62. For consideration of the relationship between the concept of law and adjudication see J Waldron, 'The Concept and the Rule of Law' (2008) 43 *Georgia Law Review* 1.

[6] Contrast R Dworkin, *Taking Rights Seriously* (Cambridge, MA: Harvard University Press 1977) and HLA Hart, *The Concept of Law* (2nd edn, Oxford: OUP 1997) 95. See also N Lacey, 'Philosophy, Political Morality and History: Explaining the Enduring Resonance of the Hart-Fuller Debate' (2008) 83 *New York University Law Review* 1059; N Lacey, 'Populism and the Rule of Law' (2019) 15 *Annual Review of Law and Social Science* 79.

[7] Dyzenhaus, 'The Very Idea of a Judge' (n 5) 67 and 79–80, referring to N MacCormick, 'Rhetoric and the Rule of Law' in D Dyzenhaus (ed), *Recrafting the Rule of Law: The Limits of Legal Order* (Oxford: Hart Publishing 1999) 163 and suggesting that legality is dependent on the existence of judges precisely because 'law must claim not only authority but also *legitimate* authority over its subjects'. See also D Dyzenhaus, *Judging the Judges, Judging Ourselves: Truth, Reconciliation and the Apartheid Legal Order* (Oxford: Hart Publishing 1998) suggesting that '[j]udges who fail to recognise their obligation to uphold the rule of law fail in some sense in their role as judges'. For discussion see J Přibáň, 'Review of David Dyzenhaus, *Judging the Judges, Judging Ourselves*' (1999) 26 *Journal of Law and Society* 577, 580 noting that 'Dyzenhaus, like Dworkin, seems to give extraordinary power to judges operating within the framework of a constitutional, liberal democratic regime'. See also LL Fuller, 'Forms and Limits of Adjudication' in KI Winston (ed) *The Principles of Social Order: Selected Essays of Lon L Fuller* (Oxford: Hart Publishing 2001) 101.

[8] Montesquieu, The Spirit of the Law (T Nugent tr, first published 1750, Berkeley, CA: University of California Press 1977) 209. See also A Barak, 'A Judge on Judging: The Role of a Supreme Court in a Democracy' (2002) 116 *Harvard Law Review* 19, 23. Some committed positivists accept a limited role in the context of the rule of law: see eg H Arthurs, 'Rethinking Administrative Law: A Slightly Dicey

concept.[9] Those that favour a thin conception argue that it encompasses a series of formal values, such as clarity, non-retroactivity, publicity, and universality.[10] For others, the rule of law sets out a number of procedural or structural commitments which make up the 'inner morality of law'.[11] Others still see the rule of law as encompassing more substantive demands, including commitment to constitutionalism and to the separation of powers and human rights.[12]

This conflict at the heart of the judicial role between activism and restraint in the interpretation of the law[13] takes on particular resonance at the sentencing stage. Concern about the potential for judges to overstep their institutional mandate mirrors anxiety about judges usurping the will of the majority.[14] Sentencing is an emotive, political issue and judges are frequently subject to claims that they 'enjoy too much discretion, are too soft, and pander to criminals at the expense of victims'.[15] It will be argued here that notwithstanding such concerns, sentencing provisions must be framed in such a way as to ensure that judges have sufficient room to prevent the imposition of punishment which violates the principles of legality, equality,[16] or the respect for certain human rights, notably the prohibition on the imposition of inhuman or degrading punishment.

This understanding of the importance of the judge at sentencing is challenged by a number of sentencing practices and laws. Some challenges to the role of the judge at sentencing are structural in nature and serve to call into question the judicial role at sentencing per se. Is a sentence imposed by an

Business' (1979) 17 *Osgoode Hall Law Journal* 1, 22 accepting that judges are 'ultimately, the custodians of 'fundamental constitutional values'.

[9] See J Waldron, 'Is the Rule of Law an Essentially Contested Concept (in Florida)?' (2002) 21 *Law and Philosophy* 137.

[10] See notably J Raz, 'The Rule of Law and its Virtue' in J Raz (ed), *The Authority of Law: Essays on Law and Morality* (Oxford: Clarendon Press 1979).

[11] See notably LL Fuller, The Morality of Law (2nd edn, New Haven, CT: Yale University Press 1969) and J Waldron, 'The Concept and the Rule of Law' (2008) 43 *Georgia Law Review* 1.

[12] See eg BZ Tamanaha, *On the Rule of Law: History, Politics, Theory* (Cambridge: Cambridge University Press 2012); T Bingham, *The Rule of Law* (London: Allen Law 2010); S Baer, 'The Rule of—and not by any—Law. On the Need to Explain and Defend Constitutionalism Today' (2019) 71 *Current Legal Problems* 335.

[13] See the lecture of Lord Hodge, Justice of The Supreme Court of the United Kingdom at the Max Planck Institute of Comparative and International Private Law, Hamburg, Germany, 'The Scope of Judicial Law-making in the Common Law Tradition', 28 Oct 2019 available at <https://www.supremecourt.uk/docs/speech-191028.pdf> (accessed 26 Mar 2021).

[14] See Dyzenhaus, 'The Very Idea of a Judge' (n 5) 62.

[15] See C French, 'The Role of the Judge in Sentencing: From Port-Soaked Reactionary to Latte Liberal' [2015] *Otago Law Review* 5; G Mackenzie and others, 'Sentencing and Public Confidence: Results from a National Australian Survey on Public Opinions towards Sentencing' (2012) 45 *Australian and New Zealand Journal of Criminology* 45, 56.

[16] In the sense of Art 1 ECHR, see further Ch 4.

administrative authority or by the prosecutor in plea-bargaining proceedings, for instance, to be considered by definition to be unfair or to lack justification? Other challenges, such as mandatory sentencing provisions might be seen as an attempt to rein in judicial discretion,[17] but might nevertheless call into question the ability of a judge to intervene to prevent the imposition of unjust or arbitrary punishment.

In order to consider the importance of the role of the judge at sentencing, it is useful to begin by investigating the judicial role in the context of the right to a fair trial as guaranteed by Article 6(1) ECHR. This will be followed by consideration of whether Article 7(1) ECHR might be taken to require some sort of judicial oversight of the system of punishment, and by an examination of the special regulation of sentences of imprisonment implied by Article 5(1)(a) ECHR. This will provide the basis for considering the compatibility of various sentencing practices and laws with the right to the judicial imposition of punishment.

II. Procedural Fairness and the Judicial Role at Sentencing

It is well established that the responsibility for setting the sentence lies with the judge. Even in common law jurisdictions, where juries are often charged with determining whether the prosecution has successfully established its case,[18] the sentencing exercise usually falls within the sole competence of the judiciary.[19] It is useful to consider to what extent the judicial responsibility for sentencing is deemed necessary to protect the right to a fair trial as guaranteed by Article 6(1) ECHR. According to Article 6(1) ECHR, those accused of criminal offences have the right in the 'determination' of a 'criminal charge' to an independent and impartial tribunal. The assessment of the application of Article 6(1) ECHR in the sentencing context requires consideration of two particular

[17] See S Krasnostein and A Freiberg, 'Pursuing Consistency in an Individual Sentencing Framework: If You Know Where You're Going, How Do You Know When You've Got There?' (2013) 76 *Law and Contemporary Problems* 265: referring to the 'perennial conflict' between individualized justice and consistency. See too ME Frankel, *Criminal Sentences: Law Without Order* (New York, NY: Hill & Yang 1972) 5: 'the almost wholly unchecked and sweeping powers we give to judges in the fashioning of sentences are terrifying and intolerable for a society that professes devotion to the rule of law.'

[18] 'Conferring discretion on a jury is not in itself inconsistent with the requirements of the Convention, provided that the scope of the discretion and the manner of its exercise are indicated with sufficient clarity' see *Jobe v UK* (dec) App no 48278/09, 14 June 2011; *O'Carroll v UK* (dec) App no 35557/03, 15 Mar 2005.

[19] See, though, RE Barkow, 'Recharging the Jury: The Criminal Jury's Constitutional Role in an Era of Mandatory Sentencing' (2003) 152 *University of Pennsylvania Law Review* 33; SB Kaufman, 'Citizenship and Punishment: Situating Death Penalty Jury Sentencing' (2011) 13 *Punishment and Society* 333.

issues. First, whether the sentencing exercise might be said to constitute part of the 'determination' of a criminal charge, and second, the implications of the right to an independent and impartial tribunal in this context.

A. The Sentencing Decision as Part of the Determination of a Criminal Charge

The principle that criminal trials be presided over by a judicial authority is a fundamental tenet of procedural fairness and is set out in the various conventions created to protect fundamental human rights.[20] The ECtHR has insisted on an autonomous definition of criminal charge and thus has held that the fair trial guarantees applicable to criminal proceedings will apply to a whole range of proceedings, such as disciplinary,[21] administrative,[22] tax,[23] customs,[24] or anti-competition proceedings,[25] if they are considered to involve the determination of a criminal charge for the purposes of Article 6(1) ECHR. The ECtHR has held that Article 6(1) ECHR is applicable throughout the 'entirety of proceedings' which concern the determination of a criminal charge and includes 'the proceedings whereby a sentence is fixed'.[26] In the *Eckle* case, the ECtHR held unequivocally that the fair trial guarantees of the Convention extended to the 'whole of the proceedings ... including appeal proceedings and the determination of sentence'.[27] The definition of the 'determination of the sentence' is of particular significance precisely because it provides the basis for delineating the boundaries of judicial control. In this regard, it is useful to consider the types of decision-making which have been deemed not to constitute part of the sentencing decision.

Proceedings involving *amnesty* fall outside the scope of the criminal charge. In a case challenging the extent and scope of amnesty provisions enacted in Spain following the end of the Civil War and the death of General Franco, the Strasbourg authorities held 'that where the person concerned has already been convicted, any dispute concerning the existence or extent of an amnesty falls

[20] See eg Art 14(1) ICCPR; Art 8(1) ACHR: Art 6(1) ECHR: in the determination of his civil rights and obligations or of any criminal charge against him, everyone is entitled to a fair and public hearing within a reasonable time by an independent and impartial tribunal established by law.
[21] *Engel and Others v Netherlands*, 8 June 1976, Series A no 22.
[22] *Lutz v Germany*, 25 Aug 1987, Series A no 123, para 182.
[23] *Jussila v Finland* [GC] App no 73053/01, ECHR 2006-XIV, para 38.
[24] *Salabiaku v France*, 7 Oct 1988, Series 141-A.
[25] *A Menarini Diagnostics SRL v Italy* App no 43509/08, 27 Sept 2011.
[26] See eg *Findlay v UK*, 25 Feb 1997, Reports 1997-I, 279, para 69.
[27] *Eckle v Germany*, 15 July 1982, Series A no 51, paras 76–77.

outside the scope of Article 6 of the Convention since the dispute has ceased to involve a criminal charge against the applicant within the meaning of Article 6'.[28] Similarly, in a case involving an accused convicted of a speeding offence who was deemed not to qualify for amnesty under the provisions of an Act which excluded minor traffic offences from its scope, the ECtHR held that Article 6 ECHR did not apply. It ruled that the proceedings did not concern the determination of a criminal charge but instead involved 'an issue relating to the execution of the sentence'. It held that as proceedings involving amnesty may 'concern a person who has been convicted in a final judgment, they no longer relate to a criminal charge against that person within the meaning of Article 6 of the Convention'.[29]

The ECtHR has consistently held that proceedings concerning the enforcement of a sentence imposed by a court do not fall within the scope of Article 6(1) ECHR.[30] In *A v Austria*, the Commission held that:

> proceedings concerning the execution of a sentence imposed by a competent court, including proceedings on the grant of conditional release, are not covered by Article 6 paragraph 1 of the Convention. They neither concern the determination of "a criminal charge" nor of "civil rights and obligations" within the meaning of this provision.[31]

Sometimes, though, the boundaries between the determination of the sentence itself and the enforcement of the sentence are not entirely clear. In the cases of *T and V v United Kingdom*, the applicants were convicted of murder and sentenced to an indeterminate sentence of 'detention during her Majesty's Pleasure'. The trial judge was required to recommend a tariff, the part of the sentence designed to satisfy the elements of deterrence and retribution, which the applicants were required to serve before they would be eligible for release. This recommendation was passed to the Home Secretary, who ultimately had the responsibility for setting the tariff. The applicants argued that allowing the Home Secretary to fix the 'tariff' amounted to an unacceptable and unlawful interference in the sentencing decision. The setting of the tariff constituted

[28] *Asociación de Aviadores de la República and Others v Spain* (dec) App no 10733/84, 11 Mar 1985, DR 41, 211.

[29] *Montcornet de Caumont v France* (dec) App no 59290/00, 13 May 2003.

[30] *Enea v Italy* [GC] App no 74912/01, 17 Sept 2009, para 97.

[31] *A v Austria* (dec) App no 16266/90, 7 May 1990, 65 DR 337; see too *Plischke v Austria* (dec) App no 1446/62, 7 Mar 1964, 8 YB 455, 463; *X v Austria* (dec) App no 1760/63, 23 May 1966, 9 YB 167, 175; *X v Austria* (dec) App no 2306/64, 19 July 1966, 21 Coll 23, 31; *X v UK* (dec) App no 4133/69, 13 July 1970, 13 YB 780, 790.

a judicial function and the transferring of that task to the executive violated Article 6 ECHR. The UK government countered by arguing that 'upon being convicted of murder, the applicant was automatically subject to the sentence of detention during Her Majesty's pleasure ... and that the fixing of the tariff was merely an aspect of the administration of the sentence already imposed by the court'.[32] The ECtHR was not convinced by this argument. It noted that the sentence of detention during her Majesty's pleasure was open-ended and that in view of the fact that the tariff was intended 'to satisfy the requirements of retribution and deterrence', the offender's continued detention after this period could only be justified for reasons of public protection.[33] This meant that in cases in which the offender was not determined to be dangerous, the tariff represented the maximum period of detention which he could be required to serve. Consequently, the 'fixing of the tariff' constituted part of the 'sentencing exercise'.[34]

The relationship between transfer proceedings under the Convention on the Transfer of Sentenced Persons and the sentencing decision has also called for consideration. In a number of cases, such proceedings were deemed to fall outwith the sentencing decision.[35] In *Szabó*, for instance, the applicant argued that the sentence that he would have to serve upon transfer to Hungry was longer than that provided for in Swedish law. The ECtHR was not convinced that the transfer impacted on the sentence itself, noting that while the 'applicant's transfer was 'likely to delay the date of his conditional release' and might 'subject him to harsher prison conditions', these issues went to the 'manner of the implementation' of the prison sentence rather than to the sentence itself. In view of the fact that 'proceedings concerning the execution of a sentence' were not covered by Article 6(1) ECHR, the provision was not applicable in the case at issue.[36]

In *Buijen*, though, the ECtHR took a different approach.[37] In this case, the applicant complained that he had only confessed to the offence following assurances that he would be able to serve the sentence in the Netherlands, which would have led to his earlier release. The ECtHR noted that 'in the particular circumstances of this case it has to be taken into account that the proceedings

[32] *T v UK* [GC] App no 24724/94, 16 Dec 1999, para 107.

[33] ibid para 109.

[34] ibid para 110. See too the distinction between the sentence and its enforcement in cases such as *Del Río Prada v Spain* [GC] App no 42750/09 ECHR 2013, discussed in Ch 2.

[35] *Szabo v Sweden* (dec) App no 28578/03, 27 June 2006; *Csoszánski v Sweden* (dec) App no 22318/02, 27 June 2006; *Veermae v Finland* (dec) App no 38704/03, 15 Mar 2005.

[36] *Szabó v Sweden* (dec) App no 28578/03, 27 June 2006; see also *Homann v Germany* App no 12788/04, 9 May 2007.

[37] *Buijen v Germany* App no 27804/05, 1 Apr 2010, paras 40–45.

relating to the applicant's transfer request were very closely related to the criminal proceedings and to the final determination of the sentence'. It noted that the 'applicant gave a full confession leading to his criminal conviction' on the strength of reassurance by the Public Prosecutor that they had 'no reservations about the transfer of the defendant to the Netherlands'. The ECtHR held that while the German court had 'imposed a criminal sentence based on the applicant's conviction, this was not to be considered as final having regard to the possibility of converting the sentence following a transfer to the applicant's home country'. It distinguished the earlier cases[38] on the basis that 'in those cases the Transfer Convention was not prospectively influencing the course of the trial and the fixing of the sentence, because no assurance was given by the public prosecutor before or during the criminal proceedings'.[39] This meant that the proceedings concerning the applicant's transfer request insofar as they related to the assurance given by the public prosecutor during the criminal proceedings fell within the 'determination of the charge' for the purposes of Article 6 ECHR.[40]

These cases demonstrate that the imposition of punishment, like the determination of guilt or innocence, falls within the scope of judicial control. They also delineate to some extent the scope of the 'sentencing decision'. Here, though, it is important to keep in mind that even though matters involving the administration or enforcement of the sentence do not fall within the scope of Article 6(1) ECHR, this does not necessarily mean that they will automatically fall within the competence of executive or administrative bodies.[41]

B. Independent and Impartial Tribunal

The imposition of the sentence, as part of the determination of the criminal charge, must be undertaken by an independent and impartial tribunal. The

[38] *Csoszánski v Sweden* (dec) App no 22318/02, 27 June 2006; *Szabo v Sweden* (dec) App no 28578/03, 27 June 2006; *Veermae v Finland* (dec) App no 38704/03, 15 Mar 2005.

[39] *Buijen v Germany* App no 27804/05, 1 Apr 2010, para 43.

[40] ibid para 44.

[41] See eg the right to judicial review inherent in Art 5 ECHR; *Vinter and Others v UK* [GC] App nos 66069/09, 130/10, and 3896/10, ECHR 2013-III, para 124, in which the ECtHR suggested that a *Vinter* review was different from that undertaken by the sentencing judge and *Murray v Netherlands* [GC] App no 10511/10, ECHR 2016, para 99, in which the ECtHR implied that the form of the review (executive or judicial) was a matter for the domestic authorities. This gives rise to difficult questions regarding compatibility with the right to *habeas corpus* in Art 5(4) ECHR. Here, the ECtHR has insisted that while the body responsible for *habeas corpus* proceedings need not be a tribunal in the sense of Art 6(1) ECHR, but it should have 'judicial character' and should inter alia be independent of the executive and the parties. For discussion see Trechsel, *Human Rights* (n 2) 479.

right to an independent and impartial tribunal established by law is 'by far the most important guarantee enshrined in Article 6' and underpins the rule of law.[42] It is an absolute right and must not be subject to exceptions or derogations.[43] The ECtHR typically considers the criteria of independence and impartiality together and has stressed that only those called upon to determine the charge are subject to the requirement. The independence requirement demands freedom from subordination to any other organs of the state, in particular to the executive,[44] but also to the legislature.[45] Compliance with the requirement is assessed in accordance with various criteria, including: the manner of appointment of its members and the duration of their term of office, the existence of guarantees against outside pressures, and whether the body presents an appearance of independence.[46] The ECtHR will consider whether an 'objective observer' would have cause for concern. Impartiality, which is best defined as the absence of bias,[47] requires both that 'judges must not harbour preconceptions about the matter put before them, and that they must not act in ways that promote the interests of one of the parties'.[48] The lack of impartiality may be a result of personal bias on the part of the judge or it may be based on facts which give rise to doubts as to the tribunal's impartiality which are not related at all to the personal conduct of any of the members of the tribunal.[49] Such concerns might arise in the context of 'the exercise of different functions within the judicial process by the same person, or hierarchical or other links with another person involved in the proceedings'.[50]

A number of cases have dealt with the issues of the independence and impartiality of the sentencing judge. In the cases of *T and V v United Kingdom*, the

[42] Trechsel, *Human Rights* (n 2) 46.

[43] HRC, *Gonzalez de Rio v Peru* App no 263/1987, UN Doc CPR/C/40/D/263/1987.

[44] See *Ringeisen v Austria*, 16 July 1971, Series A no 13, para 95: 'Besides, the Court observes that the Regional Commission is a "tribunal" within the meaning of Article 6, paragraph (1), of the Convention as it is independent of the executive and also of the parties, its members are appointed for a term of five years and the proceedings before it afford the necessary guarantees'; *T v UK* [GC] App no 24724/94, 16 Dec 1999, para 113: 'The Court notes that Article 6 § 1 guarantees, *inter alia*, "a fair ... hearing ... by an independent and impartial tribunal ...". "Independent" in this context means independent of the parties to the case and also of the executive. The Home Secretary, who set the applicant's tariff, was clearly not independent of the executive, and it follows that there has been a violation of Article 6 § 1' (references omitted).

[45] See also Trechsel, *Human Rights* (n 2) 49 and 53 discussing *Demicoli v Malta*, 27 Aug 1991, Series A no 210, para 40.

[46] *Findlay v UK*, 25 Feb 1997, Reports 1997-I, 263, para 73; see also *Mustafa Tunç and Fecire Tunç v Turkey* [GC] App no 24014/05, 14 Apr 2015, para 221; *Incal v Turkey*, 9 June 1998, Reports 1998-IV, 1547, para 71.

[47] Trechsel, *Human Rights* (n 2) 61.

[48] *Karttunen v Finland* App no 1685/10, 10 May 2011, para 72.

[49] *Castillo Algar v Spain*, 28 Oct 1998, Reports 1998-VIII, 3103, para 45; *Kyprianou v Cyprus* [GC] App no 73797/01, ECHR 2005-XIII, para 121.

[50] *Kyprianou v Cyprus* [GC] App no 73797/01, ECHR 2005-XIII, para 121.

applicants argued that the fact that the tariff period of his sentence was fixed by the Home Secretary rather than a tribunal within the meaning of Article 6(1) of the ECHR gave rise to a violation of their right to a fair trial. The Grand Chamber agreed with this assessment holding that Article 6(1):

> guarantees, inter alia, "a fair ... hearing ... by an independent and impartial tribunal ...". "Independent" in this context means independent of the parties to the case and also of the executive ... The Home Secretary, who set the applicant's tariff, was clearly not independent of the executive, and it follows that there has been a violation of Article 6.[51]

The provision guaranteed the right to an independent and impartial tribunal, which required independence of the parties and the executive. In view of the fact that the Home Secretary was clearly not independent of the executive, there had been a violation of Article 6(1) ECHR.[52]

This emphasizes the close connection between the definition of 'tribunal' and the issues of independence and impartiality. The tribunal is understood in the case law as a body exercising judicial functions, 'that is to say determining matters within its competence on the basis of rules of law and after proceedings conducted in a prescribed manner'.[53] According to the ECtHR, only a body which has 'full jurisdiction' and is able to 'quash in all respects, on questions of fact and law, the decision of the body below' will be regarded as a tribunal for the purposes of Article 6 ECHR.[54] The tribunal, which can consist of professional judges, lay judges, or jurors,[55] must meet the obligations of independence and impartiality. The initial sentencing decision will usually be determined and imposed by a judge. In the context of certain proceedings, though, the initial decision might be taken by another authority, such as an administrative authority. It is important to consider to whether this is compatible with Article 6(1) ECHR.

[51] *T v UK* [GC] App no 24724/94, 16 Dec 1999, para 113. The Home Secretary received a petition signed by over 250,000 people urging him to take account of their belief that the boys, who had been convicted of murdering a small child, should never be released; in addition, he received a petition from a Member of Parliament signed by almost 6000 people calling for the imposition of at least twenty-five years and 21,000 coupons from the *Sun* newspaper arguing in favour of the imposition of a whole life tariff. He imposed a tariff period of fifteen years.

[52] ibid.

[53] *Belilos v Switzerland*, 29 Apr 1988, Series A no 132, para 64 citing *H v Belgium*, 30 Nov 1987, Series A no 127, para 50.

[54] *Schmautzer v Austria*, 23 Oct 1995, Series A no 328-A, para 36.

[55] See eg *Holm v Sweden*, 25 Nov 1993, Series A no 279-A, para 30.

C. Subsequent Judicial Control of a Sentence

1. Sentences Imposed by an Administrative Authority

The development of the notion of criminal charge has meant that a variety of proceedings, which are not (necessarily) labelled criminal in domestic law (such as administrative proceedings), have been considered by the ECtHR to fall within the scope of the criminal limb of Article 6(1) ECHR. In these proceedings, the initial sentencing decision is usually taken by some sort of administrative authority, such as a tax,[56] anti-competition,[57] or customs authority.[58]

The case law on the application of Article 6(1) ECHR in such proceedings might be characterized charitably as a work in progress and less benevolently as rather incoherent. The ECtHR has suggested that these types of proceedings might be subject to less stringent standards of procedural fairness than 'ordinary' criminal proceedings or 'criminal proceedings in the strict sense of the term'.[59] In *Jussila,* for instance, it held that:

> Notwithstanding the consideration that a certain gravity attaches to criminal proceedings, which are concerned with the allocation of criminal responsibility and the imposition of a punitive and deterrent sanction, it is self-evident that there are criminal cases which do not carry any significant degree of stigma. There are clearly 'criminal charges' of differing weight … Tax surcharges differ from the hard core of criminal law; consequently, the criminal-head guarantees will not necessarily apply with their full stringency.[60]

This has led the ECtHR to depart from an insistence in such proceedings on some of the established principles of fairness in criminal proceedings, such as the right to an oral hearing.

The ECtHR has held that the imposition of a criminal penalty by an administrative authority in these types of proceedings is not in itself incompatible with Article 6(1) ECHR, providing that the decision of this authority is subject to the control of a court, which has 'full jurisdiction', in the sense of the power

[56] *Jussila v Finland* [GC] App no 73053/01, ECHR 2006-XIV.

[57] *Société Stenuit v France*, 27 Feb 1992, Series A no 232-A.

[58] *Salabiaku v France*, 7 Oct 1988, Series A no 141-A.

[59] *A Menarini Diagnostics SRL v Italy* App no 43509/08, 27 Sept 2011, para 62: '*la Cour rappelle que la nature d'une procédure administrative peut différer, sous plusieurs aspects, de la nature d'une procédure pénale au sens strict du terme*.'

[60] *Jussila v Finland* [GC] App no 73053/01, ECHR 2006-XIV, para 43, references omitted. Citing in particular Bendenoun and Janosevic respectively, where it was found compatible with Art 6(1) for criminal penalties to be imposed, in the first instance, by an administrative or non-judicial body, and, *a contrario*, *Findlay v UK*, 25 Feb 1997, Reports 1997-I, 263.

to adjudicate on all aspects of fact and law.[61] In *A Menarini Diagnostics*, for instance, in which the initial sentence had been imposed by the Italian anti-competition authority, the ECtHR held that it was sufficient, for the purposes of Article 6(1) ECHR, that the courts were able to consider all elements of fact and law, that the review went beyond a 'mere review of lawfulness' and extended to establishing whether the competition authority had used its powers in an appropriate fashion.[62] In addition, it pointed to the fact that the courts were able to review the proportionality of the sentence and impose a different sanction if necessary.[63]

The ECtHR's position that a penalty may legitimately be imposed in administrative proceedings by an administrative authority, providing that the individual concerned has the opportunity to challenge the imposition of the sentence in a court with full jurisdiction, gives rise to the question whether such a review actually has to take place. In other words, is an individual entitled to waive their right to a judicial review of the sentence?

2. Waiver of the Right to a Review of by a Court of a Sentence Imposed by an Administrative Authority

In a number of early cases, the ECtHR had to consider the imposition of minor penalties by administrative authorities, particularly in the context of road traffic offences and breaches of regulatory laws. In *Deweer*, the ECtHR held that the 'right to a court' was 'no more absolute in criminal than in civil matters'.[64] It cited approvingly the examples referred to by the Commission in its report of situations in which there was no right to a trial, namely in the context of the discontinuation of proceedings and decisions not to prosecute.[65] In these cases, though, as the Commission noted, the result was entirely in favour of the accused, in the sense that the proceedings did not result in a criminal conviction.[66] Proceedings concluded by way of a settlement were obviously of a different nature, in that they resulted in the imposition of a conviction. Nevertheless, the ECtHR held that such proceedings also had the potential to

[61] *A Menarini Diagnostics SRL v Italy* App no 43509/08, 27 Sept 2011, para 59.

[62] ibid para 63–64: '*la Cour note que la compétence des juridictions administratives n'était pas limitée à un simple contrôle de légalité. Les juridictions administratives ont pu vérifier si, par rapport aux circonstances particulières de l'affaire, l'AGCM avait fait un usage approprié de ses pouvoirs. Elles ont pu examiner le bien-fondé et la proportionnalité des choix de l'AGCM et même vérifier ses évaluations d'ordre technique.*'

[63] See, *a contrario*, *Silvester's Horeca Service v Belgium* App no 47650/99, 4 Mar 2004, para 28. For criticism see the dissenting opinion of Judge Pinto de Albuquerque, attached to the judgment in *A Menarini Diagnostics SRL v Italy* App no 43509/08, 27 Sept 2011.

[64] *Deweer v Belgium*, 27 Feb 1980, Series A no 35, para 49.

[65] ibid.

[66] ibid.

meet the interests of the individual and of society more broadly.[67] In view of this, it held that an accused person was entitled to accept this type of settlement and that such acceptance could constitute a waiver of the right to a trial.[68]

It also noted, however, that:

> in a democratic society too great an importance attaches to the 'right to a court' for its benefit to be forfeited solely by reason of the fact that an individual is a party to a settlement reached in the course of a procedure ancillary to court proceedings. In an area concerning the public order (*ordre public*) of the member States of the Council of Europe, any measure or decision alleged to be in breach of Article 6 calls for particularly careful review ...'[69]

Member States were required to be 'vigilant' when assessing compliance with the right to a fair trial in those cases in which 'someone formerly "charged with a criminal offence" challenges a settlement that has barred criminal proceedings'.[70]

In determining whether the acceptance of a settlement constituted a waiver of the right to a criminal trial, the ECtHR held that it was necessary to ensure, inter alia, that the decision had been made freely: 'Absence of constraint is at all events one of the conditions to be satisfied; this much is dictated by an international instrument founded on freedom and the rule of law.'[71] In the case at issue, the applicant, who was the owner of a butcher's shop, was found by a visiting economic inspector to have violated a law on 'fixing the selling price to the consumer of beef and pig meat'. He was given the option of paying 10,000 Belgian francs (around €250) and settling the case—thereby avoiding a criminal prosecution. At the same time, he was informed that the failure to accept the settlement would result in his shop being shut.[72] He complained that his waiver of the right to trial was tainted by constraint. The ECtHR agreed. It noted that 'while the prospect of having to appear in court is certainly liable to prompt a willingness to compromise on the part of many persons "charged with a criminal offence", the pressure thereby brought to bear is in no way incompatible with the Convention'.[73] Nevertheless, it held that the constraint in

[67] See too the Recommendation of the Committee of Ministers of the Council of Europe on the Simplification of Criminal Justice R (87), adopted on 17 Sept 1987.

[68] *Deweer v Belgium*, 27 Feb 1980, Series A no 35, para 49.

[69] ibid references omitted.

[70] ibid.

[71] ibid.

[72] ibid paras 8–9.

[73] ibid para 51.

the case was unlawful, noting that there was '"flagrant disproportion" between the two alternatives facing the applicant'.[74]

In subsequent cases, the ECtHR has confirmed and expanded on these principles. In *Öztürk v Germany*, the situation was somewhat different in that the applicant, rather than accepting a settlement, had been issued with a fine. Here the ECtHR held that:

> Having regard to the large number of minor offences, notably in the sphere of road traffic, a Contracting State may have good cause for relieving its courts of the task of their prosecution and punishment. Conferring the prosecution and punishment of minor offences on administrative authorities is not inconsistent with the Convention provided that the person concerned is enabled to take any decision thus made against him before a tribunal that does offer the guarantees of Article 6.[75]

The ECtHR has developed a series of principles governing the waiver of procedural rights. It has held that 'the waiver of a right guaranteed by the Convention—insofar as it is permissible—must be established in an unequivocal manner'.[76] In addition, in order to be 'effective for Convention purposes', the waiver must be accompanied by 'minimum guarantees commensurate to its importance'[77] and must not run counter to any important public interest.[78] In particular, it must be shown that the accused could reasonably have foreseen the consequences of their conduct.[79] This means, for instance, that in those cases in which a person charged with a criminal offence was not notified in person, it cannot simply be inferred that they waived the right to appear at the trial.[80] Some guarantees in Article 6 ECHR are deemed so important to the notion of a fair trial and to ensuring the effectiveness of the rest of the guarantees set forth in Article 6 as to 'require the special protection of the "knowing and intelligent waiver" standard'.[81]

[74] ibid.

[75] *Öztürk v Germany*, 21 Feb 1984, Series A no 73, para 56.

[76] *Oberschlick v Austria*, 23 May 1991, Series A no 204, para 51

[77] *Pfeifer and Plankl v Austria*, 25 Nov 1992, Series A no 227, para 37.

[78] *Hermi v Italy* [GC] App no 18114/02, ECHR 2006-XII, para 73; *Sejdovic v Italy* [GC] App no 56581/00, ECHR 2006-II, para 86; *Dvorski v Croatia* [GC] App no 25703/11, ECHR 2015-VI, para 100.

[79] *Hermi v Italy* [GC] App no 18114/02, ECHR 2006-XII, para 74; *Jones UK* (dec) App no 30900/02, 9 Sept 2003.

[80] *Colozza v Italy*, 12 Feb 1985, Series A no 89, para 28; *Sejdovic v Italy* [GC] App no 56581/00, ECHR 2006-II, para 86.

[81] See *Dvorski v Croatia* [GC] App no 25703/11, ECHR 2015, para 101; see *Pishchalnikov v Russia* App no 7025/04, 24 Sept 2009, paras 77–79 (right to counsel cases).

In *Deweer* and in the subsequent cases, the proceedings were essentially regulatory in character and the penalties imposed were all of a financial nature.[82] In this sense, while there is no doubt that they concerned criminal charges for the purposes of Article 6 ECHR,[83] the offences were all minor offences imposed by administrative authorities. The distinction between administrative proceedings and 'core' criminal proceedings adopted in cases such as *A Menarini Diagnostics* might be characterized as rather dubious.[84] Nevertheless, for our purposes, it is important to note that the argument of the ECtHR is not that all criminal proceedings should be subject to lesser safeguards, but rather that certain administrative proceedings do not necessarily have to meet the standards to be applied to core criminal proceedings. In view of this, it is necessary to consider whether the initial sentencing decision in criminal proceedings in the 'strict sense' of the term must be made by a judge.

D. Judicial Regulation of Plea-Bargaining Proceedings

In many jurisdictions, it is the prosecutor, in the context of plea-bargaining or summary punishment proceedings, who is essentially responsible for the determination of the sentence. It is important to consider the compatibility of these types of proceedings with the right to the judicial imposition of punishment. It goes without saying that a prosecutor cannot be regarded as a judge or tribunal.[85] The question is whether the possibility of an appeal to a court with full jurisdiction might also serve to meet the requirements of Article 6(1) ECHR in these cases.

Plea-bargaining proceedings differ from the administrative proceedings discussed earlier in that they involve criminal investigations conducted by the police and/or the prosecution authorities. These authorities have considerably more powers than administrative authorities, including coercive investigatory powers, as is well illustrated by the case of *Natsvlishvili and Togonidze*. In this case, the first applicant was accused of embezzlement and detained on remand

[82] See also *Öztürk v Germany*, 21 Feb 1984, Series A no 73, para 56.

[83] See *Öztürk v Germany*, 21 Feb 1984, Series A no 73, for a clear repudiation of the government's claim to have 'decriminalized' the offence thus bringing it outside the scope of protection of Art 6 ECHR.

[84] *A Menarini Diagnostics SRL v Italy* App no 43509/08, 27 Sept 2011.

[85] See also in the context of Art 5(4) ECHR, Trechsel, *Human Rights* (n 2) 479: 'It is obvious, for example, that a prosecutor cannot be regarded as a court', referring to a series of Turkish cases and *Varbanov v Bulgaria* App no 31365/96, ECHR 2000-X para 60.

for many months during the initial criminal investigation before being convicted and fined.[86]

The ECtHR noted that it was a 'common feature of European criminal-justice systems for an accused to obtain the lessening of charges or receive a reduction of his or her sentence in exchange for a guilty or nolo contendere plea in advance of trial or for providing substantial cooperation with the investigative authority'.[87] It also confirmed its earlier position to the extent that there was nothing 'improper in the process of charge or sentence bargaining in itself'[88] and that:

> plea bargaining, apart from offering the important benefits of speedy adjudication of criminal cases and alleviating the workload of courts, prosecutors and lawyers, can also, if applied correctly, be a successful tool in combating corruption and organised crime and can contribute to the reduction of the number of sentences imposed and, as a result, the number of prisoners.[89]

It held that:

> where the effect of plea bargaining is that a criminal charge against the accused is determined through an abridged form of judicial examination, this amounts in substance, to the waiver of a number of procedural rights. This cannot be a problem in itself, since neither the letter nor the spirit of Article 6 prevents a person from waiving these safeguards of his or her own free will.[90]

It noted, though, that 'it is also a cornerstone principle that any waiver of procedural rights must always, if it is to be effective for Convention purposes, be established in an unequivocal manner and be attended by minimum safeguards

[86] RK Helm, 'Constrained Waiver of Trial Rights? Incentives to Plead Guilty and the Right to a Fair Trial (2019) 46 *Journal of Law and Society* 423; L Bachmaier, 'The European Court of Human Rights on Negotiated Justice and Coercion' (2018) 26 *European Journal of Crime, Criminal Law and Criminal Justice* 236.

[87] See the comparative legal study in *Natsvlishvili and Togonidze v Georgia* App no 9043/05, 29 Apr 2014 at paras 62–75; see also *Slavcho Kostov v Bulgaria* App no 28674/03, 27 Nov 2008, para 17 and *Ruciński v Poland* App no 33198/04, 20 Feb 2007, para 12. See also *Navalnyy and Ofitserov v Russia* App nos 46632/13 and 28671/14, 23 Feb 2016; *Scoppola v Italy (no 2)* [GC] App no 10249/03, 17 Sept 2009, para 135.

[88] *Babar Ahmad and Others v UK* (dec) App nos 24027/07, 11949/08, and 36742/08, 6 July 2010.

[89] *Natsvlishvili and Togonidze v Georgia* App no 9043/05, 29 Apr 2014, para 90.

[90] ibid para 91 citing *Scoppola v Italy (no 2)* [GC] App no 10249/03, 17 Sept 2009, para 135.

commensurate with its importance. In addition, it must not run counter to any important public interest.'[91]

In its (admittedly rather superficial) 'comparative study' of plea-bargaining in the contracting states, the ECtHR noted that:

> Plea agreements leading to a criminal conviction are, without exception, reviewed by a competent court. In this sense, courts have an obligation to verify whether the plea agreement has been reached in accordance with the applicable procedural and substantive rules, whether the defendant entered into it voluntarily and knowingly, whether there is evidence supporting the guilty plea entered by the defendant and whether the terms of the agreement are appropriate.[92]

This led it to conclude that any decision to agree to a plea agreement had to be

> accompanied by the following conditions: (a) the bargain had to be accepted by the first applicant in full awareness of the facts of the case and the legal consequences and in a genuinely voluntary manner; and (b) the content of the bargain and the fairness of the manner in which it had been reached between the parties had to be subjected to sufficient judicial review.[93]

This judgment leaves open the question whether there must be an automatic judicial review of the plea agreement or whether it is sufficient that the accused is able to appeal against the decision to a court with full cognition. This was not discussed in the case at issue, as domestic law in any case required the prosecutor to submit the plea to the court for approval.[94] A clear distinction ought to be drawn here between administrative proceedings and proceedings involving plea-bargaining or other forms of accelerated proceedings. Merely providing an individual with the opportunity to contest a plea agreement is not sufficient. It is essential that there be automatic judicial supervision of any plea bargain or agreement.

[91] *Natsvlishvili and Togonidze v Georgia* App no 9043/05, 29 Apr 2014, para 91 citing *Scoppola v Italy (no 2)* [GC] App no 10249/03, 17 Sept 2009, paras 135–36; *Poitrimol v France*, 23 Nov 1993, Series A no 277-A, para 31; *Hermi v Italy* [GC] App no 18114/02, ECHR 2006-XII, para 73.

[92] *Natsvlishvili and Togonidze v Georgia* App no 9043/05, 29 Apr 2014, para 66.

[93] ibid para 92.

[94] See too *VCL and AN v UK* App nos 77587/12 and 74603/12, 16 Feb 2021, para 201.

III. Legality and the Judicial Imposition of Punishment

In its case law on legality, as protected by Article 7(1) ECHR, the ECtHR has referred to the 'element of judicial interpretation' inherent in 'any legal system' and to the 'decision-making function entrusted to the courts'.[95] The ECtHR has also referred to Article 7(1) ECHR as 'an essential element of the rule of law', noting that it 'occupies a prominent place in the Convention system of protection',[96] and there is an important sense in which the ECtHR's understanding of legality presupposes a certain understanding of the rule of law.

The ECtHR's case law underlines the importance of the relationship between law and the legal system and suggests that the institution and operation of the court system is inherent in any system of *law*. It is clear, too, in the reference to 'courts', that what is meant here is not just any form of adjudication,[97] but a distinctive process involving an independent and impartial adjudicator.[98] An adjudicatory body which does not meet these requirements is by definition not a court.[99] In a similar sense, it might be said that regulatory systems which do not provide for independent and impartial courts are not to be understood as *legal* systems.[100] This seems to reflect a vision of the rule of law which is closely tied to the definition or concept of law rather than, as is sometimes suggested,[101] merely a restraint on law.

Legality demands that punishment be imposed within the rule of law. The imposition of punishment by an authority other than an independent and impartial judge, such as by way of a decision of a police or executive authority, cannot be understood to constitute *lawful* punishment for the purposes of Article 7(1) ECHR. Equally, proceedings conducted in absentia following a decision of the state which prohibits the accused from participating in the trial

[95] *Kafkaris v Cyprus* [GC] App no 21906/04, 12 Feb 2008, para 141.

[96] *Del Río Prada v Spain* [GC] App no 42750/09, ECHR 2013, para 77 referring to the fact that the right is non-derogable.

[97] As seems to be implied by some accounts of law, see notably HLA Hart, *The Concept of Law* (2nd edn, Oxford: Clarendon Press 1994) 97 (secondary rules of adjudication); J Raz, *Practical Reason and Norms* (Princeton, NJ: Princeton University Press 1975) 136 ('primary norm-applying organs').

[98] Art 6(1) ECHR.

[99] *Belilos v Switzerland*, 29 Apr 1988, Series A no 132, para 64. See also Trechsel, *Human Rights* (n 2) 48 who notes that the definition of tribunal is superfluous in that the 'properties which, according to the text of Article 6(1), are attached to the term, are referred to as elements of definition'.

[100] See on this Waldron, 'The Concept and the Rule of Law' (n 11) 20: 'I do not think we should regard something as a legal system absent the existence and operation of the sort of institutions we call courts.' This reflects Waldron's understanding of law 'as a mode of governing people that treats them with respect, as though they had a view of their own to present on the application of a given norm to their conduct or situation', 23. See also Fuller, *The Morality of Law* (n 11) 39.

[101] eg Raz, 'The Rule of Law and its Virtue' (n 10) 214.

will not constitute lawful punishment.[102] It is important to stress, here, that the concern is with substance, not just form. The normative underpinning of the legality (and indeed legitimacy) of punishment lies in respect for the autonomy of the individual. The concept of legality set out in the ECtHR's case law makes it clear that the imposition of punishment is an exclusively judicial function. In order to meet the requirement of legality, punishment must be imposed by the judiciary in proceedings with appropriate safeguards. The importance of this understanding of the lawful imposition of punishment takes on particular importance in the context of sentences of imprisonment.

IV. Lawful Detention after Conviction by a Competent Court

Article 5(1)(a) ECHR allows for an exception to the prohibition on deprivation of liberty in those cases in which an individual has been detained following 'conviction by a competent court'. The notion of 'court' in this context is given the same meaning as in Article 6(1) ECHR.[103] In particular, it refers 'to a body "established by law" satisfying a number of conditions which include independence, particularly vis-à-vis the executive, impartiality, the duration of its members' terms of office and guarantees of a judicial procedure'.[104] The ECtHR has also held that:

> a court belonging to the judicial system of an entity not recognised under international law may be regarded as a tribunal 'established by law' provided that it forms part of a judicial system operating on a 'constitutional and legal basis' reflecting a judicial tradition compatible with the Convention, in order to enable individuals to enjoy the Convention guarantees.[105]

102 See eg the case of Sarah Mardini who was tried in absentia after a judge refused to temporarily lift a seven-year travel ban barring her re-entry to Greece, H Smith, 'On Trial for Saving Lives: The Young Refugee Activist Facing a Greek Court', 14 Nov 2021, available at <https://www.theguardian.com/world/2021/nov/14/on-trial-for-saving-lives-the-young-refugee-activist-facing-a-greek-court> (accessed 16 Nov 2021).

103 See Trechsel, *Human Rights* (n 2) 440. See *Dacosta Silva v Spain* App no 69966/01, 2 Nov 2006, para 43: 'The detention must be imposed by a competent court, which has power to try the case, is independent of the executive and affords adequate judicial guarantees.' It is worth noting that a prosecutor cannot be regarded as a court, even in the context of *habeas corpus* proceedings under the Art 5(4) ECHR standard, Trechsel, *Human Rights* (n 2) 479.

104 *De Wilde, Ooms, and Versyp v Belgium*, 18 June 1971, Series A no 12, para 78.

105 See *Ilaşcu and Others v Moldova and Russia* [GC] App no 48787/99, ECHR 2004-VII, para 460.

In *Dacosta*, the applicant, who was a member of the Guardia Civil, complained about the lawfulness of his house arrest. The detention had been imposed by a senior officer in the Guardia Civil and thus did not meet the judicial guarantees of Article 5(1)(a) ECHR.[106] Similarly, detention ordered by an applicant's 'military superiors, who exercised their authority within the chain of command and who, as such, were subject to the authority of the military hierarchy and therefore did not enjoy any independence from it' did not meet the test in the provision.[107] Competence 'falls to be examined *ratione loci, personae, temporis* and *materiae*', but the scope of review is limited in that the ECtHR will only intervene in cases in which the court's competence was obviously lacking.[108]

In *Ilaşcu*, the ECtHR held that lawfulness in Article 5(1)(a) ECHR required compliance with the Convention, 'including the general principles expressed or implied in it, particularly the principle of the rule of law, which is expressly mentioned in the Preamble to the Convention'. It stated that the 'notion underlying the expression "in accordance with a procedure prescribed by law" is one of fair and proper procedure, namely that any measure depriving a person of his liberty should issue from and be executed by an appropriate authority and should not be arbitrary'.[109] In addition, it noted that 'as the purpose of Article 5 is to protect the individual from arbitrariness, a "conviction" cannot be the result of a flagrant denial of justice'.[110] The fact that none of the applicants had been convicted by a 'court' meant that the sentence of imprisonment imposed by the body could not be regarded as 'lawful detention', imposed 'in accordance with the law' and thus violated Article 5(1)(a) ECHR.[111]

This suggests that in order for a sentence of imprisonment to comply with the guarantee in Article 5(1) ECHR, it must be imposed by a court. It might be argued that an individual might choose to waive the right in Article 5(1)(a) ECHR, for instance in the context of plea-bargaining proceedings. It is instructive in this regard, though, that the ECtHR has suggested that an individual cannot waive their right to be lawfully detained. In *De Wilde*, it held that

> the right to liberty is too important in a 'democratic society' within the meaning of the Convention for a person to lose the benefit of the protection

[106] *Dacosta Silva v Spain* App no 69966/01, 2 Nov 2006, para 44.
[107] *Koç and Demir v Turkey* App no 26793/08, 20 Mar 2012.
[108] See Trechsel, *Human Rights* (n 2) 440.
[109] *Ilaşcu and Others v Moldova and Russia* [GC] App no 48787/99, ECHR 2004-VII, para 461.
[110] ibid citing *Drozd and Janousek v France and Spain*, judgment of 26 June 1992, Series A no 240, para 110.
[111] *Ilaşcu and Others v Moldova and Russia* [GC] App no 48787/99, ECHR 2004-VII, paras 462, 463.

of the Convention for the single reason that he gives himself up to be taken into detention. Detention might violate Article 5 even although the person concerned might have agreed to it.[112]

Individuals may waive their right to a trial,[113] but they cannot waive their right to be lawfully detained. Sentences of imprisonment will only be compatible with Article 5(1)(a) ECHR if they are imposed by a judge. The possibility of a further judicial review at some point will not be sufficient to meet the demands of the right to freedom from unlawful detention.

V. Sentencing Practices which Interfere with the Right to Judicial Determination of the Sentence

A. Summary Judgments and Penalty Orders

It is useful to consider whether the imposition of punishment by the prosecutor can be considered compatible with human rights. In Switzerland, the vast majority of cases are determined in summary punishment order proceedings.[114] In these cases, the sentence is unilaterally imposed by a prosecutor. The prosecutor's power is substantial.[115] The prosecutor has a statutory obligation to impose a summary punishment order in those cases in which a sentence of up to six months' imprisonment, a financial penalty of 180-day units, or a fine is appropriate, providing that the accused has confessed to the offence or the facts of the case have been otherwise sufficiently established.[116] An objection to the decision to issue a summary punishment order has to be lodged within ten days.[117] This time limit is conspicuously short, particularly when compared to the usual thirty-day period for appealing against fines issued in relation to

[112] *De Wilde, Ooms, and Versyp v Belgium*, 18 June 1971, Series A no 12, para 65.

[113] Although see *VCL and AN v UK* App nos 77587/12 and 74603/12, 16 Feb 2021, para 202 in which it is noted that a waiver of trial rights is not permitted if this would impinge on important public interests.

[114] See M Thommen, *Kurzer Prozess—Fairer Prozess? Strafbefehls- und Abgekürzte Verfahren zwischen Effizienz und Gerechtigkeit* (Bern: Stämpfli 2013); C Schwarzenegger, 'Art 352' in A Donatsch and others (eds), *Kommentar zur Schweizerischen Strafprozessordnung* (3rd edn, Zurich: Schulthess 2020) N 2; T Hansjakob, 'Zahlen und Fakten zum Strafbefehlsverfahren' (2014) *forumpoenale* 160–64.

[115] See eg BGer 6B_941/2015, 2 Mar 2016 in which the prosecutor imposed a series of summary punishment orders on the individual for remaining in Switzerland without a valid residence permit amounting to a total of 495 days of imprisonment. At no point did the individual have the assistance of counsel.

[116] Art 352(1) Swiss Criminal Code.

[117] Art 354(1) CC.

regulatory-type offences, such as some minor traffic violations. In the event that an objection is lodged, the summary punishment order forms the basis of the indictment and the case proceeds to trial in accordance with the rules governing ordinary criminal proceedings.[118]

The dichotomy here between theory and practice is important and requires closer consideration. The formal legitimacy of such proceedings, and thus their compatibility with Article 6(1) ECHR, is said to be guaranteed by the right of the accused to reject the summary punishment order and to demand ordinary criminal proceedings.[119] The decision to accept the summary punishment order is deemed to constitute a waiver of the right to a criminal trial. It is questionable, however, whether this procedural set-up is sufficient to satisfy the demands of fairness in the sense of Article 6 ECHR.[120]

First, a failure to lodge an objection will not automatically constitute a waiver of the right to a trial. Any waiver must be established in an unequivocal manner and be attended by minimum safeguards commensurate with its importance. This requires that the accused be aware of the summary punishment order and choose to accept it in the knowledge of the procedural consequences of this acceptance. In many cases, however, this will not be the case. Instructive in this regard are a number of factors, including the fact that the prosecutor is not obliged to conduct a hearing with the accused before issuing the order,[121] the fact that the order will not be translated into a foreign language,[122] and the fact that the order does not have to be personally served on the accused.[123] It is unsurprising therefore that the Swiss courts have had to consider a number of cases in which the accused missed the deadline to file an objection. The Swiss

[118] Art 356(1) CC.

[119] Thommen, *Kurzer Prozess* (n 114) 116–22; Schwarzenegger, 'Art 352' (n 114) N 1; see also BGer 6B_152/2013, 27 Feb 2 2013, E 3.1.

[120] For criticism see A Nosetti-Kaufmann, 'Strafbefehl, Abgekürztes Verfahren und Fehlende Unmittelbarkeit: Festhalten am Status Quo—eine Verpasste Chance?' (2020) 138 *Schweizerische Zeitschrift für Strafrecht* 248–67; G Gilliéron and M Killias, 'Strafbefehl und Justizirrtum: Franz Riklin hatte Recht' in MA Niggli, J Hurtado Pozo, and N Queloz (eds), *Festschrift für Franz Riklin, Zur Emeritierung und zugleich dem 67. Geburtstag* (Zurich: Schulthess 2007) 379; M Schubarth, 'Zurück zum Grossinquisitor?, Zur Rechtsstaatlichen Problematik des Strafbefehls' in MA Niggli, J Hurtado Pozo, and N Queloz (eds), *Festschrift für Franz Riklin, Zur Emeritierung und zugleich dem 67. Geburtstag* (Zurich: Schulthess 2007) 527.

[121] See eg F Riklin, 'Art 352' in MA Niggli, M Heer, and H Wiprächtiger (eds), *Schweizerische Strafprozessordnung Basler Kommentar* (2nd edn, Basel: Helbing Lichtenhahn 2014) N 2: '*In der allermeisten Fällen befragt die Staatsanwaltschaft die beschuldigte Person zuvor nicht persönlich und kennt sie nur aus den Polizeiakten*'; M Thommen, 'Unerhörte Strafbefehle, Strafbefehle ohne Einvernahme—ein Plädoyer für Kommunikation mit Beschuldigten' (2010) 128 *Schweizerische Zeitschrift für Strafrecht* 373.

[122] See eg F Riklin, 'Art 353' in MA Niggli, M Heer, and H Wiprächtiger (eds), *Schweizerische Strafprozessordnung Basler Kommentar* (2nd edn, Basel; Helbing Lichtenhahn 2014) N 8.

[123] According to Art 88(4) Swiss Criminal Procedure Code, for instance, according to which summary punishment orders come into force even if they have not been served.

Federal Supreme Court has proved reluctant to accept arguments in favour of extending or restoring the time limit.[124]

Second, and perhaps even more importantly, there is no automatic judicial scrutiny of the summary punishment order built into the system. In this sense, the Swiss system differs considerably from those in other continental European countries where the orders are automatically subject to judicial scrutiny.[125] There is no suggestion that the prosecutor can be considered to be a judicial authority. The prosecutor is a party to the proceedings and cannot meet the requirements of judicial independence and impartiality.[126] In a number of cases, the ECtHR has held that Article 6 ECHR does not guarantee the right to an independent or impartial prosecutor,[127] not least because it would make little sense to attempt to apply the guarantee to those who are parties to the proceedings.[128] The more recent case law on plea-bargaining suggests that any settlement or bargain must automatically be reviewed by a court.[129] This is not the case in Switzerland. This means that punishment is imposed in the vast majority of cases by a prosecutor and in the absence of any judicial supervision. The lack of judicial review of the summary punishment orders imposed by the prosecutor is so serious that it calls into question entirely the lawfulness of this practice. Such proceedings are simply incompatible with the right to judicial determination of the sentence and cannot meet the requirements of fairness as set out in Article 6 ECHR.

Even more problematic are those cases in which a sentence of imprisonment is imposed by the prosecutor in such proceedings. Here the lack of automatic

[124] See eg BGer 6B_110/2016, 27 July 2016 (accused failed to pick up a registered letter; accused should have arranged to have his post collected while he was on holiday); BGer 6B_390/2020, 23 July 2020 (accused should have indicated to the authorities that he was unable to understand the order).

[125] See eg Art 407 and Art 408 of the German Criminal Procedure Code, where the penal order is only served on the accused after it has been sanctioned by a judge.

[126] *Kontalexis v Greece* App no 59000/08, 31 May 2011, para 57: 'La Cour rappelle que les garanties d'indépendance et d'impartialité propres au procès équitable fixées par l'article 6 § 1 de la Convention concernent uniquement les juridictions appelées à décider d'une accusation en matière pénale, et ne s'appliquent pas au représentant du parquet, ce dernier étant notamment l'une des parties d'une procédure judiciaire contradictoire', citing *Priebke v Italie* (dec) App no 48799/99, 5 Apr 2001; *Forcellini v Saint-Marin* (dec) App no 34657/97, 28 May 2002. See also A Donatsch, 'Der Strafbefehl sowie Ähnliche Verfahrenserledigungen mit Einsprachemöglichkeit, Insbesondere aus dem Gesichtswinkel von Art. 6 EMRK' (1994) 112 *Schweizerische Zeitschrift für Strafrecht* 317: '*Dass Verfahrenserledigungen mit Einsprachevorbehalt unter dem Gesichtswinkel von Art. 6 EMRK wenig zu reden geben, ist vor allem deshalb nicht selbstverständlich, weil das täterschaftliche Verhalten dabei in der Regel nicht von einem Richter bzw. nicht im Hauptverfahren beurteilt und sanktioniert wird, obschon es sich bei der zu beurteilenden Sache um eine strafrechtliche Angelegenheit im Sinne von Art. 6 Ziff. 1 EMRK handelt*.'

[127] *Haarde v Iceland* App no 66847/12, 23 Nov 2017, para 94: the Court observes that the Convention does not guarantee a right to an impartial prosecutor.

[128] These cases demonstrate clearly the close relationship between the requirements of independence, impartiality, and 'tribunal established by law'. For discussion see Trechsel, *Human Rights* (n 2) 49.

[129] *Natsvlishvili and Togonidze v Georgia* App no 9043/05, 29 Apr 2014.

judicial scrutiny of the decision calls into question the lawfulness of the detention as required by Article 5(1(a) ECHR, which requires that the detention follow conviction by a 'competent court'. It is notable that the vast majority of sentences in Switzerland are imposed in such proceedings and that only a fraction of individuals challenge the decision of the prosecutor in subsequent judicial proceedings.[130]

Finally, real questions arise as to whether the legality principle is sufficiently protected. Legality demands that punishment be imposed by the judiciary in the context of proceedings with appropriate safeguards. The development of a system of punishment to be routinely enforced by the executive without systematic judicial control or recourse to the safeguards associated with criminal proceedings is incompatible with the understanding of lawful punishment as defined by Article 7(1) ECHR and with the rule of law.

B. Mandatory Sentences

The problem with mandatory provisions, as the ECtHR has discussed in other contexts,[131] is that judicial control is inherent in 'certain procedural and substantive guarantees'.[132] Mandatory sentencing provisions have the potential to interfere with the right to the judicial imposition of punishment by restricting the ability of the judge to impose the sentence that they deem appropriate, thereby calling into the question the independence of the judge from the legislature.[133] In this sense, they are difficult to reconcile with many of the substantive individual rights of the Convention, to the extent that they prohibit proper consideration of the lawfulness or proportionality of the interference with the right.[134] In spite of such issues, mandatory sentencing provisions do not seem to have given rise to much concern in practice.

[130] See M Thommen and D Eschle, 'Was Tun Wir Juristinnen und Juristen Eigentlich, Wenn Wir forschen? Klassische Dogmatik versus Empirische Rechtsforschung als Innovativer Weg' in J Meier, N Zurkinden, and L Staffler (eds), *Recht und Innovation* (Zurich: Dike 2020) 3, 8.

[131] Notably in relation to the supervision of detention inherent in Art 5(3) ECHR *Caballero v UK* App no 32819/96, ECHR 2000-II: Here, the applicant complained about the automatic statutory refusal of bail in relation to those charged with certain criminal offences (murder, attempted murder, manslaughter, rape, and attempted rape). The ECtHR held that the automatic refusal of bail in the applicant's case was incompatible with the essence of the Art 5(3) ECHR which necessitated judicial review of the lawfulness of pre-trial detention.

[132] *SBC v UK* App no 39360/98, 19 June 2001, paras 22 and 23.

[133] See too K Roach, 'Searching for Smith: The Constitutionality of Mandatory Sentences' (2001) 39 *Osgoode Hall Law Journal* 367.

[134] See further Ch 3.

A number of offences in Switzerland, for instance, carry mandatory minimum sentences.[135] Examples include intentional killing, which proscribes a sentence of imprisonment of no less than five years;[136] rape, which is to be punished with a sentence of imprisonment of at least one year;[137] and theft on a commercial scale, which attracts a financial penalty of at least ninety daily units.[138] In all of these cases, the usual sentencing provisions apply. This means that the sentencing judge is obliged to assess the culpability of the offender and is entitled, for instance in cases of diminished culpability, to impose a sentence lower than the mandatory minimum.[139]

Mandatory minimum sentencing provisions also exist in the laws of England and Wales. Examples include section 314 of the Sentencing Act 2020, which imposes a mandatory minimum of three years' imprisonment for a third domestic burglary 'unless the court is of the opinion that there are particular circumstances which—(a) relate to any of the offences or to the offender; and (b) would make it unjust to do so in all the circumstances'.[140] In determining the appropriate sentence, the sentencing judge is required to 'go through the proper sentencing exercise in accordance with the sentencing guidelines and then cross-check to ensure that the sentence was no less than the minimum term required'.[141] Other provisions are even more restrictive. According to section 311 of the Sentencing Act 2020,[142] the court is obliged to impose a sentence of at least five years in respect of offenders who were older than eighteen years at the time of the commission of the offence (firearms possession), 'unless the court is of the opinion that there are exceptional circumstances which—(a) relate to the offence or to the offender, and (b) justify not doing so'.[143]

In *Rehman*, the defendant pleaded guilty to the offence of having in his possession a 'Kimar Beretta venting handgun which was less than 60 centimetres long overall and with a barrel less than 30 centimetres long'. Although it was a replica blank-firing handgun, it could easily have been altered 'so as to be

[135] For detailed consideration of recent reforms and criticism of mandatory minimums see F Bommer, 'Anmerkungen zum Versuch der Strafrahmenharmonisierung' (2019) 137 *Schweizerische Zeitschrift für Strafrecht* 267, 289.

[136] Art 111 of the Swiss Criminal Code.

[137] Art 190 of the Swiss Criminal Code

[138] Art 139(2) of the Swiss Criminal Code.

[139] See Art 48a(1) of the Swiss Criminal Code: if the court chooses to reduce the sentence, it is not bound by the minimum penalty that the offence carries.

[140] Sentencing Act 2020, s 314(2). See *R v Jerome Carlon Stevenson* [2014] EWCA Crim 1023, which involved the same provision, previously set out in s 111(1) of the Powers of Criminal Court (Sentencing) Act 2000.

[141] *R v Andrews* [2012] EWCA Crim 2332; *R v McKay (Gordon Thomas)* [2012] EWCA Crim 1900;

[142] Previously s 51A(1)(a)(2) of the Firearms Act 1968.

[143] Sentencing Act 2020, s 311(2).

capable of firing live ammunition'.[144] The gun had not been converted for use, there was no ammunition for it, and it was still in its original wrapping. The defendant was a man of previous good character and a collector. He purchased the replica firearm online, planning to display it. The police had information that the defendant had bought the firearm in question and on searching his house found it under the bed. The defendant told the police officers that he did not think that it was illegal to own the gun. In holding that exceptional circumstances justified the decision not to impose the minimum term, the court referred in particular to the defendant's good character and the fact that 'he had no knowledge of the unlawfulness of the one weapon that he had in his possession which contravened the provisions of section 5 of the Firearms Act and therefore resulted in the application of section 51A'.[145] The five-year sentence imposed by the sentencing judge was reduced to twelve months.[146]

In *Wood*, the defendant was a collector of guns and was described by the court as being 'of extremely good character' and 'a most responsible and impressive individual'.[147] The court noted that he had 'extremely impressive references', 'was the manager of a surveillance company', 'had carried out important work with Army cadets', and had 'provided help to the police'. He was sentenced to the minimum term of five years' imprisonment for possession of 'a single barrelled hammerless shotgun with a barrel less than 30 centimetres long', which he had apparently inherited from his grandfather.[148] The Court of Appeal refused to substitute the minimum term, noting that although there was 'a great deal to be said in the appellant's favour', it had 'reluctantly come to the conclusion that we would not be properly applying the statutory provision imposed by Parliament if we interfered with the sentence of five years' imprisonment'. It held that the defendant 'of all people should have understood that this was not the sort of weapon which should have been in his possession' and had failed to 'take the action which he should have done to check whether it was lawful to possess it'.[149] The exceptional circumstances proviso was central to the Court of Appeal's finding that the legislation was not incompatible with Article 3 or Article 5 ECHR.[150]

[144] *Regina v Rehman; Regina v Wood* [2005] EWCA 2056, para 17.
[145] ibid para 30.
[146] ibid para 31.
[147] ibid para 23.
[148] ibid para 25.
[149] ibid para 32.
[150] ibid Lord Woolf CJ held that circumstances were exceptional '... if it would mean that to impose five years imprisonment would result in an arbitrary and disproportionate sentence ... A holistic approach is needed. There will be cases where there is one single striking feature, which relates either to the offence or the offender, which causes that case to fall within the requirement of exceptional circumstances. There can be other cases where no single factor by itself will amount to exceptional

This suggests that many 'mandatory' sentencing provisions, such as those discussed above, are not in fact mandatory in nature and are probably better described as statutory assumptions, which provide for some judicial discretion enabling the judge to depart from the rule in certain circumstances.[151] By introducing some discretion for the judge to intervene, the provision was not to be characterized as truly mandatory. The exceptional circumstances exception essentially renders such provisions non-mandatory in nature, thereby bringing them within the realm of compliance by allowing judicial consideration of the appropriate sentence.[152] This may well be why Ashworth suggests that, while 'unwise', there is 'nothing unconstitutional about the enactment of mandatory sentences'.[153] The judgment in *Wood* makes it clear, though, that exceptional circumstances will only rarely be accepted and some have suggested that the courts have since adopted an even more restrictive approach.[154] This calls into question the extent of such provisos and the extent to which they truly allow for consideration of the interests of justice or at the very least are sufficient to guard against a flagrant denial of justice. Restrictive clauses must afford sufficient discretion to the sentencing judge to guarantee the judicial role at sentencing and to ensure that they are able to avoid passing a sentence which is arbitrary or disproportionate.[155]

circumstances, but the collective impact of all the relevant circumstances truly makes the case exceptional.' See also *James, Wells, and Lee v UK* App nos 25119/09, 57715/09, and 57877/09, 18 Sept 2012, para 203: although '[r]estrictions on judicial discretion in sentencing do not *per se* render any ensuing detention arbitrary and therefore incompatible with the provisions of Article 5(1) ECHR' provisions which prevent genuine consideration of the correlation between the aim of the detention and the detention itself may well be incompatible with Art 5 ECHR.

[151] See also eg UK sentencing guidelines: s. 125: '(1) Every court: (a) must, in sentencing an offender, follow any sentencing guidelines which are relevant to the offender's case, and (b) must, in exercising any other function relating to sentencing of offenders, follow any sentencing guidelines which are relevant to the exercise of that function, unless the court is satisfied that it would be contrary to the interests of justice to do so.' For discussion see A Ashworth and J Roberts, 'The Evolution of Sentencing Policy and Practice' (2016) 45 *Crime and Justice* 307.

[152] In contrast, for instance, to the provisions deemed unconstitutional by the Canadian Supreme Court in *Nur* [2015] 1 RCS 773 at [44]: s 95(2)(a) of the Canadian Criminal Code imposed mandatory minimum sentences of three years for a first offence and five years for a subsequent offence for possession of a prohibited or restricted firearm when the firearm is loaded or kept with readily accessible ammunition. See also *Lloyd* [2016] SCC 13.

[153] A Ashworth, 'Changes in Sentencing Law' [1997] *Criminal Law Review* 1, 2.

[154] See further M Wasik, 'Time to Repeal the Firearms Minimum Sentencing Provision' [2017] *Criminal Law Review* 203, 206, discussing, inter alia, *Jordan* [2004] EWCA Crim 3291 and *Wilkinson* [2009] EWCA Crim 1925.

[155] See also *Cochrane v HM Advocate* [2010] HCJAC 117 in which the court noted that exceptional circumstances had to be discussed in the context of 'the need to avoid sentences which are arbitrary and disproportionate', at [19] per Lord Reed, Lord Carloway dissenting. The facts of the case were described as follows: 'police officers went to the appellant's house in order to look for her son, for whom they had an outstanding arrest warrant. The appellant allowed the officers to search the house. Her son was not there, but during the search the officers found a handgun underneath the mattress of the appellant's bed. She told the police that it belonged to her and that it had previously belonged to her father, who

In the English case of *R v Offen*, the Court of Appeal considered whether the application of a mandatory sentencing provision violated Article 5(1) ECHR.[156] The 'two strikes and you're out' provision required judges to impose an automatic life sentence in those cases in which the defendant had been found guilty of a second serious offence.[157] At issue here was whether the mandatory nature of the provision impinged unacceptably on the competence of the judge, thereby precluding consideration of the reasonableness of the sentence of imprisonment. In *R v Offen*, the court held that it did not, noting that the legislation allowed for deviation from the provisions in 'exceptional circumstances'.[158] The Lord Chief Justice held that this offered sufficient scope to consider the situations in which the statutory assumption was to be overruled.[159] In particular, there was scope to ensure that the provision should be interpreted in such a way as to ensure that the punishment was not arbitrary in the sense of Article 5 ECHR or in contravention of Article 3 ECHR.[160]

As we have seen, the imposition of a mandatory sentence of imprisonment might amount to gross disproportionality in violation of Article 3 ECHR, 'particularly if it requires the court to disregard mitigating factors which are generally understood as indicating a significantly lower level of culpability on the part of the defendant, such as youth or severe mental health problems'.[161] This

had died about 28 years previously. She believed it to be a real gun. She had no ammunition for it. On examination by a firearms expert, the gun was found to be a self-loading automatic pistol which had been manufactured in Czechoslovakia. It was believed to have been made in about 1927 or shortly afterwards. It was in poor external condition, with scratches and corrosion. It had a faulty safety catch and trigger mechanism but was in working order and capable of firing bullets.' She said that it did not occur to her that she needed a licence for it: she regarded it as a war trophy. On appeal, a majority determined that exceptional circumstances justified a reduction of the minimum term and imposed a community service order.

[156] *R v Offen* [2001] 2 All ER 154.

[157] The policy was justified in the following terms: 'Too often in the past, those who have shown a propensity to commit serious violent or sex offences have served their sentences and been released only to offend again. In many such cases, the danger of releasing the offender has been plain for all to see—but nothing could be done, because once the offender has completed the sentence imposed, he or she has to be released. Too often, victims have paid the price when the offender has repeated the same offences. The Government is determined that the public should receive proper protection from persistent violent or sex offenders. That means requiring the courts to impose an automatic indeterminate sentence, and releasing the offender if and only if it is safe to do so.' White Paper, *Protecting the Public, The Government's Strategy on Crime in England and Wales* (Cm 3190, 1996), para 10.11.

[158] For discussion see D Woodhouse, 'The Law and Politics: More Power to the Judges—and to the People? (2001) 54 *Parliamentary Affairs* 223, 229.

[159] ibid.

[160] Citing *R v Governor of Brockhill Prison, ex p Evans* (No 2) [2000] 3 WLR 843, 858 per Lord Hope of Craighead: 'assuming that the detention is lawful under domestic law, it is nevertheless open to criticism on the ground that it is arbitrary because, for example, it was resorted to in bad faith or was not proportionate.'

[161] See eg *Vinter and Others v UK* App nos 66069/09, 130/10, and 3869/10, 17 Jan 2012, para 93. See further Ch 3.

emphasizes the importance of judicial discretion at sentencing, which is sufficient to ensure that such issues are afforded appropriate consideration.

C. Indeterminate Sentences

The imposition of an indeterminate sentence also has the potential to interfere with the responsibility of the judge for determining the sentence. These sentences are particularly problematic if an executive as opposed to judicial authority is responsible for making the decision on release. The ECtHR has held that it 'cannot accept that a decision-making power by the executive to detain the applicant on the basis of perceived fears of future non-violent criminal conduct unrelated to his original murder conviction accords with the spirit of the Convention, with its emphasis on the rule of law and protection from arbitrariness'.[162]

In 2016, a whopping 19% of prisoners in England and Wales were serving indeterminate sentences (ie sentences of no fixed length).[163] This was principally a result of the imposition of the imprisonment for public protection (IPP) sentence, introduced in 2005.[164] The sentencing judge was obliged to impose an indeterminate sentence under certain circumstances and to set a minimum term (tariff) which the prisoner was to serve before being eligible for release. The decision on release, like the sentence of life imprisonment, was within the discretion of the Parole Board, if it was satisfied that detention was no longer necessary for the purposes of public protection.[165] The tariff was often relatively short. In 2006, for instance, the median tariff for IPP prisoners was thirty months, and 70% of IPP sentences imposed involved tariffs of three years or less.[166] The sentence was abolished in 2012 but not for existing prisoners. The former Home Secretary Michael Gove noted that, '[i]n terms of pure justice and fairness, there are far too many prisoners, who were sentenced under the IPP—Imprisonment for Public Protection—indeterminate sentence provisions who have served far longer than the gravity of their offence requires and who should be released'.[167]

162 *Stafford v UK* [GC] App no 46295/99, ECHR 2002-IV, para 82.
163 See Ashworth and Roberts, 'The Evolution of Sentencing Policy' (n 151) 307.
164 Criminal Justice Act 2003, s 225. For discussion see J Beard, *Sentences of Imprisonment for Public Protection*, House of Commons Briefing Paper No 6086, 6 June 2019.
165 See Crime (Sentences) Act 1997, s 28.
166 See *James, Wells, and Lee v UK* App nos 25119/09, 57715/09, and 57877/09, 18 Sept 2012, para 6.
167 M Gove, 'What's Really Criminal about the Criminal Justice System?' Longford Lecture 2016.

The ECtHR has held that determination of the 'tariff' or punishment part of an indeterminate sentence was to be considered part of the sentencing exercise and not part of 'the administrative implementation of the sentence of the court as can be seen in cases of early or conditional release from a determinate term of imprisonment'.[168] It held that after the expiry of this punishment part:

> continued detention depends on elements of dangerousness and risk associated with the objectives of the original sentence of murder. These elements may change with the course of time, and thus new issues of lawfulness arise requiring determination by a body satisfying the requirements of Article 5 § 4. It can no longer be maintained that the original trial and appeal proceedings satisfied, once and for all, issues of compatibility of subsequent detention of mandatory life prisoners with the provisions of Article 5 § 1 of the Convention.[169]

The principles espoused in these cases focus attention on the definition of punishment. In the context of life sentences, the offender's punishment is based on the initial judicial determination of the punishment. If the offender continues to be detained after the expiry of the 'tariff' or 'punishment part' and the lawfulness of this (continued) detention is not considered to be inherently incorporated in the original sentencing judgment, is this continued detention 'punishment' or is it preventative detention? The question is not just whether such sentences are compatible with legality as guaranteed by Article 7(1) ECHR but also whether the scope of review is sufficient. In cases such as *James, Wells, and Lee*, in which the punishment part of the sentence was comparatively short and the offenders remained in prison long after the expiry of the tariff, it seems questionable whether the sentence itself was truly within the competence of the sentencing judge.[170]

Indeterminate sentences are difficult to reconcile with the principle of legality in the sense of ensuring that the sentence which is to be imposed is sufficiently clear and foreseeable and imposed in response to a criminal act or omission.[171] They also conflict with the idea that the sentence must be imposed

[168] *Stafford v UK* [GC] App no 46295/99, ECHR 2002-IV, para 87.

[169] ibid.

[170] *James, Wells, and Lee v UK* App nos 25119/09, 57715/09, and 57877/09, 18 Sept 2012, para 232: the combination of the Parole Board and judicial review proceedings was considered sufficient to meet the requirements of Art 5(4) ECHR. It might be argued, thus, that the standard of review in these cases should be that of Art 6(1) ECHR and not that of Art 5(4) ECHR.

[171] For discussion see Ch 2.

by a judge. In this regard it is notable that the problem here is not unrestrained judicial discretion but insufficient judicial control of the length of the sentence.

VI. The Role of the Judge and Human Rights at Sentencing

The responsibility of the judge for the determination of the sentence is well established. It is true that judges are 'not alone in judging'. They are surrounded by a 'whole series of subsidiary authorities' whose involvement might be said in the criminal justice context to 'fragment the legal power to punish'.[172] Psychiatrists, psychologists, prison personnel, social workers, and others involved in the implementation of the sentence might not have the right to judge, but are all involved in the process of the determination of the sentence.[173] The responsibility for the verdict and the sentence nevertheless rests in the hands of the judge. It is interesting that in spite of the widespread acceptance of the characterization of the sentencing decision as a judicial exercise, a number of practices and laws actually significantly undermine the role of the judge at the sentencing stage.

The judicial responsibility for the determination of the sentence is an important requirement of procedural fairness. An offender has the right to have their sentence determined by an independent and impartial court. It is also of considerable importance, though, to ensuring that the sentence is lawful and just. The requirement of judicial review inherent in many of the substantive rights of the Convention requires that a judge is able to ensure that the sentence does not violate important human rights.[174] Ensuring sufficient scope for judicial consideration of the sentence is central to the protection of fairness and legality. Any discussion of the appropriate boundaries of judicial discretion must therefore take account of the constitutional importance of the judge in upholding the human rights of the accused at the sentencing stage. The judge plays a crucial role in the justification of punishment as a practice.

[172] M Foucault, *Discipline and Punish: The Birth of the Prison* (London: Penguin Books 1991) 21.

[173] ibid: 'as soon as the penalties and the security measures defined by the court are not absolutely determined, from the moment they may be modified along the way ... one is handing over to them mechanisms of legal punishment to be used at their discretion: subsidiary judges they may be, but judges all the same.'

[174] eg Art 3 ECHR.

6

The Justification of Punishment and Human Rights

I. Introduction: Sentencing Theory and Human Rights

Human rights play an important role in the regulation of punishment. In view of this, the lack of sustained consideration of their relevance is surprising.[1] Although human rights principles provide state authorities with little guidance in determining the 'appropriate sentence',[2] they nevertheless set important limits on the choice and imposition of punishment. These restrictions differ in scope and importance from the type of limits most frequently discussed in sentencing theory. The notions of justice or fairness in punishment theory are often portrayed as matters of intuition and connected to the idea of proportionality between the sentence and the offence: 'People have a sense that punishments scaled to the gravity of offenses are fairer than punishments which are not.'[3]

The notion of justice from a human rights perspective looks quite different. In this context, the idea of proportionality between the severity of the offence and the sentence is of limited relevance; there is no right to a proportionate sentence.[4] The human rights principles nevertheless exert clear restrictions on

[1] See RS Frase, 'Comparative Perspectives on Sentencing Policy and Research' in M Tonry and RS Frase (eds), *Sentencing and Sanctions in Western Countries* (Oxford: OUP 2001) 279 referring to the 'human rights gap'.

[2] *Vinter and Others v UK* [GC] App nos 66069/09, 130/10, and 3896/10, ECHR 2013-III, para 106: 'it is not its role to decide what is the appropriate term of detention applicable to a particular offence or to pronounce on the appropriate length of detention or other sentence which should be served by a person after conviction by a competent court.'

[3] A von Hirsch, 'Proportionality in the Philosophy of Punishment' (1992) 16 *Crime and Justice* 55, 56; see also M Tonry, *Sentencing Matters* (New York, NY: OUP 1996) 184; G Giannoulis, *Studien zur Strafzumessung: Ein Beitrag zur Dogmatik, Rechtstheorie und Rechtsinformatik mit Vertiefung in den Eigentums- und Vermögensdelikten* (Tübingen: Mohr Siebeck 2014) 15: 'Man könnte die TP als eine Sache der Fairness beschreiben'; W Frisch, A von Hirsch, and HJ Albrecht (eds), *Tatproportionalität. Normative und Empirische Aspekte einer Tatproportionalen Strafzumessung* (Heidelberg: CF Müller 2001).

[4] See further Ch 3. See too *Öneryıldız v Turkey* [GC] App no 48939/99, ECHR 2004-XII, para 116 and *Nachova and Others v Bulgaria* App nos 43577/98 43579/98, ECHR 2005-VII, para 147; *Nikolova*

Sentencing and Human Rights. Sarah J Summers, Oxford University Press. © Sarah J Summers 2022.
DOI: 10.1093/oso/9780192870384.003.0006

the power of the state to punish. Punishment, as we have seen, will only be compatible with human rights if it is imposed on a culpable individual for the commission of an act or omission, which is clearly and prospectively defined as criminal. In addition, it must be free from arbitrariness, must not constitute a disproportionate interference with—or fundamentally violate—certain human rights, and must be imposed by a judge in the context of criminal proceedings.[5]

Consideration of the nature and importance of human rights principles at sentencing draws attention to the role of rights as limitations on punishment. If these principles simply constrain punishment, however, to what extent might they be said to be of broader relevance to the debate on the justification of punishment? In other words, what can human rights principles contribute to our understanding of punishment and its justification? In order to consider this in more detail, it is important to examine first the most important rationales for the imposition of punishment in sentencing theory. This will provide the basis for the consideration of the relationship between human rights and the justification of punishment.

II. Justifying Punishment: Punishment and its Purpose(s)

There is widespread acknowledgement that punishment is problematic and requires justification.[6] Consequentialist accounts of punishment find the justification in the likely consequences (such as deterrence, rehabilitation, or incapacitation) of punishing the offender,[7] while for the retributivist, the punishment of an offender is a fitting (just) social response to the commission of an offence, regardless of the consequences of the punishment.[8] The retributivist

and Velichkova v Bulgaria App no 7888/03, 20 Dec 2007, para 61; *Vinter and Others v UK* [GC] App nos 66069/09 and 130/10 and 3896/10, ECHR 2013-III.

[5] See Chs 2–5.

[6] See eg D Boonin, *The Problem of Punishment* (Cambridge: CUP 2008); V Tadros, *The Ends of Harm: The Moral Foundations of the Criminal Law* (Oxford: OUP 2011) ch 1.

[7] Famous accounts include C Beccaria, *On Crimes and Punishment* (R Bellamy ed, R Davis tr, 5th edn, first published 1766) (Cambridge: CUP 1995) and J Bentham, *An Introduction to the Principles of Morals and Legislation* (JH Burns and HLA Hart eds, first published 1789) (London: Athlone Press 1970).

[8] Important accounts include those of I Kant, *Groundwork of the Metaphysics of Morals* (ed M Gregor and J Timmerman first published 1785) (Cambridge: CUP 2014) and GWF Hegel, *The Philosophy of Right* (FM Knox tr, Oxford: OUP 1942); HLA Hart, *Punishment and Responsibility: Essays in the Philosophy of Law* (J Gardner, 2nd edn, Oxford: OUP 2008) 231 defines 'a model of retributive theory' in the following terms: 'Such a theory will assert three things: first, that a person may be punished if, and only if, he has voluntarily done something morally wrong; secondly, that his punishment must in some way match, or be the equivalent of, the wickedness of his offence; and thirdly, that the justification for

account of punishment was rejected for a large part of the twentieth century as 'vulgar' or 'barbaric'.[9] For consequentialists, any suggestion that the suffering of the guilty should serve to justify punishment was essentially immoral, precisely because suffering was always to be understood as a cost rather than a benefit of the criminal justice system.[10] In the words of Glueck: 'The old argument was that punishment was necessary as "just retribution" or requital of wickedness. No thoughtful person today seriously holds this theory of sublimated social vengeance.'[11] The pursuit of the 'suffering of the guilty as an intrinsic good' was viewed as 'immoral because considered intrinsically (ie aside from its consequences) suffering is always and only an evil'.[12] Instead a welfarist model prevailed which focused largely on the rehabilitation of the offender.[13]

This post-war consequentialist consensus in the theoretical literature[14] was dramatically overturned in the 1970s by a 'retributivist revival'[15] which was accompanied by a corresponding 'decline of the rehabilitative ideal'.[16] This shift has been explained both with reference to 'general anti-consequentialism' in the philosophical literature,[17] and as a response to the perceived injustices of

punishing men under such conditions is that the return of suffering for moral evil voluntarily done, is itself just or morally good.'

[9] See J Gardner, 'Introduction' in HLA Hart (ed), *Punishment and Responsibility: Essays in the Philosophy of Law* (J Gardner, 2nd edn, Oxford: OUP 2008) xiv, xvii. See also H Sidgwick, *Methods of Ethics* (6th edn, London: Macmillan 1901) 281: 'Personally I am so far from holding this view that I have an instinctive and strong moral aversion to it; and I hesitate to attribute it to Common Sense, since I think that it is gradually passing away from the moral consciousness of educated persons in the most advanced communities: but I think it is still perhaps the more ordinary view.' An excellent illustration of the status of retributivist thought is found in the description in *Lucky Jim* of Mrs Welch, who is characterized by 'her attitude towards "so-called freedom in education", her advocacy of retributive punishment, her fondness for reading what Englishwomen wrote about how Parisians thought and felt', Kingsley Amis, *Lucky Jim* (first published 1954, London: Penguin 2010) 184. See too the discussion in KG Armstrong, 'The Retributivst Hits Back' (1961) 70 *Mind* 471.

[10] See eg HLA Hart, 'Prolegomenon to the Principles of Punishment' in HLA Hart (ed), *Punishment and Responsibility: Essays in the Philosophy of Law* (J Gardner, 2nd edn, Oxford: OUP 2008) 9.

[11] S Glueck, 'Principles of a Rational Penal Code' (1928) 41 *Harvard Law Review* 453, 456.

[12] See Gardner, 'Introduction' (n 9) xiv, xvii.

[13] See eg H Wechsler, 'Sentencing, Correction, and the Model Penal Code' (1961) 109 *University of Pennsylvania Law Review* 465, 468.

[14] M Tonry, 'Can Twenty-first Century Punishment be Justified in Principle' in M Tonry (ed), *Retributivism as a Past: Has it a Future?* (Oxford: OUP 2011) 3–29 suggests penal practice was more complicated.

[15] For discussion of this shift see M Matravers, 'Is Twenty-first Century Punishment Post-desert'? in M Tonry (ed), *Retributivism as a Past: Has it a Future?* (Oxford: OUP 2011) 30; M Tonry, 'Fairness, Equality, Proportionality and Parsimony' in A du Bois-Pedain and AE Bottoms (eds), *Penal Censure: Engagements Within and Beyond Desert Theory* (Oxford: Hart Publishing 2019); D Garland, *The Culture of Control: Crime and Social Order in Contemporary Society* (New York, NY: OUP 2001); Giannoulis, *Studien zur Strafzumessung* (n 3).

[16] FA Allen, *The Decline of the Rehabilitative Ideal* (New Haven, CT: Yale University Press 1981). This shift is described in D Garland, *Culture of Control* (n 15) 8 as 'astonishing'.

[17] Matravers, 'Twenty-first Century Punishment' (n 15) 31, referring in particular to the importance of the 'Rawls led neo-Kantian revival' and the publication of *A Theory of Justice* with its 'systematic alternative to utilitarianism' as 'the dominant philosophical event of the period', J Rawls, *A Theory of*

a model of punishment, which focused on indeterminate sentencing and early release.[18] The problem with the rehabilitative approach was said to be that '[l]ooking to the good that will follow from punishment distracts the attention of the judges from the past and, in particular, from the particular offense that the defendant has committed'.[19] This reflects a much-discussed problem for consequentialist theories of punishment in establishing the relevance of guilt and innocence. Here the concern is whether according to such theories it might be justifiable to convict an innocent if to do so would deter others. In the words of Rawls: 'The real question ... is whether the utilitarian, in justifying punishment, hasn't used arguments which commit him to accepting the infliction of suffering on innocent persons if it is for the good of society.'[20] Attempts to address such concerns by arguing that innocent people cannot be deterred[21] or that punishment of the innocent cannot be considered to constitute punishment[22] have garnered little support.

Rawls attempts to resolve this conflict between consequentialism and retributivism by suggesting that that the justification of the punishment of an offender for particular wrongdoing comprises two distinct issues: the justification of 'a practice as a system of rules to be applied and enforced' and the justification of 'a particular action which falls under these rules'.[23] Whereas utilitarian arguments are to be considered appropriate to the issue of justifying punishment as an institution ('why do people punish one another rather than, say, always forgiving one another'),[24] retributive arguments 'fit the application of particular rules to particular cases (why was J punished rather than someone else and what was he punished for)'.[25] He suggests that retributivism does not

Justice (Harvard, MA: Harvard University Press 1971) although Rawls is commonly regarded as a non-consequentialist rather than an anti-consequentialist.

18 See Garland, *Culture of Control* (n 15) 12, who also points to the 'new and urgent need emphasis on the need for security, the containment of danger, and the identification and management of any kind of risk'.

19 GP Fletcher, *Rethinking Criminal Law* (Oxford: OUP 2000) 415.

20 J Rawls, 'Two Concepts of Rules' (1955) 64 *The Philosophical Review* 3, 9.

21 Eg Bentham, *Principles of Morals and Legislation* (n 7) ch XIII, para 9. For criticism see Hart, 'Prolegomenon' (n 10) 19 referring to Bentham's argument as a 'spectacular non sequitur'.

22 Eg FH Bradley, *Ethical Studies* (2nd edn, Oxford: Clarendon Press 1927) 26–27, who suggests defining punishment as punishment only when it is deserved: 'We pay the penalty, because we owe it, and for no other reason; and if punishment is inflicted for any other reason whatever than because it is merited by wrong, it is a gross immorality, a crying injustice, an abominable crime, and not what it pretends to be.' For criticism of this type of 'definitional stop' see Hart, 'Prolegomenon' (n 10) 5–6.

23 Rawls, 'Two Concepts of Rules' (n 20) 5. This is connected to his later argument in that utilitarianism has problems with justice particularly in the context of distribution and fails to 'take seriously the distinction between persons', J Rawls, *A Theory of Justice* (Cambridge, MA: Harvard University Press 1971) 26.

24 Rawls, 'Two Concepts of Rules' (n 20) 6.

25 ibid 5.

necessarily advocate 'as an institution, legal machinery whose essential purpose is to set up and preserve a correspondence between moral turpitude and suffering' and thus that retributivism is not necessarily concerned with justification of the institution of punishment.[26] This view, which suggests a 'retributive rule but no underlying retributive value',[27] has received little support.[28] The 'standard objection' to Rawls' view is that 'any broadly utilitarian defence of the rule against punishment of innocents leaves that rule too vulnerable to exigencies at the margins. One can always imagine extreme cases in which punishing the innocent would bring more benefit than following the rule itself and the value of its combination with other rules.'[29]

HLA Hart seems to agree with Rawls (and Quinton[30]) on the importance of proceeding in stages, distinguishing between the *General Justifying Aim* of punishment (why do we punish and in what circumstances is it a good institution) and its *Distribution* (who should be punished and how much).[31] He insists that 'it is one thing to use the word Retribution ... in order to designate the General Justifying Aim of the system, and quite another to use it to secure that to the question, "To whom may punishment be applied?" (the question of Distribution), the answer given is "Only to an offender for an offence".'[32] The general aim of the criminal law, according to Hart, is reducing future wrongdoing:

> Much confusing shadow-fighting between utilitarians and their opponents may be avoided if it is recognized that it is perfectly consistent to assert both that General Justifying Aim of the practice of punishment is its beneficial consequences and that the pursuit of this General Aim should be qualified or restricted out of deference to the principles of Distribution which require that punishment should be only of an offender for an offence.[33]

[26] ibid 7: 'Does a person who advocates the retributivist view necessarily advocate, as an institution, legal machinery whose essential purpose is to set up and preserve a correspondence between moral turpitude and suffering? Surely not.'

[27] Gardner, 'Introduction' (n 9) xxvii, also xxviii: 'the retributivism here is no mere Rawlsian veneer.'

[28] For criticism see eg JA Corlett, 'Making Sense of Retributivism' (2001) 76 *Philosophy* 77, 82.

[29] Gardner, 'Introduction' (n 9) xx.

[30] AM Quinton, 'On Punishment' (1954) 14 *Analysis* 512.

[31] Hart, 'Prolegomenon' (n 10) 4. For a more recent defence of this distinction see T Hörnle, *Tatproportionale Strafzumessung* (Berlin: Duncker & Humblot 1999) 125; and for criticism see K-L Kunz, 'Tatproportionalität aus der Perspektive eines Normativ Begründeten Strafrechts' in Frisch, von Hirsch, and Albrecht (eds), Tatproportionalität (n 3) 209.

[32] ibid 9.

[33] ibid.

Hart's approach (like that of Rawls) is often said to represent a 'mixed theory' of punishment and has been criticized as suffering from incoherence.[34] Gardner, in his introduction to *Punishment and Responsibility*, suggests however that the 'real problem' is not that 'the Hartian defence of punishment is too mixed but that it is not mixed enough ... He needs to stir a more authentic retributive ingredient into the mix.'[35] Central to this conclusion is the argument that the rule against punishing the innocent is not necessarily a rule in favour of punishing the guilty:

> There is nothing even slightly retributive about Hart's distributive rule, for under Hart's rule the guilt of the guilty does not count in favour of punishing them; it merely eliminates an objection to punishing them. The only Hart-approved rule in favour of punishing the guilty (or anyone else) is the reason given by punishment's general justifying aim, *viz* that future wrongdoing is thereby reduced.[36]

In the course of the 1970s, the development of new theories of retributivism 'sounded the death-knell of traditional, consequentialist approaches to criminal justice'.[37] The retributivist revival encompassed a wide range of theories[38] including 'rectificatory' or 'fair play' theories, according to which a criminal offence disturbs the balance between burdens and benefits in society and falls thus to be rectified,[39] and expressive[40] or communicative theories.[41] According to the extremely influential communicative account, moral wrongdoing deserves censure. In the words of Duff: 'whatever puzzles there might be about

[34] See eg N Lacey, *State Punishment: Political Principles and Community Values* (London: Routledge 1988) 49.

[35] Gardner, 'Introduction' (n 9) xxix.

[36] ibid xxv. See also J Cottingham, 'Varieties of Retribution' (1979) 29 *Philosophical Quarterly* 238, 241.

[37] J Braithwaite and P Petit, *Not Just Deserts: A Republican Theory of Criminal Justice* (Oxford: Clarendon Press 1990) 209.

[38] See eg Cottingham, 'Varieties of Retribution' (n 36) 46 referring to nine varieties.

[39] See eg H Morris, Persons and Punishment' (1968) 52 *The Monist* 475–501; J Murphy, 'Three Mistakes about Retribution' (1971) 31 *Analysis* 166; J Murphy, 'Marxism and Retribution' (1973) 2 *Philosophy and Public Affairs* 217–43; J Finnis, *Natural Law and Natural Rights* (Oxford: OUP 1980) 263–64.

[40] J Feinberg, 'The Expressive Function of Punishment' in J Feinberg, *Doing and Deserving: Essays in the Theory of Responsibility* (Princeton, NJ: Princeton University Press 1970) 95–118.

[41] RA Duff, *Trials and Punishments* (Cambridge: CUP 1986); RA Duff, 'Punishment, Communication and Community' in M Matravers (ed), *Punishment and Political Theory* (Oxford: Hart Publishing 1998); J Hampton, 'An Expressive Theory of Retribution' in W Cragg (ed), *Retribution and its Critics* (Stuttgart: Franz Steiner Verlag 1992); J Tasioulas, 'Punishment and Repentance' (2006) 81 *Philosophy* 279–322; A von Hirsch, *Doing Justice: The Choice of Punishments* (Report of the Committee for the Study of Incarceration) (New York: NY Hill & Wang 1976).

the general idea that crimes "deserve" punishment ... there is surely nothing puzzling about the idea that wrongdoing deserves censure.'[42] Such arguments differ importantly from a desert-based theory that 'we ought to punish offenders, because, and only because, they deserve to be punished'.[43] Desert theories such as that of Moore which are based on metaphysical commitments of the kind found in Kant or Hegel are 'widely regarded by liberals as an inappropriate basis on which to ground public policy in pluralistic societies'.[44] The difficulty for such theorists lies in explaining why censure is to be conveyed by 'hard treatment' (punishment).[45] If hard treatment is not intrinsically connected to censure, then some additional argument is necessary.[46]

One theory which has famously sought to 'supplement the censure-based account with an independent justification of hard treatment'[47] is the just desert theory developed by von Hirsch. Unlike Duff or Kleinig,[48] von Hirsch does not agree that some degree of hard treatment is necessary to make censure credible, contending instead that the 'hard treatment element in punishment rests on preventive grounds'.[49] The suggestion is that the hard treatment in censure is necessary to prevent future crimes.[50] Hirsch introduces the 'principle of proportionality', which he takes to be a basic requirement of fairness or justice. It is instructive, though, that this assumption seems to rest on intuition[51] rather than any particular account of justice or fairness. According to this notion of proportionality, the severity of punishment is to be linked solely to the seriousness of the crime, which is defined as consisting of two components: harm

[42] Duff, 'Punishment, Communication and Community' (n 41) 50.

[43] See eg M Moore, 'The Moral Worth of Retribution' in R Schoemann (ed), *Responsibility, Character and the Emotions* (New York, NY: CUP 1987).

[44] Matravers, 'Twenty-first Century Punishment (n 15) 36 citing J Rawls, *Justice as Fairness: Political not Metaphysical* (J Rawls and SR Freeman eds, Collected Papers) (Cambridge, MT: Harvard University Press 1999).

[45] See Duff, 'Punishment, Communication, and Community' (n 41) 51; RA Duff, *Punishment, Communication, and Community* (Oxford: OUP 2001) and for criticism M Matravers, 'Duff on Hard Treatment' in R Croft, MH Kramer, and MR Reiff (eds), *Crime, Punishment and Responsibility: The Jurisprudence of Anthony Duff* (Oxford: OUP 2011).

[46] Matravers, 'Twenty-first Century Punishment' (n 15) 34.

[47] ibid.

[48] J Kleinig, *Punishment and Desert* (The Hague: Martinus Nijhoff 1973).

[49] See von Hirsch, 'Proportionality' (n 3) 73–74; A von Hirsch, *Past or Future Crimes: Deservedness and Dangerousness in the Sentencing of Criminals* (New Brunswick, NJ: Rutgers University Press 1985); A von Hirsch, 'Proportionality in the Philosophy of Punishment: From Why Punish to How Much?' (1990) 1 *Criminal Law Forum* 259, 275; see also N Jareborg, *Essays in Criminal Law* (Uppsala: Iustus 1998) ch 5.

[50] See von Hirsch, 'Proportionality' (n 3) 74: 'Had punishment no usefulness in preventing crime, then one would not need to visit material deprivation on those who offend.'

[51] ibid 56: 'People have a sense that punishments scaled to the gravity of offenses are fairer than punishments that are not.'

and culpability.[52] This proportionality principle requires both ordinal proportionality, in the sense that 'persons convicted of crimes of comparable gravity should receive punishments of comparable severity' and cardinal proportionality, in the sense that 'a reasonable proportion must be maintained between overall levels of punitiveness and the gravity of the criminal conduct'.[53]

The problem with this account is that while it was designed to limit the imposition of punishment,[54] it has not been able to do so. Matravers suggests that the reason for this was because it was not based on 'a sound theoretical account of desert'.[55] By tying censure to hard treatment and insisting that because an offender deserves blame, the state is entitled to choose the appropriate punishment, the theory loses control of the cardinal scale 'because the translation of appropriate moral disapproval into the appropriate hard treatment is a matter of social convention'.[56] In the words of van Haag:

> Just deserts fails even more fundamentally to tell us what is deserved for any crime. Suppose we agree that murder is a serious crime and burglary a less serious one. Thus murder deserves more punishment than burglary, though nothing tells us how much more. But what does murder deserve in the first place? Execution? Life in prison? Twenty years? Ten? Just deserts cannot tell.[57]

The 'specialised literature on punishment has reached a kind of stalemate'.[58] Few—if any—modern retributivist writers support the traditional (Kantian or Hegelian) notion of retributivist theory that we are 'obliged rather than entitled to punish offenders because they deserve it'.[59] Equally, 'the old Benthamite confidence in fear of the penalties threatened by the law as a powerful deterrent has waned with the growing realization that the part played by calculation of any sort in anti-social behaviour has been exaggerated'.[60] The boundaries between

[52] von Hirsch, *Doing Justice* (n 41) 79; see also A von Hirsch, *Past or Future Crimes?* (New Brunswick NJ: Rutgers University Press 1985) 64.

[53] von Hirsch, *Doing Justice* (n 41) 75–79. See also Hörnle, *Tatproportionale Strafzumessung* (n 31).

[54] See A von Hirsch, *Deserved Criminal Sentences: An Overview* (Oxford: Hart Publishing 2017) 108 noting that the principle of proportionality 'was offered as a means for restricting the state's authority to punish'.

[55] M Matravers, 'Rootless Desert and Unanchored Censure' in A du Bois-Pedain and AE Bottoms (eds), *Penal Censure: Agreements within and Beyond Desert Theory* (Oxford: Hart Publishing 2019) 187, 190.

[56] ibid 201.

[57] E van den Haag, 'Punishment, Desert and Crime Control' (1987) 85 *Michigan Law Review* 1250, 1254.

[58] L Zaibert, *Rethinking Punishment* (Cambridge: CUP 2018) 2.

[59] T Honderich, *Punishment: The Supposed Justifications* (New York, NY: Harcourt, Brace & World 1970) 133.

[60] Hart, 'Prolegomenon' (n 10) 1.

retributivism and consequentialism have become 'blurred': it is not simply the case that many supposedly monist accounts of punishment are not that monist; mixed accounts are not that mixed.[61]

Zaibert suggests that one reason for this is the focus on justifying state punishment at the expense of justification of punishment more broadly. There can be little doubt that the problem of punishment is particularly pronounced in the context of state punishment. It is thus unsurprising that the majority of those writing about the justification of punishment are interested primarily (if not solely) in state punishment.[62] This gives rise to the question whether state punishment is 'merely the attempt to institutionalise a moral practice that already exists quite apart from the law and its institutions?'[63] or whether 'the morality of state punishment is dictated first by the morality of punishment in general, and only second (by way of modification) by the rule of law and similar specialized moral considerations?'.[64]

While Zaibert criticizes the narrow focus on state punishment, for Thorburn the leading justifications of punishment pay insufficient attention to the determination of who should carry out the punishment.[65] Criminal punishment is 'an essential part of the state-citizen relationship under the rule of law'. This means that a 'criminal justice system controlled by anyone other than the state would undermine the most basic promise of the liberal state'.[66] In his view, the rationale underpinning the state monopoly on punishment is not merely instrumental but 'flows from the fact that only the state has standing to act in the name of the system of rights itself rather than in some narrower, partisan interest'.[67] Such arguments suggest that there might be something distinctive about state punishment, which calls for particular justification. In this sense

[61] L Zaibert, *Punishment and Retribution* (London: Routledge 2006) 2; see also Zaibert, *Rethinking Punishment* (n 58) 18, where he argues that 'Rawls's and Hart's "mixed justifications" are revealed to be as monistic as Bentham's utilitarianism'. At 17 he argues that a truly plural justification of punishment would recognize both the value of suffering and the value of forgiveness. See also J Tasioulas, 'Mercy' (2003) 103 *Proceedings of the Aristotelian Society* 101–32. See also J Gardner, 'The Virtue of Justice and the Character of Law' (2002) 53 *Current Legal Problems* 1, 29; J Tasioulas, 'Punishment and Repentance' (2006) 81 *Philosophy* 279.

[62] Zaibert, *Rethinking Punishment* (n 58) cites, inter alia, Hobbes, Hegel, Rawls, Flew, Hart, Duff, Honderich, and Kleinig.

[63] Gardner, 'Introduction' (n 9) xlix.

[64] ibid.

[65] M Thorburn, 'Proportionate Sentencing and the Rule of Law' in L Zedner and JV Roberts (eds), *Principles and Values in Criminal Law and Criminal Justice: Essays in Honour of Andrew Ashworth* (Oxford: OUP 2012) 274: 'All three dominant theories of punishment today—utilitarian, retributivist, and communicative—proceed in this two-step way, treating the question of who should carry out the punishment as a secondary and quite separate one to be answered simply by reference to considerations of expedience.'

[66] ibid 282.

[67] ibid.

they focus attention on what exactly it is that requires justification and on the relationship between the definition and justification of punishment.

III. The Definition and the Justification of Punishment

The definition of punishment and its justification are usually taken to be two different issues (one classificatory, the other justificatory) and it is often taken for granted that 'the logical order is first to decide what punishment is, then, to decide whether this thing is morally justifiable or not'.[68] There is good reason to suppose, though, that this 'appearance of separateness' is illusory and that 'clarification of the concept of punishment may have to be achieved by considering both together'.[69] This can be illustrated by considering two of the most well-known definitions of punishment.

Hobbes famously defined punishment as 'an evil inflicted by public authority, on him that hath done, or omitted that which is judged by the same authority to be a transgression of the law; to the end that the will of men may thereby the better be disposed to obedience'.[70] Here the aim of punishment is quite obviously included in the definition. The imposition of evil by public authority for reasons other than deterrence seems to fall outside the definition of punishment.

HLA Hart, building on the earlier work of Flew and Benn,[71] defines the 'standard or central case of punishment' with reference to five criteria: (i) It must involve pain or other consequences normally considered to be unpleasant; (ii) It must be for an offence against legal rules; (iii) It must be of an actual or supposed offender for his offence; (iv) It must be intentionally administered by human beings other than the offender; (v) It must be imposed and administered by an authority constituted by a legal system against which the offence is committed'.[72] Punishment imposed in other contexts—such as

[68] See KG Armstrong, The Retributivist Hits Back' (1961) 70 *Mind* 476.

[69] See T McPherson, 'Punishment: Definition and Justification' (1967) 28 *Analysis* 21, 21 and 25.

[70] T Hobbes, *Leviathan* (C Brooke ed, first published 1651, London: Penguin 2017) I, ch xxviii, 257.

[71] A Flew, 'The Justification of Punishment' (1954) 29 *Philosophy* 291; SI Benn, 'An Approach to the Problems of Punishment' (1958) 33 *Philosophy* 325; Hart, 'Prolegomenon' (n 10).

[72] Hart, 'Prolegomenon' (n 10) 4–5. See also the definition of Rawls, 'Two Concepts of Rules' (n 20) 7 who defines punishment in the following manner: 'A person is said to suffer punishment whenever he is legally deprived of some of the normal rights of a citizen on the ground that he has violated a rule of law, the violation having been established by trial according to the due process of law, provided that the deprivation is carried out by the recognized authorities of the state, that the rule of law clearly specifies both the offence and the attached penalty, that the courts construe statues strictly and that the statute was on the books prior to the commission of the offence.' In addition, he notes: 'utilitarians agree that punishment is to be inflicted only for the violation of law. They regard this much as understood from the concept of punishment itself.'

'breaches of non-legal rules or orders (punishment in a family or school)'—is described by Hart as 'sub-standard' or 'secondary' in nature.[73]

Hart explains the importance of defining punishment principally in terms of maintaining a conceptual distinction between the definition and justification of punishment and preventing recourse to 'the definitional stop', whereby the definition of punishment is altered to ensure that whatever constitutes punishment is automatically justified. In this regard, he was responding to consequentialist theorists, who had suggested that punishment 'by its nature' involved 'guilt as well as suffering'.[74] By defining punishment as the imposition of suffering only on those found guilty of committing a criminal offence, the 'definitional stoppers' removed the imposition of suffering on non-culpable individuals from the realm of punishment. Hart is adamant that the criticism that consequentialism allows the punishment of the innocent if this were to serve the 'greater good' could not be solved simply by defining one's way out of the problem. He notes that the 'wrong reply' to the retributivist objection is '[t]hat, by definition, would not be punishment'.[75] This type of response prevents investigation of 'the very thing which modern scepticism most calls into question: namely the rational and moral status of our preference for a system of punishment under which measures painful to individuals are to be taken against them only when they have committed an offence'.[76]

The Hart-Flew-Benn definition of punishment has proved hugely influential.[77] One explanation for this is that it is generally considered to be value-neutral. It is certainly the case that, unlike earlier definitions such as that of Hobbes, it eschews reference to consequentialist aims. As others have pointed out, though, the definition of punishment does seem to encompass an element of justification and this is particularly pronounced in the context of state punishment.[78] The criteria legitimize punishment on legal grounds 'since it is how the rules have been infringed and the authority that decides and executes the sanction are described' and on moral grounds 'since it concerns an offense and applies to the offender'.[79] It is notable that the justificatory element here involves the reasons for the imposition of punishment rather than its aim(s).

[73] Hart, 'Prolegomenon' (n 10) 5.

[74] Gardner 'Introduction' (n 9) xvii, noting that the *locus classicus* of this argument is AM Quinton, 'On Punishment' (1954) 14 *Analysis* 512.

[75] Hart, 'Prolegomenon' (n 10).

[76] ibid 5–6.

[77] See L Farmer, 'Crime and Punishment' (2020) 14 *Criminal Law and Philosophy* 289, 296, noting that the definition is often taken as 'foundational' in contemporary literature.

[78] See eg D Fassin, *The Will to Punish* (C Kutz ed, The Berkeley Tanner Lectures, New York, NY: OUP 2018).

[79] ibid.

This emphasizes the special character of state punishment. Punishment can be imposed for all sorts of reasons (failure to keep a promise; disobedience etc) and in all sorts of contexts (between partners; by parents on children), but state punishment can only be imposed (and thus is only justifiable) in certain circumstances, notably when it is imposed by the state for a violation of the criminal law.[80] This suggests that state punishment is different from other types of punishment and calls into question the existence of some sort of notion of 'punishment-in-general',[81] which falls to be rationalized by some sort of general justification.[82] The justification of state punishment must involve consideration not just of its aims, but also of the reasons for its imposition.

State punishment is special not just because it is subject to a different kind of justificatory burden, but because, as Hart recognizes, it is mediated by and through law. This means that it is essential to focus not only on the aims of punishment, but also on the means and processes. In this sense, it is necessary to reflect on how the 'criminal offence' and 'state punishment' have been conceptualized in human rights law.

IV. Conceptualizing State Punishment

A. The Definition of a Criminal Offence and Article 6 ECHR

State punishment is commonly understood as a response to a violation of the criminal law. This means that a useful starting point in conceptualizing punishment is the definition of 'criminal charge' in Article 6(1) ECHR. In *Engel*, the ECtHR famously drew attention to the asymmetrical nature of the extent of the states' entitlement 'in the performance of their function as guardians of the public interest' to define the boundaries of the criminal law.[83] While states were 'free to designate as a criminal offence an act or omission not constituting the normal exercise of one of the rights that it protects', the decision

[80] See eg McPherson, 'Punishment' (n 69) 26: punishment can turn up in any human relationship. Lovers punish each other; parents punish their children; the State punishes criminals. Punishment takes physical forms and it takes 'mental' forms. What might in practice be given as its 'justifications' are various: 'She was unfaithful to me'; 'He disobeyed me'; 'They broke the law'.

[81] ibid.

[82] *Pace* Gardner, who suggests, for instance, that Hart by focusing on state punishment and asserting political philosophy's relative autonomy from the rest of moral philosophy 'loses sight of some of the logic of his subject-matter' and that 'the morality of state punishment' is 'dictated first by the morality of punishment in general, and only second (by way of modification) by the rule of law', Gardner 'Introduction' (n 9) xlix. See also Zaibert, *Rethinking Punishment* (n 58).

[83] *Engel and Others v Netherlands*, 8 June 1976, Series A no 22, para 81: 'the "autonomy" of the concept of "criminal" operates, as it were, one way only.'

to designate conduct as non-criminal in nature was considered to be 'subject to stricter rules'.[84] The reason for this is clear: the designation of an act or omission as criminal brings the matter within the scope of the right to a fair trial. Were a state free to designate an act or omission as non-criminal—and, say, as disciplinary or preventative in nature—the operation 'of the fundamental clauses of Articles 6 and 7 would be subordinated to their sovereign' thereby leading to results which would be 'incompatible with the purpose and object of the Convention'.[85]

The criteria for determining whether a matter is to be designated as 'criminal' in nature for the purposes of Article 6 ECHR are thus of principal importance in determining those cases where the proceedings have been designated as non-criminal by the state, but the applicant argues that they should nevertheless be understood in fact as criminal in nature. In these cases, the ECtHR applies the *Engel* criteria and examines, in particular, the legal classification of the offence under national law,[86] the nature of the offence, and the degree of severity of the penalty.[87] The characterization of the 'nature' of the rule is particularly important.[88] Rules which are defined by a contracting state as regulatory (and thus non-criminal) in nature and imposed by administrative authorities may nevertheless be considered by the ECtHR as criminal. This is well illustrated by the judgment in *Öztürk*, which concerned the classification of 'regulatory offences' (*in casu* a minor traffic violation).

In *Öztürk*, the German government sought to argue that the purpose of the criminal law was to safeguard the 'foundations of society' and 'the rights and interests essential for the life of the community'.[89] Regulatory rules (*Ordnungswidrigkeiten*) on the other hand, such as those at issue, were designed 'to maintain public order'. It argued that, '[a]s a general rule and in any event in the instant case, commission of a "regulatory offence" did not involve a degree of ethical unworthiness such as to merit for its perpetrator the moral value-judgment of reproach (*Unwerturteil*) that characterised penal punishment (*Strafe*)'.[90]

[84] ibid.
[85] ibid.
[86] ibid 82 'This however provides no more than a starting point.'
[87] This is of little relevance at the lower end of the scale in that a small fine will be sufficient in this regard, see eg *Ziliberberg v Moldova* App no 61821/00, 1 Feb 2003, para 12: MDL 36 (the equivalent of €3.17 (EUR) at the time; *Öztürk v Germany*, 21 Feb 1984, Series A no 73, para 54: 'The relative lack of seriousness of the penalty at stake ... cannot divest an offence of its inherently criminal character'.
[88] *Öztürk v Germany*, 21 Feb 1984, Series A no 73, para 52—referring to this criterion as 'a factor of appreciation of greater weight' [ie than the classification in domestic law].
[89] ibid 52.
[90] ibid.

The government drew attention to the fact that the simplified procedural rules 'greatly limited the possibilities of restricting the personal liberty of the individual at the stage of the preliminary investigations', that the regulatory fine would and could not be converted into an alternative sentence of imprisonment in the event of a failure to pay in cases in which the offender was unable to pay, and that the fine was not listed in the judicial criminal records. Finally, it noted that the aim of the designation of the fine as administrative was essentially the decriminalization of offences which was of benefit to the individual and to society in the context of 'the effective functioning of the courts'.[91]

The ECtHR was not convinced by these arguments. It noted in particular that 'according to the ordinary meaning of the terms, there generally come within the ambit of the criminal law offences that make their perpetrator liable to penalties intended, inter alia, to be deterrent and usually consisting of fines and of measures depriving the person of his liberty'. In addition, it noted that, '[w]hilst the latter penalty appears less burdensome in some respects than Geldstrafen, it has nonetheless retained a punitive character, which is the customary distinguishing feature of criminal penalties'. In addition, it noted that the sanction was 'directed, not towards a given group possessing a special status—in the manner, for example, of disciplinary law—, but towards all citizens in their capacity as road-users' and thus 'prescribes conduct of a certain kind and makes the resultant requirement subject to a sanction that is punitive'.[92] It held that:

> It matters little whether the legal provision contravened by Mr Öztürk is aimed at protecting the rights and interests of others or solely at meeting the demands of road traffic. These two ends are not mutually exclusive. Above all, the general character of the rule and the purpose of the penalty, being both deterrent and punitive, suffice to show that the offence in question was, in terms of Article 6 of the Convention, criminal in nature.[93]

The case law on the notion of a criminal charge suggests that rules which are punitive in nature, even if they also have a preventative element, will be considered to be criminal. The definition of the criminal charge and of the concept of a penalty are thus inherently linked.[94] In essence, the determination

[91] ibid.
[92] ibid 53.
[93] ibid.
[94] See also *GIEM SRL and Others v Italy* [GC] App nos 1828/06, 34163/07 and 19029/11, 28 June 2018, dissenting opinion, attached to the judgment.

of whether the rule is criminal turns on the answer to the determination of whether the sanction imposed for the violation of the norm is really a penalty (punishment).

B. The Definition of Penalty and Article 7(1) ECHR

The definition of punishment is of central importance in the context of Article 7(1) ECHR, to the extent that the guarantee applies to penalties imposed following the commission of a criminal offence. In order to establish whether a sanction constitutes 'a penalty' the ECtHR will 'go behind appearances and assess for itself whether a particular measure amounts in substance to a "penalty" within the meaning of [the] provision'.[95] The reason for the development of this 'autonomous' definition of 'penalty' is clear. A state must not be permitted to restrict the application of the legality guarantee simply by unilaterally defining a sanction as non-punitive (not a penalty) as this could lead to results incompatible with the guarantee in Article 7 ECHR.[96] In the absence of an autonomous definition of punishment, states would be able to alter the definition of punishment in order to restrict the scope of application of the right to legality.

The starting point for determining whether a sanction constitutes a penalty is consideration of 'whether the measure in question is imposed following a decision that a person is guilty of a criminal offence'. Other factors, which are also of relevance in this regard, include 'the nature and purpose of the measure in question; its characterisation under national law; the procedures involved in the making and implementation of the measure; and its severity'.[97] These criteria are (unsurprisingly) very similar to those applied in the determination of a criminal charge. As is the case in relation to Article 6(1) ECHR, the criteria are not all of equal weight. The severity of the measure, in particular, is of limited importance. Minor sanctions might be considered to be punitive, while extremely onerous sanctions might be considered to be non-punitive in nature. Although some have argued that the constitutional debate might lead

[95] ibid para 210.

[96] *Welch v UK*, 9 Feb 1995, Series A no 307-A, para 27 and *Jamil v France*, 8 June 1995, Series A no 317-B, para 30; *GIEM SRL and Others v Italy* [GC] App nos 1828/06, 34163/07 and 19029/11, 28 June 2018, para 211 discussed in detail in Ch 2.

[97] ibid 211 citing *Welch v UK*, 9 Feb 1995, Series A no 307-A, para 28; *Jamil v France*, 8 June 1995, Series A no 317-B, para 31; *Kafkaris v Cyprus* [GC] App no 21906/04, ECHR 2008-I, para 142; *M v Germany* App no 19359/04, 19359/04, ECHR 2009, para 120; *Del Río Prada v Spain* [GC] App nos 42750/09, 42750/09 ECHR 2013, para 82; *Société Oxygène Plus v France* (dec) App no 76959/11, 17 May 2016, para 47. For detailed discussion see Ch 2.

to a 'potentially broader view of punishment than one would generate under a philosophical analysis that stresses the purpose for which the punishment is imposed',[98] the overview of the case law of the ECtHR[99] suggests that the Court has resisted the temptation to focus on the nature of the sanction rather than the reasons for its imposition in the definition of punishment. The most important factor in determining whether a measure constitutes a penalty is whether it was imposed either expressly or indirectly as a response to the commission of a criminal offence. There is an inescapable circularity here: the determination of the criminal nature of a rule turns on its punitive nature; the determination of whether a sanction is punitive turns on whether it was imposed for a violation of the criminal law.

Sanctions, which are expressly imposed as a response to a violation of the criminal law, will obviously constitute punishment. The difficulties arise in relation to the determination of the nature of sanctions, such as those in the *Öztürk* case, which are not officially classed as punishment in domestic law. In these cases, it is extremely difficult to determine whether a rule is criminal in nature, precisely because of the circularity of the relationship between the criminal offence and punishment. The definition of the criminal offence is established with regard to the punitive character of the sanction, while the definition of punishment is to be determined with regard to the criminal nature of the rule.

C. The Definition and Justification of State Punishment

The definition and justification of punishment are linked in that altering the definition of punishment will inevitably impact on its justification. To what extent, though, might the definition of state punishment be said to encompass an element of justification? Consideration of this question involves reflection on the various components of the justification of state punishment. State punishment, as we have seen, might be said to be justified if it follows an appropriate aim. In this regard, it is notable that Hart's widely accepted definition of punishment avoids reference to the aims of punishment. This is unsurprising in view of the fact that, '[as] a matter of logic, anything that is included in the

[98] Fletcher, *Rethinking Criminal Law* (n 19) 414: This is because 'tension between the state's purpose and the objective impact of the sanction pervades constitutional deliberations about the concept of punishment' and has led to a 'subtle shift away from what the court regards as the euphemism of treatment, to the impact of confinement on the individual'.

[99] See Ch 2.

definition of punishment cannot be used in its justification'.[100] In this sense, the definition of punishment must be kept separate from any justification expressed in terms of aims.

The justification of state punishment, though, involves more than just reference to its aims. Punishment might also be said to be justified if it is lawful (in the sense of being in compliance with the principle of legality) or legitimate (in the sense of conforming to the various human rights principles). Here is important to consider to what extent this requirement of lawfulness is inherent in the notion of punishment: in other words, is punishment by definition only lawful punishment? In addition, it is important to consider whether punishment as a practice ought to be considered by definition to be justified, simply by virtue of the fact that it is a state-sanctioned institution.

1. Lawful and Unlawful Punishment

The definition of punishment propagated in Article 7(1) ECHR says very little about the definition or constituent parts of criminal offences. Punishment is punishment if it is imposed in response to a violation of a criminal law. In particular, the definition of punishment does not necessarily imply the commission of a criminal act (or omission[101]) nor even of a *prior* criminal act or omission. A sanction imposed for a violation of a criminal law that does not require that an act has been committed will still constitute punishment, albeit unlawful punishment. Equally, if a criminal law were to prohibit some notion of future dangerousness, some likelihood of a propensity to commit a serious act in the future, the imposition of a sanction for a violation of this law must be understood as constituting punishment, albeit once again punishment which is unlawful in the sense of being incompatible with Article 7(1) ECHR.

This issue is best illustrated by example. In *Robinson*, for instance, the legislation at issue criminalized the fact of being a drug addict (rather than the act of drug taking) and led to Robinson being convicted and sentenced to 90 days of imprisonment.[102] The sanction imposed on Robinson might be characterized as unjust or unlawful, but few would claim that it did not constitute 'punishment'. Similarly, in *Parmak and Bakır*, the applicants were convicted of the offence 'of being members of a terrorist organisation' (dubiously defined on the sole basis of the nature of the organization's written declarations and potential

[100] McPherson, 'Punishment' (n 69) 25 suggests that the definition sets out an understanding of punishment in 'largely retributivist terms', which is interesting if questionable.

[101] See M David, 'How Much Punishment Does the Bad Samaritan Deserve?' (1996) 15 *Law and Philosophy* 93–116.

[102] *Robinson v California*, 370 US 660 (1962).

for 'moral coercion' and despite the absence of violent acts attributable to that organization) and sentenced to two years and six months' imprisonment.[103] Here again, there can be little doubt that the sanctions imposed on the applicants constituted punishment, even though the punishment was held by the ECtHR to be incompatible with Article 7(1) ECHR. This emphasizes that the definition of punishment does not imply lawful punishment and that any definition of punishment framed in terms of an *antecedent criminal act or omission* is too narrow.

It is important, too, to consider the issue of sanctions, which while labelled non-punitive in national law, might nevertheless be considered to constitute de facto punishment. The ECtHR has held that the imposition of a sanction on an innocent person or on a person in the absence of a finding of personal responsibility might thus constitute punishment, despite not being expressly described as such in law, if the reason for its imposition is tied to the commission of a criminal offence.[104] In such a case, the sanction is understood as being imposed as a response to the alleged conduct, despite the acquittal. Sanctions imposed on an individual who cannot be held culpable for the violation of a criminal law might thus still constitute punishment, albeit punishment which violates Article 7(1) ECHR. In *GIEM*, for instance, the reasons for the imposition of a confiscation order on the applicants were the same as those relied on by the prosecution in proceedings, which led to the applicant's acquittal. The imposition of these sanctions despite the acquittal of the applicants was thus viewed as *de facto punishment*, albeit under a different name.[105] This again highlights the fact that punishment is not necessarily (ie per definition) lawful.

This suggests that the issue of whether punishment is lawful must be kept apart from the issue of definition. This is of considerable importance, as can be illustrated by the consequences of failing to separate these issues. As Article 7(1) ECHR only applies in the context of the imposition of punishment, were punishment were to be narrowly defined as 'lawful' punishment, then the guarantee in Article 7(1) ECHR would not apply in cases such as *Robinson*, *Parmak*

[103] *Parmak and Bakır v Turkey* App nos 22429/07 and 25195/07, 3 Dec 2019, para 28.

[104] *GIEM SRL and Others v Italy* [GC] App nos 1828/06, 34163/07, and 19029/11, 28 June 2018, para 251; Art 7 precludes the imposition of a criminal sanction on an individual without his personal criminal liability being established and declared beforehand. Otherwise, the principle of the presumption of innocence guaranteed by Art 6(2) of the Convention would also be breached. See for detailed discussion Ch 2. These problems are demonstrated most clearly by those cases, such as *Ilnseher v Germany* [GC] App nos 10211/12 and 27505/14, 4 Dec 2018 or *James, Wells, and Lee v UK* App nos 25119/09, 57715/09 and 57877/09, 18 Sept 2012, in which the state seeks to punish those who have committed crimes for longer than the actual offence would warrant on grounds of dangerousness and the corresponding notion of public protection.

[105] *GIEM SRL and Others v Italy* [GC] App nos 1828/06, 34163/07, and 19029/11, 28 June 2018. For detailed consideration see Ch 2.

and Bakır, or *GIEM*. This highlights the hazards associated with attempts to define punishment. The danger of a narrow definition of punishment, in particular, is that practices which look like and feel like punishment are excluded and that the state is given free rein, unencumbered by the restraints of legality. Just as the definition of punishment cannot set out the aims to be achieved, neither can it include any requirement that punishment conform to notions of legality or legitimacy.

2. Punishment as a Practice

The justification of punishment might be understood to involve more than consideration of the lawfulness or legitimacy of the sentence in particular cases, but also to concern its role as a state institution. In this regard, it is important to note that punishment as a practice is not 'value-neutral', but rather that its connotations are essentially favourable in the sense that '[p]art of what we mean by punishment is justifiable infliction of unpleasantness'.[106] As Rawls notes: '[m]ost people have held that, freed from certain abuses, [punishment] is an acceptable institution.'[107] The definition of punishment allows for some sort of justification of the practice simply by virtue of the fact that punishment is distinguished from other forms of state power or violence. By accepting that the state is entitled to impose punishment as a response to a violation of the criminal law, the imposition of punishment by the state for other reasons is marked as unlawful or unjustified.

The definition of state punishment serves to legitimize the institution of punishment by providing 'a means of means of distinguishing between legitimate (and hence justified) restrictions of liberty, and those which cannot be justified as a form of punishment, and which are prima facie illegitimate'.[108] Some have called attention to various state practices which seem punitive in nature, despite not being imposed for the commission of a criminal offence, thereby challenging traditional understandings of punishment.[109] This gives rise to the question: 'when does punishment of the innocent or illegal punishment cease to be properly called punishment at all?'.[110] The problem with

[106] McPherson, 'Punishment' (n 69) 26.

[107] Rawls, 'Two Concepts of Rules' (n 20).

[108] L Farmer, 'Punishment in the Rule of Law' in J Meierhenrich and M Loughlin, *The Cambridge Companion to the Rule of Law* (Cambridge: CUP 2021).

[109] See eg the thought provoking essays of Fassin, *Will to Punish* (n 78). Another example might be Art 221(2) of the Swiss Code of Criminal Procedure which allows for the preventative detention of individuals if there is a serious risk that a person will make good on a threat to commit a serious offence. There is no requirement that such a threat must reach the level of a criminal offence for the purposes of the Swiss Criminal Code.

[110] See A Flew, 'The Justification of Punishment' (1954) 29 *Philosophy* 291, 191.

accepting a broader definition of punishment, however, is that this might make 'it more difficult to define specific acts of state officials as being unlawful abuses of power'.[111] In the words of Garland: 'The existence of state practices that ignore law's restraints and impose unlawful punishments is not a reason to doubt or deconstruct the conventional definition of legal punishment. It is a reason to apply it vigorously and insist on upholding it in the representational and political struggles that, today more than ever, swirl around issues of policing and punishment.'[112]

In this regard, while there may well be state practices which (from a human rights perspective) appear as problematic as punishment and which are insufficiently regulated,[113] the response should not be to argue that they should fall within the definition of punishment,[114] but rather to insist on the development of appropriate rules to regulate such practices. It is important to think carefully about these practices and about their relationship to punishment, while staying alert to the extent to which the designation of sanction as punishment serves to legitimize the practice of punishment more broadly through its differentiation from other forms of state violence.

V. Human Rights as Limits

State punishment is different from other types of punishment in that it will only be justified if it fulfils a series of conditions. A state is permitted to impose punishment as a response to the commission of an offence, but it is not entirely free in imposing punishment. Punishment will only be justified if it conforms to the limits set by human rights. The principle of legality acts as an important constraint on punishment. It prohibits the imposition of punishment for reasons other than the commission by a culpable individual of a clearly and prospectively defined criminal offence. This requirement demands that punishment be imposed *for* (in the sense of 'by reason of') the commission of the offence.[115]

[111] D Garland, 'The Rule of Law, Representational Struggles and the Will to Punish' in D Fassin, *The Will to Punish* (C Kutz ed, New York, NY: OUP 2018) 162.

[112] See Garland, 'The Rule of Law' (n 111) 163, noting that the distinction between lawful punishment and lawless state violence is 'crucial to the project of extending legality and taming arbitrary state power'.

[113] Fassin, *The Will to Punish* (n 78).

[114] Another example might be Art 221(2) of the Swiss Criminal Procedure Code, which allows for the preventative detention of individuals if there is a serious risk that a person will make good on a threat to commit a serious offence. There is no requirement that such a threat must reach the level of a criminal offence for the purposes of the Swiss Criminal Code.

[115] See Hart, 'Prolegomenon' (n 10) 5 and for discussion Gardner, 'Introduction' (n 9) xxv.

Legality limits the *maximum* punishment which can be imposed by the state and defines it as that which corresponds to the culpability of the offender for the offence. This means that a state is prohibited from imposing a more severe sentence than is warranted by the offender's culpability. Importantly, though, the state is not obliged to impose this sentence.[116] The state is entitled (and perhaps even required[117]) to mitigate the sentence. This explains the asymmetry between the regulation of aggravating and mitigating factors (such as previous convictions) at sentencing, an asymmetry which many theories (both retributivist and consequentialist) have difficulty accommodating. This emphasizes too a key difference between legality as an asymmetrical restraint and any notion of proportionality between the sentence and the offence.

The idea of 'commensurability' or 'proportionality'[118] between the severity of the offence and the sentence is often said to be a principle of 'fairness' or 'justice' and sometimes understood as a restriction on the sentence.[119] Proportionality in the human rights context, though, is quite different from the requirement that punishment be commensurate with the offence committed.[120] Instead, it requires that the sentence does not constitute a disproportionate interference with an offender's fundamental rights, such as freedom of expression or property. Put in other terms, there is no right to an 'appropriate' or 'proportionate' sentence, in the sense of a sentence which 'fits the crime'.[121] There is a right, however, not to be punished in a grossly excessive manner or in a manner which constitutes an unacceptable interference with a right, such as the right to freedom of expression. In this sense, human rights restrictions from proportionality are quite different (and indeed much narrower) in that they act to constrain the sentence which can be imposed in certain (limited) circumstances. This indicates that, contrary to other indications in the literature, any

[116] The only restrictions here involve the importance of protecting the fundamental human rights either of the defendant (see Ch 3) or of others, see *Nikolova and Velichkova v Bulgaria* App no 7888/03, 20 Dec 2007, para 62: 'while the Court should grant substantial deference to the national courts in the choice of appropriate sanctions for ill-treatment and homicide by State agents, it must exercise a certain power of review and intervene in cases of manifest disproportion between the gravity of the act and the punishment imposed.'

[117] See eg *Murray v Netherlands* App no 10511/10, 26 Apr 2006, para 115 discussing the rehabilitative aim of imprisonment, particularly in the context of long sentences of imprisonment.

[118] See eg N Lacey and H Pickard, 'The Chimera of Proportionality: Institutionalising Limits on Punishments in Contemporary Social and Political Systems' (2015) 78 *Modern Law Review* 216, fn 2: 'The concepts of proportionality and commensurability are interchangeable.'

[119] See notably von Hirsch, 'Proportionality' (n 3) 56. For criticism see Tonry, *Sentencing Matters* (n 3) 184.

[120] See further Ch 3.

[121] It is instructive that the only instances in which the ECtHR has intervened on the grounds 'of manifest disproportion between the gravity of the act and the punishment imposed' involve instances where the sentence was considering to be unduly lenient, see eg *Nikolova and Velichkova v Bulgaria* App no 7888/03, 20 Dec 2007, para 62.

notion of proportionality or commensurability between the severity of the offence and the punishment cannot be understood as a restriction on the imposition of punishment, or at least not one based on human rights.

The human rights principles provide important limits on the state in its imposition of punishment. Punishment will only be just if it is imposed on a culpable individual for the commission of an act or omission which is clearly and prospectively defined as criminal, is free from arbitrariness, does not constitute a disproportionate interference with—or fundamentally violate—certain human rights, and is imposed by a judge in the context of criminal proceedings. These requirements are preconditions of justice, but it is important to note that ensuring that these requirements are met will not necessarily mean that the punishment can be classed as just.[122] This all calls into question the idea that proportionality between the sentence and the offence acts as a constraint on the sentence.

VI. Revisiting Punishment Theory

What conclusions can be drawn from these thoughts on the conceptualization of state punishment and human rights for the broader theoretical discussion of the justification of state punishment? Central to much of the modern writing on punishment is the underlying belief that retributivist accounts are better placed than their consequentialist counterparts to accommodate and explain why only the guilty should be punished. Retributivism is said to be able to explain the focus on punishment of the guilty because of its 'backward-looking' reliance on a prior criminal offence. In the words of Rawls: 'What retributivists have rightly insisted upon is that no man can be punished unless he is guilty, that is, unless he has broken the law.'[123] Here it is notable, though, that the terms 'offence' and 'wrongdoing' are often used interchangeably. This is well illustrated by Rawls' definition of retributivist theory:

[122] Duff, *Trials and Punishments* (n 41) 294. See also M Tonry, 'Proportionality, Parsimony and Interchangeability' in RA Duff and others (eds), *Penal Theory and Practice: Tradition and Innovation in Criminal Justice* (Manchester: Manchester University Press 1994) 65: 'punishment is not justifiable within our present system' and it will not be 'unless and until we have brought about deep and far-reaching social, political, legal and moral changes in ourselves and our society'. See also JG Murphy, 'Marxism and Retribution' in AL Simmons and others (eds), *Punishment* (Princeton, NJ: Princeton University Press 1995) 2.

[123] Rawls, 'Two Concepts of Rules' (n 20) 7.

> [P]unishment is justified on the grounds that wrongdoing merits punishment. It is morally fitting that a person who does wrong should suffer in proportion to his wrongdoing. That a criminal should be punished follows from his guilt, and the severity of the appropriate punishment depends on the depravity of his act.[124]

The terms 'wrongdoing' and 'offence' are not synonymous, though, because while 'wrongdoing' implies a past act, this is not necessarily the case in the context of a criminal offence. Actual or supposed wrongdoing is not (necessarily), *pace* Gardner, 'a logically necessary feature of punishment'.[125] This is not simply a matter of semantics. Any conceptualization of state punishment framed in terms of 'past acts of wrongdoing' is too narrow in that it serves to exclude criminal offences which criminalize future harm or status offences from the definition of punishment. The fact that a criminal offence was committed in the past does not necessarily imply the commission of an antecedent act or omission.

Theories which understand punishment as a response to a prior act of wrongdoing are without doubt 'backward-looking' in their insistence on antecedent conduct. On these accounts, punishment is 'borne by the guilty because of and in proportion to their guilt, where "guilt" designates some relationship that a wrongdoer has or had to a wrong that she already committed'.[126] The positive reason for the imposition of suffering here is the 'guilt' for wrongdoing. The problem with this approach, though, is that by defining punishment in these (narrow) terms, it fails to justify what might be considered to be clear cases of punishment. This is clearly a problem because 'if one's would-be definition of punishment fails to defend a logically necessary feature of punishment, then it is not a defence of punishment after all'.[127]

It might be argued that many retributivist accounts refer not to wrongdoing but to the offence. RA Duff, for instance, defines punishment, as 'something intended to be burdensome or painful, imposed on a supposed offender for a (supposed) offence by someone with (supposedly) the authority to do so'.[128] If it is accepted, though, that offences which do not encompass any notion of

124 ibid 4–5.

125 Gardner, 'Introduction' (n 9) xxvi.

126 ibid xxvii. Discussing both the rectificatory view that punishment serves as 'an annulment of the ill-gotten gains or ill-taken liberties' and the expressive view that punishment is a way 'of expressing or communicating the judgment of guilt and thereby, in some versions, censuring the guilty wrongdoer and/or denouncing the guilty wrong'.

127 ibid xxvi.

128 RA Duff, *Punishment, Communication and Community* (Oxford: OUP 2001) xiv–xv.

a prior act of wrongdoing fall within the definition of punishment, then such theories do not seem to contain any particular commitment to the idea that punishment can only be imposed for an antecedent act or omission. In such cases, the punishment seems to be justified even if it is imposed simply for the status or social dangerousness of the offender. These accounts do not explain why only antecedent wrongdoing can be justly punished.

This suggests that it is incorrect to assume that there is something inherently retributivist about the claim that proper punishment must necessarily involve reference to a prior criminal act or omission.[129] In the words of Cottingham: 'A retrospective or backward-looking element in a theory is never normally characterized as "retributive"; it is only in the literature on punishment that these two notions are muddled (so that, in some discussions, "retributive" becomes virtually an antonym of "teleological")'.[130] This suggests that the thesis that only those guilty of prior criminal acts or omissions are to be punished does not seem to be inherently retributivist, though clearly retributivists (like their consequentialist counterparts) can hold this notion as a principle of natural justice or human rights. This all suggests that, in the focus on aims, insufficient attention has been paid to the reasons for the imposition of punishment and the conceptualization of *state* punishment in particular. It also suggests that the intuitive appeal of retributivism might simply be the appeal of adherence to legality.

VII. The Justification of State Punishment and Human Rights

What can human rights contribute to our understanding of the justification of punishment? These principles do not, of course, explain why the fact that someone has committed an offence should be a reason to make them suffer. In other words, they explain the conditions under which punishment cannot be imposed, rather than providing any positive reason for its imposition. To paraphrase Gardner, such rules do not count in favour of punishing offenders but merely eliminate an objection to punishing them under certain circumstances.[131] This examination of the importance of human rights as limits is

[129] Cottingham, 'Varieties of Retribution' (n 36) 240.

[130] ibid 240, noting that it seems 'both arbitrary and inappropriate' to signal the claim that 'proper punishment must necessarily involve reference to a past offence' by labelling it as 'retributivist'.

[131] Gardner, 'Introduction' (n 9) xxv.

nevertheless of relevance in that it points to the importance of the reasons for the imposition of punishment and to the special nature of state punishment.

State punishment is best understood as part of 'the state-citizen relationship under the rule of law'.[132] At the heart of the justification of state punishment is thus a conflict between the liberal focus on protecting rights by preventing the commission of future crimes and the restrictions from justice that require, inter alia, that punishment be imposed only on a culpable individual for a prior criminal act or omission.[133] This is not necessarily best understood as a conflict between retributivism and consequentialism.

Any justification of state punishment must account for the reasons for its imposition, precisely because the state is only entitled to impose punishment in certain circumstances. Here, the principal limitation is from legality. It is noticeable in this regard that the notion of justice most frequently discussed in sentencing theory—the idea that punishment should be proportionate to the offence, of commensurability between the seriousness of the criminal offence and the severity of the punishment—plays an extraordinarily minor role in the human rights account on justified state punishment. Instead, justice at sentencing is guaranteed principally by the requirement from legality that the maximum sentence which can be imposed is that determined by an offender's culpability for a criminal act or omission.

This is certainly not to argue that the aims of punishment are irrelevant to the issue of the justification of state punishment, only to point out that other important parts of the justification of state punishment have been neglected and that this might be connected to the focus on the aims of punishment-in-general. The 'concentration' on the aims of punishment 'suggests what is certainly a limited, and is very probably a mistaken, view of punishment: as if punishment were something designed to fulfil a certain purpose'.[134] This is clearly evident

[132] M Thorburn, 'Proportionate Sentencing and the Rule of Law' in L Zedner and JV Roberts (eds), *Principles and Values in Criminal Law and Criminal Justice: Essays in Honour of Andrew Ashworth* (Oxford: OUP 2012) 282. T Metz, 'How to Reconcile Liberal Politics with Retributive Punishment' (2007) 27 *Oxford Journal of Legal Studies* 683, 700–1; See also J Waldron, 'Kant's Theory of the State' in P Kleingeld (ed), *Towards Perpetual Peace and Other Writings on Politics, Peace and History* (New Haven, CT: Yale University Press 2006) 183.

[133] T Metz, 'How to Reconcile Liberal Politics with Retributive Punishment' (2007) 27 *Oxford Journal of Legal Studies* 683, 689 arguing in favour of a conception of 'expressive liberalism' which defines the sole aim of the liberal state as 'to act for the sake of (innocent) people's equal rights to live as they see fit' and relying on J Raz, *The Morality of Freedom* (Oxford: OUP 1988) 156–57. See T Metz, 'How to Reconcile Liberal Politics with Retributive Punishment' (2007) 27 *Oxford Journal of Legal Studies* 683, 685: Liberalism demands that 'the sole basic end that the state ought to pursue is the protection of people's own ability to choose their own conceptions of the good'. J Rawls, *Political Liberalism* (New York, NY: Columbia University Press 1993) 156–57: '[T]he most reasonable political conception of justice for a democratic regime will be, broadly speaking, liberal. That means that it protects the familiar basic rights and assigns them a special priority.'

[134] McPherson, 'Punishment' (n 69) 26.

in the cases considered in Strasbourg and in the somewhat elusive references in the case law of the ECtHR to the 'penological purposes' of punishment.[135] It is not simply the case that punishment often follows a multitude of aims,[136] but rather that the balance of these aims may, and in the context of lengthy prison sentences almost certainly will, change in the course of the sentence.[137] This explains the Nietzschean dictate that it is 'impossible to say precisely why anyone is punished'.[138]

Consideration of the limits on punishment is of central importance because it highlights the values underpinning the system of punishment. Only by first establishing the aims and values on which the sentencing system is based is it possible to examine and evaluate the scope and legitimacy of the various sentencing practices.[139] The failure to focus on the role of the state in the justification of punishment is also a failure to take seriously the limits on the state's power to punish. It is also to overlook the central problems of sentencing practice which are concerned not so much with the punishment of the innocent, but rather with the over-punishment of the guilty.[140]

[135] See *Vinter and Others v UK* [GC] App nos 66069/09, 130/10 and 3896/10, ECHR 2013-III, para 111.

[136] See also Fassin, *Will to Punish* (n 78).

[137] *Vinter and Others v UK* [GC] App nos 66069/09, 130/10 and 3896/10, ECHR 2013-III, para 111.

[138] F Nietzsche, *On the Genealogy of Morals* (Walter Kaufman tr, first published 1887, New York, NY: Vintage Books 1989) second essay, section 13.

[139] See N Lacey, 'Discretion and Due Process at the Post-Conviction Stage' in IH Dennis (ed), *Criminal Law and Justice* (London: Sweet & Maxwell 1987) 221, 226.

[140] Garland, 'The Rule of Law' (n 111).

Bibliography

Adelman L and Dietrich J, 'Marvin Frankel's Mistakes and the Need to Rethink Federal Sentencing' (2008) 13 *Berkeley Journal of Criminal Law* 239

Albrecht P, 'Die Strafzumessung im Spannungsfeld von Theorie und Praxis' [1991] *Schweizerische Zeitschrift für Strafrecht* 45

Alexy R, *A Theory of Constitutional Rights* (Oxford: OUP 2002)

Allen F, *The Decline of the Rehabilitative Ideal* (New Haven, CT: Yale University Press 1981)

—— 'The Erosion of Legality in American Criminal Justice: Some Latter-Day Adventures of the Nulla Poena Principle' (1987) 29 *Arizona Law Review* 385

—— *The Habits of Legality: Criminal Justice and the Rule of Law* (New York, NY: OUP 1996)

Allen RJ and others, *Comprehensive Criminal Procedure* (4th edn, New York, NY: Wolters Kluwer 2016)

Alschuler A, 'The Failure of Sentencing Guidelines: A Plea for Less Aggregation' (1991) 58 *University of Chicago Law Review* 901

Ambos K, 'Punishment without a Sovereign? The Ius Puniendi Issue of International Criminal Law: A First Contribution towards a Consistent Theory of International Criminal Law' (2013) 33 *Oxford Journal of Legal Studies* 1

Amis K, *Lucky Jim* (first published 1954, London: Penguin 2010)

Amsterdam AG, 'Constitutional Restrictions on the Federal Punishment of Crimes of Status, Crimes of General Obnoxiousness, Crimes of Displeasing Police Officers, and the Like' (1967) 3 *Criminal Law Bulletin* 205

Aristotle, *Nicomachean Ethics* (WD Ross tr, L Brown ed, Oxford: OUP 2009)

Armstrong KG, 'The Retributivist Hits Back' (1961) 70 *Mind* 476

Arthurs H, 'Rethinking Administrative Law: A Slightly Dicey Business' (1979) 17 *Osgoode Hall Law Journal* 1

Arzt G, 'Geständnisbereitschaft und Strafrechtssystem' (1992) 110 *Schweizerische Zeitschrift für Strafrecht* 233

—— 'Strafzumessung Revolution in der Sackgasse' (1994) 12 *Recht* 141 (part 1) and 234–48 (part 2)

Ashworth A, 'Changes in Sentencing Law' [1997] *Criminal Law Review* 1

—— 'Departures from the Sentencing Guidelines' [2012] *Criminal Law Review* 81

—— *Sentencing and Criminal Justice* (6th edn, Cambridge: CUP 2015)

—— and Roberts JV, 'The Origins and Nature of the Sentencing Guidelines in England and Wales' in A Ashworth and JV Roberts (eds), *Sentencing Guidelines: Exploring the English Model* (Oxford: OUP 2013)

—— and Roberts JV, 'The Evolution of Sentencing Policy and Practice' (2016) 45 *Crime and Justice* 307

—— and van Zyl Smit D, 'Disproportionate Sentences as Human Rights Violations' (2004) 67 *Modern Law Review* 541

Auer A, 'L'Égalité dans l'Illégalité' (1978) 79 *Schweizerisches Zentralblatt für Staats- und Verwaltungsrecht* 281

Bachmaier L, 'The European Court of Human Rights on Negotiated Justice and Coercion' (2018) 26 *European Journal of Crime, Criminal Law and Criminal Justice* 236

Baer S, 'The Rule of—and not by any—Law. On the Need to Explain and Defend Constitutionalism Today' (2019) 71 *Current Legal Problems* 335

Bagaric M, Gopalan S, and Florio MR, 'A Principled Strategy for Addressing the Incarceration Crisis: Redefining Excessive Imprisonment as a Human Rights Abuse' (2017) 38 *Cardozo Law Review* 1663

Baker E, 'Dangerousness, Rights and Criminal Justice' (1993) 56 *Modern Law Review* 528

—— and Ashworth A, 'The Role of Previous Convictions in England and Wales' in J Roberts and A von Hirsch (eds), *Previous Convictions at Sentencing* (Oxford: Hart Publishing 2010)

Barak A, 'A Judge on Judging: The Role of a Supreme Court in a Democracy' (2002) 116 *Harvard Law Review* 19

—— 'Proportionality (2)' in M Rosenfeld and A Sajó (eds), *The Oxford Handbook of Comparative Constitutional Law* (Oxford: OUP 2012)

Bargaric M and Brebner J, 'The Solution to the Dilemma Presented by the Guilty Plea Discount: The Qualified Guilty Plea – I'm Pleading Guilty Only Because of the Discount' (2002) 30 *International Journal of the Sociology of Law* 51

Barkow RE, 'The Court of Life and Death: The Two Tracks of Constitutional Sentencing Law and the Case for Uniformity' (1996) 107 *Michigan Law Review* 1145

—— 'Recharging the Jury: The Criminal Jury's Constitutional Role in an Era of Mandatory Sentencing' (2003) 152 *University of Pennsylvania Law Review* 33

—— 'Institutional Design and the Policing of Prosecutors: Lessons from Administrative Law' (2009) 61 *Stanford Law Review* 869

—— *Prisoners of Politics: Breaking the Cycle of Mass Incarceration* (Cambridge, MA: Harvard University Press 2019)

Bazyler M and Tuerkheimer F, *Forgotten Trials of the Holocaust* (New York, NY: New York University Press 2015)

Beccaria C, *On Crimes and Punishment* (R Bellamy ed, R Davis tr, 5th edn, first published 1766, Cambridge: CUP 1995)

Beetham A, 'Whole Life Orders and Article 3' (2017) 81 *Journal of Criminal Law* 236

Benn SI, 'An Approach to the Problems of Punishment' (1958) 33 *Philosophy* 325

Bentham J, *An Introduction to the Principles of Morals and Legislation* (JH Burns and HLA Hart eds, first published 1789, London: Athlone Press 1970)

Berman HJ, 'Principles of Soviet Criminal Law' (1947) 56 *Yale Law Journal* 803

Besson S, 'Gender Discrimination under EU and ECHR Law: Never the Twain Shall Meet?' (2008) 8 *Human Rights Law Review* 647

—— 'Evolutions in Non-Discrimination Law within the ECHR and the ESC Systems: "It Takes Two to Tango in the Council of Europe"' (2012) 60 *American Journal of Comparative Law* 147

Betschart M, 'Erstaunliches, Ungereimtes und Gesetzgeberisches Versehen im Neuen Bundesgesetz über die Einführung der Straflosen Selbstanzeige' [2009] *Steuer Revue* 519

Bettinson V and Dingwall G, 'Challenging the Ongoing Injustice of Imprisonment for Public Protection: *James, Wells and Lee* v *The United Kingdom*' (2013) 76 *Modern Law Review* 1094

Bibas S, *The Machinery of Criminal Justice* (New York, NY: OUP 2012)

Bierschbach RA and Bibas S, 'What's Wrong with Sentencing Equality?' (2016) 102 *Virginia Law Review* 1447

Bild J, 'The Whole Life Sentence in England and Wales' (2015) 74 *Cambridge Law Journal* 1

Bilionis LD, 'Process, the Constitution, and Substantive Criminal Law' (1988) 96 *Michigan Law Review* 1926
Bingham T, *The Rule of Law* (London: Allen Law 2010)
Bommer F, 'Die Strafrechtliche Rechtsprechung des Bundesgerichts im Jahr 2010' (2015) 151 *Zeitschrift des Bernischen Juristenvereins* 350
—— Anmerkungen zum Versuch der Strafrahmenharmonisierung' (2019) 137 *Schweizerische Zeitschrift für Strafrecht* 267
Boonin D, *The Problem of Punishment* (Cambridge: CUP 2008)
Bottoms A, 'Five Puzzles in von Hirsch's Theory of Punishment' in A Ashworth and M Wasik (eds), *Fundamentals of Sentencing Theory* (Oxford: OUP 1998)
Bottoms AE, 'The Philosophy and Politics of Punishment and Sentencing' in C Clarkson and R Morgan (eds), *The Politics of Sentencing Reform* (Oxford: Clarendon Press 1995) 40
—— 'Reflections on the Criminological Enterprise' (1995) 46 *Cambridge Law Journal* 240
Bowers J, 'What's Wrong with Sentencing Equality'? Sentencing Legality: A Response to Professors Bierschbach and Bibas' (2016) 102 *Virginia Law Review Online* 120
Bradley FH, *Ethical Studies* (2nd edn, Oxford: Clarendon Press 1927)
Braithwaite J and Petit P, *Not Just Deserts: A Republican Theory of Criminal Justice* (Oxford: Clarendon Press 1990)
Byrne Hessick C and Hessick A, 'Double Jeopardy as a Limit on Punishment' (2011) 97 *Cornell Law Review* 45
Callenwert J, 'L'Article 3 de la Convention Européenne: Une Norme Relativement Absolue ou Absolument Relative?' in *Liber Amicorum Marc-André Eissen* (Brussels: Bryulant 1995)
Cartuyvels Y, 'Les Droits de l'Homme, Frein ou Amplificateur de Criminalisation?' in H Dumont, F Ost, and S Van Drooghenbroeck (eds), *La Responsabilité, Face Cachée des Droits de l'Homme* (Brussels: Bruylant 2005)
—— and Cliquennois G, 'The Punishment of Mentally Ill Offenders in Belgium: Care as Legitimacy for Control' (2015) 12 *Champ Pénal* N 6
Cédras J, 'La Constitutionnalisation de la Procédure Pénale en France et aux États-Unis' (2011) 82 *Revue Internationale de Droit Pénal* 445
Chiao V, *Criminal Law in the Age of the Administrative State* (New York, NY: OUP 2019)
Christofferson J, *Fair Balance: Proportionality, Subsidiarity and Primarity in the European Convention of Human Rights* (Leiden: Martinus Nijhoff 2009)
Cole D and Roberts JV, '*R v FHL*: What's the Point in Pleading Guilty?' (2018) 44 *Criminal Reports* 44
Corlett JA, 'Making Sense of Retributivism' (2001) 76 *Philosophy* 77
Cottingham J, 'Varieties of Retribution' (1979) 29 *The Philosophical Quarterly* 238
Cox M, 'Remorse and Reparation: "To double business bound"' in M Cox (ed), *Remorse and Reparation* (London: Jessica Kingsley 1998)
David M, 'How Much Punishment Does the Bad Samaritan Deserve?' (1996) 15 *Law and Philosophy* 93
Delmas-Marty M, 'Le Paradoxe Pénal' in M Delmas-Marty and C Lucas de Leyssac (eds), *Libertés et Droits Fondamentaux* (Paris: Seuil 1996)
Donatsch A, 'Der Strafbefehl sowie Ähnliche Verfahrenserledigungen mit Einsprachemöglichkeit, Insbesondere aus dem Gesichtswinkel von Art. 6 EMRK' (1994) 112 *Schweizerische Zeitschrift für Strafrecht* 317
—— and Frei M, 'Allgemeine Strafmilderungs- und Strafbefreiungsgründe im Steuerstrafrecht' [2010] *Steuer Revue* 12
—— and Tag B, *Strafrecht I: Verbrechenslehre* (9th edn, Zurich: Schulthess 2013)

—— and Wohlers W, *Strafrecht IV: Delikte gegen die Allgemeinheit* (4th edn, Zurich: Schulthess 2011)
Dubber MD, 'Toward a Constitutional Law of Crime and Punishment' (2004) 55 *Hastings Law Journal* 509
—— 'Common Civility – The Culture of Alegality in ICL' (2011) 24 *Leiden Journal of International Law* 923
Duff RA, *Trials and Punishments* (Cambridge: CUP 1986)
—— 'Law, Language and Community: Some Preconditions of Criminal Liability' (1998) 18 *Oxford Journal of Legal Studies* 189
—— *Punishment, Communication and Community* (Oxford: OUP 2001)
—— 'Choice, Character and Criminal Liability' (2003) 12 *Law and Philosophy* 345
—— 'Responsibility, Citizenship, and Criminal Law' in RA Duff and SP Green (eds), *Philosophical Foundations of Criminal Law* (Oxford: OUP 2011)
—— *The Realm of the Criminal Law* (Oxford: OUP 2018)
—— and others, *The Trial on Trial: Volume 3: Towards a Normative Theory of the Trial* (Oxford: Hart Publishing 2007)
Dwarris F, *A General Treatise on Statutes* (Albany, NY: W Gould 1873)
Dworkin R, *Taking Rights Seriously* (Cambridge, MA: Harvard University Press 1977)
—— *Law's Empire* (Harvard, MT: Harvard University Press 1986)
Dyzenhaus D, *Judging the Judges, Judging Ourselves: Truth, Reconciliation and the Apartheid Legal Order* (Oxford: Hart Publishing 1998)
—— 'The Very Idea of a Judge' (2010) 60 *University of Toronto Law Journal* 61
Edel F, *The Prohibition of Discrimination under the European Convention on Human Rights* (Strasbourg: Council of Europe Publishing 2010)
Farmer L, 'Criminal Responsibility and Proof of Guilt' in L Farmer and MD Dubber (eds), *Modern Histories of Crime and Punishment* (Stanford, CA: Stanford University Press 2007)
—— *Making the Modern Criminal Law: Civil Order and Criminalisation* (Oxford: OUP 2016)
—— 'Crime and Punishment' (2020) 14 *Criminal Law and Philosophy* 289.
—— 'Punishment in the Rule of Law' in J Meierhenrich and M Loughlin (eds), *The Cambridge Companion to the Rule of Law* (Cambridge: CUP 2021)
Fassin D, *The Will to Punish* (C Kutz ed, The Berkeley Tanner Lectures, New York, NY: OUP 2018)
Feeley MM and Simon J, 'Actuarial Justice: The Emerging New Criminal Law' in P O'Malley (ed), *Crime and the Risk Society* (New York, NY: Ashgate 1998)
Feinberg J, 'The Expressive Function of Punishment' in J Feinberg, *Doing and Deserving: Essays in the Theory of Responsibility* (Princeton, NJ, Princeton University Press 1970)
—— 'Noncomparative Justice' (1974) 83 *Philosophical Review* 297
—— *Doing and Deserving: Essays in the Theory of Responsibility* (Princeton, NJ: Princeton University Press 1974)
Feldbrugge FJ, 'Soviet Criminal Law—The Last Six Years' (1963) 54 *Journal of Criminal Law and Criminology* 249
Feuerbach PJA, *Lehrbuch des Gemeinen in Deutschland Gültigen Peinlichen Rechts* (11th edn, Giessen: Heyer 1832)
Finkelstein C, 'Positivism and the Notion of an Offence' (2000) 88 *California Law Review* 335
Finnis J, *Natural Law and Natural Rights* (Oxford: OUP 1980)
Fletcher GP, *Rethinking Criminal Law* (New York, NY: OUP 2000)
Flew A, 'The Justification of Punishment' (1954) 29 *Philosophy* 291

Foran MP, 'Discrimination as an Individual Wrong' (2019) 39 *Oxford Journal of Legal Studies* 901
Foster S, 'The Great Review and Release Swindle: The European Court, Whole Life Sentences and the Possibility of Review and Release' (2015) 20 *Coventry Law Journal* 53
Foucault M, 'About the Concept of the "Dangerous Individual" in the 19th-Century Legal Psychiatry' [1978] *International Journal of Law and Psychiatry* 1
—— *Discipline and Punish: The Birth of the Prison* (London: Penguin Books 1991)
Frankel ME, *Criminal Sentences: Law Without Order* (New York, NY: Hill & Yang 1972)
Frase RS, 'Comparative Perspectives on Sentencing Policy and Research' in M Tony and RS Frase (eds), *Sentencing and Sanctions in Western Countries* (Oxford: OUP 2001)
—— 'Excessive Prison Sentences, Punishment Goals, and the Eighth Amendment: 'Proportionality' Relative to What?' (2005) 89 *Minnesota Law Review* 571
—— 'What Explains Persistent Racial Disproportionality in Minnesota's Prison and Jail Populations?' in M Tonry (ed), *Crime and Justice: A Review of Research*, vol 38 (Chicago, IL, University of Chicago Press 2009)
—— *Just Sentencing* (New York, NY: OUP 2013)
French C, 'The Role of the Judge in Sentencing: From Port-Soaked Reactionary to Latte Liberal' [2015] *Otago Law Review* 5
Frisch W, von Hirsch A, and Albrecht HJ (eds), *Tatproportionalität. Normative und Empirische Aspekte einer Tatproportionalen Strafzumessung* (Heidelberg: CF Müller 2001)
Fuller LL, *The Morality of Law* (2nd edn, New Haven, CT: Yale University Press 1969)
—— 'Forms and Limits of Adjudication' in KI Winston (ed) *The Principles of Social Order: Selected Essays of Lon L Fuller* (Oxford: Hart Publishing 2001)
Fullinwider RK, *The Reverse Discrimination Controversy: A Moral and Legal Analysis* (Totowa, NJ: Rowman and Littlefield 1980)
Gardner J, 'The Virtue of Justice and the Character of Law' (2002) 53 *Current Legal Problems* 1
—— 'Introduction' in HLA Hart (ed), *Punishment and Responsibility: Essays in the Philosophy of Law* (J Gardner, 2nd edn, Oxford: OUP 2008)
Garland D, 'Philosophical Argument and Ideological Effect' (1983) 7 *Contemporary Crises* 79
—— *Punishment and Modern Society: A Study in Social Theory* (Oxford: OUP 1990)
—— *The Culture of Control: Crime and Social Order in Contemporary Society* (New York, NY: OUP 2001)
—— 'The Rule of Law, Representational Struggles and the Will to Punish' in D Fassin, *The Will to Punish* (C Kutz ed, New York, NY: OUP, 2018)
Gerards J, 'The Discrimination Grounds of Article 14 of the European Convention on Human Rights' (2013) 13 *Human Rights Law Review* 99
Germann OA, *Das Verbrechen im Neuen Strafrecht* (Zurich: Schulthess 1942)
Giannoulis G, *Studien zur Strafzumessung: Ein Beitrag zur Dogmatik, Rechtstheorie und Rechtsinformatik mit Vertiefung in den Eigentums- und Vermögensdelikten* (Tübingen: Mohr Siebeck 2014)
Gilliéron G and Killias M, 'Strafbefehl und Justizirrtum: Franz Riklin hatte Recht' in MA Niggli, JH Pozo, and N Queloz (eds), *Festschrift für Franz Riklin, Zur Emeritierung und Zugleich dem 67. Geburtstag* (Zurich: Schulthess 2007)
Gless S, 'Strafe ohne Souverän?' (2007) 125 *Schweizerische Zeitschrift für Strafrecht* 24
Glueck S, 'Principles of a Rational Penal Code' (1928) 41 *Harvard Law Review* 453
Gordon G, *The Criminal Law of Scotland* (3rd edn, Edinburgh: W Green 2000)
Graham L, 'From Vinter to Hutchinson and Back Again' (2018) 3 *European Human Rights Law Review* 258

Graven P and Sträuli B, *L'Infraction Pénale Punissable* (2nd edn, Bern: Stämpfli 1995)
Hall J, 'Nulla Poena Sine Lege' (1937) 47 *Yale Law Journal* 165
Hampton J, 'An Expressive Theory of Retribution' in W Cragg (ed), *Retribution and its Critics* (Stuttgart: Franz Steiner Verlag 1992)
Hansjakob T, 'Zahlen und Fakten zum Strafbefehlsverfahren' (2014) 3 *forumpoenale* 160
Harel A, 'Why Only the State May Inflict Criminal Sanctions: The Case against Privately Inflicted Sanctions' (2008) 14 *Legal Theory* 113
Harris D and others, *Harris, O'Boyle, and Warbrick: Law of the European Convention on Human Rights* (4th edn, Oxford: OUP 2018)
Harris L, 'Comment on R v Price' (2019) 1 *Sentencing News* 3
Hart HLA, 'Between Utility and Rights' (1989) 79 *Columbia Law Review* 828
Hart HLA, *The Concept of Law* (2nd edn, Oxford: Clarendon Press 1994)
—— *Punishment and Responsibility: Essays in the Philosophy of Law* (J Gardner, 2nd edn, Oxford: OUP 2008)
—— 'Legal Responsibility and Excuses' in HLA Hart (ed), *Punishment and Responsibility: Essays in the Philosophy of Law* (J Gardner, 2nd edn, (Oxford: OUP 2008)
—— 'Prolegomenon to the Principles of Punishment' in HLA Hart (ed), *Punishment and Responsibility: Essays in the Philosophy of Law* (J Gardner, 2nd edn, Oxford: OUP 2008)
—— 'Punishment and Elimination of Responsibility' in HLA Hart (ed), *Punishment and Responsibility: Essays in the Philosophy of Law* (J Gardner, 2nd edn, Oxford: OUP 2008)
—— 'Responsibility and Retribution' in HLA Hart (ed), *Punishment and Responsibility: Essays in the Philosophy of Law* (J Gardner, 2nd edn, Oxford: OUP 2008)
Hart HM, 'The Aims of the Criminal Law' (1958) 23 *Law and Contemporary Problems* 410
Hart N, 'Whole Life Sentences in the UK: Volte-Face at the European Court of Human Rights?' (2015) 74 *Cambridge Law Journal* 205
Hegel GWF, *The Philosophy of Right* (FM Knox tr, first published 1820, Oxford: OUP 1942)
Helm RK, 'Constrained Waiver of Trial Rights? Incentives to Plead Guilty and the Right to a Fair Trial' (2019) 46 *Journal of Law and Society* 423
Hobbes T, *Leviathan* (N Malcolm ed, first published 1651, Oxford: Clarendon Press 2012)
Hodgson J and Tadros V, 'How to Make a Terrorist out of Nothing' (2009) 72 *Modern Law Review* 984
Honderich T, *Punishment: The Supposed Justifications* (New York, NY: Harcourt, Brace & World 1970)
Honoré T, 'Social Justice' (1962) 8 *McGill Law Journal* 77
Horder J, 'Criminal Law: Between Determinism, Liberalism and Criminal Justice' (1996) 49 *Current Legal Problems* 159
—— *Ashworth's Principles of Criminal Law* (9th edn, Oxford: OUP 2019)
Hörnle T, *Tatproportionale Strafzumessung* (Duncker & Humblot: Berlin 1999)
Jackson J and Summers S, *The Internationalisation of Criminal Evidence: Beyond the Common Law and Civil Law Traditions* (Cambridge: CUP 2014)
Jareborg N, *Essays in Criminal Law* (Uppsala: Iustus 1998)
Jeffries Jr JC and Stephan III PB, 'Defences, Presumptions, and the Burden of Proof in Criminal Law' (1979) 88 *Yale Law Journal* 1325
Jositsch D, Ege G, and Schwarzenegger C, *Strafrecht II: Strafen und Massnahmen* (9th edn, Zurich, Schulthess 2018)
Kadish SH, 'Fifty Years of Criminal Law: An Opinionated Review' (1999) 87 *California Law Review* 943
Kadish SH, Schulhofer S, and Barkow RE, *Criminal Law and its Processes* (10th edn, New York, NY: Aspen Publishers 2016)

Kannai R, 'Proportionality in Sentencing: Constitutional or Criminal Issue' (2005) 9 *Canadian Criminal Law Review* 315

Kant I, *Groundwork of the Metaphysics of Morals* (M Gregor and J Timmerman eds, first published 1785, Cambridge: CUP 2014)

Kaufman SB, 'Citizenship and Punishment: Situating Death Penalty Jury Sentencing' (2011) 13 *Punishment and Society* 333

Kennefick L, 'Introducing a New Diminished Responsibility Defence for England and Wales' (2011) 74 *Modern Law Review* 750

Killias M and others, *Grundriss des Allgemeinen Teils des Schweizerischen Gesetzbuchs* (Bern: Stämpfli 2009)

Kleinig J, *Punishment and Desert* (The Hague: Martinus Nijhoff 1973)

Krasnostein S and Freiberg A, 'Pursuing Consistency in an Individual Sentencing Framework: If You Know Where You're Going, How Do You Know When You've Got There?' (2013) 76 *Law and Contemporary Problems* 265

Kremnitzer M, 'Constitutionalization of Substantive Criminal Law: A Realistic View' (1999) 33 *Israel Law Review* 720

Kuckes N, 'Civil Due Process, Criminal Due Process' (2006) 25 *Yale Law and Policy Review* 8

Kunz K-L, 'Tatproportionalität aus der Perspektive eines normativ begründeten Strafrechts' in W Frisch, A von Hirsch, and H-J Albrecht (eds), *Tatproportionalität. Normative und Empirische Aspekte einer Tatproportionalen Strafzumessung* (Heidelberg: CF Müller 2001)

Kurki L, 'International Standards for Sentencing and Punishment' in M Tonry and RS Frase (eds), *Sentences and Sanctions in Western Countries* (Oxford: OUP 2001)

Lacey N, 'Discretion and Due Process at the Post-Conviction Stage' in I Dennis (ed), *Criminal Law and Justice: Essays from the WG Hart Workshop 1986* (London: Sweet & Maxwell 1987)

—— *State Punishment: Political Principles and Community Values* (London: Routledge 1988)

—— 'Philosophy, Political Morality and History: Explaining the Enduring Resonance of the Hart-Fuller Debate' (2008) 83 *New York University Law Review* 1059

—— 'The Resurgence of Character: Responsibility in the Context of Criminalization' in A Duff and S Green (eds), *Philosophical Foundations of Criminal Law* (Oxford: OUP 2011)

—— *In Search of Criminal Responsibility: Ideas, Interests and Institutions* (Oxford: OUP 2016)

—— 'Socializing the Subject of Criminal Law? Criminal Responsibility and the Purposes of Criminalization' (2016) 99 *Marquette Law Review* 541

—— 'Populism and the Rule of Law' (2019) 15 *Annual Review of Law and Social Science* 79

—— and Pickard H, 'The Chimera of Proportionality: Institutionalising Limits on Punishments in Contemporary Social and Political Systems' (2015) 78 *Modern Law Review* 216

Lagodny O, 'Basic Rights and Substantive Criminal Law: The Incest Case' (2011) 61 *University of Toronto Law Journal* 761

L Lavrynsen, 'Don't Open the Floodgates: Fines and Article 1 Protocol 1' Strasbourg Observers Blog, available at: <https://strasbourgobservers.com/2015/11/09/dont-open-the-floodgates-fines-and-article-1-protocol-1/> (accessed 15 Apr 2021).

Lee Y, 'Why Proportionality Matters' (2012) 160 *University of Pennsylvania Law Review* 1835

Lippke RA, 'Response to Tudor: Remorse-based Sentence Reductions in Theory and Practice' (2008) 2 *Criminal Law and Philosophy* 259

Lydon M, 'Criminal Law – Rehabilitation, A Thesis; Punishment, the Antithesis – Insanity Defence in the Balance (1969) 19 *DePaul Law Review* 140

MacCormick N, 'Rhetoric and the Rule of Law' in D Dyzenhaus (ed), *Recrafting the Rule of Law: The Limits of Legal Order* (Oxford: Hart Publishing 1999)

—— and Garland D, 'Sovereign States and Vengeful Victims: The Problem of the Right to Punish' in A Ashworth and M Wasik (eds), *Fundamentals of Sentencing Theory* (Oxford: OUP 1998)

Mackenzie G and others, 'Sentencing and Public Confidence: Results from a National Australian Survey on Public Opinions Towards Sentencing' (2012) 45 *Australian and New Zealand Journal of Criminology* 45

Maes E, 'Del Rio Prada v Spain and the Execution of a Penalty under Article 7: Shifting Conception of Punishment?' (2017) 5 *European Human Rights Law Review* 443

Mahlmann M, 'One Step Too Far – Some Philosophical and Political Reflections on the Current Critique of Human Rights' in A Sajó and R Uitz (eds), *Critical Essays on Human Rights* (The Hague: Eleven International Publishing 2020)

Mancano L, *The European Union and Deprivation of Liberty: A Legislative and Judicial Analysis from the Perspective of the Individual* (Oxford: Hart Publishing 2019)

Manderson D and Sharp N, 'Mandatory Sentences and The Constitution: Discretion, Responsibility, and Judicial Process' (2000) 22 *Sydney Law Review* 585

Marchesi D, 'Imprisonment for Life at the International Criminal Court' (2018) 14 *Utrecht Law Review* 97

Maslen H, *Remorse, Penal Theory and Sentencing* (Oxford: Hart Publishing 2015)

Maslan H and Roberts JV, 'Remorse and Sentencing' in A Ashworth and JV Roberts (eds), *Sentencing Guidelines: Exploring the English Model* (Oxford: OUP 2013)

Mathys H, *Leitfaden Strafzumessung* (2nd edn, Basel: Helbing & Lichtenhahn 2019)

Mathys M, 'Zur Technik der Strafzumessung' (2004) 100 *Schweizerische Juristen Zeitung* 173

Matravers M, 'Duff on Hard Treatment' in R Croft, MH Kramer, and MR Reiff (eds), *Crime, Punishment and Responsibility: The Jurisprudence of Anthony Duff* (Oxford: OUP 2011)

—— 'Is Twenty-first Century Punishment Post-desert?' in M Tonry (ed), *Retributivism as a Past: Hast it a Future?* (Oxford: OUP 2011)

—— 'Rootless Desert and Unanchored Censure' in A du Bois-Pedain and AE Bottoms (eds), *Penal Censure: Agreements within and Beyond Desert Theory* (Oxford, Hart Publishing 2019)

Mavronicola N, 'Inhuman and Degrading Punishment, Dignity and the Limits of Retribution' (2014) 77 *Modern Law Review* 292

—— 'Crime, Punishment and Article 3 ECHR: Puzzles and Prospects of Applying an Absolute Right in a Penal Context' (2015) 15 *Human Rights Law Review* 721

—— *Torture, Inhumanity and Degradation under Article 3 of the ECHR: Absolute Rights and Absolute Wrongs* (Oxford: Hart Publishing 2021)

McDonald S, 'Involuntary Detention and the Separation of Judicial Power' (2007) 35 *Federal Law Review* 25

McPherson T, 'Punishment: Definition and Justification' (1967) 28 *Analysis* 21

Metz T, 'How to Reconcile Liberal Politics with Retributive Punishment' (2007) 27 *Oxford Journal of Legal Studies* 683

Meyer F, *Systematischer Kommentar zur Strafprozessordnung: Band X EMRK* (5th edn, Cologne: Carl Heymanns Verlag 2019)

Miller ML and Wright RF, 'Your Cheatin' Heart(land): The Long Search for Administrative Sentencing Justice' (1999) 2 *Buffalo Criminal Law Review* 723

Montesquieu, *The Spirit of the Law* (T Nugent, tr, first published 1750, Berkeley, CA: University of California Press 1977)

Moore M, 'Causation and the Excuses' (1985) 73 *California Law Review* 1091

—— 'The Moral Worth of Retribution' in R Schoemann (ed), *Responsibility, Character and the Emotions* (New York, NY: CUP 1987)

Morris H, 'Persons and Punishment' (1968) 52 *The Monist* 475
Morse SJ and Hoffman MB, 'The Uneasy Entente between Insanity and Mens Rea: Beyond Clark v Arizona' (2007) 97 *Journal of Criminal Law and Criminology* 143
Murphy J, 'Three Mistakes about Retribution' (1971) 31 *Analysis* 166
—— 'Marxism and Retribution' (1973) 2 *Philosophy and Public Affairs* 217
—— 'Marxism and Retribution' in AL Simmons and others (eds), *Punishment* (Princeton: Princeton University Press 1995)
Murphy JS, 'Well Excuse Me!—Remorse, Apology, and Criminal Sentencing' (2006) 38 *Arizona State Law Journal* 371
Nestler C, 'Constitutional Principles, Criminal Law Principles and German Drug Law' (1998) 1 *Buffalo Criminal Law Review* 661
Nietzsche F, *On the Genealogy of Morals* (Walter Kaufman tr, first published 1887, New York, NY: Vintage Books 1989)
Niggli MA and Maeder S, 'Was Schützt Eigentlich Strafrecht (und Schützt es Überhaupt Etwas)?' (2011) *Aktuelle Juristische Praxis* 443
Noll P, *Der Strafrechtliche Handlungsbegriff* (Kriminologische Schriftenreihe, vol 54) (Kriminalistik Verlag: Heidelberg 1971)
Nosetti-Kaufmann A, 'Strafbefehl, Abgekürztes Verfahren und Fehlende Unmittelbarkeit: Festhalten am Status quo - eine Verpasste Chance?' (2020) 138 *Schweizerische Zeitschrift für Strafrecht* 248
O'Connell R, 'Cinderella Comes to the Ball: Article 14 and the Right to Non-discrimination in the ECHR' (2009) 29 *Legal Studies* 211
Packer HL, 'Mens Rea and the Supreme Court' [1962] *Supreme Court Review* 107
—— *The Limits of the Criminal Sanction* (Stanford, CA: Stanford University Press 1968)
—— 'The Aims of the Criminal Law Revisited: A Plea for a New Look at "Substantive Due Process"' (1971) 44 *California Law Review* 490
Padfield N, 'Exploring the Sentencing Guidelines' in A Ashworth and JV Roberts (eds), *Sentencing Guidelines: Exploring the English Model* (Oxford: OUP 2013)
—— 'Justifying Indefinite Detention: On What Grounds?' [2016] *Criminal Law Review* 797
—— 'Advancing Human Rights: Levelling Up or Levelling Down?' [2017] *Criminal Law Review* 423
Paizes A, 'A Closer Look at the Presumption of Innocence in our Constitution: What is an Accused to be Presumed *Of*?' (1998) 11 *South African Journal of Criminal Justice* 409
Palmer S, 'A Wrong Turning: Article 3 ECHR and Proportionality' (2006) 65 *Cambridge Law Journal* 438
Parein L, 'Exécution des Sanctions: La Réserve de Dangerosité Met-elle en Danger le Principe *ne bis in idem*?' (2020) 2 *Neue Zeitschrift für Kriminologie und Kriminalpolitik* 48
Pérez Manzano M and others, *Multilevel Protection of the Principle of Legality in Criminal Law* (Springer: Cham 2018)
Peters CJ, 'Foolish Consistency: On Equality, Integrity, and Justice in Stare Decisis' (1996) 105 *Yale Law Journal* 2031
—— 'Equality Revisited' (1997) 110 *Harvard Law Review* 1210
Peterson J, 'A Review of Hannah Maslen: Remorse Penal Theory and Sentence' (2019) 13 *Criminal Law and Philosophy* 667
Pettigrew M, 'A Vinter Retreat in Europe: Returning to the Issue of Whole-Life Sentences in Strasbourg' (2017) 8 *New Journal of European Criminal Law* 128
Phillips D, *Equality, Justice and Rectification* (New York, NY: Academic Press 1979)
Popelier P, Lambrecht S, and Lemmens K (eds), *Criticism of the European Court of Human Rights* (Antwerp: Intersentia 2016)

Pratt J, *Penal Populism* (London: Routledge 2006)
—— 'Penal Populism and the Contemporary Role of Punishment' in T Anthony and C Cuneen (eds), *The Critical Criminology Companion* (Annandale: Hawkins Press 2008)
Přibáň J, 'Review of David Dyzenhaus, *Judging the Judges, Judging Ourselves*' (1999) 26 *Journal of Law and Society* 577
Quinton AM, 'On Punishment' (1954) 14 *Analysis* 512
RA Duff, 'Punishment, Communication and Community' in M Matravers (ed), *Punishment and Political Theory* (Oxford, Hart Publishing 1998)
Rawls J, 'Two Concepts of Rules' (1955) 64 *The Philosophical Review* 3
—— *Justice as Fairness* (1958) 67 *Philosophy Review* 164
—— *A Theory of Justice* (Cambridge, MA: Harvard University Press 1971)
—— *Political Liberalism* (New York, NY: Columbia University Press 1993)
—— *Justice as Fairness: Political not Metaphysical*, J Rawls and SR Freeman (eds), Collected Papers (Cambridge MT, Harvard University Press 1999)
Raz J, *Practical Reason and Norms* (Princeton, NJ: Princeton University Press 1975)
—— 'The Rule of Law and its Virtue' in J Raz (ed), *The Authority of Law: Essays on Law and Morality* (Oxford: Clarendon Press 1979)
—— *The Morality of Freedom* (Oxford: OUP 1988)
Reed R and Murdoch J, *Human Rights Law in Scotland* (4th edn, West Sussex: Bloomsbury 2017)
Reid K, *A Practitioner's Guide to the European Convention on Human Rights* (6th edn, London: Sweet & Maxwell 2019)
Reitz KR, 'Comparing Sentencing Guidelines: Do US Systems Have Anything Worthwhile to Offer England and Wales?' in A Ashworth and JV Roberts (eds), *Sentencing Guidelines: Exploring the English Model* (Oxford: OUP 2013)
Renzo M, 'Responsibility and Answerability in the Criminal Law' in RA Duff and others (eds), *The Constitution of the Criminal Law* (Oxford: OUP 2013)
Riklin F, 'Art 352' in MA Niggli, M Heer, and H Wiprächtiger (eds), *Schweizerische Strafprozessordnung Basler Kommentar* (2nd edn, Basel: Helbing Lichtenhahn 2014)
—— 'Art 353' in MA Niggli, M Heer, and H Wiprächtiger (eds), *Schweizerische Strafprozessordnung Basler Kommentar* (2nd edn, Basel: Helbing Lichtenhahn 2014)
Ristroph A, 'Proportionality as a Principle of Limited Government' (2005) 55 *Duke Law Review* 263
Roach Anleu S, Brewer R, and Mac K, 'Locating the Judge within Sentencing Research' (2017) 6 *International Journal for Crime, Justice and Social Democracy* 46
Roach K, 'Searching for Smith: The Constitutionality of Mandatory Sentences' (2001) 39 *Osgoode Hall Law Journal* 367
Roberts JV 'Aggravating and Mitigating Factors at Sentencing: Towards Greater Consistency of Application' [2008] *Criminal Law Review* 264
—— Sentencing Guidelines and Judicial Discretion: Evolution of Duty of Courts to Comply in England and Wales' (2011) 51 *British Journal of Criminology* 997
—— and Bradford B, 'Sentence Reduction for a Guilty Plea in England and Wales: Exploring New Trends' (2015) 12 *Journal of Empirical Legal Studies* 187
—— and others, *Penal Populism and Public Opinion: Lessons from Five Countries* (Oxford: OUP 2002)
Roberts P, 'Strict Liability and the Presumption of Innocence: An Exposé of Functionalist Assumptions' in A Simester (ed), *Appraising Strict Liability* (Oxford: OUP 2005)
Robinson PH, 'Fair Notice and Fair Adjudication: Two Kinds of Legality' (2005) 154 *University of Pennsylvania Law Review* 335

Romano M, 'Divining the Spirit of California's Three Strikes Law' (2010) 22 *Federal Sentencing Reporter* 171

Roth R, 'Libres Propos sur la Subsidiarité du Droit Pénal' in A Auer and others (eds), *Aux Confins du Droit: Essais en l'Honneur du Professeur Charles-Albert Morand* (Basel: Helbing & Lichtenhahn 2001)

Roux J-A, *Cours de Droit Criminel Français* (2nd edn, Paris: Sirey 1927)

Roxin C, 'Prevention, Censure and Responsibility: The Recent Debate on the Purposes of Punishment' in AP Simester, A du Bois-Pedain, and U Neumann (eds), *Liberal Criminal Theory: Essays for Andreas von Hirsch* (Oxford: Hart Publishing 2014)

Saltzman S, 'Strict Criminal Liability and the United States Constitution: Substantive Criminal Law Due Process' (1978) 24 *Wayne Law Review* 1571

Schäfer G, Sander GM, and van Gemmeren G, *Praxis der Strafzumessung* (6th edn, Munich: Beck 2017)

Schlink B, 'Proportionality (1)' in M Rosenfeld and A Sajó (eds), *The Oxford Handbook of Comparative Constitutional Law* (Oxford: OUP 2012)

Schmidt E, 'Zur Theorie des Unbestimmten Strafurteils' (1931) 45 *Schweizerische Zeitschrift für Strafrecht* 227

Schmidt PJ, *Probleme der Rückfallkriminalität* (Dissertation, Göttingen 1974)

Schottlaender A, *Die Geschichtliche Entwicklung des Satzes: Nulla Poena Sine Lege* (Heidelberg: Ruprecht-Karls-Universität Heidelberg 1911)

Schubarth M, 'Zurück zum Grossinquisitor?, Zur Rechtsstaatlichen Problematik des Strafbefehls' in MA Niggli, J Hurtado Pozo, and N Queloz (eds), *Festschrift für Franz Riklin, Zur Emeritierung und zugleich dem 67. Geburtstag* (Zürich: Schulthess 2007)

Schultz H, *Einführung in den Allgemeinen Teil des Strafrechts*, vol II (Bern: Stämpfli 1982)

Schwander V, *Das Schweizerische Strafgesetzbuch* (2nd edn, Zurich: Polygraphischer Verlag 1964)

Schwarzenegger C, 'Art 352' in A Donatsch and others (eds), *Kommentar zur schweizerischen Strafprozessordnung* (3rd edn, Zurich: Schulthess 2020)

Sidgwick H, *Methods of Ethics* (6th edn, London: Macmillan 1901)

Small J, 'Structure and Substance: Developing a Practical and Effective Prohibition on Discrimination under the Convention on Human Rights' (2003) 6 *European Journal of Discrimination and the Law* 45

Snacken S and van Zyl Smit D, 'European Penology and Penal Policy-Making' in T Daems, D van Zyl Smith, and S Snacken (eds), *European Penology?* (Oxford: Hart Publishing 2017)

Spohn C, *How do Judges Decide?: The Search for Fairness and Justice in Punishment* (Thousand Oaks, CA: Sage 2009)

Stewart H, 'Bedford and the Structure of Section 7' (2015) 60 *McGill Law Journal* 575

Steyn J, 'The Weakest and Least Dangerous Department of Government' [1997] *Public Law* 84

Stith K and Koh SY, 'The Politics of Sentencing Reform: The Legislative History of the Federal Sentencing Guidelines' (1993) 28 *Wake Forest Law Review* 223

Stratenwerth G, 'Die Bedeutung der Finalen Handlungslehre für das Schweizerische Strafrecht' (1965) 81 *Schweizerische Zeitschrift für Strafrecht* 179

—— *Schweizerisches Strafrecht, Allgemeiner Teil I: Die Straftat* (4th edn, Bern, Stämpfli, 2011)

—— and Bommer F, *Schweizerisches Strafrecht, Allgemeiner Teil II: Strafen und Massnahmen* (3rd edn, Bern: Stämpfli, 2020)

Streiker CS, 'Foreword: The Limits of the Preventive State' (1998) 88 *Journal of Criminal Law and Criminology* 771

Stuntz WJ, 'Substance, Process and the Civil-Criminal Line' (1996) 7 *Journal of Contemporary Legal Issues* 1

—— 'The Pathological Politic of Criminal Law' (2000) 100 *Michigan Law Review* 505

—— 'The Political Constitution of Criminal Justice' (2006) 119 *Harvard Law Review* 780

—— 'Unequal Justice' (2008) 121 *Harvard Law Review* 1969

Sullivan G, 'Strict Liability for Criminal Offences in England and Wales Following Incorporation into English Law of the European Convention on Human Rights' in A Simester (ed), *Appraising Strict Liability* (Oxford: OUP 2010)

Summers S, *Fair Trials: The European Court of Human Rights and the European Criminal Procedural Tradition* (Oxford: Hart Publishing 2007)

Tadros V, *Criminal Responsibility* (Oxford: OUP 2007)

—— *The Ends of Harm: The Moral Foundations of the Criminal Law* (Oxford: OUP 2011)

—— and Tierney S, 'Presumption of Innocence and the Human Rights Act' (2004) 67 *Modern Law Review* 402

Tamanaha BZ, *On the Rule of Law: History, Politics, Theory* (Cambridge: Cambridge University Press 2012)

Tasioulas J, 'Mercy' (2003) 103 *Proceedings of the Aristotelian Society* 101

—— 'Punishment and Repentance' (2006) 81 *Philosophy* 279

Tata C, 'The Struggle for Sentencing Reform' in A Ashworth and JV Roberts (eds), *Sentencing Guidelines: Exploring the English Model* (Oxford: OUP 2013)

Thommen M, 'Unerhörte Strafbefehle, Strafbefehle ohne Einvernahme—ein Plädoyer für Kommunikation mit Beschuldigten' (2010) 128 *Schweizerische Zeitschrift für Strafrecht* 373

—— *Kurzer Prozess—Fairer Prozess? Strafbefehls- und Abgekürzte Verfahren zwischen Effizienz und Gerechtigkeit* (Bern: Stämpfli 2013)

—— and Eschle D, 'Was Tun Wir Juristinnen und Juristen Eigentlich, Wenn Wir Forschen? Klassische Dogmatik versus Empirische Rechtsforschung als Innovativer Weg' in J Meier, N Zurkinden, and L Staffler (eds), *Recht und Innovation* (Zurich: Dike 2020)

Thorburn M, 'Proportionate Sentencing and the Rule of Law' in L Zedner and JV Roberts (eds), *Principles and Values in Criminal Law and Criminal Justice: Essays in Honour of Andrew Ashworth* (Oxford: OUP 2012)

Timmer A, 'Judging Stereotypes: What the European Court of Human Rights can Borrow from American and Canadian Equal Protection Law' (2015) 63 *American Journal of Comparative Law* 239

Tomlin P, 'Extending the Golden Thread? Criminalisation and the Presumption of Innocence' (2013) 21 *Journal of Political Philosophy* 44

Tonry M, 'The Success of Judge Frankel's Sentencing Commission' (1993) 64 *University of Colorado Law Review* 713

—— 'Proportionality, Parsimony and Interchangeability' in RA Duff and others (eds), *Penal Theory and Practice: Tradition and Innovation in Criminal Justice* (Manchester: Manchester University Press 1994)

—— *Malign Neglect: Race, Crime and Punishment in America* (New York, NY: OUP 1995)

—— *Sentencing Matters* (New York, NY: OUP 1996)

—— 'The Questionable Relevance of Previous Convictions' in JV Roberts and A von Hirsch (eds), *Previous Convictions at Sentencing* (Oxford: Hart Publishing 2010)

—— 'Can Twenty-first Century Punishment be Justified in Principle' in M Tonry (ed), *Retributivism as a Past: Has it a Future?* (Oxford: OUP 2011)

—— 'Fairness, Equality, Proportionality and Parsimony' in A du Bois-Pedain and AE Bottoms (eds), *Penal Censure: Engagements Within and Beyond Desert Theory* (Oxford: Hart Publishing 2019)

Trechsel S, 'Die Entwicklung der Mittel und Methoden des Strafrechts' (1974) 90 *Schweizerische Zeitschrift für Strafrecht* 271
—— *Die Europäische Menschenrechtskonvention, ihr Schutz der Persönlichen Freiheit und die Schweizerischen Strafprozessrechte* (Bern: Stämpfli 1974)
—— 'Why Must Trials be Fair?' (1997) 31 *Israel Law Review* 94
—— *Human Rights in Criminal Proceedings* (Oxford: OUP 2005)
—— and Jean-Richard M, 'Art 1' in S Trechsel and M Pieth (eds), *Schweizerisches Strafgesetzbuch: Praxiskommentar* (3rd edn, Zurich: Dike 2018)
—— and Jean-Richard M, 'Art. 19' in S Trechsel and M Pieth (eds), *Schweizerisches Strafgesetzbuch: Praxiskommentar* (3rd edn, Zurich: Dike 2018)
—— Noll P and Pieth M, *Schweizerisches Strafrecht, Allgemeiner Teil I: Allgemeine Voraussetzungen der Strafbarkeit* (7th edn, Zurich: Schulthess 2017)
—— and Thommen M, 'Art 47' in S Trechsel and M Pieth (eds), *Schweizersiches Strafgesetzbuch: Praxiskommentar* (3rd edn, Zurich: Dike 2018)
—— and Thommen M, 'Art 48a' in S Trechsel and M Pieth (eds), *Schweizerisches Strafgesetzbuch, Praxiskommentar* (3rd edn, Zurich: Dike 2018)
Tschannen P, 'Die Gleichheit im Unrecht: Gerichtsstrafe im Grundrechtskleid' (2011) 112 *Schweizerisches Zentralblatt für Staats- und Verwaltungsrecht* 57
Tudor SK, 'Why Should Remorse be a Mitigating Factor in Sentencing?' (2008) 2 *Criminal Law and Philosophy* 241
Tulkens F, 'The Paradoxical Relationship between Criminal Law and Human Rights' (2011) 9 *Journal of International Criminal Justice* 577
van den Haag E, 'Punishment, Desert and Crime Control' (1987) 85 *Michigan Law Review* 1250
van Zyl Smit D, 'Human Rights and Sentencing Guidelines' (2001) 5 *Law, Democracy and Development* 45
—— *UN Handbook on Basic Principles and Promising Alternatives to Prison* (New York, NY: UN 2007)
—— and Ashworth A, 'Disproportionate Sentences as Human Rights Violations' (2004) 67 *Modern Law Review* 541
—— and Snacken S, *Principles of European Prison Law and Policy: Penology and Human Rights* (Oxford: OUP 2009)
—— Weatherby P, and Creighton S, 'Whole Life Sentences and the Tide of European Human Rights Jurisprudence: What Is to Be Done?' (2014) 14 *Human Rights Law Review* 59
Vannier M, 'Caught between a Rock and a Hard Place—Human Rights, Life Imprisonment and Gender Stereotyping: A Critical Analysis of Khamtokhu and Aksenchik v Russia' (2017) in S Walklate and others (eds), *Emerald Handbook on Feminism, Criminology and Social Change* (Bingley: Emerald Publishing 2020)
Veitch S, 'Judgment and Calling to Account: Truths, Trials and Reconciliations' in RA Duff and others (eds), *The Trial on Trial II: Judgment and Calling to Account* (Oxford: Hart Publishing 2007)
Villiger M, *Handbuch der Europäischen Menschenrechtskonvention* (3rd edn, Zurich: Schulthess 2020)
von Hirsch A, *Doing Justice: The Choice of Punishments* (Report of the Committee for the Study of Incarceration) (New York, NY: Hill & Wang 1976)
—— *Past or Future Crimes: Deservedness and Dangerousness in the Sentencing of Criminals* (New Brunswick, NJ: Rutgers University Press 1985)
—— 'Proportionality in the Philosophy of Punishment: From Why Punish to How Much?' (1990) 1 *Criminal Law Forum* 259

—— 'Proportionality in the Philosophy of Punishment' (1992) 16 *Crime and Justice* 55
—— *Censure and Sanctions* (Oxford: Clarendon Press 1993)
—— 'Proportionate Sentences: A Desert Perspective' in A von Hirsch, A Ashworth, and J Roberts (eds), *Principled Sentencing: Readings on Theory and Policy* (Oxford: Hart Publishing 2009)
—— *Deserved Criminal Sentences: An Overview* (Oxford: Hart Publishing 2017)
—— and Ashworth A, *Proportionate Sentencing: Exploring the Principles* (Oxford: OUP 2005)
Waldmann B, 'Das Strafrecht im Spannungsfeld zwischen Grundrechtverwirklichung und Grundrechtsbindung' in MA Niggli, J Hurtado Pozo, N Queloz (eds), *Festschrift für Franz Riklin* (Zurich: Schulthess 2007)
Waldron J, 'Is the Rule of Law an Essentially Contested Concept (in Florida)?' (2002) 21 *Law and Philosophy* 137
—— 'Kant's Theory of the State' in P Kleingeld (ed), *Towards Perpetual Peace and Other Writings on Politics, Peace and History* (New Haven, CT: Yale University Press 2006)
—— 'The Concept and the Rule of Law' (2008) 43 *Georgia Law Review* 1
Ward BH, 'Sentencing Without Remorse' (2006) 38 *Loyola University of Chicago Law Journal* 131
Ward T, 'Magistrates, Insanity and the Common Law' [2017] *Criminal Law Review* 796
Wasik M, 'Towards Sentencing Guidelines in England' in I Dennis (ed), *Criminal Law and Justice: Essays from the WG Hart Workshop 1986* (London: Sweet & Maxwell 1987)
—— 'Time to Repeal the Firearms Minimum Sentencing Provision' [2017] *Criminal Law Review* 203
Wechsler H, 'Sentencing, Correction, and the Model Penal Code' (1961) 109 *University of Pennsylvania Law Review* 465
Wells C and Quick O, Lacey, Wells and Quick Reconstructing Criminal Law (4th edn, Cambridge: CUP 2010)
Welzel H, *Das Deutsche Strafrecht: Eine Systematische Darstellung* (11th edn, Berlin: De Gruyter 1969)
Wendell Holmes O, *The Common Law* (New York, NY: Barnes and Noble 2004)
Wermink H and others, 'The Effects of Punishment on Criminal Behavior' in C Damboeanu (ed), *Sociological Studies on Imprisonment: A European Perspective* (Bucharest: Tritonic 2016)
—— and others, 'Short-Term Effects of Imprisonment Length on Recidivism in the Netherlands' (2018) 64 *Crime & Delinquency* 1057
Westen P, 'The Empty Idea of Equality' (1982) 95 *Harvard Law Review* 537
—— 'Two Rules of Legality in Criminal Law' (2007) 26 *Law and Philosophy* 229
Wheeler S, *Sitting in Judgment: The Sentencing of White-Collar Criminals* (New Haven, CT: Yale University Press 1988)
Wiprächtiger H and Keller S, 'Art 47' in MA Niggli and H Wiprächtiger (eds), *Basler Kommentar: Strafrecht I* (4th edn, Basel: Helbing & Lichtenhahn 2019)
—— and ——, 'Art 48a' in MA Niggli and H Wiprächtiger (eds), *Basler Kommentar: Strafrecht I* (4th edn, Basel: Helbing & Lichtenhahn 2019)
Woodhouse D, 'The Law and Politics: More Power to the Judges—and to the People?' (2001) 54 *Parliamentary Affairs* 223
Zaibert L, *Punishment and Retribution* (London: Routledge 2006)
—— *Rethinking Punishment* (Cambridge: CUP 2018)
Zhong R and others, 'So You're Sorry? The Role of Remorse in Criminal Law' (2014) 42 *Journal of American Academy of Psychiatry and the Law* 39

Index

For the benefit of digital users, indexed terms that span two pages (e.g., 52–53) may, on occasion, appear on only one of those pages.